Re-imagining African Christologies

Princeton Theological Monograph Series

K. C. Hanson, Charles M. Collier, and D. Christopher Spinks, Series Editors

Recent volumes in the series:

David H. Nikkel
Radical Embodiment

Eliseo Pérez-Álvarez
A Vexing Gadfly: The Late Kierkegaard on Economic Matters

Oscar Garcia-Johnson
The Mestizo/a Community of the Spirit: A Postmodern Latino/a Ecclesiology

Samuel A. Paul
The Ubuntu God: Deconstructing a South African Narrative of Oppression

Linden J. DeBie
Speculative Theology and Common-Sense Religion: Mercersburg and the Conservative Roots of American Religion

Gabriel Andrew Msoka
Basic Human Rights and the Humanitarian Crises in Sub-Saharan Africa: Ethical Reflections

Re-imagining African Christologies

Conversing with the Interpretations and Appropriations
of Jesus Christ in African Christianity

VICTOR I. EZIGBO

☛PICKWICK *Publications* · Eugene, Oregon

RE-IMAGINING AFRICAN CHRISTOLOGIES
Conversing with the Interpretations and Appropriations of Jesus Christ in African
Christianity

Princeton Theological Monograph Series 132

Pickwick Publications
An Imprint of Wipf and Stock Publishers
199 W. 8th Ave., Suite 3
Eugene, OR 97401

www.wipfandstock.com

ISBN 13: 978-1-60608-822-7

Cataloging-in-Publication data:

Ezigbo, Victor I.

Re-imagining African Christologies : Conversing with the Interpretations
and Appropriations of Jesus Christ in African Christianity / Victor I. Ezigbo ;
foreword by Andrew F. Walls.

Princeton Theological Monograph Series 132

xviii + 338 p. ; 23 cm. Includes bibliographical references and index.

ISBN 13: 978-1-60608-822-7

1. Jesus Christ — Person and offices. 2. Theology, Doctrinal — Africa, Sub-
Saharan. 3. I. Walls, Andrew F. II. Title. III. Series.

BT205 .E95 2010

Manufactured in the U.S.A.

To Adamma Rita Ezigbo

Contents

Foreword

THEOLOGY IS AN ACADEMIC DISCIPLINE, TO BE PURSUED, LIKE OTHER disciplines, with rigor; but its sources lie, not in the study or the library, but in the nature of Christian life. The mainspring of theology is in the decisions that Christians—all Christians—have to make, simply because they are Christians.

The first theological decisions to be made usually involve the question "What, as a Christian, should I do?" in certain specific circumstances. Of this order are the questions that the Christians of Corinth asked the apostle Paul, such as "Should I accept an invitation from a pagan friend to go to dinner when I think he may have got the meat from a sacrifice in a pagan temple?" It is noteworthy that Paul's answers to this question range not only through a series of possibilities about the meat, but through a series of theological themes, including the ontological status of pagan gods, the nature of Christian freedom, the status of apostles and the need for mutual responsibility within the Body of Christ.[1]

But if "What, as I Christian, should I do?" about some specific issue is the usual beginning of theological enquiry, a further stage of theological activity, "What, as a Christian, should I be thinking?" soon presents itself. Any thinking we do, in theology as in other matters, will be done with the intellectual materials to hand. When the Lord asked his disciples the question that lies at the heart of christology, "Who do you say that I am?" Peter answered in the terms of his Jewish background, "You are the Messiah."[2] Asking the same question in a Greek context, in the Greek language, in a setting in which Greek intellectual materials formed the discourse, produced the centuries of heart-searching debate issuing in the declarations of Nicaea and Chalcedon. Even now, we can recognize in those declarations discoveries about Christ calling us to

---

1. The argument on this and associated questions occupies 1 Corinthians chapters 8 to 10.

2. Mark 8:29.

worship as we recite the words. Statements about the One who is "begotten of his Father before all worlds . . . being of one substance with the Father," do not replace the word Messiah or make it obsolete. But even if we argue that all that the creeds say is contained in the word Messiah, it remains true that only the long process of enquiry, study of Scripture, investigation and debate using the intellectual materials to hand—the theological process, that is—made the discovery plain.

Africa is a theological laboratory now, in the way that the Mediterranean world was then. Dr. Ezigbo's thought-provoking book reveals the astonishing degree of current theological activity on the African continent. He uncovers the works of a multitude of theological writers, from West and East and Southern Africa, of Catholic and Protestant background, and a whole spectrum of theological positions within those traditions. But he does not confine himself to the theologians who write books and articles; he examines the working theology of what he calls the "grassroots," that is ordinary Christians, Catholic, historic Protestant, Evangelical, Charismatic, and those from the African-Instituted Churches. All of these are necessarily integrating the question "Who do you say that I am?" into their daily lives, and he underlines the importance for these informal theologians of the figure of Jesus the Problem Solver. The theological workshop never closes; the exposure to changing human life that we call culture continues to force the questions on us, first "What, as a Christian, should I do?," and then "What, as Christians, should we think?" The business of theology is to learn to think in a Christian way, and African Christians are at work on these questions.

It is one of the many merits of Dr. Ezigbo's book that he does not isolate this ferment of African theological thought, but brings it into engagement with theological thought in the West. Here, too, he covers a wide range, geographically and confessionally, including representatives of that special category of theological thought characteristic of Latin America; and there is a hint towards the end of the book that he believes that Asian theology should also be at the table. At the end of the day, all theology is contextual; modern Western theology arises from centuries of Biblical and Christian interaction with the languages and cultures of Europe. The universal Christian confession is that in Christ, divinity assumed humanity; yet there is no such thing as generalized humanity; in practice, we meet only culture-specific humanity, humanity under the conditions of particular times and places. Yet there is only one Christ; it is our expressions of humanity, not his, that are partial and incomplete; only together can we hope to understand the full stature of Christ.

This leads to another important aspect of the book. It is not simply descriptive and analytical, but constructive and innovative. Dr. Ezigbo proposes for our attention a christological model of Christ as Revealer. One issue addressed in this connection is the dangerous gap that Dr. Ezigbo identifies between what the academic theologians are doing in Africa and the popular christology of ordinary Christians. Both groups are "contextualizing"; but, as he puts it, "whereas many theologians attend to the need to produce a contextualized Jesus by 'dressing him up' in the indigenous metaphors; the majority of lay Christians seek to experience a Jesus who has the power to solve their existential questions." The Revealer model can be used to critique both modes of thinking; for, though we may seek to understand Christ in terms of humanity as we know it, in truth, we can truly understand humanity, not to speak of divinity, only in the light of Christ the Revealer.

Models, of course, are ways of approaching and understanding reality, rather than reality itself; but Dr. Ezigbo has provided an immense amount on which to reflect, much to engage with, and much to employ the best theological resources of that complete, six-continent humanity that Christ has assumed.

Andrew F. Walls
University of Edinburgh and Liverpool Hope University

Preface

IN CONTEMPORARY AFRICAN CHRISTIANITY, MANY THEOLOGIANS AND Christians who do not have a formal theological training perceive Jesus Christ primarily as a solution to the problems that confront humanity.[1] They expect Jesus Christ to inspire the conversations that will deconstruct and overthrow Western theological hegemony, to rekindle the quest to preserve some indigenous traditions, to liberate the oppressed, poor and powerless, to expose the oppressors and all evildoers, to liberate and protect people from the attacks of the malevolent spirits, and to save people from being eternally separated from God. But what these solution-oriented Christologies have overlooked is that the Christ-Event is a paradox: it creates simultaneously a problem and a solution for the Christian community which confesses that God has revealed God's self in this event. The contextual Christology that I develop in this book probes the theological, christological and anthropological consequences of this claim for interpreting and appropriating Jesus Christ in the African contexts. To achieve this task, I will converse with and critique some selected constructive Christologies and grassroots Christologies that exist in Africa.

I argue that the Christology that aims to engage concretely with both the Christ-Event and the complex contexts of Africa should construe Jesus the Christ simultaneously as a *question* and an *answer* to the theological, cultural, religious, anthropological, spiritual and socio-economic issues which confront, shape, and inform these contexts. Viewed from this perspective, I will argue that the Christ-Event may sometimes upset, unsettle, critique, and reshape the solution-oriented Christologies of African Christianity. I will explore this claim within

1. Although I use the expressions *African Christianity* and *Nigerian Christianity* throughout this book, I am aware that there are different and sometimes competing versions of Christianity within Africa. It is a mistake therefore to assume that the emerging Christologies from Africa are homogenous. This is one of the reason I have used the term *Christologies* to describe the existing interpretations and appropriations of Jesus Christian African Christianity.

the circumference of the overarching assumption of this book; namely, as both a question and an answer, Jesus Christ confronts us as a *revealer* of divinity and humanity. Therefore, he mediates and interprets divinity and humanity for the purpose of enacting and sustaining a relationship between God and human beings. I will construct within this christological parameter a model that will engage concretely with some of the key issues that are shaping African Christianity.

In chapter 1, I explore the major christological presuppositions that inform and shape the interpretations of the Christ-Event in African Christianity. Most of these presuppositions overlap. They illuminate the complexity of the backgrounds of the majority of the Christologies that exist in contemporary Africa. As we will see later, the theologians that I examined have drawn insights from most of the presuppositions. Therefore, the theologians cannot be neatly categorized under any single one of the presuppositions. I examine in chapter 2 the major christological models some key theologians have developed. Although I focused primarily on Nigerian theologians, I interacted with some other African theologians who either share or disagree with the models of neo-missionary Christology, the culture-oriented Christology, and the liberation-oriented Christology. In chapter 3, I examine the grassroots Christologies that emerged from the qualitative research I carried out among five churches in Aba, a city in the southeast of Nigeria, from February to July 2006.[2] I analyzed and interacted critically with the emerging christological issues and themes.

I articulate in chapter 4 a christological model that I will be referring to in this book as *Revealer Christology*. I explore also the christological meaning of the word *revealer* and locate it within the broader context of the theological discussions on revelation. In addition, I examine the contextual and christological grounds on which an adequate African Christology can be constructed. I also engage with the two major potential christological problems that can obstruct a successful construction of a Revealer Christology model for the African contexts. Chapters 5, 6, and 7 contain the main substance of this model. In chapter 5, I examine some indigenous understandings of the Supreme Being and how this Being correlates to the Christian God. I also explore the ways in which Jesus Christ interprets and mediates God and also provides the con-

---

2. See chapter three for discussion on the methodology I used for data collection and analysis.

text for constructing a contextual Christology for the African contexts. Building on chapter 5, in chapter 6 I interact with the understandings of the malevolent spirit beings as construed in Christianity and the indigenous religions. This is an area that has been largely neglected by many African theologians who write Christologies. But any Christology that neglects how Jesus Christ interacts with the malevolent spirits will hardly connect with the existential questions and experiences of the majority of African Christians who have continued to believe that such spirit beings influence their daily affairs. In chapter 7, I investigate and critique some of the major understandings of humanity and the human world in both Christianity and the indigenous religions, locating them within a Revealer Christology model that I develop in this book. In the conclusion, I articulate the christological and contextual warrants of the Revealer Christology model. Appendix 1 contains the pre-set questions I asked the interviewees and Appendix 2 contains the names of the churches, the interviewees, and the date of the interviews.

Acknowledgements

THIS BOOK IS LARGELY THE PRODUCT OF MY PhD RESEARCH DEGREE AT the School of Divinity, University of Edinburgh, Scotland. I am grateful to Dr. John C. McDowell, my principal supervisor, for teaching me how to research, develop and construct a theology from a systematic approach. Dr. T. Jack Thompson, my second supervisor, guided me into the world of African theological literature.

I am indebted to several scholars outside and within the School of Divinity, University of Edinburgh who read some sections of my research and offered helpful comments. They are Dr. Afe Adogame, Professor Andrew Walls, Professor David Kerr, Dr. Eolene Boyd-Macmillan, Margret Acton, Billy Norton, and Dr. Ben Fubura-Manuel. I wish also to thank some of my colleagues at the University of Edinburgh for asking some penetrating questions that helped me to reformulate some of the arguments I presented in this dissertation. They are Martin Lunde, Israel Akanji, Joshua Ralston, Elijah Brown, Janice McLean, and Rosemary Okoli.

I must thank Jon Semke and Debbie Cornett for their significant financial support. In addition, the School of Divinity, University of Edinburgh, Daily Prayer Charitable Trust and Fintan Ufomadu have all given me financial support. I am also grateful to LUPKI for its financial assistance. ECWA English Church, ECWA Theological Seminary Aba, Bruntsfield Evangelical Church and African Caribbean Christian Fellowship gave me spiritual support and encouragement throughout my four years postgraduate study in Edinburgh. I thank all the members of these churches, the fellowship group and the seminary for their immeasurable help.

My deepest gratitude goes to my parents Rev. and Mrs. ISLO Ezigbo for their enormous spiritual and financial support. I am also grateful to the members of my family for their immeasurable support and encouragement. Finally, I thank my wife, Adamma Rita Ezigbo, for bringing enormous joy, support, and kindness to my life. She has comforted and encouraged me throughout the rigorous stages of this research. I also thank her for her editorial advice.

Abbreviations

AACC	All African Conference of Churches
AICs	African Indigenous (or Independent) Churches
AFER	African Ecclesiastical Review
CPM	Christian Pentecostal Mission
EAEP	East African Educational Publishers
ECWA	Evangelical Church of West Africa
EATWOT	Ecumenical Association of Third World Theologians
IJST	International Journal of Systematic Theology
NASR	Nigerian Association for the Study of Religions

Introduction

Historical Contexts of Christological Discourse in Sub-Saharan Africa

THE EARLY ECUMENICAL COUNCILS OF THE CLASSICAL CHRISTIAN church through painful processes—controversies, fierce debates, physical abuse, and voting—created what can be referred to as a standard resilient circumference within which many Christian theologians have explored the meaning and significance of Jesus Christ.[1] Since the Chalcedonian Council, many theologians have wrestled rigorously with the issue of how to hold in tension the claim that Jesus Christ is both divine and human and how to explain this highly troubling christological assertion and confession.[2] The interpretations, reactions, and appropriations of this christological claim have varied depending on the contexts of different Christian communities. For too long, however, many North American and European theologians have hijacked christological discourses and have (consciously or unconsciously) constituted a Western christological hegemony.[3] But with the influence of postmodernity infiltrating almost unrestrained into theological and christological discourses, forcing many theologians to be more suspicious of metanarratives, many non-Western theologians now seek for ways to dismantle what seems to be the imperialist empire of Western Christologies. In what follows, I will explore how some Nigerian and other African theologians have reacted against Western Christologies,

1. See Kelly, *Early Christian Doctrines*; Ayres, *Nicaea and Its Legacy: An Approach to Fourth-Century Trinitarian Theology*. For a book on the Christologies of the early Christian councils by a Nigerian theologian, see Ezeh, *Jesus Christ the Ancestor*.

2. In this book, the expressions and names *Jesus the Christ, Jesus Christ, Christ, Jesus* are used interchangeably with no theological distinction intended.

3. The word *Western* in this book refers to North America and Europe.

and also how they have proceeded to explain the Christ-Event to befit their local contexts.[4]

Discovering the Missing Gene: Awareness of the Import of African Pre-Christian Worldviews and African Identity for Contextual Christology

African contextual Christologies are weaved together into a complex political, cultural, economic, and religious web. A helpful way to unpack this complexity is to locate it within the broader historical context of the emergence of what has been described (for lack of a better expression) as *African theology*.[5] Since the focus of this book is a systematic and contextual examination of some African Christians' (particularly Nigerian theologians') interpretations of the Christ-Event, and not an historical examination, I will not discuss extensively the history of the development of Christologies in Africa. But it is important to note that some theologians began to wake up from their theological slumber in the 1950s to raise some questions that concerned their dual identities; namely, the issues that concerned their African *and Christian* heritages. Since the 1950s, many theologians have continued to seek for some novel and relevant ways to express the Christ-Event in their contexts.[6] Inspired by the rise of *pan-Africanism* and nationalism, the complex ideologies promoted by individuals such as Nnamdi Azikiwe (Nigerian) and Kwame Nkrumah (Ghanaian) which aimed to promote the one-

---

4. The expression *Christ-Event* is used in this book to refer to the birth, life, ministry, death, resurrection, and ascension of Jesus Christ.

5. Some contemporary African theologians have argued that the existing theological discussions in Africa cannot be described in the singular due to the variety of issues that inform the discussions. Thus, they speak of *African theologies* and not *African theology*. The same principle is also applied to christological discourses in Africa. See Nyamiti, "Contemporary African Christologies," 62–77.

6. Scholars of Christianity in Africa disagree on who pioneered African theology, and what it means. Whilst John Parratt is willing to associate African theology with Bishop Samuel Ajayi Crowther and Holy Johnson, Benezet Bujo sees Placide Tempels as the father of African theology. Bujo also sees Mulago's 1955 dissertation titled "Life Unity Among the Bashi, Banyarwanda and Barundi" as a template of an African Theology. See Bujo, *African Theology in Its Social Context*, 58; John Parratt, *Reinventing Christianity*, 5–10. John Mbiti sees Harry Sawyerr as the first African theologian "to publish a substantial book in the area of indigenous theology." Mbiti, *New Testament Eschatology in African Background*, 187.

ness of African peoples, to empower them to fight against Western imperialism and domination, and to encourage them to promote their cultural heritage,[7] some theologians began to construct contextual theologies that promoted and defended the dignity of Africans in "a world that denigrated black humanity."[8] The 1955 conference organized by the Christian Council of Gold Coast in Accra, Ghana (to explore the theme "Christianity and African Culture") provided a platform for some Anglophone theologians such as C. Baeta to present arguments for the co-existence of African indigenous religions and Christianity.[9] A year later, in 1956, some Francophone theologians including Vincent Mulago and Engelbert Mveng began to launch attacks against the Europeanization of African Christianity.[10] Thus, from the 1960s through the mid 1970s, there were steady streams of theological articles, treatises, and books written by African theologians to defend the possibility of engaging in a Christian theological discourse from an African vantage point. Most of these theologians were also critical of the relevance of Western-shaped theologies and Christologies for Africa.[11]

The Nigerian theologian, Bolaji Idowu, in 1969 summarized what can be considered the underlying task of African theology.

> We seek, in effect, to discover in what way the Christian faith could best be presented, interpreted, and inculcated in Africa so that Africans will hear God in Jesus Christ addressing Himself immediately to them in their own native situation and particular circumstances.[12]

Idowu's summation is, of course, broad for it does not specify exactly what he means by "African situation and particular circum-

---

7. Nkrumah, *Africa Must Unite*; *Neo-colonialism*; Azikiwe, "Future of Pan-Africanism," 302–27; Hastings, *History of African Christianity*, 14–16.

8. Martey, *African Theology*, 7.

9. See Baeta, ed. *Christianity and African Culture*. In 1958, a similar conference took place in Ibadan, Nigeria. According to Uchenna Ezeh, the conference led to the formation and inauguration of All Africa Council of Churches (AACC) in Kampala in 1963. Ezeh, *Jesus Christ the Ancestor*, 104–7.

10. Baur, *2000 Years of Christianity in Africa*, 291.

11. Ibid.

12. Idowu, "Introduction," 16. Concerned with the plurality and differences of the cultures of Africa, Aylward Shorter argues that an "African Christian Theology . . . will correspond to a culturally fragmented Africa, albeit with many chains of possible comparison and actual, historical interaction." Shorter, *African Christian Theology*, 27.

stances." But at the time he was writing, some theologians were well aware of the particular situations and circumstances to which he was referring: the dehumanized, disgraced, oppressed, and colonized conditions of African peoples which were the consequences of their contact with Western slave traders, colonialists and missionaries. Almost a decade later after Idowu's summation, some theologians who convened in Ghana signed a christological communiqué on the task of African theology. The communiqué's description of the task of theology in some ways corresponds with Idowu's understanding of the task of theology.

> African theology must reject . . . the prefabricated ideas of North Atlantic theology by defining itself according to the struggles of the people in their resistance against the structures of domination. Our task as theologians is to create a theology that arises from and is accountable to African people.[13]

Kwame Bediako, one of the leading Ghanaian theologians, has in most of his writings explored the fragmented identity of African peoples after they encountered the West.[14] He accuses many Western slave traders, colonizers, and missionaries for collaborating to promote the "general European *Afrikaanschauung*"—the Western estimation of Africans as "savage, ignorant, and superstitious."[15] For Bediako and many other theologians who were dissatisfied with some Westerners' derogatory estimation of the cultures, traditions, and personality of Africans, the primary task of an African theologian is to deconstruct Western colonialists' and missionaries' perceptions of Africans with the intent to rediscover (and rescue) the identity and heritage of Africa.[16]

---

13. "Final Communiqué," in *African Theology en route*, 193.

14. See Bediako, *Theology and Identity*.

15. Bediako, *Christianity in Africa*, 6.

16. It is important to note that the attitudes the Western missionaries in the nineteenth and early twentieth centuries exhibited toward African peoples were ambivalent. Some of the missionaries, perhaps due to their theological anthropology, viewed and treated the people of Africa in a more respected manner than some of their Western colleagues who primarily construed and treated them as sub-humans. I am indebted to T. Jack Thompson for discovering this ambivalence in some Western missionaries' estimations of African peoples. It is equally important to note that some African theologians have viewed Western missionaries differently. Whilst some are highly critical of the missionaries and have promoted anti-missionary literature, others have continued to see the Western missionary presence in Africa from an ambivalent perspective. See Parratt, *Reinventing Christianity*, 7–13.

Within the Christian theological circle, the quest to criticize the presence of Westerners in Africa (both in the political and ecclesial arenas) inspired some theologians to interpret and appropriate God and Jesus Christ intelligibly, culturally, and contemporarily to confront the dehumanized and oppressive conditions of many African peoples. Some of the theologians started to interpret and explain Jesus Christ as the one who identified with the oppressive conditions under which most of their people lived. The corollary of these theological explorations is the development of numerous christological and theological typologies. But it was not until the 1970s that constructive christological discourse began to find its way in the theological works of some African theologians.[17] By the early 1990s, christological discourse flourished so much that in 1994 Charles Nyamiti, a Tanzanian theologian, wrote: "Christology is undoubtedly the most advanced subject in African theology today."[18] Christology has since the 1990s become the most developed topic in sub-Saharan Africa.

Interestingly, the emergence of constructive African contextual Christology is indebted to the writings of some Western missionaries, particularly the British missionary John V. Taylor. In the early 1950s, some Western historians of religions and anthropologists began to be highly suspicious of the negative attitude of some Western missionaries towards the indigenous religions of Africa. The writings of Edwin Smith and Geoffrey Parrinder became popular among some African theologians who considered the indigenous religions to be compatible with Christianity. Parrinder, like Smith, argued that Christianity functions as a sort of fulfillment to the religious aspirations of the indigenous religions.[19]

> The old attitude of missionaries was usually destructive; the indigenous religion was not studied, it was not thought to have any divine revelation or inspiration, and little effort was made to use any part of it as a basis for fuller teaching. But it is not necessary to deny that the old religion both taught some truths

17. In 1972, the Kenyan theologian, John Mbiti, observed: "African concepts of Christology do not exist." What Mbiti seems to be saying is that at the time African theologians have not started to engage critically with the Christ-Event from the perspective of the indigenous worldviews of Africa. Mbiti, "Some African Concepts of Christology," 51.

18. Nyamiti, "Contemporary African Christologies," 70.

19. See chapter one for an examination of the fulfillment presupposition.

and produced some spiritual values and living. There was some general revelation of the God who has never left Himself without witness, even if it is now superseded by the full and unique revelation of Jesus Christ.[20]

But it is John Taylor's writing that has stimulated some contextual christological discussions among many African theologians since the mid twentieth century.[21] In 1963, Taylor posed a series of questions that provokingly summarized the christological condition (created by most Western Christian missionaries) within which African Christians experienced and expressed the Christ-Event.[22] In *The Primal Vision: Christian Presence amid African Religion*, Taylor asked the following questions that triggered a paradigm shift in Jesus-talk among African theologians.

> Christ has been presented as the answer to the questions a white man would ask, the solution to the needs that Western man would feel, the Savior of the world of the European world-view, the object of adoration and prayer of historic Christendom. But if Christ were to appear as the answer to the questions that Africans are asking, what would he look like? If he came into the world of African cosmology to redeem Man as Africans understand him, would he be recognizable to the rest of the Church Universal?[23]

These questions have continued to inspire many theologians to undertake constructive Christologies from a contextual spectrum. I will refer to Taylors' rhetorical questions in this book as the *Taylorian christological presupposition*. Reacting to the presupposition, particularly, Taylor's claim that many Western missionaries presented Jesus Christ as the answer to the questions the Western peoples were asking,

20. Parrinder, "Theistic Beliefs of the Yoruba and the Ewe Peoples of West Africa," 239.

21. See Bediako, *Jesus and the Gospel in Africa*; Ayegboyin, "Li Oruko Jesu: Aladura Grass-root Christology," 11–21; Bahemuka, "Hidden Christ in African Traditional Religion," 1–15; Stinton, *Jesus of Africa*; Mbiti, *New Testament Eschatology in African Background*, 1.

22. In the same year, John Mbiti completed his doctoral dissertation at the University of Cambridge. Unsurprisingly, he referenced Taylor's writing. The dissertation has been published by the Oxford University Press as the *New Testament Eschatology in African Background: A Book of the Encounter between New Testament Theology and African Traditional Concepts*.

23. Taylor, *Primal Vision*, 16.

Ukachukwu Chris Manus, a Nigerian theologian, contends: "For over a century of missionary work and intensive evangelization, this image of Christ had been planted in Africa."[24] Manus goes on to argue that many Western missionaries failed to present Jesus Christ in the ways that were recognizable to many African peoples.[25]

The theologians who adopt the *Taylorian christological presupposition* seek, among many other things, to construct the Christologies that are designed to undo Western theological hegemony and imperialism, and to rediscover the import of the indigenous worldviews for doing contextual theologies and Christologies. The Tanzanian theologian, Andrea Ng'Weshemi, observes:

> African theology comes out of a search for freedom from the domination and imperialism of western theology, which not only has been dumb on the African experiential reality, but also has perpetuated the disorientation and oppression of African people, and the expansionist agenda and attitude of the West.[26]

The Kenyan theologian, J. N. K. Mugambi, essentially says the same thing in *From Liberation to Reconstruction*. He notes that liberation has been the dominant theme in African Christian theology, and that the primary issue has been how "African Christians can be liberated from domination by the missionary legacy on which they have been nurtured, to enable them participate as full members of the international community."[27] Like the majority of African theologians, Mugambi is highly suspicious of the ways some Western missionaries in the nineteenth and twentieth centuries presented the gospel message in Africa. I will now turn to examine how the majority of contextual theologians have understood and re-expressed the Missionary Christology.

Beyond Western Christology: African Theologians' Articulation and Estimation of Missionary Christology

The locution *Missionary Christology*, as used in this book, refers to what the majority of African theologians believe to be the predominant un-

---

24. See Manus, *Christ the African King*, 119.

25. Ibid., 118.

26. Ng'weshemi, *Rediscovering the Human*, 82.

27. Mugambi, *From Liberation to Reconstruction*, 23.

derstandings and portrayals of Jesus Christ by most Western missionaries who worked in Africa in the nineteenth and twentieth centuries. Many of these theologians have construed the Missionary Christology as suppressive and oppressive. Douglas Waruta is a representative of the theologians who are seeking to demonstrate to their Western peers and African peoples their right to construct the Christologies that can fit more properly into their own contexts. He writes, "I contend that Africans have every right to formulate their own Christology, their own response to who Jesus is to them. Such response should reflect their consciousness as to who the Messiah really is."[28]

It is important to keep in mind that the activities of the Western missionaries and their estimations of African peoples are ambivalent. Therefore, it is misleading to speak of the Missionary Christology as a congruent unit. We must recognize that the missionaries did not write books on Christology for their converts. The theologian who undertakes the task of articulating the structure and content of the Missionary Christology will encounter the following difficulties. First, since the missionaries did not write a constructive Christology, it is extremely difficult to know if the theologians who charge them with the crimes of non-contextualization and insensitivity to the indigenous cultures and religions have correctly judged them. Even when we depend on the reports, sermons and journals of the missionaries, it is vital to note that the problem with depending on such material is that they were never intended to be theological writings or treatises and as such cannot represent a systematic view of the missionaries on the person and work of Jesus Christ.[29] Second, the theologian would need to depend on the christological stories of some Christian converts who lived under the tutelage of the missionaries. The danger is that some of the stories seem to have been preserved in distorted forms in the traditions of the mission churches.[30] Thus, the theologian will face the obstacle of misrepresentation. This is because it is possible that some Christian converts unintentionally misinterpreted the Christology of

28. Waruta, "Who is Jesus Christ for Africa Today? Prophet, Priest and Poten-tate," 53.

29. We should also keep in mind that the missionaries came from different missionary agencies which were connected with some church denominations that had different theological and christological views.

30. Mission Churches are the churches some Western missionaries established.

the missionaries because of language problems,[31] or intentionally did so with the intent to castigate the missionaries whom they already saw as posing some serious threats to their indigenous traditions and customs.[32] In light of these difficulties, it is important for the theologian who wants to reconstruct the Missionary Christology to examine the following questions: What kind of images of Jesus did the missionaries preach and embody? And what are the ideologies and contexts that shaped them? In what follows I will explore the images of Jesus Christ that existed in the Missionary Christology.

THE ENLIGHTENED JESUS: MISSIONARY CHRISTOLOGY AND THE INTELLECTUAL MINDSETS OF THE MISSIONARIES

The Nigerian theologian and ethicist, Yusufu Turaki, once wrote that a "mixture of Western Christian worldview was what [the missionaries] transmitted to Africa."[33] Similarly, Ogbu Kalu, a prominent Nigerian church historian, has argued that the "conflict with African cultures occurred precisely because missionaries came with a different worldview."[34] But what is it that constitutes the worldviews of the missionaries? It must include socio-political, historical, theological, doctrinal, and philosophical factors. Kalu provides a helpful summary of what many African scholars refer to as the Western worldview. He writes:

> Reasons for the nineteenth-century revival of the missionary enterprise include scientific discoveries, voyages of exploration, new and aggressive mercantilist economic theories, scientific theories of racism, and competition for plantation of colonies, as well as humanitarianism, anti-slavery movements, resettle-

31. Language barrier could be a major reason. Africans who learned under the missionaries undoubtedly had difficulty understanding their language. The missionaries too would have experienced a great difficulty in understanding the languages of Africans. However, the translation of the Bible into some African vernaculars, initiated by some missionaries, gave African converts the opportunity to hear the message of Jesus in their own languages. See Sanneh, *Translating the Message*, 105–25, 157–64.

32. An excellent book that describes the disintegration of the cultures and traditions of the Nigerian people when they encountered the missionaries is Chinua Achebe's *Things Fall Apart*.

33. Turaki, *Unique Christ for Salvation*, 86.

34. Kalu, "Church Presence in Africa: A Historical Analysis of the Evangelization Process," 19.

ment of liberated slaves, and the desire to convert souls alleg-
edly headed for perdition.[35]

My concern here is the intellectual ideology of the missionaries, a factor
many theologians have ignored. In some ways the intellectual ideology
of the missionaries functioned as a hub around which most of the other
factors revolved.

In *Culture and Imperialism* Edward Said has described the intellectual mindset that undergirded scholarship in eighteenth-century
Europe and North America. Central to this intellectual mindset is "the
belief that mankind formed a marvelous, almost symphonic whole
whose progress and formations . . . could be studied exclusively as a
concerted and secular historical experience, not as an exemplification
of the divine."[36] This mindset is what principally underscores the project of the Enlightenment that began with the works of individuals such
as Francis Bacon (1561–1626) and René Descartes (1596–1650).[37] For
many advocates of the Enlightenment, the West has for too long lived
under the shackles and shadows of religious beliefs or, as Alvin Plantinga
puts it, under "the religious and intellectual ferment generated (in part)
by the Reformation . . ."[38] But the proponents of the Enlightenment in-
sisted that a new intellectual era was en route. They compelled some
Westerners to seek an alternative hermeneutic to understand the world.[39]
Thus, the stage was set for the pursuit of a scientific way to know and to
explain the universe from the perspective of the individual self.[40] With
the breakthroughs in both science and in philosophy, the *Age of Reason*
was firmly inaugurated in the West. To use the words of Colin Greene,
"science replaced religion as the final arbiter of truth" and became the
most acceptable way of understanding the world and manipulating

---

35. Ibid., 17.

36. Said, *Culture and Imperialism*, 50.

37. Gunton, *Enlightenment and Alienation*, 3.

38. Plantinga, *Warranted Christian Belief*, 71.

39. Immanuel Kant defined the Enlightenment as the era of human beings' "emergence from self-incurred immaturity." And by *immaturity* Kant meant "the inability to
use one's understanding without the guidance of another." Thus, he construed the motto
of the Enlightenment as "*Sapere aude!* Have courage to use your own understanding!"
See Kant, "Answer to the Question," 54.

40. Gunton, *Enlightenment and Alienation*, 71.

it for human purposes.[41] And consequently, "omnicompetent human reason"[42] became the universal test of all knowledge.[43]

The causes of the Enlightenment, its relations to modernity, and its influence on Christianity are complex. An exhaustive examination of these phenomena is beyond the scope of this book. However, it suffices to note, as Alister McGrath has done, that the "interplay between the 'Enlightenment' and 'modernity' is notoriously complex,"[44] a phenomenon that has resulted in the misrepresentation of the uniqueness and similarity of modernism and the Enlightenment. The claim that modernism is "a cultural movement" and that the Enlightenment is its "ideational or intellectual core"[45] remains open to criticism. But many scholars seem to accept that the Enlightenment derived impetus from a modernistic worldview—a cultural mood that emerged from the will "to achieve autonomous self-definition" and "to achieve emancipation from any form of intellectual or social bondage."[46]

The extent to which the Enlightenment has shaped Western Christianity is ambivalent.[47] But some theologians have continued to claim that the Enlightenment ideologies have influenced Western Christianity.[48] For example, McGrath argues that Western Christianity absorbed the Enlightenment's fraudulent theme of supremacy of human reason which reflected on its views of Scripture, spirituality, apologetics and evangelism.[49] Regarding the influence of the Enlightenment on Western Christians' understanding of mission, He writes,

> Evangelism, on the basis of an Enlightenment worldview, is about persuading people of the *truth* of the gospel—with that crucial word "truth" being understood in a strongly rational manner as "propositional correctness." Evangelism thus con-

41. Greene, *Christology in Cultural Perspective*, 75.

42. Ibid., 74.

43. Newbigin, *Foolishness to the Greeks*, 25.

44. McGrath, *Passion for Truth*, 165.

45. Ibid.

46. Ibid., 31.

47. The expressions Western Christianity, African Christianity, and Nigerian Christianity are used in this book with caution. This is because there are different versions of Christian expressions within each of these contexts.

48. See Gunton, *Enlightenment and Alienation*, 112.

49. McGrath, *Passion for Truth*, 166–79.

cerns the proclamation of the cognitive truth of the gospel, with a demand for its acceptance.[50]

Although the extent to which Western Christians embraced the Enlightenment ideologies has remained a subject of massive debate, it is important to recognize that the Enlightenment forced many Western Christians to make some theological adjustments in order to become relevant to the intellectual culture the Enlightenment created. For Ng'Weshemi, this adjustment had a dual effect on the Western missionary expedition to Africa. On the one hand, the missionaries feared that the future of Christianity was under serious threats and therefore wanted "to reach out to unchristian populations, [to] evangelize them" and also "to check the spread of secularism and other consequences of the Enlightenment." On the other hand, the missionaries considered Africans as people who were "living in darkness and backwardness" and as people who were "irrational, ignorant, irreligious, and uncivilized."[51]

Armed with the idea of propositional understanding of the truth of the gospel, the intellectual and scientific methods of knowing, dualistic understanding of the spiritual and physical worlds, common sense, and Jesus as the "Teacher of Common Sense,"[52] many Western missionaries set off on a missionary journey to the sub-Saharan Africa.[53] And holding tenaciously unto their intellectual worldview that was deeply shaped by the Enlightenment, some of the missionaries presented to their converts the image of an enlightened Jesus who denounced most of their indigenous religious customs and traditions. The key issue here is that many of the missionaries failed to see that their cultures and traditions were not indissolubly united with the gospel message of Christianity. This made them to be highly suspicious of and to discourage the peoples of Africa from creating an African church. For example,

50. Ibid., 177.

51. Ng'Weshemi, *Rediscovering the Human*, 40–41.

52. As Greene argues, "Jesus ceased to be regarded as the Logos incarnate, or the Divine Son of the Father and became instead the great example of moral excellence or the simple teacher of common sense religion." Greene, *Christology in Cultural Perspective*, 75. See also Pelikan, *Jesus Through the Centuries*, 182–93.

53. What many Western missionaries failed to take seriously, to use the words of Veli-Matti Karkkainen, was that "the average African Christian takes the story [about Jesus] at face value. The kind of critical-historical questioning so common in the West is foreign to African Christians. African culture is at home with the stories of unusual events, miracles, visions, prophecies, and healing." See Karkkainen, *Christology*, 248.

a missionary with the Church Missionary Society (CMS) who worked in Nigeria in the 1920s lamented that the quest for an African Church "is exercising a most baneful influence . . . and threatens to sap the very life of the Church in Nigeria. Its low moral standards, and its readiness to baptize every would-be applicant at a shilling a head, are a scandal to the Christian faith."[54]

This is an example of the suspicion and hostility of some missionaries toward the desire of some African Christians to contextualize their faith. When the indigenous religious tenets such as the ancestral cult failed the scientific and intellectual tests of the West, many missionaries dismissed them as mere superstitions, claiming that they were incapable of contributing positively to Christianity's messages about the Christ-Event.[55] The sole purpose of the enlightened Jesus of the Missionary Christology, as some African theologians see it, is to teach the barbaric and unschooled people the civilized ways of the West. The influence of the intellectual ideology of the West on the Missionary Christology will become even more evident as I explore some missionaries' estimation of the identity, cultures, and indigenous religions of Africa.

JESUS THE IMPERIALIST: MISSIONARY CHRISTOLOGY AND THE PERSONALITY OF THE PEOPLES OF AFRICA

Like the colonizers, many missionaries viewed Africans as barbaric people without the knowledge of God, uncivilized, and objects to be conquered. To cite one example, the missions' manifesto of Pringle, a Scottish missionary, in 1820 represented this sort of dehumanizing view of African peoples.

> Let us enter upon a new and nobler career of conquest. Let us subdue and salvage Africa by justice, by kindness, by talisman of Christian truth. Let us thus go forth, in the name and under the blessing of God, gradually to extend the moral influence . . . the territorial boundary also of our colony, until it shall become an empire.[56]

54. Quoted in the Annual Report of CMS of Committee in May 3, 1921—*Proceedings of the Church Missionary Society for African the East, 1920-1921*, 5.

55. Bujo, *African Theology in its Social Context*, 43–49; King, "Angels and Ancestors," 11–14.

56. Quoted in Hammond and Atla Jablow, *Myth of Africa*, 44.

The words of Pringle reveal a predominant Western estimation of Africans in the nineteenth century, and a cluster of hegemonic prospects that were executed through colonization and evangelization. In V. Y. Mudimbe's assessment, Pringle was a template of many classical Western missionaries, whose objectives were "coextensive with [their] country's political and cultural perspectives on colonization, as well as the Christian view of mission."[57] He went on to argue that the majority of the missionaries served with enthusiasm as agents of political empires, representatives of civilization and envoys of God. He concluded that there was "no essential contradiction" in these three functions because they "implied the same purpose: the conversion of African minds and space."[58]

It is important to note that although Pringle's understanding of the evangelization of Africa was popular in the nineteenth and twentieth centuries, there were some Western missionaries who believed that Christian evangelization must be distanced from the Western political ambition to colonize and rule African peoples. John Robson's address to Hope Waddell as the latter was preparing to leave for Nigeria in 1845 on a mission trip is a vivid contrast to Pringle's mission theory. In this address, Robson encouraged Waddell with the following inspiring words: "You go to prosecute there [Christianity's] peaceful and bloodless conquest, to subdue hearts to the obedience of the faith, and to bring them to bow in submission to the scepter of the 'Prince of Peace.'"[59] Although the language of warfare appears in this charge, such as, subdue, conquest, and scepter, it is clear that Robson locates the victory of evangelism within the context of the "kingdom of God," which in his thinking, "must prevail" but not through a political conquest of a colonial kingdom or rule.[60]

The relationship between the missionaries and colonial masters is complex and an extensive examination of this phenomenon is not a task of this book.[61] However, what is worth noting is that although the

---

57. Mudimbe, *Invention of Africa*, 47.

58. Ibid.

59. Robson, "Address by Rev. J. Robson, D. D., to the Rev. H. M. Waddell, on the Occasion of his leaving for Africa," 23–24.

60. Ibid.

61. For scholars like Bolaji Idowu and Benezet Bujo, the missionaries and the imperialists worked hand-in-hand in disintegrating African cultures, and in siphoning

missionaries may have criticized and rejected some of the policies of the colonizers, the majority of contemporary African theologians have consistently accused many classical missionaries and imperialists of sharing a dehumanizing concept of the identity of Africans. Evidently, Pringle was not the only Westerner who considered Africans to be inferior to Westerners. To cite another figure that was highly influential in the West, Georg Hegel, in *The Philosophy of History*, trivializes the ancestral cult of Africa and describes Africans as cannibals and as people with "barbarous sensuality."[62]

Many African scholars and theologians have remained highly critical of some Westerners' derogatory estimation of Africans. According to Chukwudi Njoku, the missionaries "embraced the idea of a civilizing mission, the idea of being heirs of a culturally superior people going out to share the riches and glories of their culture with people from cultures they generally assumed to be inferior to their own."[63] Teresia Hinga concurs and argues that the missionaries degraded the cognitive faculties of Africans by presuming that they were *tabula rasa*: "The conquest of Africa implied erasing most of what Africans held dear. The missionaries, in the name of Christ, sought to create a spiritual and cultural *tabula rasa* upon which they could inscribe a new culture, a new spirituality."[64]

Jesus the Imperialist, therefore, arrived in Africa with his Western workers with the intent to capture the land, the mind, and the indigenous worldviews of the local people. For this Jesus, in the thinking of many theologians, Africans must drop their unique identity and adopt the theological mindsets and religious hermeneutics of the West in order for them to qualify as his true disciples. A serious implication of the imperialist Christology of some missionaries is that many theologians

---

Africa's resources. However, as Ogbu Kalu and T. Jack Thompson have rightly observed, to assume that the missionaries were always in agreement with the colonial masters is reductionistic and amounts to an oversimplification of a complex phenomenon. They argue that some missionaries were sometimes highly critical of some of the policies of the colonizers when the policies conflicted with their evangelistic work and occasionally with the rights of Africans. Bujo, *African Theology in Its Social Context*, 43–49; Idowu, *African Traditional Religion*; Kalu, "Ethiopianism in African Christianity," 260; Kalu, "Color and Conversion," 67–74; Thompson, *Christianity in Northern Malawi*.

62. Hegel, *Philosophy of History*, 218–19.

63. Njoku, "Missionary Factor in African Christianity, 1884–1914," 228.

64. Hinga, "Jesus Christ and the Liberation of Women in Africa," 187.

have considered the imperialist Jesus to be an enemy of the traditional society.

Many African theologians continue to contend that the majority of the missionaries construed Africans to be inferior cognitively and spiritually because they view African cultures and traditions to be inferior to theirs. A consequence of this estimation of African cultures and religions is the idea that embracing Jesus Christ entails depriving oneself of the indigenous framework.[65] Lamin Sanneh laments this state of affairs: "Notions of Western cultural superiority found a congenial niche in the Christian missionary enterprise where spiritual values were assumed to enshrine concrete Western cultural forms, so that the heathen who took the religious bait would in fact be taking it from the cultural hook."[66]

Among the cultures and religious practices of Africa the missionaries condemned were polygamy, the ancestor cult, and some traditional festivals such as the New Yam festival.[67] By failing to engage constructively with the indigenous traditions, most of the missionaries succeeded in imposing a strange Jesus on their converts. Their derogatory attitudes toward the indigenous cultures and religions suggest strongly that for some of them Jesus was too enlightened to approve of or associate with the indigenous cultures and religions they labeled uncivilized. It is noteworthy that the understanding of Christianity as anti-African cultures continues to haunt many African churches.[68] One example is the element which many mission churches use when they celebrate the Eucharist. In the Missionary Christology, (Western) wine signified the blood of Jesus. Many missionaries did not encourage the use of the traditional wine, such as palm wine, in the celebration of the Eucharist.[69] Instead, they imposed the use of Western brands of wine on the local Christians.[70] Another effect of some missionaries' insensi-

---

65. Schreiter, "Introduction: Jesus Christ in Africa Today," viii.

66. Sanneh, *Encountering the West*, 22.

67. See Ajayi, *Christian Missions*, 105–10; Anyanwu, "Why the Igbos Abandoned Their Gods," 91–99.

68. Therefore, Luke Mbefo's claim that the impact of Western Christianity on African Christianity "has been broken down with the emergence of non-Western churches" is certainly misleading. See Mbefo, "Christian Theology and African Heritage," 7.

69. Bujo, *African Theology in Its Social Context*, 47.

70. This action only helped to perpetuate the idea that white people (Westerners) are superior and holier, and black people (Africans) are inferior and incapacitated of producing some original and adequate interpretations of the Christ-Event. The major-

tive attitudes toward the indigenous worldviews is that it has created a *religious schizophrenia* in many Christians.[71] Many of them live with "dual religious minds." The Nigerian theologian, Osadolor Imasogie, expresses this state of affairs when he argues that the "superficiality of the African Christian's commitment is evidenced by the fact that when he is faced with problems and uncertainties he often reverts to traditional religious practices."[72] The point he makes is that many Christians devote themselves, not only to Jesus Christ, but also to the indigenous religions. When they are inside the church, they sing songs and pray in the ways that express their allegiance to Jesus Christ, but when they are outside the church, some of them act in the manner that demonstrates their trust and belief in some of the teachings of the indigenous religions.

Rethinking African Christologies: Towards a New Context

My main aim in this book is to construct a christological model that engages with and critiques the major christological models some key African theologians have developed since the 1980s. Also, I will interact with and critique some of the grassroots Christologies that exist in Nigerian Christianity. The three major assumptions that I explore are: (1) the majority of the constructive and grassroots Christologies that exist in African Christianity are solution-oriented; (2) an adequate contextual Christology will construe Jesus Christ simultaneously as the question and solution to the needs, aspirations, and problems of humanity, and (3) a contextual Christology that hopes to be relevant to many lay Christians will interact with the grassroots Christologies that are embedded in their testimonies, songs, and prayers.

The majority of African contextual theologians who construct Christologies have been driven by the quest to interpret and explicate the Christ-Event to befit the history and experience of their people. On the basis of this quest, they have continued to locate their Christologies within the context of the ambivalent interaction between the local people and many missionaries who worked among them in the nineteenth

---

ity of the mission-churches in Nigerian today never use palm wine to celebrate the Eucharist or the Holy Communion.

71. Udoh, "Guest Christology,"

72. Imasogie, *Guidelines for Christian Theology in Africa*, 14.

and some part of the twentieth centuries. Following the *Taylorian christological presupposition*, many African theologians have continued to construct the Christologies that seek, on the one hand, to deconstruct the Missionary Christology and, on the other hand, to re-explain the Christ-Event within the indigenous cultural and religious thought. But many of these theologians have failed to examine and engage with the key christological questions that the majority of contemporary lay Christians are asking today. Consequently, an unwarranted dichotomy exists between the contextual Christologies that many theologians are developing and the existing grassroots.

The reactions of some theologians to the Missionary Christology, as I have already argued, reflect the impact of the *Taylorian christological presupposition* on the understandings of the nature of contextual Christologies. These theologians aim to discover and articulate what Jesus will look like when they present him as the answer to the questions the African peoples are asking, and as the solution to their needs. But an adequate Christology must aim to articulate, explicate, and explore the Christ-Event in an intelligibly relevant way, allowing it to engage with the new questions that arise from the new shifts and new historical conditions in the context-of-life of a given people. Therefore, I argue that although Taylor's provoking questions were appropriate at the time he posed them, they are now somewhat obsolete and can no longer adequately inspire the kind of Christologies that are needed and required in contemporary Africa. A new kind of Christology, which arises from a new set of christological questions, is what is needed in African Christianity. In this book, I will raise one such new questions and construct a christological model that is informed and shaped by it. The question is: since many African theologians have expressed Jesus Christ to befit the indigenous worldviews and the experiences of their people and have presented Jesus as an answer to some of the social, cultural, and religious questions that some people are asking, if Jesus were also to be presented simultaneously as a question and solution to needs of the people, what would he and they look like?

It is important to articulate the relationship between the key question that I have asked and Taylor's questions which have informed, imbued, and shaped most of the existing contextual Christologies in Nigeria. The background of the new christological question that I have asked is partly the *Taylorian christological presupposition*. But the key issue here is what has changed from the historical context in which Taylor posed his questions when the *Taylorian christological presupposition* is examined in light of the twenty-first century Nigerian context. Although we cannot speak definitively of the post-colonial era, the post-missionary era, and the post-racism era, since some individuals and organized systems may (indirectly) continue to think and act in a way that perpetuates such outdated ideologies, I argue that the majority of the Nigerian people are no longer living in the imperialist and racist eras, which arguably were the eras the Missionary Christology constituted an unchallenged hegemony.[73]

The major problems that confront contemporary Nigerian and many other African Christians are no longer the Western missionaries and colonialists who devalued the dignity of Africans, demeaned their cultures and traditions, and imposed and enforced some Western ideologies and interpretations of the Christ-Event on the Christian converts. The Ghanaian theologian, Kwame Bediako, captures this state of affairs and consequently predicts a new shift of direction in African theological discourse.

> The era of African theological literature as reaction to Western misrepresentation is past. What lies ahead is a critical theological construction which will relate more fully the widespread African confidence in the Christian Faith to the actual and ongoing Christian responses to the life expression of Africans.[74]

Bediako made this observation as African Christianity and its theologians neared the end of the twentieth century. It must be said that in this twenty-first century, the perennial challenge that faces many African theologians is not the Missionary Christology, but rather how to move on to engage the *new contexts* in which African peoples now live. Surprisingly, Bediako who predicted the new shift in christological discourse has continued to write and wrestle with the deep cultural issues that stem from the Western derogatory estimation of the African pre-Christian traditions. Thus, his Christology and theology

---

73. Therefore, Tite Tienou is correct when he contends that "as long as Europe and the West continue to dominate the economy and educational systems of Africa," it remains a legitimate quest by African peoples to seek for "self-hood and identity." Tienou, "Search for the 'African Past,'" 48.

74. Bediako, "Understanding African Theology in the 20th Century," 64.

have largely remained heavily influenced by the *Taylorian christological presupposition*.[75]

Nigerians (and many other African peoples) now live in a new era: an era in which they enjoy a political independence, an era in which theologians and African churches are no longer dependent entirely on Western theologies and spirituality, an era in which their theologians have succeeded in rescuing some indigenous cultures and religions from disappearing from the consciousness of many people, and an era in which some people are now seeking to re-evangelize the Western world. Since every era has its own challenges, this new era stimulates new forms of challenges that are different from the challenges of the era of Western imperialism, the missionary cultural and theological hegemony, and apartheid. But what are the challenges that this new era poses to African Christianity and Christologies, particularly for the Nigerian contexts? I will highlight three major challenges.

First, African Christians need to engage with the challenge posed by the intellectualist and dichotomist tendencies that have compelled many theologians to construct abstract Christologies that fail to interact with the grassroots Christologies. The majority of the Christologies that theologians have constructed (as we shall see in chapters two and three) have been written not with the laity in mind, (and most times) not for the theological students in Nigeria, but for the Western academia.[76] Most of these Christologies are peer-driven and escape some key existential christological questions that the majority of lay Christians are asking.

Second, African Christians face the challenge posed by pragmatism. Many theologians and lay Christians tend to explain Jesus Christ only in terms of what he can do for them, such as providing solutions to their cultural, political, social, and religions problems. I will examine some Nigerian grassroots Christologies in chapter three. It will become evident that many Christians primarily see Jesus Christ as a *Solution* to their problem, and interestingly, as a *Solution* which they hope to control. This explains why many of them will seek for a solution to their problems from the indigenous sources (such as native doctors) when Jesus seems not to solve their problems.

---

75. See Bediako, *Jesus and Gospel in Africa*.

76. This is a serious theological problem that is widespread in Africa. See Tienou, "Theological Task of Church in Africa," 7; Onaiyekan, "Christological Trends in Contemporary African Theology," 366.

Third, the task of constructing the Christologies that are not restricted to the African context is another challenge that faces a contextual theologian. Any Christology that hopes to be relevant in this twenty-first century will, on the one hand, be relevant to its immediate context and, on the other hand, interact with and contribute to the development of Christology outside of its immediate context. Manus has encouraged African theologians to undertake christological discussions that are relevant to Africa in isolation "from the prevalence of Western European and North American Christologies . . ."[77] But statements such as this can be misleading and can cause many African theologians not to give sufficient recognition to the positive aspects of the Missionary Christology. Manus' statement can also cause an African theologian to ignore the christological conversations that are going on in the West today. A Christology that does not aim to contribute to the development of christological discourses universally is parochial and can hardly have any impact on the twenty-first century world. If it is true that Africa has contributed immensely to the (demographic) shift of the centre of Christianity's gravity from the West to the non-Western world, as Andrew Walls, Bediako, Philip Jenkins, and others have argued,[78] it follows that African theologians face the challenge, not only of evangelizing the West, but also the task of challenging and contributing to the development of Christologies that are designed for the Western communities. I will now move on to explore in chapter one the presuppositions that inform the majority of christological discourses in sub-Saharan Africa.

77. Manus, *Christ, the African King*, 10.

78. See Walls, "Towards Understanding Africa's Place in Christian History," 180–89; P. Jenkins, *Next Christendom*.

PART ONE

Jesus-Talk in Contemporary
African Christianity

1

Major Presuppositions of African Christologies

IN THE INTRODUCTION, I SHOWED THAT THE *TAYLORIAN CHRISTOLOGI-cal presupposition* has provoked some serious christological conversations among African Christian theologians.[1] A critical examination of these conversations unveils some other complex presuppositions that inform and shape most of the existing christological models in African Christianity. The following three observations are noteworthy.

First, the theologians and the lay Christians I will examine here cannot be categorized neatly under any of these presuppositions. This is because some of them draw insights from all or most of the presuppositions, albeit in different ways.[2] In addition, although the presuppositions have their unique contents and agendas, they overlap. For example, they share the ideology of contextualization. I will highlight their points of difference and agreement throughout the chapter. Second, I will discuss the contents and the implications of these Christologies extensively in chapters two and three. However, it is important to examine first the presuppositions that function as the backdrop to these Christologies. Without these presuppositions it will be difficult to understand and appreciate the contemporary interpretations and appropriations of the Christ-Event in African Christianity. And third, these presuppositions should not be confused with the *actual* contents of each of the christological models that I will examine in chapters two and three.

---

1. See the introduction for the discussion on John Taylor's christological questions and assumptions and their impact on African Christologies.

2. For example, while the theologians who adopt the reconstructionist and gap and fulfillment presuppositions may be highly suspicious of some of the claims of the theologians who use primarily the destructionist presupposition, they all employ the solution presupposition. This will become clearer as I interact with the theologians and their articulations and reactions to the presuppositions.

Also, the presuppositions should not be conceived as being independent of the christological models. Instead, they should be taken as the general assumptions and ideologies that underlie the interpretations and appropriations of Jesus the Christ.

Every theologian operates with some assumptions. In some cases, these assumptions are clearly defined and the theologian is able to detect them and manage their influence on the texture of his or her work. Sometimes the theologian fails to clearly identify and articulate his or her assumptions and, therefore, is unable to properly manage them. Some African theologians and the majority of Christian laity hardly bother to articulate clearly the presuppositions that shape their understandings of the Christ-Event. This makes it difficult and sometimes daunting for people who are not familiar with African Christianity to understand and appreciate the emerging Christologies. The presuppositions I examine in this chapter have emerged from the struggles of many Christians to construct an adequate engagement with the Christian faith and the indigenous religions, and to practice their faith within their multicultural, multi-religious, political, and socio-economic context. I will classify and explore these presuppositions under four major categories: namely, Gap and Fulfillment, Destructionist, Reconstructionist, and Solution.

Gap and Fulfillment Presupposition

The gap and fulfillment presupposition is one of the oldest apologetic tools that some African theologians have employed to engage with the theological tension that emerges as they try to set out a theological meeting point for Christianity and the indigenous religions.[3] This presupposition posits that there are gaps in the indigenous religious understandings of God's revelatory activities. The proponents of this view argue that there is a necessity to fill these religious gaps if African peoples are to make sense of God's purpose and salvific history, and also to appreciate the purpose and limits of their God-given cultures and traditions. For them, the indigenous religions contain only some

---

3. For an earlier discussions on the fulfillment and sublimation theories for the African context see Smith, *African Beliefs and Christian Faith*; McVeigh, *God in Africa*, 155–62. Some North American black theologians have argued for the necessity of rooting Black theology in the indigenous religions of Africa. See Roberts, *Black Theology in Dialogue*, 41.

fragments of divine truth, and as such, are incomplete and are in dire need for a supreme and definitive fulfiller.[4] The majority of the theologians who operate with this mindset contend that the Christ-Event can effectively and definitively fill these religious gaps. Consequently, they introduce Jesus as the only one who can bring to a total fulfillment the religious aspirations of Africans which they struggle to fulfill through some indigenous religious ways.

In the gap and fulfillment presupposition, Jesus does not need to destroy all the core values and beliefs of the indigenous religions. The majority of the theologians and lay Christians who employ the gap and fulfillment presupposition have continued to agitate for the need to recognize the existence of God's imprints in the indigenous religions. The backdrop to this agitation is the attempt to discredit the view that considers the indigenous religions to be completely incompatible with Christianity. Therefore, it is important to articulate the content of the so-called divine imprints in the indigenous religions and to examine how they relate to Christianity's views of the Christ-Event.

The Nigerian theologian Luke Mbefo, for example, has called upon African Christians to excavate the divine imprints in their cultures and religions. He challenges them to engage in this enormous task with a positive mindset: "instead of a negative inference from the criticism of the early missionary Christianity, we are reminded with force and vigor of the values and the meanings of the heritage that is properly African—which were never called into dialogue in the colonial period of Christianity."[5] By heritage, Mbefo means the religious and cultural traditions that the ancestors embodied. Since these traditions define the identity of African peoples, to require them to dissociate themselves from such traditions almost entails requiring them to forego their identity. For him, it is the determination to retain this identity that inspired some theologians to warn their colleagues against the danger of making Christianity a foreign and superficial religion in Africa.[6]

But what precisely are the traditions that define African peoples? The response to this question will differ depending on the theologian, his interest and contexts. Mercy Oduyoye subsumes these traditions

---

4. Imasogie, *Guidelines for Christian Theology in Africa*, 78.

5. Mbefo, "Christian Theology and African Heritage," 10.

6. Ibid.

into a ten-point category.[7] These are: the belief in the divine origin of the universe, the belief that human beings are the custodians of the earth, the sense of wholeness of the person, the inquiry into "whether women are an integral part of humanity or merely appendages to the male,"[8] the belief that God delegates authority to intermediary beings, the concept of covenant-making, the belief in the power of evil, the concept of reconciliation, some rites of passage such as marriage, naming ceremony, and burials; and the traditional liturgical practices such as drumming, dancing, and extemporaneous prayer.

Returning to Mbefo's understanding of the heritage of Africa, it is important to highlight his reconstruction of some of the possible issues that worried the elders when they encountered some Western missionaries.

> A typical question the elders posed was: such and such ancestor who stood for truth and justice, who never poisoned anybody and who was famous for his [or] her hospitality, is he [or] she in this heaven you preach even without your baptism? If he is in heaven, then it is sufficient without your baptism to follow him there. If he is in hell, we do not want to be separated from such a good man. Our ancestors have left us a way that gives fulfillment to our life.[9]

The issue of reuniting with their ancestors was undoubtedly a primary concern of the majority of African peoples in the early era of the Western missionary expeditions. It is, however, doubtful if it is still a major concern of many of the present-day Africans who are seriously losing their grasp of the sense of community that characterized the traditional societies.[10] My task here is to explore the indigenous traditions that some theologians believe are the consequences of divine manifestation. At the heart of these traditions are ethics and morality. And for some theologians, the notion of morality comes from God's self-disclosure. As Bolaji Idowu argues:

7. Oduyoye, "Value of African Religious Beliefs and Practices for Christian Theology," 91. See also Pobee, *Toward an African Theology*, 109–16.

8. It is not clear if this feminist ideology is part of the traditional African religious beliefs and practices.

9. Ibid.

10. This does not mean that a community orientation is no longer visible, but rather that it is gradually disappearing. And the possible causes are numerous, including urbanization, modernization, globalization and the influence of individualism.

> We find that in every age and generation, there is a direct contact of God with the human soul, the personal awareness of God on the part of man through God's own initiative. What man knows of God, what he discovers about God, comes as a result of this self-disclosure.[11]

The key idea here is divine revelation, and I will discuss it extensively in chapter four. At this point it is essential to note that in the thinking of some theologians who employ the gap and fulfillment presupposition, it is the divine revelation that is responsible for the ancestors' traditional ethics and morality. And the traditional way of life, to use the expression of Idowu, constitutes the "spiritual and cultural treasures" of Africans.[12]

The relationship between the indigenous heritage and the Christian gospel has continued to cause a fierce theological tension among many theologians. While some like Idowu lean heavily toward a separatist view of the indigenous religions and Christianity, others agitate for a dialogue between them. The key problem of a theologian, Chris Ukachukwu Manus argues, is how to take seriously the divine revelations that are manifested in the indigenous religions and the command of Jesus to his followers to go and make disciples.

> Throughout history, Christian scholars have established the fact that Christian revelation had been expressed in various circumstances and in different cultural settings. The deposit of faith had often been articulated in hardware concepts and propositions. But the Risen Lord charges his Church to go into the wide world to preach the gospel and to make disciples (Matt 28:16–20). Thus, revealed truth must, of necessity, encounter other nations, their values, and cultures.[13]

As we will see later, some theologians who use the destructionist presupposition such as Yusufu Turaki will agree with Manus' argument. The point of contention is how to achieve this task while at the same time preserving the integrity of the gospel. According to Mbefo, one of the ways to embark on a meaningful proclamation of the Christ-Event in Africa is to acknowledge that "there are aspects of African heritage that are totally for Christ and his Church."[14] For him, an African theologian

---

11. Idowu, *African Traditional Religion*, 56.

12. Ibid., 205.

13. Manus, *Christ the African King*, 14–15.

14. Mbefo, "Christian Theology and African Heritage," 10.

needs to explore the indigenous heritage with the intent "to formulate a Christianity that is African in its expression."[15] He argues that to achieve this great task, the theologians and all Christians must see Christianity as the fulfillment of the indigenous religions: "By adopting these elements of traditional heritage through affirmation and denial we carry forward into Christianity those authentic interpretations of God who already revealed himself to our ancestors before Christianity came as fulfillment."[16]

The concept of fulfillment vis-à-vis Christianity and other religions was already in existence in the West in the early half of the twentieth century. Kenneth Cracknell has noted that this theory was prominent during the Edinburgh 1910 world missionary conference.[17] But it was the groundbreaking work of John Nicol Farquhar's *The Crown of Hinduism* that made the concept popular in the missionary circles in the early twentieth century.[18] In this inspiring work, Farquhar compared some of the major themes of Christianity and Hinduism. His conclusion was radical:

> We have already seen how Christ provides the fulfillment of each of the highest aspirations and aims of Hinduism. . . . Every true motive which Hinduism has found expression in unclean, debasing, or unhealthy practices finds in Him fullest exercise in work for the downtrodden, the ignorant, the sick, and the sinful. In Him is focused every ray of light that shines in Hinduism. He is the Crown of the faith of India.[19]

Edwin Smith, however, was one of the earliest individuals who proposed that Christianity fulfills rather than destroys the indigenous religions of Africa. In 1926, he wrote: "Christianity comes to Africans with greater power when it is shown to be not destructive but a fulfillment of the highest aspirations which they have tried to express in their beliefs and rites."[20]

The majority of the theologians who use the gap and fulfillment presupposition see Jesus the Christ as the fulfillment of the religious

---

15. Ibid.

16. Ibid., 18.

17. See Cracknell, *Justice, Courtesy and Love*, 221.

18. Farquhar, *Crown of Hinduism*.

19. Ibid., 457–58.

20. Smith, *Christian Mission in Africa*, 40.

longings and practices of their people. Most of these theologians argue that Jesus himself associated with and operated within the Jewish indigenous culture and religion. Jesus told his disciples that he did not "come to destroy the Law or the Prophets" but instead to "fulfill them."[21] This is the key passage most African theologians normally cite in support of their fulfillment theory. Justin Ukpong is an example. He writes, "Jesus' attitude toward the Torah was basically positive and transcended prevailing Jewish attitudes. Jesus introduced a new understanding of the Law and pointed to himself as its fulfillment."[22] Since Matthew 5:17 is an important biblical texts on which many theologians build their fulfillment theory it merits a close examination. What exactly did Jesus mean by the Law and Prophets? How did he fulfill the Law and the Prophets? These are vital questions that can provide us with a helpful exegetical and theological framework for examining the connection between the fulfillment Jesus meant in this context and the fulfillment theory of some African theologians. Most biblical scholars agree that the Law and Prophets in the Matthean context refer to the Hebrew Scripture.[23] John Nolland notes that the "Law defined the identity of the Jewish people."[24] And it is most likely that it is the Law, and not the Prophets, that is the primary focus in this passage. Nolland observes,

> The law was clearly central in all streams of Jewish faith, and the reading of the Law had primacy in the synagogue; it was the role of the Law to regulate Jewish life and practice. For all the Jewish groups of which we are aware the prophetic books had a supporting secondary role which no doubt was capable of being variously conceived . . . [25]

The Law, therefore, defined the culture and the religion of the Jewish community. It is the "prophetic perspective [that] enabled the Law to be correctly apprehended" by the Jewish people.[26] It is difficult to know exactly what prompted Jesus' comments on his relationship to the Law and the Prophets since Mathew does not state clearly the situation.

21. Matthew 5:17.

22. Ukpong, "Christology and Inculturation," 53.

23. See Davies, *Matthew*, 51; Smith, *Augsburg Commentary on the New Testament: Matthew*, 89.

24. Nolland, *Gospel of Matthew*, 218.

25. Ibid.

26. Ibid.

Some have suggested that the passage indicates a polemic against antinomians. Others have argued that some legalistic Jews who intended to scandalize Jesus were the most likely group of people that Matthew had in mind.[27] However, what is clear in this passage is that Matthew negates the view that Jesus has come to annul the Law or the Prophets. On the contrary, he argues that Jesus has come to fulfill the Law or the Prophets. But is it exegetically legitimate to say that Jesus fulfils the indigenous religious aspirations and practices of African peoples on the basis of Matthew 5:17? Clearly, it will require a radical shift away from the context of the passage to make such a claim. Christologically, however, it is possible to construe Jesus as the one who fulfils the indigenous religious aspirations of African peoples. But this requires appealing to the universality of the Christ-Event. While the particularity of the Christ-Event, strictly speaking, limits Jesus only to his Jewish origin and context, its universality locates him beyond the parameters of his Jewish context. It is precisely on the ground of the universality of the Christ-Event that theologians can extend Jesus' role of fulfillment to all cultures of the world. As Adeolu Adegbola argues:

> The gospel is not primarily a new teaching about a way of life; it is not a new philosophy. Rather, it is a proclamation that in Jesus Christ, God has himself achieved the fulfillment of his purpose for the world, his rule has triumphed over all, in him, new creation has come into being, the new age has begun.[28]

Some difficulties emerge when the gap and fulfillment presupposition is examined in light of the Christ-Event. One of the christological difficulties of the fulfillment theory is how to construe the fulfillment work of Jesus vis-à-vis the indigenous religious aspirations of the African peoples. Unlike Judaism, there is no anticipation of a Messiah or someone who will fulfill the purported religious aspirations that are contained in the indigenous religions of Africa. Perhaps the idea of fulfillment falls into the category which John Mbiti, a prominent Kenyan theologian, has described as the christological concepts that are "historically rooted . . . and bound up with the Jewish eschatological hope" but which do not have any "parallels in African thought-forms, histories

---

27. France, *Gospel According to Matthew*, 113.

28. Adegbola, "A Christian Interpretation of the African Revolution," 39.

and traditions."[29] Within the Jewish context, the idea of fulfillment fits perfectly well into the hope of a Messiah. Thus, for example, when Peter describes Jesus as the Christ,[30] he anticipates that the rest of the disciples (who are Jewish) and even the earliest Jewish followers of Jesus will understand the messianic concept and how Jesus fulfils this highly exalted position. The idea of fulfillment, in the sense the gap and fulfillment theoreticians use it, is therefore strange to the indigenous religions of Africa. There are no indications of some gaps and the anticipations of a fulfiller in the indigenous religions. Even in the case of the ancestor cult, it will require a massive distortion of this religious phenomenon to understand it as myth, which has arisen from the religious aspirations that is in need of fulfillment.[31] The fulfillment theory, therefore, appears to be a foreign thought that has no real bearing on the indigenous religious values, beliefs and practices.

Another problem with the gap and fulfillment presupposition is connected with the way in which Jesus fulfils the purported gaps in these religious aspirations. Even if it is granted that there are religious aspirations in African indigenous religions which Jesus can fulfill, the question that remains is: how does Jesus fulfill these aspirations or purported gaps? Is it by merely completing the previous religious traditions and values of the ancestors? Or is it by replacing the previous religious values and traditions with a new one? In other words, should we understand the fulfillment in a qualitative sense (i.e., to change or correct the aspirations and values) or in a quantitative sense (i.e., to add to, to complete, or perfect the aspirations and values)?[32] Since Matthew has not clearly articulated the meaning of fulfillment, it is difficult to establish what the word means exactly in this context. This explains the plethora of meanings that theologians and biblical scholars have assigned to it.

The proponents of the gap and fulfillment presupposition contend that Jesus does not abolish the preparatory work of the ancestors but

29. Mbiti, "Some African Concepts of Christology," 58.

30. Matthew 16:16.

31. Adeyemo, *Salvation in African Tradition*, 29; See also Bediako, *Jesus and the Gospel in Africa*, 30.

32. From the Early church through the medieval era, the predominant view of fulfillment was the idea of perfection. In this sense, Jesus perfects the imperfect elements in the Jewish Law. During the Reformation there was a shift in emphasis: it is "no longer the perfection of the law of the medieval exegesis but its correct interpretation by Jesus is now in the centre." See Luz, *Matthew 1–7*, 261–65.

fulfils them. The Congolese theologian, Francois Kabasele Lumbala, no doubt speaks for many African theologians when he argues:

> Just as Christ, the one priest, does not abolish human media-
> tions, but fulfils them in himself, so does he consummate in him
> the mediation exercised by our ancestors, a mediation that he
> does not abolish but which, in him, is revealed to be henceforth
> a subordinate mediation.[33]

For him, then, the mediatory work of Jesus supersedes that of the African ancestors. However, Jesus does not discard or abolish the work of the ancestors in order to function as the mediator between God and the African peoples. The idea of fulfillment here seems to be perfecting the previous work of the ancestors. As another Congolese theologian, Benezet Bujo, suggests, "Christ brings creation to its fulfillment and, together with the Father, leads the ancestors of African peoples into fullness of life."[34]

But for Nigerian theologian Justin Ukpong the fulfillment entails creating a new form of meaning. He contends that fulfillment in the Matthean context includes "a new understanding" of the Law,[35] which entails "restoring the original divine intention of the Law."[36] Jesus does not merely complete the gaps in the Law but introduces a new meaning of the Law. In the thinking of Ukpong, divine love stands in the center of the new meaning of the Law that Jesus has introduced. "Central to this new approach to the Law," he writes, "was love—the fact that God loves all persons both good and bad, as children, and we must likewise love all other persons to prove that we are God's children."[37] Again he postulates:

> Jesus introduced a new understanding of the Law and pointed
> to himself and the fulfillment He revealed God's love and mercy
> . . . and emphasized what was already in the Old Testament—
> that God wants repentance, mercy, love rather than the ritualis-
> tic observance of the Law . . . This is how Jesus evangelized the
> Jewish religious world with the Good News and the new vision

---

33. Lumbala, "Christ as Ancestor and Elder Brother," 126.

34. Bujo, *African Theology in Its Social Context*, 86.

35. Ukpong, "Christology and Inculturation," 53.

36. Ibid., 50.

37. Ibid., 51.

of God's kingdom—he reinterpreted the people's religious perception in a new way.[38]

An adequate understanding of Matthew 5:17 must present fulfillment as an appropriate counterpart to annul and must illuminate the
teaching of Jesus in 5:21–48.[39] Therefore, it is most likely that Matthew
wants his readers to know that Jesus does not undercut the Law and the
Prophets, but as a good teacher, he interprets the Law with the intent to
"enable God's people to live out the Law more effectively."[40] In addition,
although the concept of fulfillment in 5:17 may contain a christological
content,[41] and may be the ground to extend the effect of the work of
Jesus to the indigenous religions of Africa, it remains problematic to
construe Jesus as the fulfiller of the indigenous religious aspirations,
practices and values of the ancestors. This is partly because the fulfillment theory is prey to the relativism that informs some understandings
of religious pluralism. To argue that Jesus is required to be proposed in
order to deal with the gaps in the indigenous religions is a prey to the
growing belief in the uniqueness of every religion and its capacity to
bring to its adherents the realizations of their aspirations. The issue here
is that as more people come to conceive of the indigenous religions as
self-sufficient, there will be no more gaps for Jesus to fill up. The Christ-
Event will consequently become irrelevant to the indigenous religious
values, beliefs and practices of the people. This is a major weakness in
the gap and fulfillment presupposition. Also, the gap and fulfillment
presupposition overestimates the continuity between Christianity and
the indigenous religions but underestimates their differences. This is the
point that is highlighted in the destructionist presupposition to which
I will now examine.

Destructionist Presupposition

The destructionist presupposition not only reflects a strong incredulity
towards the idea of gap and fulfillment but also rejects its core thesis.[42]

38. Ibid.

39. Nolland, *Gospel of Matthew*, 218.

40. Ibid., 219.

41. Luz, *Matthew 1–7*, 265.

42. The Protestants and Pentecostals are the predominant advocates of the destructionist presupposition.

It is important to note that some theologians who adopt the gap and fulfillment presupposition and who also employ the reconstructionist presupposition will concede some indigenous cultures need to be eradicated. But the uniqueness of the destructionist presupposition lies in its assumption that Jesus has to destroy the core of the indigenous religious teachings and practices of Africa in order to effectively extend the benefits of his work to the people. The destructionist presupposition rejects the idea of fulfillment, arguing that Jesus does not fulfill the indigenous religious values and practices of the ancestors. Yusufu Turaki makes this point:

> God's universal way of dealing with His fallen creation and humanity was revealed in Jesus the Messiah, His redemptive and reconciling work on the cross. Can African "intermediaries" deal adequately with the theological question of the human fall and sin? There are no substitutes to Jesus the Messiah. Even where Jesus is thus recognized and admitted to be Lord and Savior, He is not a successor or a fulfillment of anything within African religious pantheon and practice, as it was the case between Jesus and the Judaic System.[43]

Tokunboh Adeyemo makes a similar point:

> Some . . . African theologians have asserted that Jesus came to fulfill not only the Old Testament but the African traditional expectations. Besides the fact that this is neither biblical nor traditionally true, it is pertinent to ask why the shadow is still embraced (that is, the Traditional Religion) when the perfect reality (Jesus Christ) has come? Why are the advocates of Traditional Religion soliciting a return to the imperfect, confused, and unrealistic mythology?[44]

Underlying the destructionist presupposition is the belief that the work of Jesus Christ is unique and stands opposed to the purported mediatory works of the ancestors. This presupposition emphasizes the discontinuity between the indigenous religions and Christianity. Byang Kato is one of the earliest Nigerian theologians who considered the Christian gospel to be radically different from the indigenous religions. According to him, the attempt by some theologians to integrate Christianity into the indigenous religions is both christologically and pragmatically dan-

43. Turaki, *Unique Christ for Salvation*, 224.

44. Adeyemo, *Salvation in African Tradition*, 29.

gerous.[45] He argues that such undertaking is equal to encouraging a Christian convert, who is supposed to be liberated from the evils and superstitions of his or her indigenous religion, to go back to them. For him, the indigenous religions cannot provide a valid solution to the Christian's spiritual problems. To use his own words, the "beliefs of African traditional religion only locate the problem; the practices point away from the solution; the Incarnate risen Christ alone is the answer. Christianity is a radical faith and it must transform sinners radically."[46]

For some destructionist theoreticians, the core of the indigenous religions and cultures is contra Christianity. This assumption, of course, is based on the idea that "culture is man-made" and is therefore under the influence of "Satan and his fallen cohorts."[47] Thus, "culture is . . . a tool of the enemy of the gospel and does not yield easily to the need of the gospel."[48] What has remained unclear is if there are some aspects of the indigenous religions that are compatible with Christianity. According to Odey,

> Those who have tried to baptize elements of African Traditional Religion into Christianity, for instance, ancestors, and communion of the saints, prove unconvincing. For one, eclectic enterprise adds too little. Then, there is a tendency towards a superficial parallelism with loss of real meaning. As it de-emphasizes the force of the gospel, namely, that Christ liberates from sin and bondage of demonic forces, all who [are] held captive. It runs against the unique claim of Christianity that there is "No other Name" and the liberating cry, "Behold, I make all things new."[49]

Many advocates of the destructionist presupposition such as Odey dismiss the idea that there are major valid areas of convergence between the gospel of Jesus Christ and the religious traditions. The logic of these suspicious attitudes toward the indigenous religions can be articulated as follows: Since culture is man-made, it follows that the indigenous religions are man-made and, therefore, cannot be equated with Christianity,

---

45. This understanding underlies what I will refer to in chapter two as Neo-Missionary Christology.

46. Kato, *Theological Pitfalls in Africa*, 38.

47. Odey, "Superstitious Beliefs and Practices," 145–64.

48. Ibid.

49. Ibid.

which is divine-made. This is precisely the argument of Kato when he bemoans the attempt of some theologians to contextualize Christianity in Africa: "Christianity cannot incorporate any man-made religion. But some theologians are seeking recognition of the so-called common ground between Christianity and African traditional religions."[50]

Those who adopt the destructionist presupposition usually locate their Christology primarily in the biblical representations of Jesus Christ and the creedal christological formulations of the early church. While acknowledging that a Christology designed for African contexts should interact with the indigenous cultures and religions, some of the advocates of the destructionist presupposition insist on the supremacy of the Bible and the christological formulations of the early church on the matter of Christology. In this sense, then, the task of the theologian is to present the Christ-Event in a way that allows the "biblical teachings" on Jesus to address the entire African "worldview and its culture and religion."[51] And rather than seeking for the areas the indigenous religions agree and conflict with Christianity, the theologian's goal should be to discover what the Bible is saying about non-Christian religions.[52] In his examination of the ancestor-Christology model, Peter Nyende, a Kenyan theologian, faults Kwame Bediako, Benezet Bujo, and others on failing to engage seriously and comprehensibly with the New Testament teaching about Jesus.[53] Nyende shares the concern of Kato and Turaki on the need for African theologians to use the Bible as the standard for testing and measuring an authentic Christian Christology. For Kato, African theologians who desire to "indigenize Christianity in Africa" must not "betray Scriptural principles of God" in the process.[54]

What is at stake in the attempt to contextualize the Christ-Event, in the thinking of some advocates of the destructionist presupposition, is the finality and supremacy of Jesus Christ. Some of them fear that the finality of Jesus as the only way through which human beings can obtain divine salvation is in danger of underestimation. For Turaki, the uniqueness and finality of Jesus Christ underlie the validity of Christianity's message of salvation. He writes, "[u]nless Christ is

50. Kato, *Theological Pitfalls in Africa*, 17.

51. Turaki, *Unique Christ for Salvation*, 5.

52. Ibid.

53. Nyende, "Jesus the Greatest Ancestor," 5–14.

54. Kato, *Theological Pitfalls in Africa*, 16.

confessed and proclaimed as the unique Lord and Savior of the whole world as attested to and affirmed by the Holy Scriptures, the prophets and the apostles, our Christian offer of salvation, peace, and justice to the world is meaningless and empty."[55]

Insofar as Jesus figures as the only Savior of the world, the proponents of the destructionist presupposition contend that there is no salvation outside of Jesus Christ. According to Kato, it "is not arrogance to herald the fact that all who are not 'in Christ' are lost." It is rather "articulating what the Scripture says."[56] For him, the indigenous religions are devoid of soteriological content and simply have "clues which only highlight human dilemma, man's craving for the Ultimate Reality, and yet constant flight from Him through the worship of idols. . . . There is emphatically no possibility of salvation through these religions."[57] Whether or not Kato's exclusivist understanding of God's salvation is conceded, it is clear that the destructionist presupposition construes Jesus not as a fulfiller of the purported religious aspirations that exist in the indigenous religions. Rather Jesus stands as a redeemer who can liberate the people from the fears, superstitions, and satanic entanglements that permeate their indigenous religions.

The destructionist presupposition has continued to reverberate in African Christianity. The reasons for this are not too hard to discern. Some Christians have internalized the Western missionaries' derogatory estimation of the indigenous cultures and traditions.[58] Others, perhaps as a result of their denominational orientation, have continued to view everything that is associated with the indigenous religions as anti-Christianity. The consequent response is that these Christians have become highly suspicious of the compatibility of the indigenous religions and Christianity, and also have become unwilling to grant that there is a positive role of the indigenous religious customs in contextualizing Christianity in Africa. Some of these Christians continue to view the core beliefs of the indigenous religions such as ancestor worship as devilish and anti-Christian gospel. Some even go to the extent of insisting that it is unchristian for a Christian to take some medicines that are prepared by native doctors. In *Christianity in Nigeria: The Way*

55. Turaki, *Unique Christ for Salvation*, 116.

56. Kato, *Theological Pitfalls in Africa*, 16.

57. Ibid., 45.

58. See the introduction.

Forward, Felix Ugochukwu narrated a story of his encounter with a Christian who was open to taking a traditionally prepared medicine to cure himself.

> A brother we reckon high in [the Christian] faith was ill and there was itching all over his body as a result of drug reaction. He took drugs but to no avail, and [the] laboratory test showed nothing. I suggested the use of coconut. He broke one, drank the water and chewed the fruit and was expecting an instant healing. I explained to him that it was not like hunger that disappears as soon as one is fed. . . . To my greatest surprise, he said how he wished he could get what is called *Nsiattu*, [a word] in Igboland meaning "poison neutralizer" or "poison destroyer." I asked: "Do you know what you are actually requesting?" [I said to him] that is a concoction prepared by a native doctor under his gods. Even if it means death, a Christian should not request that.[59]

Ugochukwu also narrated a story of a Christian woman who heeded the advice of some of her non-Christian friends to contact a particular native doctor they knew could cure her sickness.[60] According to Ugochukwu, by contacting the native doctor, the woman sinned and has failed to acknowledge that "God's healing balm remains available to faithful Christians always."[61] It is important to recognize here that many Christians associate native doctors with the indigenous religions. And since in their thinking the indigenous religions are demonic, everything that is associated with it is demonic and anti-Christianity. But this understanding of the gospel and the indigenous religious traditions seem to operate only at a surface level. At the deeper level, many Christians exhibit a dual allegiance: they leave Jesus to consult some indigenous sources for solutions to their problems when Jesus is slow to bring them solutions.[62]

The greatest problem of the destructionist presupposition is its inability to develop an adequate christological response to the issue of Christ and culture. This presupposition fits roughly into the category that N. Richard Niebuhr in his classical work *Christ and Culture* has

59. Ugochukwu, *Christianity in Nigeria*, 6.
60. Ibid.
61. Ibid.
62. See chapter three.

dubbed "Christ against culture."[63] Essential to the destructionist presupposition is the idea that loyalty to Jesus Christ entails a rejection of the indigenous cultural and religious thought forms which are believed to be under the influence and control of Satan. Since the mission of Jesus Christ in the world includes destroying the works of Satan, in order for Christians to demonstrate complete loyalty to Jesus Christ, they must continue his work by rejecting the ways of the world; that is, the world outside of the Christian church.[64]

What the proponents of the destructionist presupposition fail to take into account is the logical and practical impossibility of a "sole dependence on Jesus Christ to the exclusion of culture."[65] As Niebuhr argues,

> Christ claims no man purely as a natural being, but always as one who has become human in culture; who is not only in culture, but into whom culture has penetrated . . . If Christians do not come to Christ with the language, the thought patterns, the moral disciplines of Judaism, they come with those of Rome; if not with those of Rome, with those of Germany, England, Russia, America, India, or China.[66]

One can add to the list the cultures of African societies. The advocates of the destructionist presupposition underestimate the role of the cultures and traditions when interpreting and appropriating the meaning and significance of the Christ-Event in their contexts. The consequence is a form of docetic Christology. The proponents of the destructionist presupposition have failed to account adequately for the humanity of Jesus Christ and how the Jewish culture provided the context for his gospel. They have also failed to acknowledge the existence of the dialectics exemplified in Jesus's attitude towards human cultures. As a being that incarnated into human culture, Jesus undoubtedly took on human cultural forms although "without being dependent on or domesticated by them."[67] Jesus does not need to destroy the indigenous religious traditions of Africa in order to effectively communicate to the people the divine salvation he embodies. African theologians also do not have to

---

63. Niebuhr, *Christ and Culture.*

64. Ibid., 58–63.

65. Ibid., 80.

66. Ibid.

67. Metzger, *Word of Christ and the World of Culture,* 153.

construe the indigenous religious thought forms as totally incompatible with the person and work of Jesus Christ.

The destructionist presupposition underestimates the place of the culture of the hearers in their perceptions of the meaning of gospel of Jesus Christ. The proponents of this presupposition need to rediscover that it is not possible for people to truly appreciate and experience the meaning of the Christ-Event in isolation from their own culture. Graham Ward has argued that to "do Christology is to engage in a christological operation; to enquire is to engender Christ; to enter the engagement is to foster the economy whereby God is made know to us. To do Christology is to inscribe Christ into the times and cultures we inhabit."[68] An African Christology that fails to engage dialectically with the indigenous religions will hardly influence many Christians at a deeper level. One of the greatest needs of African Christians is to de-stigmatize the indigenous cultural forms and traditions and to use them as vital tools for re-interpreting the Christ-Event. The reconstructionist presupposition, to which I will now turn, attempts to bridge the gulf between the gap and fulfillment and destructionist presuppositions.

Reconstructionist Presupposition

Another presupposition that informs christological conversations in African Christianity, particularly amongst theologians, arises from the assumption that Jesus deconstructs the indigenous religions and reconstructs it in order to create a new religious understanding of the world. Although some proponents of the gap and fulfillment presupposition lean more toward the reconstructionist presupposition, it seeks to provide a bridge between the destructionist and the gap and fulfillment presuppositions. What the reconstructionist presupposition shares with the gap and fulfillment presupposition is the view that the indigenous worldviews of Africa provide a valid context for interpreting and explaining meaningfully the Christ-Event in the African contexts. The reconstructionist presupposition, however, agrees with the destructionist presupposition on the latter's claim that Jesus Christ does not merely fill the purported gaps in the indigenous religions.

The majority of the theologians who employ the reconstructionist presupposition perceives Jesus as the one who reconstructs the indig-

---

68. Ward, *Christ and Culture*, 2.

enous religions by challenging, sifting, transforming, and rebuilding it.[69] Justin Ukpong is a leading proponent of this view. Although he sees Jesus as a fulfiller, he construes fulfillment in the sense of reconstruction. This understanding of Jesus's relation to the indigenous cultures, for him, stems from Jesus's attitude towards the traditions of Judaism.

> Using [some] elements of Jewish culture, [Jesus] sought to instill into the Law and the Jewish religion a new vision based on the Good News that he preached. This involved a challenge to this Jewish culture and religions to respond to the Good News and a challenge to people to rethink their basic beliefs, hopes, and institutions. Jesus issued this challenge from within the culture itself and not from outside of it.[70]

According to Ukpong, an adequate Christology will create enough room for Jesus to accommodate and reconstruct the cultures and traditions of Africa. The Kenyan theologian J. K. Mugambi has articulated a theological foundation for the reconstructionist presupposition. In *From Liberation to Reconstruction: African Christian Theology after the Cold War,* Mugambi writes:

> Jesus of Nazareth enters history at a time when Judea is rife with the Messianic hope that some deliverer would come to liberate the people from the yoke of Roman imperialism. The critics of Jesus accused him of trying to destroy Judaism and its institutions. In response, Jesus replied that his mission was reconstructive rather than destructive.[71]

For Mugambi, the beauty, albeit the complexity, of reconstruction is that in the builder master plan "new specification may be made in the new designs, while some aspects of the old complex are retained in the new."[72] He argues that it is time African theologians moved from the state of liberation to reconstruction just as the people of Israel who returned with Ezra and Nehemiah reconstructed their nation. He argues that the book of Nehemiah should become the "central text of the new theological paradigm in African Christian theology as a logical

---

69. Ukpong, "Christology and Inculturation," 41.

70. Ibid., 58.

71. Mugambi, *From Liberation to Reconstruction*, 13.

72. Ibid.

development from the Exodus motif."[73] He develops a broader concept of the reconstruction model. According to him, a reconstructive theology must include a personal reconstruction, cultural reconstruction, and ecclesiastical reconstruction. Personal reconstruction refers to the transformation that begins with the individual person: "Jesus teaches that constructive change must start from within the motives and intention of the individual."[74] The cultural reconstruction includes the religious worldview of a given society. He warns that African theologians are in danger of producing the theologies that are irrelevant to their people if they ignore their cultures.

> Let each of us take our cultural background as the starting point of our theological quest. We do not have any other option, unless we intend to be superficial and redundant. If we wish to serve meaningfully and relevantly, then we must take our cultural and religious heritage seriously.[75]

The ecclesiastical reconstruction includes "management structures, financial policies, pastoral care, human resources development, research, family education, service, and witness."[76]

Although Mugambi has not fully developed a Christology that is built on a reconstructionist presupposition, his understanding of a theology of reconstruction is crucial for conceptualizing the content of this presupposition. Ukpong and many others construe Jesus as the one who has not come to destroy the indigenous traditions of Africa. On the contrary Jesus has come to reconstruct the traditions. Therefore, they contend that the Christ-Event must be interpreted to befit the cultural, religious and social needs of African Christians. The key difference between the gap and fulfillment presupposition and the reconstructionist presupposition is that whereas the former construes Jesus as the individual who fills the gaps in the indigenous religions, the latter sees Jesus as the individual who radically criticizes and destroys some parts of the indigenous religious beliefs when necessary in order to effectively

73. Ibid.
74. Ibid., 15.
75. Ibid., 25.
76. Ibid., 15.

reconstruct and rebuild a new form of cultures and traditions for the African peoples.[77]

It is important to acknowledge that the indigenous thought forms have continued to shape the beliefs and lives of African Christians. Construing Jesus as the one who destroys the indigenous worldviews therefore will perpetuate a shallow understanding of the meaning and relevance of the Christ-Event in African Christianity. But rather than simply fulfilling or completing the gaps that exist in the indigenous religions, Jesus reconstructs them radically with the intent to create a new understanding of God and his creation—a worldview that is African and at the same time Christian. Understood in this way, the story of Jesus Christ would become good news to Africans who converted to Christianity from their indigenous religions. The Christian convert would not be under the fear of being removed from the cultures and traditions that define his or her identity as an African.

Ogbu Kalu has argued that African worldviews are elastic in nature and has the "capacity to make room within [their] inherited body of traditions for new realities" or foreign worldviews.[78] A reconstructionist presupposition explores the openness of the indigenous religions. Ukpong challenges Christians to adopt the presupposition of reconstruction in their practice of evangelism.

> Correctly understood, the church's mission is to evangelize human cultures and to transform the human race through the gospel message. This means effecting change in a Christian direction in the common meanings and values that inform the way of life of people. It involves a challenge to the common thinking and shared meaning in society.[79]

Kalu agrees with Ukpong, and argues that "Christianization process must take cognizance of the element of continuity in the religious lives of Africans instead of branding everything under the umbrage of syncretism."[80]

---

77. Another difference between the gap and fulfillment presupposition and the reconstructionist presupposition is that whilst the former concentrates on the indigenous cultures and traditions, the latter goes beyond some of the obsolete indigenous cultures and traditions to engage with the contemporary concerns of Africans.

78. Kalu, "Introduction," 3.

79. Ukpong, "Christology and Inculturation," 41.

80. Kalu, "Introduction," 8.

The reconstructionist presupposition in a sense assembles some of things the destructionist presupposition dismantles, and deconstructs some of the foundations of the gap and fulfillment presupposition with the intent to create a meeting point for Christianity and the indigenous religions. However, what many reconstructionist theologians have failed to articulate is the extent to which Jesus reconstructs the indigenous religions. How can we ascertain the precise elements of the indigenous religions or cultures that need to be demolished or refurbished in order to construct an adequate African Christology? How far does Jesus need to reconstruct the indigenous traditions? Would the core elements of the indigenous understandings of the world remain untouchable after the reconstruction? Would the understandings still be recognizable after the reconstruction? Or would what is left of them after the reconstructions be only debris of a disintegrated core? These are some pertinent questions that the theologian who employs the reconstructionist presupposition must be ready to answer. The theologian must also avoid constructing a Christology on syncretistic foundations that neither adequately represents the teachings of Christianity nor the indigenous religions. This is part of the worries of the theologians who adopt primarily the destructionist presupposition. The proponents of the reconstructionist presupposition have the burden to articulate the required balance that is needed to faithfully represent the indigenous religions and the meaning and significance of the Christ-Event.[81] In what follows, I will examine presuppositions of solution and how it informs christological conversations in Africa, particularly among Nigerian Christians.

Solution Presupposition

The three presuppositions I have examined share the view that Jesus is a solution to human religious problems. For some advocates of the destructionist presupposition, human beings are in a fallen state, under the wrath of God and in need of a savior. Jesus alone, and not the ancestors or the mediators in the indigenous religions, can provide a lasting and adequate solution to this human predicament. As Turaki argues,

---

81. I will explore these issues further in chapters four, five, six, and seven.

The solution of man's condition does not lie in any religious ritual and ceremonies and sacrifices, for these are only mere human attempts at placating God (Hebrews 8–10). God cannot be appeased by any human religiosity. Man's efforts cannot be man's solution. Man needs a divine solution, which God has already provided in Jesus the Messiah. If 'intermediaries' often talked about in the African religious pantheon are meant to solve human problems, especially, man's estrangement from his Creator, this form of solution falls only within "man's making of his own god." The tradition and religion of the ancestors, even when invoked, fall under man's making of his own "bridges" to God. Jesus the Messiah is that "bridge" and the fulfillment of God's universal prophetic and messianic hope.[82]

Kato is also very critical of human nature. He contends that to be saved in the Judeo-Christian understanding "presupposes the lost condition for which salvation or deliverance is needed."[83] But Onah Odey articulates a holistic view of salvation. According to him,

Salvation [is] not necessarily a technical theological term, but simply denotes "deliverance" from almost any kind of evil, whether material or spiritual. Theologically, however, it denotes the whole process by which man is delivered from all that interferes with the enjoyment of God's highest blessing; the actual enjoyment of those blessings. The root idea in salvation is deliverance from some danger or evil.[84]

The salvation that Jesus brings, for Odey, embraces the idea of an already-not-yet tension. It actively affects the present and the future. He writes,

As in the teaching of Jesus (Matt 9:22) salvation throughout the New Testament is regarded as a present experience, but it is eschatological as well. In deed the blessing of salvation the believer has now [is] only a foretaste of what are to be [in the] coming age, after Christ comes. The salvation Christ brings is not merely deliverance from future punishment, but also from sin as a present power (Rom 6). It includes all the redemptive blessing we have in Christ, chiefly conversion, regeneration, justification,

82. Turaki, *Unique Christ for Salvation*, 145.

83. Kato, *Theological Pitfalls in Africa*, 41.

84. Odey, "Superstitious Beliefs and Practices," 145–64.

adoption, sanctification, and glorification. It provides a solution for the whole problem of sin, in all its many aspects.[85]

The proponents of the reconstructionist and gap and fulfillment presuppositions have argued that the salvation Jesus enacts and embodies affects all aspects of human exigencies. The work of Jesus is a solution to the problems caused by human sins and which have imbued the cultural and religious traditions of Africa. The functional Christology of these two presuppositions tends to lean more to the humanity of Jesus Christ. For many of these theologians, Jesus provides a perfect example of what God intends human beings and their societies to be.[86] The tasks of the theologian, in their thinking, are to present the gospel message about Jesus in a way that "exposes inhuman actions, ignorance, superstition," to "broaden the border of Christian charity" and to teach the people to "appreciate the love of God and the loftiness of human dignity and rights"[87]

At the grassroots level, the majority of lay Christians see Jesus primarily as a solution to their spiritual, economic, and social problems. The grassroots Christologies of African Christianity exist in different oral forms, including songs, testimonies, and prayer. Here I will examine a popular Christian song composed by James Arum, a popular Nigerian musician.[88] Many Christian songs composed by some Christian musicians usually have powerful theological and christological contents. In some situations, songs play a creedal role, functioning as a short theological or christological expression of the cardinal beliefs of many Christians. In this song, Arum asks Jesus to "settle him so that he can rejoice with other people" whom Jesus has already settled with prosperity and blessing.

Ude mụ na asụ;

My sobbing

Akwa nke mụ na ebe;

My crying

85. Ibid.

86. Ukpong, "Christology and Inculturation," 51.

87. Odoemene, "Church in Nigeria: Its Human Burden vis-à-vis Its Divine Mission," in *Witnessing Christ in Contemporary Nigeria*, ed. Anacletus N. Odoemene, 77.

88. This song is partly in Igbo language and *pidgin English* and is most popular in southeastern Nigeria.

Nanị Jisọs bụ onye nwe m mara mkpa mụ;

It is only Jesus that understands my need

Jisọs settle luọ nụ mụ;

Jesus, settle me

Ka mụ soro ibe mụ ñụrịa;

So that I can rejoice with others

Jisọs settle luọnụ mụ;

Jesus, settle me

Ka mụ kwụsị I nye gi nsogbu

So that that I can stop disturbing you

Mere m ihe nkem na arịọ;

Do for me the things I am requesting

One of the interesting things about this song is that Arum alludes to some of the sayings of Jesus to buttress his persistent request for a divine settlement or blessing. Arum begins by reminding Jesus of some of his promises that are contained in his Sermon on the Mount.[89]

Ọ kwa gị sị anyị rịọ, I sị na anyị ga arịọta

Na anyị kụọ aka na ụzọ, na ọnụ ụzọ ga emepe?

Did you not tell us to ask; you said, we would receive?

And that we should knock at the door, that the door would be opened?

Arum also alludes to Jesus' invitation to people to come to him with their burdens.[90]

I sịrị anyị 'biakute gi anyị bụ ndi eboro ibu dị arọ.

You said to us: come to you all of us that are carrying heavy load.

Na I ga eme ka ibu arọ anyị bu dị nfe;

That you would make our heavy loads to be weightless'

Eburuwo mụ nsogbu uwa bịa na iru gị

89. See Matthew 7:7–12; Luke 11:9–13.

90. Matthew 11:28.

I have brought my problems to your presence

Ome nma I ga ekwa ka mu buru ha laghachi?

The benevolent one, would you want me to go back with the problems?

Arum buttresses his desire for a divine settlement by alluding to the parable Jesus told about a persistent widow and "a Judge who did not fear God."[91] The word settlement which is the key to understanding this song is worthy of examination. There are several possible ways of understanding the contextual implications of the language of settlement in Nigeria. But two contexts are particularly helpful. Firstly, the language of settlement goes hand-in-hand with apprenticeship. In most cases, some young adults live with some wealthy businessmen or businesswomen to learn trade. The duration of the training varies depending on the circumstances and the conditions of the agreement. At the end of the training, the businessman (normally called master) is expected to settle or give a reasonable sum of money and other resources to settle the trainee. What is vital to remember in this context is that it is believed to be the right of the apprentice, so long as he or she completes the training without offending his or her master, to demand a settlement.

Secondly, almost anyone living in Nigeria understands the language of settlement to mean paying off ones way. A popular example is the encounter between many motorists and the majority of police officers who work at numerous road checkpoints. Normally, when a police officer stops a car or a commercial bus he or she immediately asks the driver for *papers*. For anyone that is new to the country, the *language of papers* may not make sense at all. But the majority of the people who live in the country know immediately that the officers are not really asking the driver to produce the documents of the vehicle, but rather (in most cases) to settle or to give them money. Sometimes some police officers will detain the motorists who refuse to give them money. Here the idea is: if a motorist does not want the police officers to delay or continue to disturb the flow of his or her journey, then he or she must settle them. Undoubtedly, some motorists who settle immediately do so most of the time grudgingly.

91. Luke 18:1–8.

The christological problem with using the language of settlement to explain Jesus' idea of people asking, knocking and seeking, and his invitation to the people with heavy loads, is that it distorts the generosity and graciousness that propel God's blessings. Unlike many motorists who give grudgingly to the police officers at road checkpoints, God, in the thinking of Jesus, gives generously and willingly.[92] Also, unlike the police officers who extort money from motorists, Jesus teaches that people who ask from God must do so within the confines of God's righteousness: "But seek first His kingdom and His righteousness, and other things will be added to you."[93]

Other crucial elements that need noting in Arum's song are the impatience and ungodly jealousy that subtly drive the whole concept of settlement. The following lines from the song will highlight these elements:

Oge nkem eruola. Mere mụ ihe imere ibe mụ

My time has come. Do for me what you have done for others

Ọ kwa ọna abụ emere nwatakịị ihe emere ibe ya

Isn't it [true] that when it is done for a child what has been done for others

Ọ kwa obi ga adị ya nma na elu ụwa?,

Would the child not become happy?

Ya mere chọrọ mụ my own share

Therefore, give me my own share

Ka mụ soro ibe mụ yọ ba-ị bara n'ime

So that I can rejoice with others

Ka mụ kwụ sị ị nye gị nsogbu

So that I can stop disturbing you

It is vital to highlight three major problems with the solution presupposition. First, as Arum's song has indicated, the desire to accumulate and possess health, wealth, and wellbeing stimulates and drives the idea of settlement. To use the language of John McDowell, this desire

92. Matthew 6:25–34.

93. Matthew 6:33, *NASB.*

contradicts the notions of self-giving and self-dispossessing exemplified in the Christian image of the triune God.[94] Rather than being driven by the spirit of accumulation and possessiveness, African Christians face the challenge to learn from Jesus who embodies self-giving. Second, the danger in construing Jesus as the one who settles people is that this understanding may lead a Christian into an ungodly comparison that reproduces hatred, covetousness, and jealousy. Theologians and lay Christians must begin to see Jesus Christ as both an answerer and a questioner. He does not only produce answers or solutions to human problems; he also questions people's understandings of their problems and the motives behind their desires for solutions. And third, what is at stake here is the politics of power. The quest for power partly informs Jesus-talk in contemporary African Christianity. This quest is embedded in the struggles of the majority of theologians as well as lay Christians to liberate themselves from the bondage of Western Christologies and to contextualize the Christ-Event so as to befit their history, experience, cultures, aspirations, and social location. This quest, as it will become clearer in chapters two and three, is shrewdly metamorphosing into icons of power and control that strip Jesus of the power to critique and inform the emerging contextual Christologies. The implication of this state of affairs is that the majority of theologians and the Christian laity are consciously or unconsciously disempowering Jesus in order to achieve their christological, cultural, religious, and social aspirations.

In conclusion, as I have already argued, it is a mistake to assume that African theologians can be categorized neatly under any of these presuppositions. They share the quest to imagine and express the Christ-Event in the ways that connect with some cultural and existential issues that confront their contexts. The four presuppositions I have examined are unique in some respects; but as I have shown, they also overlap. In spite of their christological problems, these presuppositions inform the majority of the existing theologies and Christologies in Africa. They have contributed immensely to the uniqueness of the christological models that have been constructed by some key theologians. Some of the presuppositions also shape some of the emerging grassroots Christologies. The Revealer Christology model I aim to construct in this book, on the one hand, will draw insights from these presuppositions and, on the other hand, will differ from them, particularly from any claim that seem

94. McDowell, *Gospel According to Star Wars*, 25.

to discourage a dialectical engagement between the Christ-Event and the indigenous religions of Africa. I will now proceed to examine in the next two chapters some of the major christological models that exist in contemporary African Christianity.

2

Constructive Christologies of Contemporary African Christianity

IN THIS CHAPTER, I EXAMINE SOME OF THE CHRISTOLOGICAL MODELS that some key African theologians have constructed. For the purpose of clarity, I examine these models under three major headings, namely, neo-missionary Christology, culture-oriented Christology and liberation-oriented Christology. Although these Christologies sometimes overlap, it is important to note that they have pursued different agendas and have generated different kinds of questions and answers. Building on the christological presuppositions I examined in chapter one, I will question, articulate, and critique these Christologies, paying attention to their historical contexts, agendas, and contents. As we shall see, these Christologies are indicative of the persistent influence of the *Taylorian christological presupposition* that I examined in the introduction.

The theologians I am going to examine have made unique contributions to the development of Christologies and theologies in Africa. But I will argue that their Christologies have remained largely inadequate. The majority of them has fallen into a dichotomist trap and has failed to engage appropriately with the dialectics that ought to characterize ontological Christology and functional Christology, and also the *tension* that shrouds the act of interpreting and appropriating the Christ-Event in human ever-shifting cultural and social contexts. Some of these theologians have continued to raise the questions which may have defined the identity of African Christianity in the nineteenth and early twentieth centuries but which no longer bother many lay Christians today. While it is important to acknowledge the contributions of these Christologies in the making and development of contextual christological discourses in Africa, it is also necessary to critique them in order to see how adequately (or inadequately) they have understood and interacted with their immediate contexts and the Christ-Event.

Neo-Missionary Christology

> Christianity does not undertake to destroy national assimilation; where there are any degrading superstitious defects, it corrects them . . .[1]

These were the words of Samuel Ajayi Crowther, a rescued Nigerian slave, who later became the first Nigerian Anglican bishop of the Niger Dioceses. Crowther's contention exemplifies one of the earliest attempts by some African Christian converts to contextualize the Christ-Event and Christianity. But it is Byang Kato who has created what I describe in this book as the Neo-missionary Christology.[2] According to Kato, while it is important for African theologians to write theologies that are relevant to their contexts, they must bear in mind that Christianity is superior to every culture and as such must remain the sole judge to determine the adequacy of their indigenous cultures and traditions.

> Some [African] church leaders today frown [at] the missionaries for declaring the unique Lordship of Christ as presented in the Scriptures . . . African Christians who have found it necessary to burn every idol have followed precedents set in the Scriptures (Acts 19). Christianity stands to judge every culture, destroying elements that are incompatible modes of expression for its advance, and bringing new life to its adherents, the qualitative life that begins at the moment of conversion and culminates eternally with the imminent return of our Lord Jesus Christ.[3]

1. Quoted in Jesse Page, *The Black Bishop: Samuel Ajayi Crowther*, 299.

2. Although Kato lived a relatively short life, he has remained the most influential Evangelical theologian in Nigeria and arguably in Africa. He was born in 1936 in Nigeria and studied theology in ECWA Theological Seminary Igbaja, Nigeria and London Bible College. He completed his doctorate studies in theology at Dallas Theological Seminary, Texas, USA, in 1974 (a year after he was elected general secretary of Association of Evangelicals of Africa and Madagascar). He became the vice-president of the World Evangelical Fellowship (WEF) in 1974 and in 1975 became the chairman of WEF's theological commission. He died in December 1975. Kato only published one book before his death but wrote and presented several theological papers on theology some of which have now been published.

3. Kato, *Biblical Christianity in Africa*, 29.

Kato's foregoing words encapsulates the Neo-missionary Christology. Although the locution neo-missionary has not yet entered into the christological discourse in Africa, it seems to be the most appropriate expression that describes the type of Christology that emerged as a reaction to the culture-oriented Christology and the missionary Christology.[4] Broadly conceived, the neo-missionary Christology tries to create a compromise between the Missionary Christology and *some* indigenous cultures of Africa.[5] It relates to the Missionary Christology dialectically: on the one hand, the neo-missionary Christology adopts some of the presuppositions of the Missionary Christology; and, on the other hand, it parts ways with the Missionary Christology by creating a new and contextually-driven hermeneutic for interpreting the Christ-Event.

Neo-Missionary Christology in Relation to Missionary Christology

Kato, technically speaking, did not write a Christology. But he was a sort of a generalist writing on different aspects of Christian theology. However, his Christology permeates his soteriology and theology of religions, and his work remains foundational to the development of the neo-missionary Christology. He sets his theological work against the backdrop of what he considers the problem of universalism and syncretism (embedded in the emerging African theology and ecumenical theology), which he perceives as a threat to the "belief in Christ as the only way of Salvation."[6] His description of this religious phenomenon and the danger it poses to Christology is sharp: "the stage is well set for universalism in Africa. Universalism means the belief that all men will eventually be saved whether they believe in Christ or not."[7]

4. See the introduction for discussions on the Missionary Christology as used in this book. I will examine the meaning and content of the Culture-oriented Christologies later in this chapter.

5. It will be misleading to assume that every Christology that belongs to the category of Neo-Missionary shares the same level of enthusiasm for the Missionary Christology.

6. Kato, *Theological Pitfalls in Africa*, 11. Kato sees African Theology as "a funeral march of Biblical Christianity and a heralding of syncretism and universalism." Ibid., 55.

7. Ibid.

Again he writes, "It is not neo-colonialism to plead the uniqueness and finality of Jesus Christ. It is not arrogance to herald the fact that all who are not 'in Christ' are lost. It is merely articulating what the Scriptures say."[8]

Regardless of what anyone thinks of Kato, his theology and Christology continue to influence African theological and christological discourses.[9] His greatest contribution to African theology is perhaps his insistence on situating the Bible in the center of Christian theology.[10] Keith Ferdinando argues that Kato "was committed to certain non-negotiable presuppositions," and fundamental among them "was the belief that the Bible was the unique Word of God, the ultimate source and authority" for theological expression.[11] Kato guarded jealously the centrality of the Bible in theological discourses so much so he warned that his contemporaries who were more open to cultural dialogue emasculated the classical view of the Bible and salvation: "Having thrown away the authoritative basis of the Word of God, man leaves the door open for a man-made message. It is no wonder that liberals cannot come to an orthodox understanding of salvation."[12]

Interpreters of Kato differ on the relevance of his work to African contextual Christology (and theology in general). But they agree that he held a high (Evangelical) view of the Bible. The Ghanaian theologian, Kwame Bediako, for example, describes Kato as a biblicist whose theology was rooted in the tradition of North American Christianity and represented a "reaction and rebuttal of" the project of African theology.[13] David Hesselgrave and Edward Rommen, on the contrary, paint

---

8. Ibid., 16.

9. Although Kato's works constituted primarily an intellectual engagement with some African theologians like Bolaji Idowu and John Mbiti, he demonstrated a keen interest in engaging with Western theological scholarship. His only Major work was *Theological Pitfalls in Africa*. Kato's influence on African theological discourse persists as evidenced in the annual lectures some Nigerian seminaries (e.g., ECWA Theological Seminary Igbaja) organize in commemoration of his theological work. Also some Nigerian influential Evangelical theologians like Tokunboh Adeyemo and Yusufu Turaki draw inspiration from Kato's theological presuppositions. See Turaki, "Theological Legacy of the Reverend Doctor Byang Kato," 133–55.

10. Bediako, *Theology and Identity*, 412.

11. Ferdinando, "Legacy of Byang Kato," 169–74.

12. Kato, *Theological Pitfalls in Africa*, 16.

13. Bediako, *Theology and Identity*, 386.

a positive picture of Kato, presenting him as a theologian whose work models an authentic biblical Christian theology.[14]

It is misleading to see Kato either as a completely anti-African theological discourse, or as the only theologian who took the Bible seriously in the construction of theology in Africa in the 1970s. To buttress this contention, I will explore his views of some indigenous cultures and religions and their relationship to Christianity. It is important to note he was sometimes critical of some missionaries' theology and cultures, although some of his critics do not always acknowledge it. In his assessment, some of the early Western missionaries were culprits of the error and arrogance of cultural hegemony. He writes, "one common error ... is the lumping together of some fundamental Biblical principles with the western culture and repudiating both. The error begins with some early missionaries who identified the kingdom of God with Western civilization. This naïve concept is rejected today."[15]

Also, he indicts a particular missionary who worked in Nigeria in 1918 for describing the ethnic group among whom he worked in a degrading way by presenting them as the "'people of low type ... [who lived] for the most part in crude nudity. The older men and women can recall the taste of human flesh. They are all lazy ... They do not know God.'"[16]

Kato employs the same standard to evaluate the compatibility of Western and African cultures with what he considers to be the gospel. For him, Western cultures or African cultures can co-exist with biblical Christianity so long as they do "not imprison the gospel."[17]

He, however, underestimates the complexity that undergirds the messages of Jesus Christ and the variant ways his followers, particularly the New Testament writers, have explained the meaning of the gospel to the people of their own contexts.[18] His failure to interact thoroughly with the complexity of the Christian gospel and cultures—even though he was aware of the complexity—informed his presenta-

---

14. Hesselgrave and Rommen, *Contextualization*, 96–112.

15. Kato, *Theological Pitfalls in Africa*, 175.

16. Ibid., 8.

17. Ibid., 176.

18. See Ukpong, "Christology and Inculturation," 40–61; Marshall, "Culture and the New Testament," 21–46; Nicholls, "Towards a Theology of Gospel and Cultured," 69–82; Apel, "Towards a Samburu Christology," 356–67.

tion of an image of Jesus Christ.[19] Like in the Missionary Christology, Kato Christology aimed to conquer and eliminate some indigenous religions and cultures of Africa. For example, he rejected Mbiti's theology on the ground that Mbiti did "not feel that African traditional beliefs should be wiped out."[20]

Neo-Missionary Christology and the Making of African Contextual Christology

The neo-missionary Christology, unlike the Missionary Christology, as we will see later in this chapter, acknowledges the need to root the gospel of Jesus Christ in the indigenous contexts.[21] Tokunboh Adeyemo, a Nigerian theologian who has embraced Kato's theological ideologies, hints at this shift. He expresses his dissatisfaction with the dependence of many African churches "on their parents in Europe and North America for their theology, liturgy, and funds."[22] He goes on to argue that the time for the African churches to break with some of the Western theological ideas, funds, and hymns is overdue.[23]

It is a misrepresentation of Kato to construe him as presenting completely an anti-contextual Christology or theology. Ferdinando has argued that Kato's "*Theological Pitfalls* itself, as well as many of [his] articles, addressed some of the issues of the Africa of 1970s and are themselves a move toward a contextual approach."[24] In one of his ten-point proposals on how to "safeguard biblical Christianity in Africa," Kato challenges Christians to "express Christianity in a truly African context, allowing it to judge African culture and never allow the culture to take precedence over Christianity. To do otherwise would isolate African Christianity from historical Christianity . . ."[25] Again he asserts, the "Evangelicals who hold the Bible as their basic source for Christian theology must learn to move beyond the divinely revealed source to the human dimension where the action is. They must discover how best to

19. Kato, *Theological Pitfalls in Africa*, 174.

20. Ibid., 70.

21. Kato, "Theological Pitfalls in Africa," 146.

22. Adeyemo, "African Evangelicals in the 80s," 33.

23. Ibid., 40.

24. Ferdinando, "Legacy of Byang Kato," 169.

25. Kato, *Theological Pitfalls in Africa*, 182.

relate to the human situation in all areas including the socio-economic arena."[26] Kato is sympathetic with the agenda of African theology only when it means relating a "Christian theology to the changing situations in Africa."[27] He rejected some of the contextual approaches some theologians such as the Kenyan theologian, John Mbiti, and the Nigerian theologian, Bolaji Idowu, have developed and argued that they were "defending African traditional religions and practices that are incompatible with biblical teaching."[28]

The reason some theologians see Kato's theological work as North American in nature and approach and perhaps even irrelevant to the project of African contextual theology is connected to his conflicting attitude toward the indigenous religions and cultures. On the one hand, he recognizes the need to promote some cultures and the identity of African peoples through constructing a contextual theology; on the other hand, he appears to be highly critical of some cultures, viewing them as incompatible with a biblical Christianity.

Kato's positive view of some indigenous cultures can be seen in the following contention:

> The attitude of Christians toward cultural renaissance need not be negative. Culture as a way of life must be maintained. Jesus Christ became a man in order to save men. In becoming incarnate, He was involved in the Jewish culture—wearing their clothes, eating their food, thinking in their thought patterns. But while He went through all that, He was without sin, addressing both Jewish and Gentile people authoritatively as the Son of God. Jesus would not have come to make Africans become American Christians [or] to cause Europeans to become Indian Christians. It is God's will that Africans, on accepting Christ as their Savior, become Christian Africans. Africans who become Christians should therefore remain Africans wherever their culture does not conflict with the Bible. It is the Bible that must judge the culture. Where a conflict results, the cultural element must give way.[29]

This lengthy quotation indicates that Kato is pro-contextual Christology. But he also seems to treat some indigenous cultures and religious belief

26. Ibid., 151.
27. Ibid., 148.
28. Ibid., 146.
29. Ibid.

harshly, and sometimes regarding them holistically as incompatible with what he construes as a biblical Christianity. He contends that when an Evangelical "rejects the veneration of African traditional religions" he or she does so for the sake of "safeguarding the unique gospel of Christ."[30] For him, Jesus relates to the non-Christian religions and cultures "not by filling up the measure of idolatry but by transformation."[31] He accuses Mbiti of giving "the impression that both Christianity and non-Christian religions are valuable and deserve co-existing."[32] In his assessment of B. Schuyler's criticism of some Westerners for their degrading conception of Africans and their indigenous understandings of the world, he dismisses the idea that the indigenous religions can contribute positively to the spiritual formation of Christians. He writes,

> For anyone who has been involved in "pagan" religion, the suggestion for "integral Christianity" or "evolution of African from pagan to Christian beliefs" is like telling an ex-cancer patient that it was a mistake that he received a complete cure. The dominating fears and superstitions concerning the spirit world are so dreadful that an instantaneous and complete cure is what Jaba people need . . . African traditional religions only locate the problem; the Incarnate risen Christ alone is the answer. Christianity is a radical faith and it must transform sinners radically.[33]

Some theologians have continued to be highly critical of Kato's theological work. To cite one example, Mercy Oduyoye, a notable feminist theologian, contends that Kato's reason for studying African indigenous religions "is to expose the idolatry that they are and to reduce their hold on the culture of the people."[34] She also argues that his condemnation of the indigenous religion of the Jaba people is based on the standard of a "Western Christian attitude toward the primal worldview of African beliefs and practices."[35]

---

30. Ibid., 177.

31. Ibid., 114.

32. Ibid., 70.

33. Ibid., 38. For Kato, Jesus Christ is a "fulfillment of the Old Testament and of the deep spiritual need of the human hearts, *but He is not the fulfillment of African traditional religions or any other non-Christian religion.*" Ibid., 155.

34. Oduyoye, *Hearing and Knowing*, 61.

35. Ibid., 62.

The neo-missionary Christology presents us with a picture of Jesus who is undergoing an identity crisis—the Jesus who is neither truly Western nor truly African. This particular image of Jesus pervades Kato's theological struggle to contextualize the Christian gospel whilst at the same time holding unto his North American-shaped theology and Christology. The difference between Kato and some of his contemporaries who constructed contextual theologies lies partly in his approach. He construed the Bible as the Word of God and as the ultimate source of Christian theology that must judge every culture.[36] For him, "Christianity should be judged by what its Founder has said in His Word . . ."[37] What he perhaps ignores is the fact that the Bible itself is influenced by several cultures. Colin Gunton has pointed out that the "biblical books emerged out of a process of human engagement with God, as Israel and the apostolic Church lived out and lived within the historical events which were determinative of faith."[38] The cultures and indigenous religions (at least Judaism and Hellenism) of the authors of the Bible inform its structures and contents. Since Kato perhaps ignores this truth about the Bible, he assumes that it is unwarranted to develop some non-biblical images or local metaphors to explain the dialectic of the universality and particularity of Jesus Christ. Also, he underestimates the importance of the reader in biblical hermeneutics. While a reader-response hermeneutic is problematic, and is by no means the only lens through which to interpret the biblical text, it nonetheless provides a helpful way to engage with the dynamic journey from an author to a text and to a reader. He, like some Western missionaries, fails to create a sufficient theological space for Africans to read the Bible from the perspectives of their history and experience. Therefore, his idea of a

---

36. It is important to recognize that the Neo-Missionary Christology is a contextual Christology like the Culture-Oriented Christology and Liberation-Oriented Christology. The difference between them is that the Neo-Missionary Christology can be regarded as "dogmatic contextualization" while Culture-Oriented and Liberation-Oriented Christologies can be classified as "existential contextualization." Bruce Nicholls defines dogmatic contextualization as the approach that "begins with a concern for biblical theology as a fixed authoritative orienting point of contextualization," and existential contextualization as the approach that begins with culture and "seeks to develop a dialectical interaction between questions" of a particular human history and the "existential understanding of the Word of God." See Nicholls, "Toward a Theology of Gospel and Culture," 69–70.

37. Kato, "Evaluation of Black Theology," 245.

38. Gunton, *Intellect and Action*, 43.

biblical Christianity should be suspected. He construes the Bible as the Word of God in a propositional sense.[39] But he undermines the nature of the Bible as a *living text*, which implies that it should not function as an oppressive tool, suppressing indiscriminately the non-Jewish and non-Greco-Roman cultures, but rather as a guide to understanding the redemptive history of God that is revealed in the Christ-Event.

The image of Jesus who is neither truly Western nor truly African poses at least three problems for African Christianity. First, this image of Jesus makes it almost impossible for many lay Christians to understand who Jesus truly is and how he can relate meaningfully to them. Second, a Jesus who is undergoing an identity crisis helps to perpetuate the religious schizophrenia that exists already in African Christianity—a situation in which many Christians continue to see Jesus as a foreign god who is only to be consulted when the indigenous gods and ancestors are unable to solve their problems. Third, a Jesus who is not contextualized to befit and at the same time critique the experiences, history, and the indigenous traditions will continue to hamper the attempt of some contextual theologians to interpret and appropriate the Christ-Event in the ways that speak concretely and relevantly to their people.

The images of Jesus Christ that some theologians have developed for African Christianity need not be exactly the same as the ones contained in the Bible. This is not to suggest a denial or a weak idea of the authority of the Bible. But we must avoid using the Bible as a tool for coercion. The Bible must not be invoked "to suppress free inquiry," to use the phrase of Daniel Migliore, into newer ways of understanding the meanings and significance of Jesus in the contemporary human contexts.[40] The mosaic of pictures of Jesus represented in the Bible should only function as elastic parameters for testing the adequacy of the representations of him that emerge from within African Christians' experiences and contexts. Therefore, the biblical representations of Jesus Christ must not repress the possibility of some new christological expressions. The task of a contextual theologian, therefore, transcends a mere translation of the christological images in the Bible into a lo-

---

39. Kato, *Theological Pitfalls in Africa*, 173. Kato fails to recognize that the expression "Word of God" technically refers to the sections of the Bible where God is presented as speaking directly through someone, for example, the prophets. See also Goldingay, *Models for Scripture*, 204.

40. Migliore, *Faith Seeking Understanding*, 44.

cal equivalence. The task must include discovering some genuine local concepts, pictures and images that have the capacity to communicate effectively and relevantly the meaning and significance of the Christ-Event to his or her context. This new christological adventure explains the rise and subsistence of the Culture-oriented and liberation-oriented Christologies. I will examine these two models in the remainder of this chapter.

Culture-Oriented Christology

The Ghanaian theologian, Kwame Bediako, in *Christianity in Africa: The Renewal of a Non-Western Religion*, poses the question: "Is Christianity suitable to the Africans?"[41] He then proceeds to delimit the task of his project, a task that underlines the thrust of the entire book, by posing another question: "Will African Christianity be able to find viable intellectual grounds upon which to validate and secure its African credentials?"[42] Bediako's questions have occurred in various forms in the writings of some other theologians. Set in the broader context of the correlation between the indigenous religions and Christianity, the following assumptions underscore the intent of these questions: the translatability of Christianity into the African cultural and religious thoughts, and the possibility of constructing some viable contextualized Christologies.[43]

The culture-oriented Christology seeks to re-express Jesus Christ in terms of some indigenous cultures and religious thought forms. I will examine two out of the major models that have emerged, namely, the Guest Christology and the Ancestor Christology models.

Guest Christology

Enyi Ben Udoh is no doubt one of the pioneers of the Culture-oriented Christology.[44] In his 1983 doctoral dissertation titled the "Guest

41. Bediako, *Christianity in Africa*, 3.

42. Ibid., 4.

43. See Sanneh, *Translating the Message*, 1–6; Sanneh, "Horizontal and the Vertical in Mission," 165–71.

44. The writings of some Nigerian theologians, such as Bolaji Idowu, of course, pre-date Udoh's work. But Udoh's work was different because it concentrated primarily on Christology whilst Idowu's works were on African theology and indigenous religions.

Christology: An Interpretative View of the Christological Problem in Africa," he develops a christological model from the indigenous notion of a guest.[45] A guest in the Nigerian indigenous societies is "considered *sacred*" and is consequently "treated with *respect* and *care*."[46] Since guests are treated with dignity and respect, Udoh argues that the construal of Jesus as a guest provides a christological platform to address the problems of "faith schizophrenia"—the dilemma of devoting simultaneously to Christianity and the indigenous religions.[47] He states that his major task is to "undertake a dialectical initiation of Christ and Africa to one another in a manner that does not alienate or dissolve the integrity of either party."[48]

For him, there are two christological problems confronting African Christians. The first is Africans' perception of Jesus Christ as an illegal alien.[49] As an illegal alien, many perceive Jesus Christ as the *unfriendly other*. He goes on to argue that the image of Jesus Christ as an alien or stranger makes him "liable to be rejected, doubted and excluded from the mainstream."[50] He traces the presentation of Jesus as a stranger to the nineteenth-century European missionary expeditions, particularly the Scottish missionary activity in Calabar.[51] Inspired by Pepper Clark's *Plays from Black Africa*, he explores the positive perception of a legal visitor or a guest for a contextual Christology. He argues that construing Jesus Christ as a legitimate guest is an effective way "to bring Africa and Christ closer to one another."[52] As a legitimate guest, Jesus Christ will become be accorded every possible honor and generosity. However, he is expected to conform to the cultures and customs of Africa.[53]

The second christological problem facing African Christians, according to Udoh, is the image of Jesus Christ as a divine being. He contends that the depiction of Jesus Christ as a divine messenger or son

---

45. Udoh, "Guest Christology." The work has been published by Peter Lang.

46. Olikenyi, *African Hospitality*, 106. Emphasis in the original.

47. Udoh, "Guest Christology," 263.

48. Ibid., 17.

49. Ibid., 212.

50. Ibid., 225.

51. Ibid., 206–8.

52. Ibid., 209.

53. Schoffeleers, "Folk Christology in Africa," 157–83.

is "problematic in African religious experience."[54] For him, this problem arises because the "African belief system discounts all claims which elevate any human individual to becoming a divinity as presumptuous and arrogant. In West Africa, this creed is compressed in pidgin English *interalia: God no bi mann, mann no bi god.*"[55] Again he writes, "because God never could become incarnate in human form or vice versa for Africans," the belief that Jesus Christ is a divine "messenger or son" escapes them.[56] Therefore, he concludes that in the indigenous religions "it is an anathema for any historical being to claim for himself . . . the divine prerogatives."[57] He cites the Ibibio cosmology as an example.[58]

> God does not need a messenger. Ibibio cosmology assigns him limitless sphere . . . an ultimate authority. There are no prophets and no temples in Ibibio religion. Directly, the clan communicates [with God] in words, and dramatic gestures but direct appeals to God are rare and confined to crisis situation. Indirectly, it is done through *elders*, dead or alive, by the use of rituals and prayers.[59]

Udoh is dissatisfied with the images of Jesus Christ as a stranger and as a divine being. Conversely, he proposes a guest christological model, which for him will bridge the gulf between Jesus Christ and Africa and the issue of faith schizophrenia. To address the problem stemming from the image of Jesus Christ as an alien, he proposes that Africans need to play the role of a host and make Jesus go through the "initiation act . . . by which [his] image as a guest is transformed into one of a constitutional citizenship."[60] Ukachukwu Chris Manus points out that Udoh sees the *rite of naturalizing* Jesus Christ in Africa as a two-way process. First, Africans must be willing to allow Jesus Christ to become "one of them" by offering him the opportunity to undergo the

---

54. Udoh, "Guest Christology," 80.

55. Ibid., 81. The expression *God no bi mann; mann no bi god* can be translated into a standard English as "Man is not a god; God is not a man."

56. Ibid.

57. Ibid., 210.

58. Ibibio is one of the ethnic groups in Nigeria.

59. Ibid., 81.

60. Ibid., 215.

rite of naturalization. And second, Jesus Christ himself needs "to submit to the process of inculturation."[61] Udoh puts it in this way:

> The Christological significance of this is that Jesus is far from knowing all the social forms and experiential road signs of the African. Like any other guest, his understanding of the new environment is limited. A host has the responsibility of taking him on a tour of his world.[62]

But to become an African, Jesus does not need to be "biologically African."[63] Through the ritual of adaptation or naturalization, he can become a full member of the African community. Once Jesus undergoes this rite, Africans will become less suspicious of him and consequently will "rely on him for answers to their deep religious questions."[64]

Udoh defines a "cultural naturalization rite" as a "ceremony which, when performed, transforms a guest into a legitimate member of the clan."[65] This ritual varies from one ethnic group to another. In some cases, as he argues, it involves "drinking cold water," and in some cultures it may be a more complex ceremony.[66] For him, the rite is very important, not only because it changes the status of Jesus Christ from that of a guest to a citizen or a kin, and possibly a lord, but the rite also compels Africans to see themselves as the hosts of Jesus as well as the Christianity.[67]

Since for Udoh, the image of Jesus Christ as a divine figure or messenger is offensive to many Africans because for them "God has no need for prophets," and God cannot become a man,[68] he argues that an adequate Christology for Africa must divest Jesus Christ of his divine garb and restore him to the status of a human being. He writes,

61. Manus, *Christ, the African King*, 57.

62. Udoh, "Guest Christology," 227.

63. Ibid., 225.

64. Ibid., 230.

65. Ibid., 194.

66. Ibid., 196.

67. He writes, "if [Africans] become aware of [their] role as host to [the Christian] faith both in terms of [their] obligation and loyalty, then there would be no need to see [themselves] as being in exiles in [their] home or strangers to the faith which [they] helped to plant and continue to nurture." Ibid., 214.

68. Ibid., 83, 211.

> A comprehensive Christology seeking to re-communicate God through Jesus of Nazareth effectively to Nigerians must make the historicity of Christ the starting point of its reflection. It would have to restore to him the full human status about which the scriptures speak. Only humans belong to human community, share human anxiety, needs, thoughts, and participate in transforming the human world.[69]

Against this backdrop, he employs a low-Christology (or Christology from below) approach.[70] But unlike some theologians who use Christology from below and then work their way up to a high-Christology (i.e., a Christology that does not divest Jesus of his divinity),[71] his Guest Christology seems to have no room at all for the divinity of Jesus Christ.[72] According to him, "'faith-schizophrenia' is rooted in the claim that Jesus is divine."[73] To buttress this contention, he argues that as "an ordinary, normal, and Jewish male, Jesus does not raise serious problems for the African. His historicity is, therefore, incontestable even among non-Christian Africans. At issue is his divinity compounded by the Scottish emphasis in Nigeria."[74] Again he argues, "Whereas the Christian creeds affirm the divinity and the universal relevance of Jesus Christ, the traditional [i.e., indigenous religious] statement—*deity no bi mann, man no bi god*—nullifies it as presumptuous and 'ungodly.'"[75] He concludes that many people have rightly rejected the divinity of Jesus Christ: "If the missionaries charged Africans with 'paganism' and religious ignorance because they rejected the divinity of Jesus, Africans consider Jesus' divinity blasphemous."[76]

It is clear that Udoh's Guest Christology seeks to express Jesus Christ in a way that resonates with the cultures and experiences of Nigerians and other African peoples. As I have argued earlier, some

69. Ibid., 222.

70. Ibid.

71. For example, see Uzukwu, "Inculturation and Liturgy (Eucharist)," 95–114; and Ukpong, "Christology and Inculturation," 40–58.

72. Udoh, "Guest Christology," 223. Also he avers, "Full humanity of Christ is a prerequisite for a proper institution of the guest ceremony. That is because this ritual process is possible only in a human world." Ibid., 224.

73. Ibid., 263.

74. Ibid.

75. Ibid., 263–64.

76. Ibid., 264.

African theologians awakened from their christological slumber to discover that the Missionary Christology does not fit properly into the history and experience of the people. Driven by the desire to make Jesus Christ meaningful, Udoh embarked on the task of exploring a new christological model for engaging with the Christ-Event.

That Jesus appeared to be an unwelcome stranger in Africa was a corollary of the way some Western missionaries in the nineteenth and twentieth centuries presented him. Udoh maintains that most of the images of Jesus exported to Africa by the missionaries differ significantly with the biblical images of him.[77] And, for him, recognizing this difference is crucially important in order for an African theologian to undertake genuinely and successfully the task of contextual theologizing.

There are, however, some major problems with Udoh's Guest Christology. He has built his Christology on two dubious assumptions; namely, that African indigenous religions and cultures do not have provisions for the possibility of a deity becoming human. It is important to highlight the two major fallacies of this assumption. First, the expression or slogan *mann, no bi god; god no bi mann*, (literally man is not a god; god is not a man) does not express the idea that God cannot penetrate the human world by coming in the form of a human being, or in any other form. Rather, the slogan expresses the magnitude of the power, benevolence, and knowledge of the Supreme Being or other gods when compared with the weakness and frailty of human beings. This idea comes out clearly in the popular Igbo name *Maduabuchukwu* (an equivalent of *mann no bi god*), which literally means 'human beings are not God'. When some Christian parents give this name or a similar name to their child, they are not suggesting that God does not have a messenger. It is rather a name that signifies the ways many Christians wrestle with the infinite power of God. For example, some mothers give the name to their children if doctors told (or people mocked) them that they could not have any children. The idea here is that God is the one who has the final say in matters of such magnitude. The slogan *mann no bi god*, whether used by Christians or indigenous religionists, is a honorific expression aimed at communicating the majestic powers of the Supreme God or the lesser gods.

The second fallacy is that it is untrue that Africans believe that God does not have and does not need messengers or prophets. One

77. Ibid., 214.

of the popular christological models in Africa today is the Ancestor Christology. I will discuss this model later in this chapter. Here it suffices to say that many ethnic groups in West Africa revere ancestors as messengers and mediators of gods, and even of the Supreme Being. As Uchenna Ezeh has argued:

> The ancestral cult is the heart of the African tradition and culture. The presence of the ancestors is felt in the daily life of the traditional African community. They are God's agents in the maintenance and control of the universe. They act as intermediaries between God and man, and between man and the divinities.[78]

In some cases, some of these ancestors are apotheosized heroes. An example is *Sango,* the god of thunder in the Yoruba cosmology.[79] To argue that the possibility of a divine messenger is strange to Africans is totally unfounded and underestimates the indigenous understandings of the interrelatedness of the spiritual world and human world. Even the Ibibio cosmology, which he cited as a proof for the absence of divine intermediaries, has provision for ancestral reverence. He recognized this, although trivialized it, when he argued that the presence of ancestors during the ritual of adaptation was only symbolic.

Another problem with his Guest Christology is that it undermines the divinity of Jesus Christ and the universal significance of his work. He fails to engage with the biblical representation of the ontology and the dialectic of the universality and particularity of the work of Jesus Christ. It is dubious and unwarranted to misrepresent the person and the extent of the work of Jesus Christ for the purpose of constructing a contextual Christology. Thus, although he aimed to develop a truly indigenous Christology that would break radically with the Missionary Christology and the Neo-Missionary Christology, he has constructed a christological model that both misrepresent African indigenous understandings of God, the ancestors, and the biblical representations of Jesus Christ.

---

78. Ezeh, *Jesus Christ the Ancestor,* 285. See also Cox, *Rational Ancestors,* 35–55.

79. Idowu, *African Traditional Religion,* 186; Idowu, *Olodumare,* 90–91; Imasogie, *African Traditional Religion,* 35–38.

Ancestor Christology

The understandings of Jesus Christ as a chief ancestor, a proto-ancestor, a brother ancestor and a true ancestor perhaps make the Ancestor Christology a popular model in the contemporary African Christian christological discourses.[80] The reason may well be connected with the claim that the cult of the ancestors proffers the best "theological meeting point" for Christianity and African indigenous religions.[81] I will concentrate primarily on the work of the Nigerian theologian, Uchenna A. Ezeh. In *Jesus Christ the Ancestor*, he undertakes the task of expressing the mystery of Jesus Christ as God-human from the perspective of the indigenous concepts of ancestors. On the basis of the assumptions that the "ancestral cult is the heart of the African tradition and culture,"[82] and that "ancestors stand as the middle point between the visible and invisible worlds,"[83] he contends that presenting Jesus Christ as an ancestor opens up "a mutually enriching encounter for a dialogue between Christianity and the African culture."[84]

One thing that distinguishes his ancestor christological model from other proponents of this view is the locating of his Christology both within an African indigenous cosmology and the christological debates of the early church.[85] After examining the christological issues leading to the Councils of Nicaea in 325 AD, Ephesus in AD 431 and Chalcedon in 451 AD, he argues that the introduction of the non-biblical expression *homoousios* by the Councils to express the view that Jesus Christ has the same nature with God the Father should propel Africans to express him "through the resources of the African cultural categories."[86] In addition, the reference to the christological circumfer-

80. A good summary of Ancestor Christology model as understood in contemporary Africa is Stinton's *Jesus of Africa*, 112–42.

81. McCarthy, "Christology from a Contemporary Perspective," 34. See also Moloney, "African Christology," 509.

82. Ezeh, *Jesus Christ the Ancestor*, 285.

83. Ibid., 17.

84. Ibid.

85. Bujo, the most influential proponent of this view in Africa, argued that his Proto-Ancestor is legitimate because the early church ascribed to Jesus Christ several titles that originated from their cultural repertoire. See Bujo, "Nos anceres, ces saints inconnus," 165–78; Bujo, *African Theology in its Social Context*, 119.

86. Ezeh, *Jesus Christ the Ancestor*, 200.

ence the Councils created provides Ezeh with a standard to test the validity of his Ancestor Christology. He writes,

> Through the resources of the core African cultural symbol of the ancestor and the analysis and the application of the Christological definitions of the Church in her first five centuries of her existence, this African confession of Christ as the ancestor is weighed on the balance of the classical Christological orthodoxy. This ancestral Christological model is truly African and no less Christian.[87]

He endeavored to remain faithful to the Chalcedonian confession of the dual natures of Jesus Christ. Again, drawing upon the insights from the council's adoption of *homoousios*, he argues that this word signifies that the "radically immanent God-man can be understood from the African sense of solidarity."[88] To him, the incarnation enables Jesus Christ to fit into the category of the ancestors.[89] Of course, the difficulty in using a local metaphor to describe the Christ-Event in Africa, as he observes, is that the "belief in Christ" is not found in the indigenous worldviews unlike the idea of the Supreme God.[90] For him, however, the non-existence of the "belief in Christ" in the indigenous cosmologies does not mean Africans are to understand and explain effectively the Christ-Event befitting to their contexts. The task of a culture-oriented Christology, therefore, is to present Jesus Christ in a way that allows him to incarnate into the African cultures in order to speak to "African 'souls' as they are as Africans in their categories that can elicit such examinations 'God has come to us in the form and language of men' (Acts 14:11) and so we can hear them proclaiming the mighty deeds of God in our own language (Acts 23:11)."[91]

Ezeh sees the Ancestor Christology model as the "attempt from the anthropo-cultural resources to develop an analogous concept of Christ."[92] Although he acknowledges the existence of some other versions of the Ancestor Christology, he seems to favor brother Ancestor Christology.

87. Ibid., 17.
88. Ibid., 201.
89. Ibid., 237.
90. Ibid., 199–200.
91. Ibid., 200.
92. Ibid., 201.

> By his incarnation Christ became one of us, our brother. He is
> in a transcendent status that enables him to mediate between
> God and the human being as Ancestor not just because of his
> redemptive death but because he stays in a special relationship
> with God the Father as God-made man who is God.[93]

The brother ancestors belong to the category of family ancestors. Family ancestors were the head of their families before they died. And since death is not believed to constitute a terminus of these ancestors, they continued to communicate with and to supervise the affairs of their families. The ancestors are responsible for protecting the property of their family members. Their families consult with them at both social and religious occasions, including at birth, puberty, marriage, and death.[94]

Ezeh, however, differentiates the ancestorhood of Jesus Christ from African brother ancestors. This difference lies in his divinity: "His being of the same nature with the Father makes him an Ancestor of special class. He is both like and unlike his brother African Ancestors. There is a kind of parallelism here. He then becomes the exemplar of the African Ancestors by his pre-eminent role of mediation."[95] Again he postulates, "[a]s a model of behavior, [Jesus] transcends the African ancestors because his transcendental status is not just that he enjoys closeness with God but that he is also God. His divinity elucidates his superiority over and above the moral standard in the African ancestral relation."[96] The Congolese theologian, Francois Kabasele Lumbala, makes a similar point. He describes Jesus Christ as the "true elder" brother ancestor.[97] For him, Jesus alone merits this title because he has truly demonstrated his elder-brother function by "taking responsibility for our wrongs [and] in performing expiation for us (Isaiah. 53:4–5; Hebrews 8–10)."[98] Charles Nyamiti, a Tanzanian theologian, is another prominent proponent of the brother Ancestor Christology model. He argues that the elder brother-ancestorhood typology bears the "clos-

93. Ibid.

94. Dickson, *Theology in Africa*, 69.

95. Ezeh, *Jesus Christ the Ancestor*, 201.

96. Ibid., 301.

97. The oldest son is believed to be genealogically and culturally closer to the ancestors in many traditional societies of Nigeria.

98. Lumbala, "Christ as Ancestor and Elder Brother," 122.

est analogy" to Christ.[99] He sees the concept of the ancestral cult as a pointer to "a relationship which is directly or immediately linked with our eternal life," and a relationship that exists between God and us.[100] In his comparison of an African ancestral brotherhood and Christ's brotherhood ancestorship, he postulates five similarities.[101] Among the striking things in his arguments are the notions that Africans share consanguinity with Christ through his "Adamite origin" and that just as "the living and their brother ancestor have common immediate father and mother," so also "the first Person of the Trinity is the common and immediate Father and mother of Christ and His earthly members."[102] Like Ezeh and Lumbala, Nyamiti highlights the need to recognize the "profound differences" between Jesus Christ and the African ancestors. To him, the difference stems from the superiority of Jesus Christ's ancestral function which is rooted in his pre-existence.[103]

Some proponents of the Ancestor Christology argue that conceiving of Jesus Christ as an ancestor emphasizes a soteriological dimension of the Christ-Event. For Ezeh, the soteriological dimension is precisely located in the death of Jesus Christ.

> Through the ancestral figure, humanity is in relationship with God. In the ancestral understanding, death is seen as a decisive means of reaching a fulfillment of the human person realized in the transcendental life with God. It belongs to the human nature but being linked with God. It is soteriological. It means salvation for man. Death belonging now to the human nature which God assumed as his own, through his incarnation in Christ, one can rightly then say that "he dies." As the Ancestor, [Jesus'] death has also this soteriological dimension. His death is life.[104]

Nyamiti agrees with Ezeh on the soteriological value of the death of Christ vis-à-vis his ancestorhood. He writes, "it is only through His death and resurrection that [Jesus] became our Brother Ancestor in fullness," and so he "could fully exercise His ancestral mediation."[105]

---

99. Nyamiti, *Christ as Our Ancestor*, 16.

100. Ibid., 17.

101. Ibid., 19–20.

102. Ibid., 21.

103. Ibid., 27.

104. Ezeh, *Jesus Christ the Ancestor*, 239.

105. Nyamiti, *Christ as Our Ancestor*, 27.

Ezeh, like many other African theologians, undertakes the task of contextual Christology with caution and a sense of awe, knowing that the Christ-Event is a mystery. He observes,

> The idea of . . . ancestor Christology is to express the mystery of Christ through the analogous ancestral African cultural symbol. Alongside the ancestor title are other titles such as the chief, the master of . . . initiation, and healer, through which the African seek[s] to express his or her faith in Christ. Each of these titles highlights some aspects of the inexhaustible nature of the incarnate Son of God who is God.[106]

An Ancestor Christology is attractive to many African theologians and is undoubtedly the model that strikes a familiar chord in the ears of many Africans. In order to appraise thoroughly the problems and contributions of the Ancestor Christology model to the development of contextual Christologies in African Christianity, I will examine the foundations on which this model is constructed.

Humanness Argument

Ezeh, as we have seen, builds his Ancestor Christology on the incarnation of Jesus Christ. He points out that the incarnation implies an amalgamation of divinity and humanity in Jesus of Nazareth, the Christ. For him, therefore, Jesus Christ qualifies as an Ancestor (although in an analogical sense) on the basis of taking on a human nature. He writes,

> Even though ancestorship is a purely human title, it can also be applied to the incarnate Christ following the same principle of the *communicatio idiomatum* . . . By making man's history become God's history, the incarnate Son of God would consequently be seen as an ancestor which is the highest perfection of human being in the African culture.[107]

Nyamiti develops his brotherhood ancestorship on the same biological ground:

> African brother-ancestorship is founded on consanguinity and the supernatural status of the ancestors after death. Christ's relationship to men is also linked with consanguinity

106. Ezeh, *Jesus Christ the Ancestor*, 307–8.
107. Ibid., 306.

...on the account of His Adamite origin. The difference here lies in the fact that being Adamite in character Christ's brotherhood transcends all family, clan, tribal or racial limitations.[108]

Ezeh moves in the same direction when he argues that "Christ the Ancestor is transcultural."[109] For him, "Jesus Christ the ancestor introduces a new relationship which is neither based on sex nor color or race."[110] According to him, Jesus "points us to the common fatherhood of God and this means the brotherhood and sisterhood of all people."[111]

Building an Ancestor-Christology on the genealogy of Jesus Christ no doubt proffers a helpful tool to express the universal effect of his work in the ancestral-oriented world such as Africa. However, it is important to note that the biological argument for an Ancestor Christology underestimates the relevance of the question: how could Jesus who was biologically a non-African become an African ancestor?[112] This question is crucially important because the ancestors are considered in many societies to be the real owners of the land and the custodian of their clan's traditions.[113] These beliefs about ancestors will only make sense if the ancestors are indigenes. Since the criteria of becoming an ancestor in the indigenous cosmologies include raising family, leading an exemplary life of obedience to the laws of the family or society, it is essential for the theologians that develop the ancestor christological models to pay serious attention to the eligibility of Jesus's ancestorhood and also to develop a meaningful theological response to address the question.[114]

MYTHOLOGICAL ARGUMENT

Ezeh does not use a mythological argument to substantiate his Ancestor Christology. But some African scholars such as Kwame Bediako use it. According to Bediako, it is necessary to construe the cult of the ances-

108. Nyamiti, *Christ as Our Ancestor*, 20.

109. Ezeh, *Jesus Christ the Ancestor*, 311.

110. Ibid.

111. Ibid.

112. The biological argument also fails to deal with the particularity of Jesus Christ, as an individual who was born into and lived in a particular context.

113. See Dickson, *Theology in Africa*, 61.

114. Parratt, *Reinventing Christianity*, 135.

tors as a groundless myth in order to see how Jesus displaces and fulfills the aspirations of African peoples.[115] He maintains that Jesus Christ displaces the ancestors because they "need saving, having originated from among us."[116] And since "there is no valid alternative to Jesus Christ," he contends that

> the question is no longer: why should we relate to Jesus of Nazareth who does not belong to our clan, family, tribe and nation? [But] how may we understand more fully this Jesus Christ who relates to us most meaningfully and most profoundly in our clan, family, tribe and nation?[117]

When examined critically, the reason Bediako provides for the displacement of the mediatory functions of the African ancestors suffers an internal incoherence. If Jesus Christ displaces the works of the ancestors because he does not "need saving" unlike the ancestors, it follows that the ancestors in the first place did not exercise any valid salvific mediation and therefore the comparison between Jesus and the ancestors cannot be on a mediatory ground. Bediako seems to have noticed this theological problem, and therefore, depicts the ancestral cult as a myth and groundless.

> Since the ancestral function, as traditionally understood, is now shown to have no basis in fact, the way is open for appreciating more fully how Jesus Christ is the only real and true Ancestor and Source of life for all mankind, fulfilling and transcending the benefits believed to be bestowed by lineage ancestors.[118]

The role of a myth in the conceptualization of some religious beliefs has generated a lot of debates.[119] To designate the ancestral cult as a myth in the sense that Bediako uses it tends to eclipse the historical reality of the cult. Many Africans continue to believe that they can communicate with their ancestors through divination and other metaphysical means. A serious researcher of this cult must come to grips with the reality that some people believe they hear from and relate to their ancestors. For

115. Bediako, *Jesus and the Gospel in Africa*, 26.

116. Ibid.

117. Ibid., 32.

118. Ibid., 31.

119. See Cox, *Rational Ancestors*, 35–55; Soyinka, *Myth, Literature and the African World*.

example, Idowu observes that many families in the traditional Nigerian societies consult with an oracle each time a child is born to discover the ancestral spirits dwelling within the child.[120] Therefore, Bediako's depiction of the cult of the ancestors as a myth, and his argument against the validity of this cult as traditionally construed is misleading.[121]

SOTERIOLOGICAL AND ETHICAL ARGUMENT

Benezet Bujo situates his Ancestor Christology on a soteriological foundation and not on a biological ground. He writes: "to call [Jesus] 'Proto-Ancestor' means precisely, that he is believed to be the 'firstborn among all the ancestors' and this is not on a biological, but in a soteriological level of re-birth to a mystical and supernatural life and mode of existence."[122] For him, the "proto-ancestrality" of Jesus Christ as the firstborn of God "makes irrelevant any racial or tribal barrier."[123] Ezeh, like Bujo, contends that to see Jesus Christ as an Ancestor has both soteriological and ethical values. He writes,

> . . . we maintain that the African cult of the ancestors epitomizes the African quest for salvation (soteriology), goodness in the community (ethics). . . . Through his incarnation, these Africa values are perfectly fulfilled in Christ as perfect God and perfect man. Hence Jesus Christ is the Ancestor par excellence, who as God-man perfectly mediates salvation to the people. His moral authority to the community is from the point of view of service. In this way he becomes the perfect fulfillment of all the African aspirations or quests integrated in the cult of the ancestors.[124]

Situating the relationship between Jesus and the ancestors on a soteriological ground is enigmatic. The primary theological difficulty with this view is that it unnecessarily overloads the cult of the ancestors with the redemptive concepts most of which derive from Christianity. While it is true that African traditionalists believe in the ancestors' mediation

---

120. Idowu, *African Traditional Religion*, 79.

121. If Bediako's contention for the invalidity of the cult of the ancestors is correct, then it follows that there is no convincing correlation between Jesus and the ancestors.

122. Bujo, *African Christian Morality at the Age of Inculturation*, 82–3.

123. Ibid., 21.

124. Ezeh, *Jesus Christ the Ancestor*, 316.

between the physical world and the spiritual world, it is misleading to deduce redemptive acts from this belief.[125] Strictly speaking, the ancestors do not function as redemptive agents, if by redemption we mean the buying back the freedom of someone or something held captive. They are rather guardians of the ethos of the land, and in some contexts the means of accessing the spiritual world.

When placed in its proper context, the mediatory work of the ancestors is didactical and ethical rather than redemptive as construed in some Christian soteriologies. The ancestors' primary concern is to ensure that the living community continues to obey the ancestral laws,[126] which is important for the joy, blessing and prosperity of the living.[127] This does not mean that there is no sense in which the mediation of the ancestors could be described as Soteriological, for part of the goals of obeying the instructions of the ancestors is to experience wellbeing and escape the anger of gods or the Supreme God. But we should recognize that the ancestors do not function as redeemers, but as guides to the knowledge of the spiritual world. It is not enough to situate the functional difference between Jesus Christ and the ancestors on the context of quantitative difference as Nyamiti has done.[128] Granted that Jesus Christ and the ancestors are models of a good life, and that as the perfect archetype of the Christian life Jesus exemplifies an unprecedented model of conduct, it is essential to acknowledge also that he functions, not only as the model of good living, but also (primarily) as the one who produces the Christian life through the believer.[129]

---

125. Soteriology in this sense incorporates both the Christian claim that it is in the death and resurrection of Jesus the Christ that God exposes and deals decisively with the sin and guilt of human race, and the cosmic, and holistic nature of God redemptive work. Salvation from the biblical point of view goes beyond mere socio-economic redemption which the majority of contemporary African theologians emphasize and almost at the expense of some other aspects. See Mana, *Christians and Churches of Africa*.

126. This includes bringing judgment on violators of the laws of the Land.

127. Cox, "Spirit Mediums in Zimbabwe," 192.

128. According to Nyamiti, "Christ is, like the African Ancestors, the model of behavior for His brethren and is the source of Christian tradition. But, here again, His divine status should alone suffice to show His eminent superiority in this regard. For being God-man He is of necessity infinitely more perfect as model of conduct than the African ancestors can ever be." See *Christ as Our Ancestor*, 21.

129. Galatians 2:20.

Furthermore, it is also important to note that the Christian life is possible through the mediatory work of Jesus Christ. On a soteriological ground, the mediatory work of Jesus Christ differs from that of the ancestors because while the former is the redeemer of the whole world including Africa (as many African Christian theologians believe), the latter's mission is non-redemptive (in the sense of dealing with the sin and guilt and appeasing God as Scripture speaks about Jesus), but rather didactical. The ancestors concentrate on guarding people to keep the laws of the land. Another theological problem with the Ancestor Christology model is that it lays heavy emphasis on the mediatory work of Jesus and African ancestors. Christologically, the danger is that this type of Christology can lead to the understanding of Jesus as a mere middleman who connects God and humans. Pannenberg rightly warns against this kind of mediatory Christology:

> There are Christologies that have no interest at all in the immediate presence of God himself in Jesus—neither accidentally nor substantially—but are simply interested in Jesus' mid-position between God and man. It can be that such Christologies presuppose the doctrine of the unity of God and man in Jesus Christ, but are nevertheless primarily concerned with the independent mid-position of Jesus and less interested in the coincidence of the divine and the human spheres. Rather, a third thing, the figure of the mediator, is inserted between these two spheres.[130]

The Ancestor Christology, therefore, needs to take the ontological question about Jesus's identity seriously. The proponents of this model must recognize that it is christologically inadequate to discuss the work of Jesus in isolation from his person.[131]

Liberation-Oriented Christologies

My interest here is to explore and critique the concept of liberation as it is used in theological discourses in Africa. However, I will focus on feminist Christology. This is because it is the major christological model and a form of liberation theology that has engaged with the liberation motive and some cultural issues which concern the contextual

---

130. Pannenberg, *Jesus—God and Man*, 123.

131. See chapter four for discussions on the problems of constructing a Christology that underestimates the ontology of Jesus Christ.

appropriations of the person and work of Jesus Christ. Although I will highlight some of the arguments of some key Latin American, South African, Asian and Western liberation theologians, and also critique some of the ideologies of liberation theology, my aim is to converse with African feminist Christologies.

The expression *liberation theology* was popularized by Latin American theologians whose works aimed to expose oppression, exploitation, and poverty as sinful and unwarranted.[132] Also, many liberation theologians seek to inspire poor people to reject their condition, to restrain from being indifferent to their situation, and to fight against all forces, individuals, and systems that perpetuate their destitute conditions. Liberation theology, as Alfred Hennelly has rightly pointed out, has transformed the "lives of persons, communities, nations, and world's Christian churches" as well as a host of people "who previously paid little attention to the life and words of Jesus Christ."[133] In Africa, the theme of liberation has continued to reverberate in the theological works of some individuals, particularly feminists and the theologians who write from the context of apartheid in South Africa.[134]

As a discourse, liberation theology is complex and difficult to articulate insofar as it includes liberation discussions that arise from the experiences of the poor and the oppressed, and also transcends the methodological boundaries created by the theologies that concentrate on abstract ideas and ignore real human experiences. For example, Jon Sobrino in *Christology at Crossroads*, criticizes the Chalcedonian christological formulation, insisting that it is too abstract and fails to resonate with people's experiences of Jesus Christ.[135] For Lisa Isherwood, liberation theologians argue that it is not enough to "create doctrines about Jesus." On the contrary, she contends that an adequate Christology must present Jesus Christ in a way that allows him to become "part of the

---

132. See Gutierrez, *Theology of Liberation*; Bonino, *Rome to Be People*; Boff, *Jesus Christ Liberator*; Sobrino, *Christology at the Crossroads*; Cone, *A Black Theology of Liberation*; and Cleage, *Black Messiah*.

133. Hennelly, *Liberation Theologies: The Global Pursuit of Justice*, 9.

134. Boesak, *Black Theology Black Power*; Oduyoye, "Christian Feminism and African Culture: The 'Hearth' of the Matter," 441–49; Moore, ed., *Black Theology*; Nicolson, *A Black Future?*, 163–212.

135. Sobrino, *Christology at Crossroads*, 3–5. See chapter four for my conversation with the Chalcedonian christological formulation.

ongoing dialogue between the oppressed and oppressors."[136] One of the key aims of liberation theologians is to create a hyphen that will connect orthopraxy and orthodoxy. For example, in *The Power of the Poor in History* Gustavo Gutierrez wrote:

> Practice is the locus of verification of our faith in God who liberates by establishing justice and right in favor of the poor. It is also the locus of verification of our faith in Christ, who laid down his life for the proclamation of the kingdom of God and the struggle for justice.[137]

In spite of its complexity and diversity, at the heart of liberation theology is the quest to construct the theologies and Christologies that are rooted in people's everyday experience of poverty, life of deprivation and their struggle against oppression and marginalization.[138] Unlike some traditional ways of doing theology or Christology that begin with abstract discussions on the ontology of God or Jesus Christ, liberation theologians begin with the experiences of people who are starving, suffering, dehumanized, exploited and oppressed. Leonardo Boff and Clodovis Boff have argued that liberation theology exists and makes sense because of its "prophetic and comradely commitment to life, cause, and struggle" of the poor.[139] "Liberation theology," for them, "was born when faith confronted the injustice done to the poor."[140] The poor in their thinking must include all people who are being "exploited by the capitalist system, the underemployed, those pushed aside by the production process . . . , the laborers of the countryside, and the migrant workers with only seasonal work."[141] Writing specifically about the African context, Laurenti Magesa argues that liberation theological discussions must engage seriously with the

> questions of excessive wealth in the midst of dehumanizing poverty and vice versa; questions of exploitation of the majority of African peoples by internal and external forces; questions of political domination by domestic and international power

---

136 Isherwood, *Liberating Christ*, 49.

137. Gutierrez, *Power of the Poor in History*, 17.

138. Rowland, "Introduction: The Theology of Liberation," 1–2; Musto, *Liberation Theologies*, xxiv.

139. Boff and Boff, *Liberation and Theology*, 3.

140. Ibid.

141. Ibid., 3–4.

brokers; questions of suppression of the African cultures by dominant conceptions of life by means of refutation and ridicule; [and] questions of monopolies of power by ecclesiastical oligarchies at the expense of the liberty of the people of God.[142]

Although the positions and emphases of liberation theologians will vary depending on their social and ecclesiastical contexts, they share the burden to critique inhuman misery and the commitment to explore the meaning of the Christ-Event, particularly how this event can bring new life and hope to people who experience injustice, poverty, and all forms of oppression.[143] Thus, Christology is central to most liberation theological discussions. The key questions are: how are Christians to speak of Jesus Christ in the face of senseless and avoidable human sufferings and poverty? How can the image of Jesus Christ as a suffering servant inspire a movement of liberation and criticism of oppression? And how are we to develop a Christology that is rooted in people's struggle for self-determination and the search for political and economic liberation?

According to Gutierrez, a theology of liberation seeks to "understand the grace and salvation of Jesus Christ in the context of the present and from the situation of the poor."[144] In *Black Theology Black Power*, Allan Aubrey Boesak, the South African theologian, highlights the theme of liberation in Black theology and locates it within Christology. He writes:

> Black Theology is the theological reflection of black Christians on the situation in which they live and on their struggle for liberation: Blacks ask: What does it mean to believe in Jesus Christ when one is black and living in a world controlled by white racists? And what if these racists call themselves Christians also?[145]

In 1989, Mercy Oduyoye posed a radical challenge to African peoples and the systems that perpetuate the dehumanizing experiences of women. She argued that any "element in African culture that is not liberating for women will not liberate all the energy required for Africans'

---

142. Magesa, "Christ the Liberator and Africa Today," 154.

143. Giblin, "Jesus Christ in Liberation Theologies," 78.

144. Gutierrez, "Task and Content of Liberation Theology," 19.

145. Boesak, *Black Theology Black Power*, 1–2.

well-being."[146] She went on to describe women feminist theologians as those "who have refused to give up the church and who are putting up resistance to the male takeover of the religion of Jesus of Nazareth."[147] Later in this chapter, I will examine some of the criticisms that some feminist theologians have directed against indigenous cultures and churches of Africa. At this point, I will move on to critique some of the approaches and objectives of liberation theology.

Several criticisms have been directed against liberation theology. An exhaustive interaction with them is beyond the scope of this chapter. However, I will highlight some of them that relate to the objectives of this chapter and the Revealer Christology model that I aim to develop. Some of these criticisms come from liberation theologians. For example, many feminist theologians criticize the liberation theologians who write against oppression and marginalization that stem from some economic systems but have ignored the oppression and suffering of many women that are rooted in some ecclesiastical and cultural systems of their societies.[148] Also, some non-liberation theologians have been highly critical of the hermeneutic and ideologies of liberation theologies and Christologies. Some of the critics have accused liberation theologians of concentrating mainly on some narrative biblical texts and ignoring prophetic texts.[149] Some have accused liberation theologians of using the "Marxist analysis of social reality as a frame of reference for reading" and interpreting the Bible and have questioned the legitimacy of this hermeneutic.[150] Roger Haight, however, has argued that although some liberation theologians have studied Marxist thought and use it as a framework to "analyze the social condition of the poor," there are many who know very little of Marx and Marxism.[151] He also argues that although some liberation theologians use Marxist language, they have "not incorporated an integral Marxist vision of reality, which would be incompatible with Christian faith."[152]

---

146. Oduyoye, "Christian Feminism," 441.

147. Ibid.

148. I will explore these criticisms later in this chapter.

149. See Rowland, "Introduction: The Theology of Liberation," 9.

150. Ibid.

151. Haight, "Liberation Theology," 573.

152. Ibid.

The key source of liberation theological discourse, as I have pointed earlier, is human experience, particularly the experience of the people who are poor. In chapter three, I will explore and critique in detail the place of religious experience in Nigerian grassroots Christologies. Here, it suffices to note that liberation theology has created a bridge to connect academic Christologies and popular or grassroots Christologies. This is one of the tasks of the Revealer Christology model I develop in this book. It is time theologians and the people who do not have any formal theological training discovered that their theologies must inform and shape each other. Jurgen Moltmann has correctly argued that academic theology and popular theology

> must relate to each other, show consideration for each other, and learn from each other. If academic theology does not find its way to ordinary people, it loses its foundation. Without the church, Christian theology cannot exist as a university discipline. It will become diffused and lose itself in the science of religions. On the other hand, popular theology loses its reasonable character if it pays no attention to academic theology, or if it despises that theology's competence.[153]

Whatever criticisms we present against liberation theology, it is vital to recognize that an adequate contextual Christology must be able to interpret and appropriate the meaning and significance of the Christ-Event in a way that engages seriously with the real life experiences of people. It must be able to locate the suffering of Jesus Christ within the suffering of the people who are dying of starvation and the people who are victims of oppressive systems. Liberation theologians have reminded us that Christians should not remain indifferent to the situation of the poor and that "following Jesus has practical social and political consequences."[154]

However, liberation theologians' emphasis on human experience and their use of the dehumanizing conditions of the poor and the oppressed as the source of their theologies and Christologies are somewhat problematic. To successfully achieve their task, most liberation theologians employ Christology from below approach.[155] The key

153. Moltmann, *Experience in Theology*, 11.

154. Webster, "Liberation Theology," 637.

155. See chapter four for discussions on the relationship between low and high Christologies.

problem with this approach is that it creates a dichotomy between the divinity and humanity and also the person and work of Jesus Christ.[156] Liberation theologians need to recognize it is inadequate to argue that human situations (particularly the experiences of the poor) must determine the meaning and significance of Jesus Christ. Whereas we cannot rediscover fresh meanings of the Christ-Event, and interpret and appropriate it relevantly in our contexts without locating it within the concrete human experiences, we make a mistake when we assume that human experiences must determine Jesus's person and work. Throughout this book, I will argue that although Jesus identifies with human the contexts (for example, experiences of suffering, pain, poverty, rejection and oppression), as the God incarnate, he escapes any attempt by us to reduce and confine him to our local images and categories.

The liberationist theme of the option for the poor or the claim that God is always on the side of the poor can be misleading. God does not identify with the poor any more than he identifies with the rich. Also, God does not criticize the rich any less than he criticizes the poor. The point I aim to establish is that the rich and the poor can engage (and historically have engaged) in the activities that are oppressive and sinful. For example, the rich people who service their wealth and status quo by exploiting other people, who use their wealth to perpetuate injustice, and who refuse to use their resources to ameliorate the condition of the poor are oppressive and sinful. The poor people who steal, kill, and engage in some despicable acts such as sacrificing parts of their body, their children, or parents in order to improve their conditions are also oppressive and sinful.[157] It is inadequate to describe sin and salvation simply as social actions. An adequate Christian theology must define sin to include human beings' (all peoples—the poor and the rich, white and black, oppressors, and oppressed) rejection of God's offer of relationship in and through the Christ-Event. Sin ought to be defined broadly to include any ideology or action that dehumanizes humanity. If human beings are God's image bearers, it follows that the actions which prohibit them *to become what God intends them to be* contravene God, and

156. In chapter four, I will develop a model that allows for a simultaneous interaction between Christology from below and Christology from above, and a simultaneous conversation between the divinity and humanity and also the person and work of Jesus Christ.

157. I will explore this claim further in chapter three under the emerging themes from the grassroots Christologies of Nigerian Christianity.

therefore such actions are sinful. Salvation also ought to be defined in a way that transcends liberation from sinful political and socio-economic structures to include God's holistic liberation of humanity.[158]

Liberation theologians must be able to move from liberation to reconstruction. They must not only become involved practically in alleviating and ameliorating the conditions of the oppressed; they must also develop their Christologies and theologies in a way that promotes self-criticism. Their theologies and Christologies must be able to raise and answer the questions: what will Jesus look like if he is interpreted and appropriated in a way that engages with the situation of the poor? And what will the situation of the poor, their struggles for liberation and the approach they use in dealing with injustice look like when they are examined in light of the Christ-Event? Throughout the remainder of this book, I will explore how these kinds of questions must inform an adequate contextual Christology that is designed for African Christianity.

Returning to African Christology, it is important to note Liberation and Inculturation are the two major approaches that are predominant in the christological discourses.[159] Three things are noteworthy. First, liberation-oriented Christologies correlate to a culture-oriented Christologies: both models discuss liberation and cultural issues.[160] Jean-Marc Ela, the Cameroonian theologian, has correctly argued for the integration of inculturation and liberation in theological discussions. He writes:

> Everything that specifically marks the Christian tradition today is questioned, if one watches those Africans who live in oppression and suffer under the injustice of ideological, social, political, and economic structures. . . . What must be deepened . . . if faith is to move ahead, is the ability of the gospel to respond to the situation that can no longer be covered up: "the powerful and most irreversible aspiration that people have for liberation." So critical reflection on the relevance of an African Christianity requires us to identify the structures or strategies of exploitation and impoverishment against which Africans have always

158. See chapter seven for discussions on sin and salvation of humanity.

159. Nyamiti, "Contemporary African Christologies," 64. In this book, I have described these models as culture-oriented and liberation-oriented Christologies.

160. Ela, *My Faith as an African.*

struggled, finding their own specific forms of resistance within their cultures.[161]

Second, although some liberation-oriented Christologies bear many features of the liberation theologies and Christologies that exist in Latin America, Asia, and North America, they differ because of the uniqueness of the questions, concerns and cultural contexts that shape them. Third, the concept of liberation has not yet occupied a central place in the constructive Christologies of most Nigerian theologians. Further research is required in this area. Among the reasons for this is a misleading understanding of the relationship between the tasks of African theology and Black theology. Some theologians have construed inculturation as the primary task of African theology and liberation as the key task of Black theology.[162] Theologians must begin to explore in their theologies and Christologies the questions that are rooted in the experiences of the people who are poor and oppressed and their struggles against poverty and all forms of political and socio-economic injustices. Two things are noteworthy. First, the theologians who separate inculturation and liberation have forgotten too quickly these concepts inspired some earliest African theologians' rejection of most Western theologies which they believed promoted or failed to critique cultural hegemony, colonial oppressive systems, racism and apartheid. Second, it is important for theologians to recognize that Jesus Christ embodies liberation. I will examine this claim further in chapters six and seven. It suffices to note here that the Christ-Event demonstrates the action of God to critique oppressive systems and to liberate the people who are oppressed. When theologians separate the concepts of liberation and inculturation they endanger the relevance of Jesus Christ, particularly how their Christologies can critique and undo the indigenous, governmental, and ecclesiastical structures that are oppressive.

As I have already indicated, I will concentrate primarily on the Christologies of some key feminist theologians. I have chosen to explore feminist Christology here because it is the key model that has integrated liberation and inculturation motives. On the one hand, some feminist theologians have criticized the Western theologies for failing to engage with the indigenous cultures and religions. On the other hand,

---

161. Ibid., xvii.

162. See Martey, *African Theology*, xi.

some of these theologians have criticized the indigenous cultures that perpetuate the oppression of women and have begun to seek a christological examination of the marginalized and impoverished conditions of women.

Feminist Christology

Feminist theology gained prominence in Christian theological discourse in the 1960s.[163] But women's involvement in biblical theology began in the nineteenth century with the works of people such as Sarah Grimke and Elizabeth Cady Stanton.[164] It was not until the 1980s that some feminist theologies and movements emerged in sub-Saharan Africa. Although African women had always used some non-public and non-academic ways to establish their significant places in their societies which the male-dominated cultures have veiled, their irruption into Christian theological discourse began in 1980. The Ibadan conference organized by Daisy Obi, who was then the director of the Institute of Church and Society of the Christian Council of Nigeria, was momentous because it signaled a new era for some Nigerian and other African women theologians.[165] Soon after, some African women began to join the Ecumenical Association of Third World Theologians (EATWOT).[166] The Worlds Women meeting in Nairobi, Kenya in 1985 also boosted the courage of some women to fight for their liberation from the oppressive actions, networks, and policies of men. Furthermore, the establishment of the Circle of Concerned African Women Theologians in 1989 also empowered and created more opportunities for African women to develop some theological and christological responses to the dehumanizing conditions of women in many African societies.[167]

---

163. Greene, *Christology in Cultural Perspective*, 220. See also Jones, *Feminist Theory and Christian Theology*, 3; Giddings, *When and Where I Enter.*

164. The publication of *The Woman's Bible* in 1895 and 1898 triggered a paradigm shift in biblical theological discourses. See Schottroff, Schroer, and Wacker, *Feminist Interpretation: The Bible in Women's Perspective*, 3–5.

165. Oduyoye, "Gender and Theology in Africa Today," available from http://www.thecirclecawt.org/focus_areas?mode=content&id=17292&refto=2629ecirclecawt.org; Internet; accessed 4 August 2006.

166. Stinton, *Jesus of Africa*, 39.

167. Oduyoye, "Jesus Christ," 153.

Feminist Christology is very difficult to define because it encompasses several contours that have both united and divided many feminists. Several concepts including queer theory, postmodernism, postcolonial theory, feminist theory, gendered body and sexual body[168] are shaping the nature and agendas of feminist theologies.[169] However, central to the feminist theological discourses is the liberation and empowerment of women: a march to rediscover the eclipsed and marginalized freedom of women to exist not as the *other*, and a march to preach the gospel of equality, mutuality and reciprocity in the patriarchal world in which they live. Serene Jones notes two concomitant goals which derive from some feminist liberative movements. The first is to "identify the various forms of oppression that structured women's lives." And the second is the attempt to create a context that will ensure "an alternative future [for women] without oppression."[170]

Some feminist Christologies launch attacks against the societal and ecclesial systems that encourage or help to perpetuate injustice, oppression, violence and marginalization carried out against women and all people. It is noteworthy that the exact targets of the feminist christological discourses vary depending on the experience and context of the theologian. But it seems, recognizing the risk of oversimplification, that the numerous targets of most feminist Christologies can be categorized into two; namely, the world of males and the world of humans. A feminist Christology, which targets the world of males, sees men as the principal antagonists of women—in this case, feminism is seen as contra andocentric ideologies. This understanding of feminism was predominant in the early development of feminist movements.[171] Some feminist theologians who belong to this category focus primarily on the liberation of women. Their works are directed specifically to women

---

168. See Althaus-Reid "'Pussy, Queen of Pirates': Acker, Isherwood and the Debate on the Body in Feminist Theology," 160; Isherwood, *Introducing Feminist Christologies*; Pui-lan, *Postcolonial Imagination and Feminist Theology*.

169. Most of these theories have not fully reflected in the Christologies of African feminists.

170. Jones, *Feminist Theory and Christian Theology*, 3.

171. For discussions on the early development of feminist movements and Western Feminist Christolog(ies), see Cott, *Grounding of Modern Feminism*; Daly, *Beyond the Father: Toward a Philosophy of Women's Liberation*; Fiorenza, *In Memory of Her: A Feminist Theological Reconstruction of Christian Origins*; Fiorenza, *Jesus*.

with the intent to ignite in them the desire to stand up and fight for their liberation from any oppressive systems created by the world of male.

Conversely, some feminist theologians who aim to reconstruct and redefine what it means to be human define broadly their target as the world of humans—they target all persons (male or female) who define humanity on the basis of gender and race. They seek for the liberation of all persons and even for ecological liberation.[172] Susan Parsons and Mercy Oduyoye are examples of such feminists whose goal is to redefine humanity. Parsons views the ethics of feminism as consisting in the attempt to provide a scheme for "understanding our identity as human persons, our place in the overall order of things, and the ways in which the fulfillment of our humanity might come about."[173] Mercy Oduyoye shares a similar idea. She argues that "feminism is not the word *of* the female, it is the word of all who are conscious of the true nature of human community as a mixture of those things, values, roles, temperaments, etc., that we dichotomize into feminine and masculine."[174]

Oduyoye insists that a feminist theology is geared toward enabling all humans to "attain the fullness of their being" and to "liberate human community from entrenched attitudes and structures that cannot operate unless dichotomies and hierarchies are maintained."[175] In the thinking of Parsons and Oduyoye, feminism is not necessarily anti-male; rather it is an inclusive terminology that conveys the agitation of some women (and men) to re-examine the nature of human beings without employing the oppressive female-male dichotomy.[176]

For some African Christians, the words feminism and feminist Christology trigger off some cultural problems.[177] A persistent suspicion has shaped this negative understanding of a feminist approach to Christology. This is the idea that feminism is a deadly western-oriented

172. Jones, *Feminist Theory and Christian Theology*, 6.

173. Parsons, "Accounting for Hope: Feminist Theology as Fundamental Theology," 1–2.

174. Oduyoye, "Feminism: A Pre-condition for a Christian Anthropology," 193–94.

175. Ibid.

176. Christologically, this is a representative understanding of the humanity of Jesus Christ in "a generic sense as that which transcends gender and is therefore inclusive of both male and female." Greene, *Christology in Cultural Perspective*, 240.

177. Oduyoye, "Feminist Theology in an African Perspective," 166–67. The harsh negative attitudes toward feminism in Nigeria may not be entirely unconnected with the indigenous estimation of females as subordinates to males.

movement which is cutting deep into the cultural structure of some indigenous customs and traditions—a cultural structure which empowered male to become strong and superior but disempowered female to become weak and inferior. Feminism, for some Christians who hold this view, is foreign and revolutionary, albeit destructive, in the sense that it is empowering women to be equal with men and even sometimes disempowering men in order to make women the stronger and superior individuals. The common saying in Nigeria "whatever a man can do a woman can equally do if not better" heightens the suspicion of such Christians. But feminism, for some Christians who are sympathetic to its history and agenda, is a helpful movement that can help women realize their full potentials as the people who are created in the image of God and who are essentially equal with men. What perhaps remains obscure to many Christians is the relevance of any Christology that is feminist-oriented. Therefore, it is important to discuss three developments that have functioned as a backdrop to the emergence of feminist Christologies in Nigerian Christianity. All of these developments are rooted in the experiences of women who are struggling to regain freedom to exist in the andocentric systems of their churches and the society at large.

PATRIARCHAL-STRUCTURED CULTURES AND CUSTOMS OF INDIGENOUS NIGERIA

In many African societies, women live under some oppressive cultures and systems. Traditionally, some men consider women and children to be inherently inferior. In some societies, word such as *men* does not simply signify gender but more importantly a class or status quo. For instance, some men are sometimes described derogatively as women because they are lazy or cowards. Conversely, the word such as *women* represents both the gender and class of people who may not have any significant leadership roles in their societies. All females are believed to have inherited a low status and should remain subordinate to men. When they want to escape from this cultural web, some men see such acts as constituting rebellion to the laws of the Supreme Being, the ancestors, the gods of the land, and ultimately a threat to the world of men. As Oduyoye observes,

> In Africa, the very idea of a "free woman" conjures up negative
> images.... The single woman who manages her affairs success-
> fully without a man, is an affront to patriarchy and a direct chal-
> lenge to the so-called masculinity of men who want to "possess"
> her. Some women are struggling to be free from this compul-
> sory attachment to the male. Women want the right to be fully
> human, whether or not they choose to be attached to men.[178]

Many indigenous cultures and traditions of Nigeria are undoubtedly male-centered. This, however, does not mean that some cultures and
traditions do not promote respect for women. The problem, it seems, is
the conditions under which many women live in their homes, clans,
and the society at large. Most indigenous cultures configure respect and
significance of women mainly in the perspectives of men. Sadly, some
men continue to see women as sex objects for the gratifications of their
sexual desires, or as wombs whose sole purpose is to bear children for
men. Oduyoye laments this state of affairs:

> We have been brought up to believe that a woman should always
> have a suzerain, that she should be "owned" by a man, be he fa-
> ther, uncle, or husband. A "free woman" spells disaster. An adult
> woman, if unmarried, is immediately reckoned to be available
> for the pleasure of all males and is treated as such.[179]

The agony of many women, which Oduyoye expresses sharply, is
the oppressiveness of the cultures and traditions that define a woman's
identity only in relation to the values and demands of men. Therefore,
the march for liberation is situated on freeing women from their "com-
pulsory attachment to men."[180] Some feminist theologians see this attachment as one of the causes of the dehumanizing treatments they
experience.

Rosemary Edet, while recognizing that the widowhood ritual imposed on women "may or may not be out of malice," contends that the
ritual exposes women to hostility, enormous sufferings and health haz-
ards.[181] The requirements of some clans for widowhood ritual are dis-
gusting and preposterous. For example, a widow is usually considered
the prime suspect in her husband's death. Under a barbaric method of

178. Oduyoye, *Beads and Strands*, 69.

179. Ibid.

180. Ibid.

181. Edet, "Christianity and African Women's Ritual," 31.

establishing if she is guilty or innocent, some cultures in Nigeria, for example, require the widow to drink part of the water that is used to wash her husband's corpse. When the widow refuses to drink the water the clan will ostracize her and subjugate her to horrendous sufferings.

EMANCIPATION OF WOMEN FROM THE OPPRESSIVE ECCLESIAL SYSTEMS

In the church, too, women feel they also suffer injustice and oppression. Some feminist theologians have given a distress call to churches to rediscover the priesthood of all believers. Edet wonders why churches "continue to choose their leaders from the educated, predominantly male, middles classes," and why there "are no women bishops."[182] Also she questions the reason in some local churches women are teachers "who do not participate to any great extent in church theological and political discussions, and whose views are not taken into account."[183] Modupe Owanikin argues that some "Nigerian custom and tradition recognize the priesthood of women." She contends that the churches which oppose women leadership in the church should learn from the indigenous religions.[184] Chukwudi Okolo is an example of some Nigerian men who are highly critical of the dehumanizing treatment of women in the church. He notes that the "Nigerian woman is fast coming of age" and gradually becoming aware of her conditions. For him, this phenomenon is justified, and the "church in Nigeria needs [to be] aware of the Nigerian woman's diverse socio-cultural realities, difficulties" threatening her existence.[185] Daisy Nwachukwu argues that this estimation of women is also apparent in the indigenous religions.[186] She challenges women to wake up from their slumber and express their dissatisfactions with the ecclesial and cultural traditions that perpetuate the "rites and rituals" which foster female oppression.[187]

Although many feminist theologians draw insights from diverse ideologies, Christology has remained central to their quest for the lib-

---

182. Ibid., 37.

183. Ibid., 37–38.

184. Owanikin, "Priesthood of Church Women in the Nigerian Context," 217.

185. Okolo, "Church and the Nigerian Woman," 368–69.

186. Nwachukwu, "Christian Widow in African Culture," 65.

187. Ibid.

eration of women from all forms of marginalization and oppression. Oduyoye argues forcefully for the need to acknowledge the liberative effect of the Christ-Event on African women.

> African women are heard loud and clear singing the redemptive love of Jesus the liberator. Jesus accomplishes God's mission by setting women free from sexism, oppression, and marginalization through his death and resurrection, and both women and men are made members of God's household and of the same royal priesthood as men.[188]

Oduyoye raises some vital christological issues here but does not explore them. However, her aim is clear: to argue that the Christ-Event is the ground on which many women who are oppressed can breathe liberation and also draw encouragement to criticize oppressions and their oppressors. At the heart of the reconstruction of African Christologies from the feminist perspective is the criticism of a problematic anthropology that is prevalent in some theological discourses and the attempt to eliminate all "limitations to the fullness of life envisaged in the Christ-Event."[189] For Oduyoye, Jesus embodies the liberation for all humanity and therefore stands in opposition to the oppression of women. She argues that "in the heightened debate surrounding the role of women, some Africans are puzzled when Christian women say that it is the will of Christ . . . that women should be free to respond to the fullness God expects of all human beings."[190]

According to her, the humiliating status of many women in Africa is a contradiction to the essence of Christianity, a religion that promotes liberation and freedom. She criticizes African Christianity for remaining largely indifferent to the ordeal of women.

> It is my experience that Christianity, as manifested in the western churches of Africa, does little to change sexism, whether in church or in society. I believe that the experience of women in the church in Africa contradicts the Christian claim to promote the worth (equal value) of every person. Rather, it shows how Christianity reinforces the cultural conditioning of compliance and submission and leads to the depersonalization of women.[191]

188. Oduyoye, "Jesus Christ," 156.

189. Oduyoye, *Beads and Strands*, 68.

190. Ibid., 70.

191. Ibid., 72.

I will explore further the concept of liberation in some of the writings of African feminist theologians in the following section.

LIBERATION FROM WESTERN COLONIZATION AND MISSIONARY CHRISTOLOGY

For many African feminist theologians, the enemies are not only the aspects of indigenous cultures and ecclesiastical systems that are oppressive, but also Western colonization, and the Missionary Christology. Rosemary Edet and Bette Ekeya underscore this assumption. According to them, women fared no better under the colonial rule for all the disabilities of Western Christian culture were added to the already burden of African situation.[192] Teresia Hinga, the Kenyan scholar, expresses the role of the West in the subjugation of African women in the following way:

> Going back to history, we recall that during the period of colonial and imperial expansionism, the prevailing image of Christ was that of Christ the conqueror. Jesus was the warrior King, in whose name and banner (the cross) new territories, both physical and spiritual, would be fought for, annexed, and subjugated. An imperial Christianity thus had an imperial Christ to match. The Christ of the missionaries was a conquering Christ.[193]

She, however, points out the ambivalence of the missionaries' attitudes toward the subjugated in Africa. She observes that some Western missionaries established "centers of refuge" where some women who were "trying to break away from unsatisfactory marriages or harsh parental control" took shelter.[194]

Relatively, Teresa Okure, a Nigerian biblical scholar, sees Jesus' post-resurrection message to Mary Magdalene for his disciples recorded in John 20:11–18 as the foundation on which the unity of Christian communities is to be built. Jesus' usage of the possessive pronouns your and my to describe the relationship that is now existing between his followers and his Father, and between him and his Father, for Okure, underscores a new relationship in which all Christians are to "relate to

192. Edet and Ekeya, "Church Women of Africa," 5.
193. Hinga, "Jesus Christ and the Liberation of Women," 187.
194. Ibid., 189.

one another in Jesus as blood brothers and sisters relate to one another."[195] She goes on to argue that this new form of relationship must inspire "the so-called Christian countries of the west to care for their less fortunate sisters and brothers in the two-thirds world."[196] But Okure's contention emerges powerfully in that she is not interested in the act of giving aid; instead she is primarily concerned with the motive underlying the act of caring or giving. A "sense of duty" and not a "sense of benevolence," she argues, should be the motive behind the caring and aid that some countries in the West provide for poor countries. She contends that the "belittling relationship that often exists between donors and receivers should give place to a genuine sharing not only of goods but of technology and skills."[197]

Some feminist Christologies present Jesus as a liberator. This image of Jesus serves two primary purposes. First, in the thinking of the majority of these theologians, Jesus is a liberator who de-stigmatizes and liberates women and all human beings from the oppressive sexist conditions, patriarchal cultures, and oppressive ecclesial traditions. Inherent in this thinking is the contention that Jesus reconstructs the sexist dichotomy of male and female and introduces a radical meaning of humanity. Jesus Christ, for them, embodies true humanity. Drawing upon the ways he related to some women in the Gospel stories and the experience of women, some feminist theologians argue forcefully for the need to eradicate any intellectual framework that degrades women. Second, the image of Jesus Christ as a liberator is intended by some feminist theologians to inspire many women to arise from their underserved state of humiliation. This is evident in the most powerful charge Okure gives to African feminist theologians. She writes: "Let us eject from our attitudes and subconscious all prejudices and inferiority complexes about ourselves as Africans and as women. Let us promptly obey Jesus who awakens us from sleep and authorizes and empowers us to undertake responsible theological action and reflection."[198] To her, women have a serious part to play in liberating themselves from their oppressive conditions. Jesus has opened a new horizon and a new way of viewing humanity and liberation. African women, therefore, are to

195. Okure, "Jesus and Mary Magdalene," 318.

196. Ibid., 324.

197. Ibid.

198. Ibid. See also Okure, "Will to Arise," 227.

draw encouragement from Jesus and must aim at achieving total liberation and true humanness.

A major element distinguishing many African feminist Christologies from some feminist Christologies emerging in Europe, Latin America, and North America is the emphasis on the *work* of Jesus Christ and not on the gender of Jesus Christ. For many Nigerian feminist theologians, the gender of Jesus does not warrant the suspicion of the possibility of a male savior effectively saving a woman.[199] They see Jesus' attitude toward some women in the Bible as persuasive evidence which he criticized and deconstructed cultures that subjugated women, and re-constructed a new model that upholds the dignity of women.[200] As Edet writes, "Jesus was revolutionary. He liberated the woman with the issue of blood and restored the son of the widow of Nain. He never tortured them, nor segregated them, nor demanded purifications rites."[201]

Some African women have always expressed their experiences which have traumatized their lives through writing, through aesthetical forums such as dancing and painting, and through speech acts such as poems and storytelling. But their experiences have not been truly heard and accorded due place in the church. Many women, represented by some women theologians, want their experiences to become a text for doing Christology. It is not that some men have not acted as spokespersons of women, for some men have condemned and called for the eradication of the indigenous cultures and traditions which empower men to maltreat their wives, widows, and indeed all women. But women want to speak for themselves. They want to be their own advocates; they want to stand up and declare their freedom themselves. As Oduyoye notes:

> Women's spirituality is qualitatively different from that of men
> because women's experience of socio-economic realities differs

199. In the West, however, the question "can a male savior be able to save women?" is one of the defining questions on which some feminist Christologies are built. It is the influence of this question that perhaps made Naomi Goldenberg to argue that in order to "develop a theology of women liberation, feminist have to leave Christ and the Bible behind." See Goldenberg, *Changing of the God*, 22. Rosemary Radford Reuther, "Can Christology be Liberated from Patriarchy?" 7–29; Hampson has also argued that no authentic Christology is compatible with feminism. See Hampson, "Feminism and Christology," 287–99.

200. See Okure, "The Will To Arise," 221–30.

201. Edet, "Christianity and African Women's Ritual," 37.

from that of men. . . . When women read the Bible, they often hear what is unheard by men. Thus, women's biblical theology originates at a different depth.[202]

Oduyoye and Musimbi Kanyoro express their suspicion of male's theology: "African women theologians have come to realize that as long as men and foreign researchers remain the authorities on culture, rituals and religion, African women will continue to be spoken of as if they were dead."[203] This suspicion of some feminist theologians seems to be justified when we consider that some of the images of Jesus Christ in the African constructive Christologies are shaped by patriarchy. One example is the Ancestor Christology model. Usually, it is only men who are readily associated with the ancestor cult. Ezeh, the key proponent of the Ancestor Christology, acknowledges that this is one of the arguments raised against the Ancestor Christology model.[204]

The quests to contribute to the academic discourse and for self-expression are not peculiar to the African women. Kwok Pui-lan explains that these quests are embedded in the struggle of all women in the world who are marginalized. Writing specifically from the context of postcolonial discourse, she asserts:

Women's articulation of their experiences of colonization is so new; these women have been much represented, but until recently have not been allowed the opportunities to represent themselves. Even if they have "spoken," their speech acts are expressed not only in words but in forms that the academic and cultural establishments either could not understand or deemed insignificant.[205]

How would an African woman speak freely about her experiences of Jesus and expect them to inform the Christology of her church or denomination without immediately putting herself in the theological line of battle with men who doubt her right and capability to engage in such enterprise? Oduyoye correctly observes that even when some African women venture to do theology "they model themselves on male theology, or else they would have to seek men's approval for what they write."[206] The emergence of feminist Christology in African Christianity

202. Oduyoye, "Feminist Theology in an African Perspective," 167.
203. Oduyoye and Kanyoro, "Introduction," in *The Will to Arise*, 1.
204. Ezeh, *Jesus Christ the Ancestor*, 310.
205. Pui-lan, *Postcolonial Imagination and Feminist Theology*, 30.
206. Oduyoye, "Feminist Theology in an African Perspective," 167.

has begun to draw out sharp criticisms against the male-dominated ways of interpreting Jesus the Christ. The legitimacy of the concern of feminist theologians is unquestionable. The liberation call which they make is unavoidable. One wonders how African Christians (both men and women) can justify some of the practices and ill-treatment women undergo in their clans, homes, and more disappointingly in the church. The ritual of widowhood has become more and more oppressive on women. Whether or not a feminist christological-talk in African Christianity has succeeded in its agenda depends on the angle one examines it. But what is undeniable is that, although gradual, some Christians are beginning to acknowledge the importance of women for the vibrant existence and subsistence of Christianity. For example, many women in some Pentecostal churches closely stand, teach and minister with their husbands who are founders of churches.

Another phenomenon that is worthy of recognition is the fact that the impact of some feminist Christologies is felt mainly on the surface level. Some of these Christologies have appealed only to a few men and women who are learned. But the idea of feminist Christology is still off-putting and inaccessible to numerous women and men who do not have any formal theological education. The irony is that the majority of African women who continue to suffer injustice and oppression have not gone through the university or any formal education at all. They live in the deep parts of some villages and have no access to the scholarly works of feminist theologians. The challenge for feminist theologians and indeed for all Christians in Africa is to reach out to such women with a liberative gospel through workshops, preaching and any other techniques that are suitable to their contexts. What this entails is that a Nigerian feminist theologian has the responsibility to bring his or her Christology down from an ivory tower (which earns him or her respect and fame in the world of academia) and direct it into the rural areas and villages where many women are still being maltreated and oppressed.[207]

Finally, an adequate contextual Christology designed for African Christianity should present Jesus Christ as the figure who dismantles all forms of oppression emanating from a gender and sexist cultural web. In addition, a feminist theologian faces is to confront the tendency to

---

207. Some feminist theologians who are members of the Circle of Concerned African Women are beginning to move in this direction, reaching out to some women in the villages.

overemphasize the particularity of Jesus Christ to the extent of reducing him to a tool for achieving some selfish agendas. The tension between Black or womanist Christologies and what could be called (for lack of a better expression) White feminist Christology exemplifies this danger. For some Black American feminist theologians, the idea of feminism has originated from and has served the need of some White middle-class women. Thus, some Black American feminist theologians differentiate the theologies which arise from the unique experiences (gender, class and race) of Black American women from the feminist theology emerging from within the experience of the White middle-class Americans.[208] African feminist theologians have the task of producing the Christologies that have the capacity to critique the oppressive concepts and ideologies which emanate from both men and women. Daisy Nwachukwu, for example, has argued that some of the humiliating customs women undergo in Nigeria were initiated by women themselves.

Some of the obnoxious and repressive roles of women, whether in religion or in social matters, were formulated in the distant past by powerful elderly women for the purposes of female discipline in the areas of wifely submission, chastity, good maternal care, and for the maintaining femininity.[209]

An African feminist Christology should, therefore, guard against the danger of an opposite error. Jesus Christ should be allowed to dismantle the oppressive customs initiated by men against women, women against men, and women against other women, and indeed every form of oppression and dehumanizing cultures.

In conclusion, I have examined in this chapter some of the major christological models that exist in contemporary African Christianity. I argued that they are concerned with the issue of contextualizing the person and work of Jesus Christ to befit the religious, cultural, political, and socio-economic conditions of the people. The Missionary Christology has provided the context for the Neo-missionary Christology, the Culture-oriented Christology and the Liberation-oriented Christologies. A key question that drives many theologians to

208. Grant, "Womanist Theology," 346. Grant has argued that "Womanist theology begins with the experience of Black women as its point of departure. The experience includes not only Black women's activities in the larger society but also in the churches, and reveals that Black women have often rejected the oppressive structures in the church as well." Ibid., 278.

209. Nwachukwu, "Christian Widow in African Culture," 66.

construct contextual Christologies is: 'what would Jesus Christ look like if he was expressed with the indigenous thought forms and if he was located within contexts of the history of the experiences of Africans?' Many theologians have wrestled with this question and have made some original contributions to the development of contextual Christologies. As we have already seen, some of these models have some serious christological problems. They have not allowed the person and work of Jesus Christ to critique their contextual approaches and agendas. In addition, while these christological models claim to be contextual, they seem not to engage seriously with the christological concerns of many Christians who do not have any formal theological training. The concerns include the existential significance of Jesus for the issues of poverty, fear of evil spirits, the danger of insecurity, and quest to achieve wellbeing. This will become evident as I explore in the next chapter some of the grassroots Christologies. I will also explore further some of the theological problems of the models I have examined in this chapter.

3

Grassroots Christologies of Contemporary African Christianity

A Case Study of Nigeria

IN THIS CHAPTER, I WILL CONCENTRATE ON SOME GRASSROOTS CHRIS-tologies which emerged from the qualitative fieldwork research (individual interviews) I conducted in Aba (one of the major cities in southeast of Nigeria) in the summers of 2003, 2004, 2005, and also from February to July 2006. The chapter is divided into two major sections. First, I begin by describing the methodology I employed. This includes the rationale for undertaking the research and the procedures I used for data collection and analysis. I also articulate the relationship of this chapter to the overarching theses and objectives of this book. Second, I will examine the christological issues and themes that emerged from the interviews and articulate the conclusions I have drawn from the analysis of the data. Under this section, I will interact with the two major sources of grassroots Christologies; namely, the Bible and religious experience. Also I will explore some of the key contexts that inform and shape the grassroots Christologies. Finally, I will examine the solution-oriented ideology underlying many of the grassroots Christologies.

Methodology

Research Rationale

> African theology . . . has remained far too academic, and is for
> the most part irrelevant to what is going on in African society
> today.[1]

The Congolese theologian, Benezet Bujo, in the foregoing observation
articulates a major problem that confronts many contextual theologies
and Christologies in Africa. For too long, Bujo laments, many theologians have written theologies and Christologies that never get "beyond
the lecture halls of universities and congresses [and] mostly outside of
Africa."[2] The observation of Bujo provides a broad context for this chapter. Many theologians have constructed some Christologies that discuss
some of the issues that bothered Christians in the nineteenth and the
early part of the twentieth centuries but have ignored the contemporary
issues many lay Christians wrestle with in their daily lives and how such
issues inform and shape their interpretations and appropriations of the
Christ-Event. But if a contextual theologian wants to be relevant to the
majority of African lay Christians, he or she must begin to construct a
Christology that moves beyond a peer-driven conversation.[3] In addition, he or she should interpret and appropriate the Christ-Event in the
ways that are rooted strongly in, to use the words of Kenneth Ross, "how
ordinary people understand the identity and meaning of Jesus Christ."[4]

The quests to discover how lay Christians in Africa perceive Jesus
Christ and how their Christologies compare to the major constructive
Christologies theologians have written are the two major reasons for
the inclusion of this chapter in this book. Theologians make a mistake
when they assume that they already know what many lay Christians in
their communities think and believe about Jesus Christ without taking
time to converse with them. I argue that no constructive Christology is
truly contextual if it fails to take seriously and engage with the living
experiences of people. A contextual Christology must go beyond "formal written expressions to include informal expressions, for example

1. Bujo, *African Theology in Its Social Context*, 70.

2. Ibid., 70.

3. Laity here refers to Christians who do not have a formal theological training.

4. Ross, "Current Christological Trends in Northern Malawi," 160–76.

in worship, prayer, preaching, artwork, drama, gesture, and symbols."[5] Although I will make reference to some written texts in this chapter, I will focus primarily on oral Christologies, particularly those existing in Nigerian Christianity.

Research Procedure

I used a qualitative field research approach.[6] This method fits the objectives of this chapter because it promotes active conversations between a researcher and the interviewees.[7] It allows the researcher, to use the words of Uwe Flick, to gain access to the experiences of the interviewees in their own natural contexts.[8] A qualitative method, unlike a quantitative method, requires a *descriptive interpretation* of the experiences of the interviewees rather than on a *statistical evaluation*.[9] As we will see later, this method allows me to use a conversation analysis approach to analyze the data.

Data Collection and Rationale for the Field Research Sites

It is impossible to cover all the churches in Nigeria in this book. Therefore, it is important to reiterate that I conducted my research in Aba, a city in southeast of Nigeria. Although the interviewees are born in Nigeria, come from different ethnic groups and are affiliated to different church denominations, there are still limitations that the selection of the field sites pose. Thus, when I speak of Nigerian Christianity, I am aware of the roles and risks of generalization. However, as it will

---

5. Stinton, "Jesus of Africa," 31.

6. The meaning and the nature of qualitative research have become more complex in the wake of the descriptions that are associated with this form of research. What is noteworthy is that many researchers have moved away from construing qualitative research as simply an alternative to quantitative research. They see qualitative research as a unique method that is most appropriate to specific forms of ethnographical research. See Flick, *Designing Qualitative Research*, 1; Silverman, *Doing Qualitative Research*, 7–11.

7. Robert C. Bogdan and Sari Knopp Biklen, *Qualitative Research for Education: An Introduction to Theory and Methods* (Boston: Ally and Bacon, 1982) 27–30.

8. Flick, *Designing Qualitative Research*, x.

9. Silverman, *Doing Qualitative Research*, 7.

become clear later in this chapter, many Christians in Nigeria, irrespective of their denominational differences, their ethnicity, and varying understandings of Christ-Event, share a solution-oriented mindset.[10]

Churches in contemporary Nigeria can be categorized roughly into two dominant groups, namely, mission churches and locally initiated churches.[11] The *mission churches* have ties with the Western churches and have to a great extent retained the theological and liturgical traditions of the mother churches. The *locally initiated churches* are those with Nigerians founders and which may not have any direct connection with Western missionaries.[12] Some of the founders of these churches may have at one time been members of the mission churches but left to found their churches for reasons such as liturgical and theological differences. I selected five churches, namely, the Roman Catholic Church, the Presbyterian Church, Evangelical Church of West Africa (hereafter ECWA), Christian Pentecostal Mission (hereafter CPM), and Christ Holy Church, a.k.a., Nation Builders (or *Odoziobodo*).

The following reasons informed my selection of the research sites. First, the churches represent the major church groups in Nigeria. Since my main objective was to gain access to the grassroots Christologies of Nigerian Christianity, it was necessary to interview Christians from the denominations representing the major church groups. The key reason is to test the regularity, variability and similarity in the responses of the interviewees.[13] Second, I have established a rapport with the pastors and priests of the selected churches. I taught theology in ECWA Theological

10. The issue of generalizability or transferability in qualitative research concerns how the findings of a given research site can be applicable to other settings or contexts. Sampling is an integral part of generalization in both qualitative and quantitative forms of research. The key assumption here is that the variables and similarities that exist in the selected research site can also occur (in some recognizable and identifiable form) in the wider population of the broader context of the book. See Marshall and Rossman, *Designing Qualitative Research.* It is only on the ground of sampling and generalization that I am able to speak of Nigerian grassroots Christologies based on the individual interviews I conducted among five churches in Aba.

11. It will be an oversimplification to think that the Christians who, for instance, identify themselves as Pentecostals do not share some theological views of the Evangelicals.

12. These churches belong to the group many African theologians and scholars of religions describe as AICs (African Independent or Indigenous Churches).

13. I have highlighted and engaged with the variables and similarities in the interviewees' responses throughout this chapter.

Seminary in Aba in the summers of 2003–2005. During this period, I visited the churches and spoke to their leaders about my plan to conduct interviews in their churches for my doctoral research.[14] Third, the members of these churches spoke Igbo and/or English languages fluently. Because I understand the two languages, I was able to deal with the practical difficulties associated with language, meaning, translation and interpretation during data analysis. Fourth, Aba is a major city which attract people from different ethnic groups reside. This made it possible for me to interview people from different ethnic groups without travelling to their hometowns.

The primary source of data collection was individual interviews. The interviewees participated voluntarily. I used a semi-structured approach revolving around six pre-set questions.[15] I asked other follow-up questions based on the interviewees' responses to the pre-set questions with the intention to probe their Christologies.[16] The questions I asked the interviewees were open-ended and were designed to elicit the interviewees' perceptions of Jesus Christ.[17] I interviewed ten volunteers from each of the five churches. In each church I interviewed a pastor (and in the case of the Roman Catholic Church, a priest) and nine lay people. I used both English and Igbo languages for the interviews, depending on the interviewee's choice. In a few cases, some of the interviewees used both English and Igbo languages. I recorded all the interviews with an audiotape recorder and transcribed them myself.[18]

14. In 2005, I conducted pilot interviews in three of the five churches—ECWA English Church Aba, Christian Pentecostal Mission and the Presbyterian Church. The pilot interviews helped me to test the objectives of the research and to modify my research and interview questions. I lived and studied in Aba for seven years. This helped me to deal with some geographical issues, particularly in locating and visiting the research sites.

15. As we will see later, this approach has informed the *conversation analysis* and *meaning of interpretation* approaches I employed in analyzing the data. See Appendix 1 for the pre-set questions.

16. I used adverbs such as *how* and *why* to introduce the subsequent questions I asked the interviewees to probe their responses to the pre-set questions.

17. The duration of the interviews varied, ranging from 20 to 50 minutes.

18. I transcribed the interviews in their original languages.

ETHICAL ISSUES

There are important ethical issues that are of paramount importance to qualitative research. These are informed consent, the rights of the interviewees, anonymity, confidentiality, fairness, and objectivity in interpreting the responses of the interviewees.[19] I observed these ethical codes during the interviews, the transcription of the interviews, and in writing up my critical analysis of the emerging themes from the interviews. Although I informally notified the pastors and priest of the selected churches in 2005 of my intention to carry out interviews in their churches, I made a formal request and got their permission before conducting the interviews in 2006.[20] I also explained the objectives and purpose of my research to the interviewees and obtained their consents before interviewing them.

I explained to all the interviewees that I would record the interviews on tape. I also told them to tell me to stop recording the interview if there were things they did not want to be on tape. In addition, I explained to them that the information they gave would be strictly confidential and will be used specifically for the purpose of book. I also explained to the interviewees who were lay Christians that their church leaders would not have access to the tapes or my transcripts of the interviews.[21] I explained to all the interviewees that I would use pseudonym in my research unless they have permitted me to use their real names.[22]

METHODS OF DATA ANALYSIS

There are several ways of analyzing an interview.[23] Steinar Kvale has identified eight modes, namely, meaning coding, meaning condensa-

---

19. Marshall and Rossman, *Designing Qualitative Research*, 69–77; Rapley, *Doing Conversation, Discourse and Document Analysis*, 23.

20. I gave all the pastors, priest, and interviewees the official *letter of introduction* I obtained from the University of Edinburgh. I also gave them the *Informed Consent Form* that I designed for the research. The form contains the ethical codes, objectives and purpose of my research.

21. I explained to the interviewees that the goal of the research is to gain access to their personal views, and not the official view of their churches, of Jesus Christ.

22. Some of the interviewees requested that I used only their first names.

23. See Tesch, *Qualitative Research*.

tion, meaning interpretation, linguistic analysis, conversation analysis, narrative analysis, discursive analysis and deconstruction analysis.[24] I have employed both the *conversation analysis* and *meaning interpretation* modes for coding and analyzing the data.[25] According to Kvale, *a meaning interpretation* approach involves interpreting "the meaning of interview text" in a way that goes beyond "a structuring of the manifest meanings of what is said to deeper and more critical interpretations of the text."[26] Conversation analysis "examines the minute details of talk-in-interaction, which has become widely accessible with the advent of a tape recorder."[27] Uwe Flick has noted that the key factor in this approach is demonstrating how conclusions are based on detailed transcription of the interviews and "how to present excerpts from the material in an accessible and readable way."[28] In "conversation analysis, comparison is in many cases oriented toward a more general model . . . which is juxtaposed to the concrete case that is being studied."[29]

These methods fit my goal of gaining access to the existing grassroots Christologies in Nigerian Christianity by interviewing a few people from the selected research sites. They also fit my goal of interacting and analyzing the data from a theological perspective by probing the responses of the interviewees. They provided me with the hermeneutical framework and context to engage in a rigorous interaction with the data. I have quoted some excerpts in the chapter. One of the reasons is to ensure a fair and objective representation of the interviewees' understandings and perceptions of Jesus Christ. What follows is a critical examination and presentation of the themes and conclusions that have emerged from my analysis of the data.

24. Kvale, *Doing Interviews*, 104.

25. I used Nvivo 7 (computer-assisted qualitative data analysis software) in coding the data.

26. Kvale, *Doing Interviews*, 107.

27. Ibid., 111.

28. Flick, *Designing Qualitative Research*, 106.

29. Ibid., 104.

Emerging Issues and Themes in Nigerian Grassroots Christologies

Sources of Grassroots Christologies

The issue of the sources of Christology has generated debates among many theologians. No consensus, however, exists among these theologians on where to draw resources and insights when interpreting the Christ-Event. The conversations on the issue of the sources of African Christology appear to exist on two related levels.[30] On the one level, there are those who concern themselves with the nature of the possible sources of a contextual Christology. Among the competing sources are the Bible, the indigenous religious understandings of the world, and church traditions. On the second level, others debate on the type of relationship that should exist among the possible sources. For example, some concern themselves with the question, should the Bible be placed above other sources of Christology? The majority of Nigerian lay Christians take the issue of the sources of Christology for granted. But a close examination reveals that the Bible and religious experience are the two major sources.[31] In what follows, I will examine how these sources function as the foundation of some of the oral Christologies of contemporary Nigerian Christianity.

THE RESOURCEFUL ROLE OF THE BIBLE

According to Benedict Ufomadu, a member of ECWA, "it is in the Bible we know about Jesus Christ." This was her response to question "from where do you get your knowledge of Jesus Christ?"[32] Amadi's (a Presbyterian) response to the same question was, "Jesus to me is the savior of the world; he is the Son of God according to what is written in the scripture, and that is what I believe."[33] The responses of Ufomadu and Amadi are representative of the predominant responses of many of the interviewees to the question on the sources of their Christologies.

---

30. See Nyamiti, "Contemporary African Christologies," 62–77. Stinton, *Jesus of Africa*, 22–24.

31. Some of my interviewees made reference to their church teaching or tradition.

32. Ufomadu, interview by author, tape recording, Aba, 28 May 2006.

33. Amadi, interview by author, tape recording, Aba, 10 April 2006.

Many of the interviewees made reference to the Bible to buttress their understandings of the person and work of Jesus Christ.

The resourceful role of the Bible, particularly the New Testament, in coming to the knowledge of Jesus Christ is not contested in christological discourses. This is not to suggest that all theologians take the representations of Jesus Christ in the Bible to be historically authentic. Rather, many of them draw upon some biblical representations of Jesus Christ when they discuss the Christ-Event. Two reasons can be advanced for this state of affairs. First, the Bible is the only major collection of books and epistles written about Jesus the Christ by some individuals who lived with him and/or experienced him in some ways.[34] John Macquarrie has argued that although "the knowledge that comes to us from the New Testament is mediated knowledge … we can experience through the language even today something of the power of that person whom we call Jesus Christ."[35] The second reason many Christians consider the Bible normally as a source of Christology is because, even when an individual claims to experience the risen Christ, the experience most times stems from some biblical christological narratives. The words of Humble Douglas, a member of ECWA, attest to this: "I call Jesus my Savior because I have experienced him, and because of what history laid down for us. And I was taught from the Bible."[36]

That many Christians consider the Bible a source of Christology is not striking. However, what is noteworthy is their understanding of the nature of the Bible. Using the Bible as a resourceful tool for gaining knowledge of the Christ-Event is the key that connects the grassroots Christologies and the constructive Christologies of theologians. But a crucial question is: do Christians who are not theologically trained read the Bible in the same manner many theologians read it? At first the question may seem too obvious to need stating. However, the complexity of the possible answers and the necessity of this question emerge sharply when we recognize that there are differences between the agenda of many contextual theologians and many lay Christians. Whereas many Christians who are not theologians are seeking to *experience* a Jesus who hears and solves their spiritual, psychological and physical problems when they pray to him, many theologians are seeking to con-

---

34. An example is the Apostle Paul (Acts 9).

35. Macquarrie, *Christology Revisited*, 85.

36. Douglas, interview by author, tape recording, Aba, 17 June 2006.

struct *contextually* and interpret the Christ-Event within the indigenous categories.[37] The key issue here is that the difference in the resourceful roles of the Bible in the Christologies of many theologians and in the grassroots Christologies is not simply hermeneutical. Rather, it chiefly lies in how they construe the nature of the Bible and their purpose in reading it. The majority of contextual theologians view the Bible as a church's special book and read it christologically with the intent to deconstruct some images of Jesus in it that are strange to the indigenous understandings of the world. On the contrary, most lay Christians view the Bible as God's book and read it christologically with the intent to experience Jesus' power to solve spiritual and physical problems.

For many Nigerian lay Christians, the Bible is the Word of God. Writing on the use of the Bible among the Igbo of southern Nigeria, Anthony Nkwoka asserts:

> To the Igbo, the Bible is a living book, the unique Word of God Almighty, Creator and Controller of the universe. Apart from the fact that it is "*Bible Nso*" (The Holy Bible), it is the Messenger-gift of an awfully holy and all-terrible God and is therefore very different from any other book! An irreverent handling of it is regarded as an insult to God, which no sane person should engage in.[38]

The question, "What do lay Christians mean when they refer to the Bible as the *Word of God* or a *divine book*?" provides us with a platform to investigate the role the Bible plays in shaping the contents of some grassroots Christologies of Nigerian Christianity. This is a very difficult question to answer because the majority of these Christians do not bother to engage in a discussion on the origin of the Bible. They seem to settle with the idea that the Bible is the *Word of God* without question. However, when pressed further, it seems that they use the expression *Word of God* in a propositional sense; that is, they see the Bible as a set of divine propositions. It is noteworthy that many Christians who hold the propositional revelatory view of Scripture are indebted partly to some North American missionaries, especially

---

37. See Adamo, "Use of Psalms in African Indigenous Churches in Nigeria," 336; Mosala, "Use of the Bible in Black Theology in South Africa," 175–99; West, "Reading the Bible Differently: Giving Shape to the Discourses of the Dominated," 21–41; West, *Academy of the Poor*.

38. Nkwoka, "Role of the Bible in the Igbo Christianity of Nigeria," 327.

those of the Evangelical tradition. Some of those missionaries who labored in Nigeria were already influenced by the propositional model of revelation espoused by theologians such as B. B. Warfield, Carl F. H. Henry, and Gordon Clark.[39]

In the thinking of some Christians who construe the Bible as the *Word of God* in a propositional sense, the content of the Bible is trustworthy. To quote Humble Douglas, when I asked him if some of the things written in the Bible about Jesus may be untrue, he responded, "Well if they are not true it means that the existence of the universe will not be true."[40] While it is not clear how the truthfulness of the christological content of the Bible is a warrant for the truthfulness of the existence of the universe, what Douglas appears to be saying is that if the existence of the universe could not be doubted then whatever the Bible says about Jesus Christ equally should not be doubted. At the heart of the propositional revelatory model of the Bible is the belief that the content of the Bible must be true and reliable because it proceeds from God. Therefore, whatever the Bible says about Jesus Christ must be true.

To seek to subsume the Bible under a single model will eclipse the diversities which characterize the collection of books and letters that constitute the Bible. African theologians are not strangers to the debates on the nature of the Bible and hermeneutics. Justin Ukpong has categorized the history of African biblical interpretation into three phases. Phase 1 (1930s–70s) is composed of a reactive and apologetic hermeneutic and "focused on legitimizing African religion and culture" through comparative studies. In phase II (1970s–90s), African biblical scholarship moved from the level of polemic to proactive. At this level they construed "African context as a resource for biblical interpretation" and employed inculturation and liberation hermeneutics. In phase III (1990s), according to his assessment, the pendulum swung to a reader-response hermeneutic—ordinary readers (and African contexts) became the "subject" of biblical interpretation.[41] Like most periodization, his three phases run the risk of superficiality. He recognizes this pitfall when he notes that these phases intersect.[42]

39. See Henry, *God, Revelation, and Authority.*

40. Douglas, interview by author, tape recording, Aba, 17 June 2006.

41. Ukpong, "Developments in Biblical Interpretation in Africa," 12.

42. Ibid.

Getting a correct hermeneutical paradigm to interpret the Bible is the least worry of the majority Nigerian lay Christians. Some of them read it with the intent to discover what God or Jesus Christ is saying to them. Most times they read the Bible literally and claim all the divine blessings contained in it. For them, these blessings are their portions and are expected to manifest in their lives. But they fail to recognize that inadequate views of the nature and the purpose of the Bible affect greatly the theologies and Christologies which are constructed from it. This will become clearer when I examine the emerging christological themes from the interviews.

RELIGIOUS EXPERIENCE

Alvin Plantinga, one of the leading philosophers in North America, has written this about religious experience: "'religious experience' is construed in a thousand different ways to cover a vast and confusing variety of cases; the question as it stands is multiple ambiguous and, in fact, we are probably better off boycotting the term."[43] A religious experience is notoriously slippery. Understandably, many people (both in the West and Africa) are reluctant to take religious experience seriously. The skepticism of people regarding most religious experiences can be explored from phenomenological, psychological, and theological spectrums. In psychology, it is difficult to know if an acclaimed religious experience is a hallucinatory experience or an experience that occurs as a result of a mental disorder.[44] For some anthropologists and sociologists, the phenomenon of religious experience posses a conundrum because it is not always clear if a given experience is a historical fact; that is, if it happened, and is authentic, original, and verifiable. Some theologians discard religious experience because they consider the cognitive input or interpretation of a given religious experience a threat to some already established traditions, especially if the interpretation suggests some new innovations.[45]

---

43. Plantinga, *Warranted Christian Belief,* 182.

44. See Clark et al., *Religious Experience*; James, *The Varieties of Religious Experience: A Book in Human Nature* (reprint, New York: University Books, 1963).

45. See Hurtado, *How on Earth Did Jesus Become a God?*, 180–86; Haight, *Dynamics of Theology*, 51–67.

In spite of the incredulity toward religious experience, this phenomenon cannot be ignored in any serious interpretation of the development of Christianity. As Ronald Nash observes:

> Based on my observation ... far more people are religious believers because of religious experiences they've had than because of arguments they've heard. Even the few Christians I've met who appear sometimes to disdain the religious experience (or at least more extreme religious experience) of others and claim that their faith is grounded not on experience but on God's revelation in Scripture overlook an important point. The revealed texts are products of the religious experiences of the inspired human authors who penned them.[46]

Nash notes the intrinsic connection between Christian scripture and religious experience. Roger Haight buttresses this connection: "The first genetic source for the scriptures . . . lies in religious experience."[47] Religious experience is difficult to test partly because it is grounded in subjectivism. In addition, the emergence of some stories of religious experiences that appear to be too extreme has made some scholars all the more skeptical about this phenomenon. My concern here is not to defend or deny the reality and validity of religious experience, but rather to explore how this phenomenon informs some grassroots Christologies of Nigerian Christians. While some Christians consider some religious experiences to be delusive, many continue to honor and accept it as a valid way of experiencing the risen Jesus Christ.

The influence of some religious experiences on how Christians construe the person and work of Jesus Christ is not peculiar to Nigerian Christianity. It goes back to early Christianity. Larry Hurtado has argued that "revelatory experiences were crucial contributing factors in producing the important religious innovations that mark early Christianity."[48] For him, it is the religious experience or encounter between Christians and the risen Christ that has fostered the "cultic devotion that is given to Christ" even at an astonishingly early period.[49] In what follows I will highlight three types of religious experiences that exist in Nigerian Christianity. The first is *conversion religious experience*. This type of

46. Nash, *Faith and Reason: Searching for a Rational Faith*, 143.

47. Haight, *Dynamics of Theology*, 94.

48. Hurtado, *How on Earth Did Jesus Become a God?* 192.

49. Ibid., 198–204.

religious experience involves an inward change of heart, deriving from an individual's decision to surrender to and trust in Jesus as the savior. Many Christians believe the Holy Spirit initiates this religious experience. This inward change (although expected to be outwardly demonstrated in lifestyle) caused by the internal instigation of the Holy Spirit, argues Plantinga, is an element in the "divine response to human sin and the human predicament, a predicament in which we human beings require healing, restoration, and salvation."[50] Ernest Mbefo, a member of Christian Pentecostal Mission, locates his knowledge of Jesus Christ within the framework of this type of religious experience. Responding to the question on the sources of his Christology, he says:

> This is by personal experience . . . because you can't tell who somebody is except you have come close to him [and have] been able to interact with him; from there you can now know who that person is. I came in contact with Jesus in 1991, 24 January, that's exactly when I gave my life to Christ.[51]

Although it is difficult to know the actual event that happened to Mbefo the moment he "gave [his] life to Jesus," what is clear, however, is that the religious experience, as he claims, has transformed his life and his view of Jesus the Christ. Again he says, "Jesus has taught me a lot of lessons by experience. When I [say] by experience, I mean [through] experience I have been able to find out that whatever he says stands."[52] It is noteworthy that this religious experience is in many cases posterior to hearing the gospel message about Jesus. The experience of John Okpara, also a member of Christian Pentecostal Mission, is an example.

> Well, I wouldn't say that people told me [about Jesus]. Nobody preached to me. I wasn't born again by preaching. Nobody preached to me. I, one day sat down, you know, looked at my life and said "no" I don't think I am getting it right. So, I went into a church; nobody talked to me. I didn't answer any altar call. I just sat down and listened to the Word of God. I compared it with how I was living my life and I knew that I was getting it wrong and I decided as a person to change. And to embrace the character of Christ and that was it. I said, yes, this is the real one and that is why I am born again today; that is why I see him as my

---

50. Plantinga, *Warranted Christian Belief*, 180.

51. Mbefo, interview by author, tape recording, Aba, 24 May, 2006.

52. Ibid.

Savior. Not just that I read him in the Scripture, not that pastor preached to me, no, it is a personal encounter. It is a personal experience.[53]

Perhaps what Okpara means when he said that "nobody preached to me" about Jesus is that he did not come to know who Jesus Christ is by having a one-on-one conversation with a anyone. Certainly, he heard about Jesus Christ when he went to the church and, to use his words, "listened to the Word of God."

It is also important to note that conversion religious experience varies from person to person depending on his or her family or denomination backgrounds. For example, many Evangelical and Pentecostal Christians readily talk about this kind of radical inward experience. Perhaps this is because in the Evangelical and Pentecostal traditions, there is emphasis on individual or personal encounter with Jesus. Conversely, many Roman Catholics rarely talked about this type of radical inward change.

The second type is revelatory *religious experience*. A revelatory religious experience can take different forms. Some of the interviewees claim that this type of religious experience can occur in a dream, vision, trance, by hearing a strange voice, and so on. This type of religious experience, however, is usually associated with a divine call to ministry and in some cases leads to theological or ecclesiological innovations. Some pastors of the African Independent or Initiated Churches (AICs) claim to have had this religious experience and use it as the reason for establishing their churches. Of course, this type of experience is not restricted to pastors of AICs. Evangelical, Presbyterian, Pentecostal pastors, and some priests of the Roman Catholic tradition also claim to have experienced a divine call to ministry. An interviewee who simply wanted to be addressed as Reverend Peter (a Presbyterian pastor) describes his call to ministry which took place in a Presbyterian church in Aba in the following way:

> When I came into the church, I now saw my dirtiness; my filthiness was all over me. And I said: "God I am not worthy to be here, look at your children singing praises unto your name. What have I got to do with them? Somebody like me, a wretched sinner" . . . A time came and the power of God came upon me [and] I started speaking things and even giving them messages,

53. Okpara, interview by author, tape recording, Aba, 24 May 2006.

which they themselves had not received at that time. God told me that there was a ring somebody invoked into that pulpit and that they should pray to destroy it. While I was releasing these messages, you know, looking at my appearance or maybe they have seen me once or twice, they did not believe me. They started beating me saying that "it was evil spirit that was troubling me"; they started beating and injured me.[54]

The testimony of Peter highlights the suspicion that is associated usually with revelatory religious experience. But for him, it was this experience that has led him to give up his business ambitions in order to become a pastor. In some cases, some of the individuals who claim to have this kind of religious experience may hesitate at first before responding to the divine call. Sometimes they respond to the call after encountering further religious experiences.

The third type of religious experience can be described as the *continuous communication or interaction* between a Christian and Jesus. Many of the interviewees claimed their experiences of Jesus do not stop with the *initial* conversion experience; such experiences, for them, continue throughout their lifetime. Jesus continues to manifest himself in their lives. Bridget Udoma, a Roman Catholic, summarizes her experience of Jesus with these words, "Jesus is good to me; today, tomorrow, and all the time, Jesus is good to me."[55] Favor Okafor, a member of Christ Holy Church, describes her experiences of Jesus in more detail. "I am living by his grace. I do everything by his grace. He is taking care of me even my family. I don't spend [money on] hospital [bills]. That name Jesus has been so wonderful to me and to my family . . . If not Jesus, I cannot do anything."[56]

Some theologians ignore the impact of religious experience on the ways many lay Christians understand and relate to Jesus Christ. But a contextual Christology that is designed for contemporary African Christianity cannot ignore the role of religious experience in the ways Christians with no formal theological training perceive the Christ-Event. Jesus's question—"who do you say I am?"—is phrased in a way that invites people to describe his person and work partly from their

---

54. Peter, interview by author, tape recording, Aba, 14 March 2006.

55. Udoma, interview by author, tape recording, Aba, 20 June 2006.

56. Okafor, interview by author, tape recording, Aba, 25 June 2006.

experience of him.[57] To put it differently, in most cases, the journey of discovering who Jesus really is begins when people encounter and experience him. For example, the pre-Damascus Saul construed Jesus Christ and his followers initially as blasphemers.[58] But his dramatic experience of Jesus on the road to Damascus changed his understanding—the one whom Paul considered a blasphemer suddenly became his Lord.[59]

Frequently, one hears many Nigerian Christians say, "when Jesus came into my life," or "when I encountered Jesus," or "when I invited Jesus to come into my life," "my life became different" or "my life changed." These expressions indicate some attempts of some Christians to explain the mystery of the union they believe occurred between them and Jesus Christ. It is unnecessary and unwarranted to see all religious ecstatic experiences as dysfunctional and false consciousness.[60] Although some religious experiences may be described as hallucination, there are numerous experiences that seem to be genuinely rooted in the works of the Holy Spirit and Jesus himself.

The major theological problem with using a religious experience as a source of Christian Christology is that a religious experience belongs primarily to the realm of subjectivism. For instance, it is very difficult to know if a given story of a religious experience derives from Jesus Christ or from other sources that are not connected with God's activities. Some Christians are aware of this difficulty and as a result are skeptical of some stories of religious experiences. The Christians who use their religious experiences as a source of their Christologies have the burden to demonstrate that their experiences derive from God's activity. And when such experiences misrepresent the meaning and significance of the Christ-Event as articulated in the Scripture, they need to be criticized. In other words, whereas a religious experience may help an individual to accept and trust in the person and work of Jesus Christ, as articulated by some writers of the Bible, the Christ-Event itself should inform and shape the experience of the individual.

---

57. Mark 8:29.

58. Acts 9:1–3.

59. Acts 9:4–31.

60. Hurtado, *How on Earth Did Jesus Become a God?*, 187. We must note that it is difficult to tell the difference between a religious experience that is as a result of dysfunctional consciousness or psychological disorder from a religious experience that is as a result of the activity of the Holy Spirit.

Contexts of Grassroots Christologies of Nigerian Christianity

I make a distinction between the sources and contexts of the grassroots Christologies of Nigerian Christianity. The Bible and religious experience, the two major sources of grassroots Christologies, differ from the *contexts* that foster the unprecedented phenomenon of interpreting and appropriating Jesus Christ. In what follows, I will answer the question, what features are responsible for the ways Nigerian Christians perceive and experience Jesus Christ?

QUESTS TO ACHIEVE WELLBEING

Studies on the indigenous religions and cultures of Africa have shown that African peoples see wellbeing as a holistic phenomenon that is intrinsically connected with a cordial relationship between the world of human beings and the world of the ancestors. James Cox made the following observation after studying the phenomenon of spirit possession and the cult of ancestors in Zimbabwe: "Although illness and misfortune are considered evil and thus act against the general wellbeing of the community, ancestors can inflict suffering on individuals and even on the community as a whole as a means of making contact with and gaining the attention of their families."[61] Like some other Africans, many Nigerians have carried on the idea of wellbeing, as construed in the indigenous religious and cultural thought, into Christianity. For these Christians, material prosperity (health, wealth, security, etc.,) is a sign that a Christian enjoys a cordial fellowship with Jesus Christ. These Christians also construe the salvation Jesus Christ embodies to be holistic. An adequate healing, for instance, includes the human and spiritual dimensions, although sometimes the human dimension is often emphasized more than the spiritual dimension. As Anacletus Odemene observes, many Christians continue to think about "heaven as a secondary concern" because in their religio-social framework, heaven "is a consequence of a happy and well-lived earthly life."[62] For example, Amadi, a Presbyterian, testifies that Jesus has always saved, provided, and protected him.

61. Cox, "Spirit Mediums in Zimbabwe," 191.

62. Odoemene, "The Church in Nigeria: Its Human Burden vis-à-vis Its Divine Mission," in Odoemene, *Witnessing Christ in Contemporary Nigeria*, 77–78.

> I came from a humble family, economically. But I know that it is through Jesus, through knowing him that I got to this height. I got to Jesus in 1975 as a young man, and I was not expected to reach this height. [But] I know that it is God's intervention that has lifted me up to this point.[63]

For him, it is Jesus that has brought him into the new economic height he now enjoys as a medical doctor, and this radical shift in status, in his thinking, is by God's intervention. His testimony reveals a holistic understanding of salvation. To him, his encounter with Jesus has transformed his economic status. What also merits noting in the testimony of Amadi is that most Christians do not make a conscious distinction between God and Jesus Christ. The majority of the interviewees quickly drifted from Jesus-talk to God-talk and vice versa. Therefore, we will misread and misrepresent them if we try to impose a strict ontological dichotomy between Jesus and God. Once we recognize the shift from God-talk to Jesus-talk among Nigerian lay Christians it will become easier to connect God and Jesus in Amadi's testimony.

The majority of the interviewees at first described Jesus as Savior, Son of God, God in human flesh, Redeemer of the world, but when pressed further, they immediately talked about how Jesus has blessed them with riches, good health, and protection. The response of Veronica Okeke, a member of Christ Holy Church, to the question "Who is Jesus to you?" underscores the readiness of many Christians to locate Jesus-talk in the context of total wellbeing.

> Jesus is the living Son of God. What he does in my life is numerous. There are at times when it seems as if I may not live, if I call upon Jesus he does not waste time, he answers me immediately. Before I came into this Christ Holy Church, I was seriously sick. I was told that if I would abide in Christ and to believe in him that the sickness in my body would disappear before three months. I stayed [in the church] and before three months I walked into the church unaided and shouted "hallelujah." And I said, "God is that how you are?" When I call upon God, he answers me. God is with me; Jesus is beside me now I am talking to you.[64]

63. Amadi, interview by author, tape recording, Aba, 10 April 2006. Amadi used the word humble figuratively to describe the state of *abject poverty* of his parents when he was born.

64. Okeke, interview by author, tape recording, Aba, 25 June 2006.

The words of Okeke highlight the solution-oriented mindset that underlies the majority of Nigerian Christians' Christologies. She seems to define who Jesus is to her on the basis of the healing she believes has come from him. According to her, Jesus is the living Son of God who does numerous things in her life. And the most significant among them is the miraculous healing she experienced because she trusted in Jesus. The corollary of this physical healing is that she radically changed her attitudes toward Jesus Christ. Prior to this miraculous healing, she considered Jesus to be "far away" from her. After encountering Jesus in such a remarkable way, she began to see Jesus as always present to her.

The idea of Jesus as a savior is not simply metaphysical, but also holistic to many Christians. To say that Jesus is a savior has become a creed in Nigerian Christianity. But this creed is not devoid of existential content. For many Christians, the work of Jesus as the bearer and dispenser of divine salvation includes both solving existential problems and restoring them to fellowship with God. Shedrach Okonkwo, a member of Christ Holy Church, again pointed out this holistic nature of the salvific work of Jesus. He said, "In my own thinking, Jesus is the Son of God, the one through whom we get all things. In any good condition human beings find themselves today it is through the grace of Jesus Christ. He is also the savior of my soul."[65] Also, Queen Mamoh, a Presbyterian, calls Jesus her "All in All" because he is always there for her.

> Sometimes when I am in a difficulty and my parents are not there, and my best friends are not there, he is always there to comfort and to encourage me. Sometimes I may be discouraged about things in life, but he is "all in all" to me, he is ever there for me to make way where there seems to be no way.[66]

Apart from the indigenous holistic idea of prosperity, there are some other contemporary factors that inform and shape the desire of many Christians to achieve wellbeing. One such factor is the *health and wealth gospel*. It is incorrect to assume that this kind of gospel exists only among charismatic churches. Different forms of *health and wealth gospel* exist in several church denominations in Nigeria. Of course, one does not even need to go to a church to hear this type of gospel. It is now readily available in most popular Christian choruses, songs, car stickers

---

65. Okonkwo, interview by author, tape recording, Aba, 25 June 2006.

66. Mamoh, interview by author, tape recording, Aba, 18 May 2006.

and movies. The variants of this type of gospel make it almost impossible to define exactly what this gospel looks like. However, what is central to this gospel is the idea that Jesus Christ is the owner of all good things and that he is always willing to bestow them upon his followers. The subtle aspect of this gospel is the idea that it is the right of Christians to request and get things from Jesus. The consequence, which is often unnoticed, is a change from the language of request to the language of demand or warfare when speaking to Jesus about problems. One hears expressions, such as, possess your possession, or if Jesus says no to your request, you need to remind him that he has not finished with you when some Christians talk to Jesus about their needs. A Presbyterian who simply wanted to be called Mrs. Comfort said:

> I see Jesus as my friend, my close friend, my all and all. And if I am praying, I talk to him personally as if I am seeing him. I will make it a mandate. I will say to him, you are doing this [for me] and you are doing it; you don't have any other choice than to do that particular thing that I want. And actually it will happen that way.[67]

Without in any way suggesting that all Christians in Nigeria command Jesus to do things for them, it is evident that Comfort speaks for many. When critically assessed, *health and wealth gospel* forms a particular christological mindset that recognizes Jesus's ability to bestow blessings on his followers but ignores how he can radically reshape and redefine the meaning of wellbeing. Consequently, Nigerian Christianity is producing at an astonishing speed some Christians who simply construct a Jesus who fits into their christological box—a Jesus who can provide what they need and when they need it, but will not critique and inform their understandings of prosperity and wealth. Some of the interviewees hinted that some people become Christians because they see Jesus primarily as the one who can make them wealthy. But when they do not get the riches, they turn immediately to other sources, such as, witch doctors, occult priests, and goddesses.

The notions of affluence and recognition are also factors that propel Christians' desire for wellbeing. Anthony Anijielo provides a helpful context for understanding the quests for affluence and recognition in Nigeria. He writes:

67. Comfort, interview by author, tape recording, Aba, 18 June 2006.

> The average contemporary Nigerian is wont to assess people by the amount of wealth they are able to display. For this reason, many of our people are not guided by pragmatic considerations but by the quest for recognition. This is the reason why many a Nigerian would build a three-floor flat in his home village even when his contacts with the village are limited to Christmas seasons and occasional ceremonies. He builds and sees his house as his own ego. He believes that people would assess him from their impressions taken from the grandeur of that structure.[68]

Whether or not the average Nigerian thinks in this way depends on who takes the demographic statistics. What is, however, evident is that the desire to command respect and to become powerful, for many Nigerians, is intrinsically imbedded in wealth and affluence. Many families feel that they are under the threat of abuse and humiliation because they are poor. Therefore, for example, as Anijielo points out, many people (of course, including Christians) build houses they neither use nor need so as to protect themselves against potential traitors and to become respected in the society.

It is not unusual to hear Christians in Nigeria pray to Jesus to make them the head and not the tail or to immensely bless them so that they can become a light to their villages or churches. Driven by this mindset, these Christians continually go to tarry nights, fast, and attend miraculous meetings organized by prominent preachers of *health and wealth gospel* with the hope to unlock the gates of heaven where their riches are stored. It is noteworthy that many lay Christians are sometimes the victims of some pastors who are driven by the spirit of affluence and who prey on their members' money and property. These pastors exploit vulnerable members, sometimes rendering them perpetually poor while they themselves continue to enjoy a life of affluence. The sermons of these pastors are usually about health and wealth, and they do so with the intent to stimulate their members to continuously donate money to the church or even to donate their cars, houses, and land. Jude Nwachukwu, a Roman Catholic priest, gives a graphic description of this state of affairs:

> If you go to many churches, you will hear the pastors prophesy: I have seen a Hummer Jeep parked in your house, a jeep parked

---

68 Anijielo, "Pastoral Perspective of the Socio-Cultural Challenges of Nigerian Priests and the Church in the Twenty-First Century," 5–6.

in your house, claim it in Jesus name, and you will say amen; yet
[in] the next ten years you are still riding *Okada*[motorcycles];
you have no bicycle and no good shoe. This is the kind of false
prophecies people are giving us today.[69]

Nwachukwu, of course, exaggerates some of the outcome of the anticipation of some Christians who believe, or claim, to use a common par-
lance in Nigerian Christianity, the prosperity-oriented prophecies given
to them by their pastors and ministers. Some of these Christians testify
that Jesus indeed blesses them because of their faith in such prophecies.
But Nwachukwu correctly articulates the kind of gospel of Jesus that is
predominant in many charismatic and some non-charismatic churches.
Sometimes the pastor of these churches (consciously or unconsciously)
presents Jesus as a mean Son of God who is ready to make one become
very poor if the one refuses to give money to the work of God. And usually, the work of God to which these Christians are induced to give turns
out to be the personal property of the pastors. Most times, and sadly so,
it is for the pastors to buy expensive cars and to build mansions.

Another ideology that drives the quests for wellbeing is a theology
of poverty. While most Christians continue to associate poverty with
inadequate leadership and unfavorable local and international policies,
the understanding of poverty as a divine curse is gaining ground in
their intellectual and religious mindsets. For some, becoming a true fol-
lower of Jesus entails crossing over the line of poverty and anything that
withholds one from achieving a total wellbeing. Inherent in this thinking is the belief that material prosperity is a consequence of spiritual
prosperity, which occurs when a person encounters Jesus the Christ.
Frequently, one hears among some Christians the expressions such as
Jesus was made poor so that I might be rich, and I have made a covenant
with Jesus therefore I have kissed poverty goodbye. In the religious, social, and intellectual mindsets of these Christians, it is not *Christian* to
be poor. Clement Ogbonnaya, the coordinator of International Gospel
Campaign and the pastor of Word of Faith International Church, in his
book *I am too Big to be Poor*, speaks for many Christians who consider
it inconceivable for a Christian to be poor. He writes:

You are involved in the kingdom of God's abundance. So, YOU
ARE TOO BIG TO BE POOR! Your father (God) is the owner

---

69. Nwachukwu, interview by author, tape recording, Aba, 22 June 2006.

of the whole world and everything in it. And in the world, all you need are there. This means that God has or is in possession of all you need. Go to Him and get what belongs to you. God is in possession of your car! God is in possession of your house! God is in possession of your education, wisdom, knowledge, and understanding! God is in possession of your children—you don't need to be barren! God is in possession of your food . . . God is in possession of everybody and everything! He has all you need, and because you have Him, you have more than you need, So YOU ARE TOO BIG TO BE POOR![70]

Whether or not the assumption that Christians are too big to be poor is practically possible remains to be seen. There is no doubt that many Nigerian Christians cannot be classified as poor. But many people who are economically poor and vulnerable continue to constitute the greater part of the population of many churches. Although poverty is not only a material issue but also a spiritual issue, the argument of Ogbonnaya points more in the direction of material poverty. Some of the themes that emerged from the fieldwork I conducted , included religious and intellectual explanations for the inability of some Christians to get their blessings from Jesus.. I will explore them under the second context of grassroots Christologies of Nigerian Christianity, namely, *Christodicy*.

CHRISTODICY

Christodicy in this book refers to the defensive reasons some Christians offer to explain why Jesus Christ sometimes fails or refuses to solve the problems of Christians. In a sense, the Christodicy of Nigerian Christians is similar to the broader issues that characterize *theodicy*, the defense of God in the face of evil. For many philosophers, as Ronald Nash argues, "the most serious challenge to theism was, is and will continue to be the problem of evil."[71] Some philosophers have argued that the belief in a theistic God and the existence of evil in the world violates the law of non-contradiction. The argument is that there seems to be an apparent contradiction in believing the existence of "evil, on the one hand," and at the same time and in the same relation in believ-

---

70. Ogbonnaya, *I am Too Big to be Poor*, 35. Emphasis is in the original.

71. Nash, *Faith and Reason*, 177.

ing the "omnipotence and perfection of God."[72] The existence of both moral and natural evil in the world of a theistic God who is believed to be wholly good, all-knowing, and all-powerful is not only problematic to philosophers but also to theologians. I will not engage in a detailed discussion of the problem of evil for Christian theism here because it is not the main concern of this book.[73]

The problem of evil also poses great difficulties to Christology. The obvious difficulty is the death of Jesus Christ on the cross. The question can be phrased as follows: if God is omni-benevolent, omniscient, and omnipotent, why did he allow or even authorize the death of Jesus Christ? Interestingly, this christological problem does not bother many Nigerian lay Christians.[74] They are rather preoccupied with the problem of how Jesus, who is wholly good, loving, and all-powerful, sometimes refuses or fails to solve the problems of his followers. A helpful way to understand the grassroots christodicies is to articulate their *christological assumptions*. The majority of the interviewees believe (a) that there is no problem Jesus cannot solve; (b) that Jesus is willing to solve their problems; (c) that Jesus wants them to present their problems to him, and (d) that not all of their problems which they presented to Jesus are solved. The possibility of Jesus not solving all the problems of Christians raises serious christological problems vis-à-vis the person and work of Jesus. It is either that the Jesus who is willing and capable to solve their problems does not exist or that he truly exists, as many of them believe, but other complex circumstances are responsible for his refusal or inability to solve some problems. In what follows, I will examine the key striking reason most of the interviewees used to explain why Jesus sometimes refuses or fails to solve some problems of his followers.[75]

A key argument that emerged from the fieldwork was that sometimes Jesus would delay in solving a particular problem of a Christian for the reason of protecting both the Christian and the blessings he

72. McCloskey, "God and Evil," 97.

73. For a discussion on the arguments for and against the problem of evil, see Plantinga, *Warranted Christian Belief*, 458–99; Plantinga, *God and Other Mind*.

74. At least the problem did not emerge in my conversation with Christians during my fieldwork.

75. Some of the interviewees talked about what can be described as a character-making Christodicy. The argument is that in order for Jesus to produce virtuous followers, the people who follow him must be prepared to face some problems that will help to mould them into the kind of people Jesus wants them to be.

would provide. Shedrach Okonkwo, a member of Christ Holy Church, articulates this argument:

> When Christians do not get what they are asking from Jesus, it does not mean that he is not able to solve their problems. Maybe God is trying to put some things in place; maybe there are enemies of progress, and he wants to take the enemies out before he can solve their problems.[76]

In Okonkwo's contention, the ability of Jesus to know the problems of Christians and the possible outcome if he solves the problems comes out vividly. I will refer to this view as *providence christodicy*. For those who hold the providence christodicy, when Jesus blesses a Christian with children or riches, for example, he also wants to protect the children and the riches. The vital assumption of providence christodicy is the belief that the gift of Jesus lasts and is profitable, unlike the gifts of Satan and his agents.[77] For these Christians, it is safer to keep on trusting in Jesus Christ even when he seems not to solve problems than to seek for solutions from *babalawo* (native doctors) or from false prophets who have founded several prayer houses. Queen Mamoh, a Presbyterian, observes:

> I have heard so many stories about some people serving the Lord, asking the Lord to give them a particular thing and after a long time ... most especially in the area of finance, somebody seeking for money, and you find out that the friends of such person are getting wealthier every day and the person is poorer. The person may want to know why his friends are getting richer and by so doing, may go to some native doctor houses to perform some rituals and sacrifices. But at the end of it, it is only a disaster because I don't think that they enjoy the money, like most of them we see in the home videos [or movies]. They don't end well and they regret it. This is because sometimes their occult societies will ask them to sacrifice their best child or their parents, you know, and even if they refuse, there is no going back because they have already stepped into it. So, it is dangerous for any Christian that puts his or her hand on the plough to look back.[78]

---

76. Okonkwo, interview by author, tape recording, Aba, 25 June 2006.

77. See chapter six for the discussions on some of the understandings of Satan and demons in Nigerian Christianity.

78. Mamoh, interview by author, tape recording, Aba, 18 May 2006.

In this lengthy quote, Mamoh attempts to explain some of the bewildering stories she has heard about some Christians who desert the church to look for solutions in some occult organizations. Anyone familiar with some of the movies and dramas produced in Nigeria will recognize immediately the phenomenon that Mamoh attempts to explain. In most of these movies, one discovers an incessant quest of some people to become wealthy, and their determination to do anything in order to become prosperous. The moral of the movies is evident in the short-lived and unhappy ending of the characters who murder their mother, children, friends, or used a part of their bodies for rituals in order to become wealthy.[79]

Interestingly, most Christians do not doubt the existence of such diabolic societies. Mamoh speaks for many Nigerians who believe that some people, including those who consider themselves Christians, are members of such occult organizations. My concern here is not to prove or disprove the existence of such diabolic organizations, but rather to show that some christodicies constitute one of the principal contexts which are shaping grassroots Christologies in contemporary Nigerian Christianity. Also, in the thinking of those who subscribe to providence christodicy, when Jesus provides or solves the problems of his followers, he protects whatever solution he has provided. In addition, some proponents of providence argument maintain that the solution Jesus gives contrasts with the solutions Christians can get from native doctors in that the former endures and brings joy whereas the latter lasts only for a short time and brings greater sorrow.

The ideologies and anticipations that shape some providence christodicy of Christians are complex. For example, it is difficult to know if the proponents of a providence christodicy are inspired by their belief in God's will and freedom to protect gifts that God has provided for them. Whereas the belief in God's wisdom, love, and freedom to protect people cannot be ruled out completely as part of the reasons some Christians believe Jesus can delay in providing things for his followers, it is also clear that the mindset of self-accumulation is another factor that informs some providence christodicies. What is noteworthy here is that the Christ-Event—the birth of Jesus Christ in a manger, the poverty of Jesus and his death on the cross, resurrection and ascension— demonstrates God's act of self-giving. Therefore, any christodicy built

79. See for example, "Blood Money."

merely on the desire for self-accumulation is in contradiction with the meaning and significance of the Christ-Event. I will explore this argument in detail in chapter five.

HOPE FOR A SECURED FUTURE

The hope that Jesus has gone to prepare a place for his followers and that he will return to take them is another major context that shapes some of the grassroots Christologies of Christians. According to Favor Okafor, a member of Christ Holy Church, her prayer always is for "Jesus to redeem" her and to give her "the grace to make heaven."[80] This was her response to the question, "If Jesus was to say to you, ask me for one thing and I would do it, what would you request from him?" Bridget Udoma, a Roman Catholic, gave the following response to the same question:

> What I will request from Jesus is everlasting life. I want him to help me to be where he is, that is what is in my mind right now. Forgetting the wealth of this world, I ask Jesus, like the thief who was crucified on the Good Friday, to remember me in his paradise. I want to be with Jesus after I finish my [Christian] race in this world.[81]

Two things are noteworthy regarding the hope for a secured future in some grassroots Christologies of Nigerian Christianity.[82] First, the hope of Christ's return to take or rapture his followers is not peculiar to some Nigerian Christians. The history of this hope goes back to the missionary era and undoubtedly Nigerian Christians draw on some of the Bible passages, which speak of Christ's return to take his followers to the mansions he has gone to prepare.[83] Second, the requirements to follow Jesus when he returns to the earth to take his followers differ from one denomination to another. Even within a given denomination the requirements will also vary from one individual to another. Thus, one will misrepresent many Nigerian Christians if the one assumes that every individual Christian in a given denomination holds the same eschatology. For some Christians, the only requirement is to experience

80. Okafor, interview by author, tape recording, Aba, 25 June 2006.

81. Udoma, interview by author, tape recording, Aba, 20 June 2006.

82. The hope *for a secured future* is a form of futuristic eschatology.

83. John 14:1–4.

Jesus Christ and trust him as Lord and savior. For others, it is not just enough to place faith in Jesus Christ. The Christian must also continue to live righteously if he or she wants to experience rapture. Yet some others claim that only those who are righteous at the moment Jesus returns will be qualified for rapture. Despite these variant views on the requirements for future reunion with Jesus Christ, what is clear in the religious mindset of many Christians is the anticipation that Jesus will come back to take his followers away from this painful world.

It is surprising that many Nigerian theologians ignore the importance of a futuristic hope for a better place beyond the earth in the Christology of lay Christians. Even when some theologians attempt to engage with this future hope, they criticize it as a mere escapist mindset that makes some Christians evade dealing with the perennial problems of poverty, poor health, and insecurity in Nigeria. Bernard Ukwuegbu, a Roman Catholic priest, is a template of such theologians. In his *Confrontational Evangelization*, he writes:

> No matter what is happening in recent times [in Nigeria], it remains a fact that there is an escapist element in the mentality which promises the poor a reward hereafter if they would patiently endure injustice in this life. . . . With this mentality, a perfect dichotomy was drawn between the spiritual and the mundane. People who purport to be holy manifest a complete indifference to the worldly, often in good will.[84]

Ukwuegbu rejects this mentality and contends that it has introduced "a spirituality" that regards "attendance of mass" as a "Christian obligation," but excludes "lifting a finger to help a brother in need." There is no doubt, as he points out, that the mentality of a better reward for the poor in the afterlife shapes the attitudes of some Christians toward earthly things. But to say that this hope for a better life in heaven is a reason some Christians refuse to help the poor is misleading. It is one thing to say that some Christians who are rich do not help the poor. It is another matter to say that the hope for the future reward of poor people after their lives here on the earth is the reason some Christians in Nigeria refuse to help the poor. Of course, there could be exceptions, but such mindset is not widespread in Nigerian Christianity. Ukwuegbu fails to recognize the principal factor that drives the futuristic eschatology of Christians; namely, the hope that Jesus is coming back to reward

84. Ukwuegbu, *Confrontational Evangelization*, 121.

his followers, especially those who obey his commands, and to punish those who reject him in hell.[85] Since helping the poor is part of the commands of Jesus, it follows that many Christians who are anticipating the return of Jesus Christ will want to help the poor.

Another factor that informs and sustains the hope for a secured future among lay Christians is the belief that the sufferings of this world are incomparable to the blissful hope of reuniting with Christ and with the loved ones who have preceded them. An excellent example is Chinyere Udoma's Christology. In her bestseller song, *Agu na eche mba*, literally, "the lion that guards a nation or city," she describes Jesus as a lion who is able to keep whatever is placed in his mouth. It might as well be possible that the image of Jesus as the "lion of the tribe of Judah" influenced her choice of this christological imagery. But the uniqueness of the song stems from the event that surrounds its composition. In the song, Udoma, a well-known Christian musician, describes the death of her son, Chukwuemeka. The incident occurred on her way home from a singing ministration. Armed bandits attempted to stop the bus on which she was traveling. When the bandits realized that the bus driver was unwilling to stop the bus, they ripped it apart with bullets, killing many of the passengers including Chukwuemeka.

In the song, Udoma recollects her horrific experience. She describes how her son died in her arms in the pool of his blood. The following excerpt from the song illustrates her futuristic eschatology.

> *Agụ na eche mba ewerela m onwe m tinye gị na aka*
>
> The lion that guards the city, I have entrusted myself into your hand
>
> *Igwe na eche ndụ mụa, ewerela m onwe mụ nye gị*
>
> The king that protects my life, I have given myself to you;
>
> *Ihe etinyere gị bụ agụ na ọ nụ Ekwensu ọ ga emetụ ya aka?*
>
> "The thing that is placed into your mouth, the lion, could Satan touch it?"[86]

---

85. As Ukweni O. Ukweni, a member of the Presbyterian Church, has argued: "My salvation, which Jesus has given [to] me, has given me a place in heaven. The Bible says afterlife there is judgment. . . . I am very sure that after here I will make heaven. And through this salvation my eyes are opened to know that heaven is real and hell is real." Ukweni, interview by author, tape recording, Aba, 18 June 2006.

86. A smoother translation is: "would Satan touch (or snatch away) something that

Ihe etinyere gị bụ agụ na ọnụ onye iro ọ ga emetụ ya aka?

"The thing that is placed into your mouth, the lion, could an enemy touch it?"

With the foregoing rhetorical questions, Udoma lays the foundation on which she expresses her trust in Jesus Christ to protect her life and the life of her son. But has Jesus failed her? Is Jesus incapable of safeguarding the life of her son? The song suggests strongly that, for Udoma, Jesus has not failed her, even though he did not save the life of her son from the attacks of the armed robbers. Her confidence in the ability of Jesus to safeguard her dead son permeates the song. In her thinking, Chukwuemeka is safe in the mouth of Jesus, the lion. This expresses her strong hope that she will see her son again someday. The majority of Christians, such as Udoma, continue to anticipate the return of Jesus and which for them will usher in a world that is free of sufferings and senseless evil like the brutal killing of Chukwuemeka. This hope for a secured future is largely shaping the interpretations and perceptions of the person and work of God in Jesus in Nigerian Christianity.

Another thing that is noteworthy, as Udoma's song suggests, is that some Christians anticipate and pray for the return of Jesus Christ because they want to escape their problems. It is hard to tell where the unselfish desire to reunite with Christ fits into their quest for the Second Coming of Jesus Christ. Again, a solution-oriented mindset plays a significant role in shaping some of the Christologies and eschatologies. I will now examine the concept of solution in some of the grassroots Christologies.

Jesus as a Solution among Other Solutions

An unprecedented conversation on Jesus Christ is taking place among many lay Christians. Signs of this talk appear everywhere—on the signposts of churches, hospitals, companies, on stickers, on television screens, in business conversations, and in the lifestyles of many Christians. The key assumption that underpins this christological thinking is the belief that Jesus Christ is a savior or a solution to the spiritual and material problems of humanity. In the thinking of the majority of lay Christians,

---

is placed into your mouth, the lion?"

Jesus is one among many solutions, but he is believed to be the most reliable solution. This is exemplified in some of the names Christians give to him, such as, ọ tụmọkpọ ndị nsọ, literally, "a powerful amulet for the holy people or Christians."

The idea of Jesus as a savior or a solution to spiritual and material problems is central to the grassroots Christologies of many Christians. The majority of the interviewees answered the question 'who is Jesus to you?' by saying "he is my Savior" or "he is the savior of the world." But if salvation is the work of God, as many of these Christians profess, it follows that when they see Jesus as a savior they ascribe to him a divine power and function. This raises a serious problem for the contextual theologian who wants to know the ontological connection between Jesus and God. Many Christians believe that God can execute his salvific functions through angels, human beings, and other ways he deems fit. But these Christians seem also to make a distinction between a case in which God delivers someone without using a human agent and a case in which God delivers someone through a human agent. For example, if God saves *Mr. A* from the attacks of some bandits through a police officer, when *Mr. A* testifies of his deliverance he will say that God has saved him by using the police officer as an instrument. Hardly will *Mr. A* say that the police officer is his savior in the sense he understands Jesus Christ as a savior. When most Christians describe Jesus Christ as a savior they mean something much deeper than a mere salvific instrument of God. They speak of Jesus in a way that suggests he enjoys an unprecedented relationship with God. For these Christians, Jesus is "the Son of God" and even God himself. And as we have already seen, the majority of lay Christians do not engage seriously in the kind of christological debates of the fourth and fifth centuries that revolved around the constitution of the person of Jesus. They are concerned primarily with the content of the salvific acts of Jesus and not on his exact ontological composition.

But what exactly do Nigerian Christians mean when they address Jesus as the savior? The majority construe Jesus as a divine figure who saves them from their sins and from ancestral traditions, which may hinder them from getting divine blessing or favor. For example, Ukweni O. Ukweni, a member of the Presbyterian Church, describes Jesus as the God incarnate who saved him from his "traditional ways of doing things."[87] When I asked him to explain what those traditional ways were, he said:

> We all have our old ways or traditional ways of doing things. Like where I come from, there is what they call *Abasi-isom*, the god of fire, and my people believe that some people come from this source. At some point Christ came to save a lot of people and I am one of the persons that Christ saved. "Saved from what?"—my ancestral belief.[88]

Iliya Habu, a member of ECWA, introduces another interesting dimension which will help us to interpret Nigerian Christians' perception of Jesus as a savior.

> I have many things to tell you about how Jesus saved me. One, he saved me because he died for me . . . When I read the Bible, I knew that somebody died for me and [that] he died for my sin. His death is a kind of punishment, which I was supposed to receive personally as a human being. But he said I should not die, and that he will now bear the punishment on my behalf. So Jesus Christ received the punishment that I was going to receive before the Almighty God who created me. Jesus Christ died for me because of Adam's sin.[89]

Blessing Madu, a member of Christ Holy Church, makes as similar point when she says:

> To me, Jesus Christ is my Lord and personal Savior. He came to the earth and died for us. He suffered on the cross of Calvary for our sins to be washed away, for all have sinned and come short of the glory of God. But because of the blood he shed we are now free from sin.[90]

Habu and Madu highlight a theological concept that theologians refer to as the Original Sin.[91] By saying that Jesus Christ died for him "because

---

87. Ukweni, interview by author, tape recording, Aba, 18 June 2006.

88. Ibid.

89. Habu, interview by author, tape recording, Aba, 29 February 2006.

90. Blessing Madu, interview by author, tape recording, Aba, 25 June 2006.

91. Theologians differ on how exactly humanity is connected to the sin of Adam. Terrance Tiessen provides a helpful definition of concept of Original Sin. He writes, "The sinfulness is original not just because it was the first human sin; that distinction would go to Eve's disobedience. But Adam's transgression is critical because it is the origin of all the human sin that followed the primal fall." Tiessen, *Who Can Be Saved,*

of Adam's sin," Habu's claim begs the questions, how is he under the punishment of God because Adam sinned? And how does the salvation Jesus gives him relate to the sin of Adam? It is vital to note that many Christians, like Habu and Madu, believe that God holds them responsible for the sin of Adam. In the thinking of these Christians, the death of Jesus Christ redeems them from the guilt and punishment the sin of Adam brings. Interestingly, these Christians do not bother to exegete this belief which functions almost like a creed. For them, as Habu and Madu have indicated, this theological assumption is true because the Bible teaches it. I have already examined the existing views of the Bible in Nigerian Christianity in the early part of this chapter and I need not rehearse these views. What needs noting is that many Christians hold a high view of the Bible. Consequently, they accept almost everything that is contained in it to be true and binding to them.

The ways the majority of lay Christians construe the person and work of Jesus will change depending on if (and how fast) he solves their problems. These Christians primarily see Jesus Christ as a solution to the spiritual, economic, ethical, and political problems they experience. What is striking and deserves exploring is that, in the thinking of some of these Christians, Jesus is the chief solution among many solutions that are available in their societies. Interestingly, some of these Christians believe that the other solutions sometimes work faster than Jesus Christ. For example, Moses Attah, who is from Nassarawa State in northern Nigeria, claims that some Christians in Northern Nigeria will consult native doctors or other powers in some situations in which Jesus may appear to be too slow to answer their prayers.

> In the North [that is, the northern part of Nigeria], you may have problems with somebody and if you call on Jesus the problems may not be solved immediately. Some people will do as we normally say: "Let me put off the shirt of Jesus Christ and put on the cultural shirt." Then they will go to the shrine or any other place to look for help forgetting that Jesus will help them. And sometimes during war either tribal war or religious war between Christians and Muslims some Christians go to the herbalists to collect some charm in order to protect themselves forgetting that Jesus is there to protect them.[92]

---

73. See chapter seven for an extensive discussion on sin and humanity.

92. Attah, interview by author, tape recording, Aba, 29 February 2006.

The act of temporarily deserting Jesus Christ in order to use other sources of solution is not a phenomenon that occurs only among Christians in Northern Nigeria. This phenomenon is happening among many Christians in all parts of the country. The majority of the interviewees, regardless of their church denominations and ethnic backgrounds, said that many Christians are consulting native doctors or other indigenous agencies when Jesus delays giving them children, healing them, protecting them from spiritual attacks, and blessing them with material things. Some of them said that many Christians no longer have to go outside of the church to get their solutions because many native doctors are now founders of churches and prayer houses.

It is noteworthy that some Christians worry about this phenomenon. One of the ways they have approached this phenomenon is to create a dichotomy between real Christians/professing Christians, true believers/non-true believers, backsliding/ true Christians, and born again Christians/church-goers. Ejim Okonkwo, a member of the Presbyterian Church, acknowledges that some Christians in Nigeria go outside of Jesus Christ to get solution to their problems, but she argues that such Christians are "people who do not know whom they are following."[93] She insists that what such Christians need to do is to "continue to have faith in Jesus Christ" even if he appears not to answer their prayers immediately.[94] Faith Ukaegbu, a member of CPM, is even more radical:

> Yes, it is happening in Nigeria. Many people go to native doctors to get solutions. Well, the problem is when we [call them] Christians. When we call them Christians we are getting it wrong, because if you are a Christian you cannot go to native doctors no matter the situation. So I don't believe that if you are a Christian you can go to that extent, except you are a backsliding Christian.[95]

The key problem with the foregoing dichotomies is that it is difficult to know who is and who is not a Christian. This is because sometimes people define a Christian on the basis of church denominational prejudice. For example, many Pentecostals see some Evangelical Christians as non-true Christians because they either do not emphasize

93. Okonkwo, interview by author, tape recording, Aba, 18 June 2006.
94. Ibid.
95. Ukaegbu, interview by author, tape recording, Aba, 6 May 2006.

speaking in tongues or do not practice it. Some Evangelicals equally accuse some Pentecostals and members of the AICs of belonging to and engaging in diabolical practices. Also, although some Christians argue that it is possible to know a true Christian through his or her lifestyle, the difficulty with this assumption is that some Christians, as most of the interviewees claimed, consult native doctors, ancestors and other diabolic sources. And some of these Christians conceal their lifestyles, making it almost impossible for people to suspect them until their secrets are uncovered. Thus, the philosophy of faith articulated in lifestyle is a misleading yardstick to define who is a Christian in contemporary Nigerian societies.

In conclusion, I have explored in this chapter some of the grassroots Christologies. Like some of the constructive Christologies of African theologians I examined in chapter two, the majority of the grassroots Christologies are driven partly by the search to discover and experience the meaning and significance of Jesus Christ. Among the things that distinguish the grassroots Christologies from the constructive Christologies, what appears to be the most significant is the radical difference in their objectives and concerns. Many theologians are preoccupied with the struggle to establish themselves as the legitimate individuals who have the right to determine the indigenous cultural practices which Christians can incorporate into Christianity. Consequently, most of these theologians, as we have seen in chapter two, have devoted a large part of their works to a severe criticism of many Western missionaries' derogatory views of the indigenous religions and cultures of Africa. On the contrary, the majority of lay Christians appear to have taken for granted the classical Westerners' derogatory estimation of African peoples. Their primary concern is to experience Jesus's liberating and providential power in their daily lives. They are poor and hungry; therefore, they want to experience Jesus who can feed them. They are in constant fear of death, spiritual attacks, assassination, and robbery. Therefore, they are in need of Jesus who has the power to protect them.

I have argued that at the grassroots level many Christians, irrespective of their church denominations, perceive and relate to Jesus Christ merely as a problem-solver. They belong properly into the category of functional Christology. It is the manifestation of Jesus Christ in the lives and situations of many lay Christians, and not their understandings of his ontology, that largely informs and shapes their interpretations of the Christ-Event. To state it differently, many lay Christians take the ontology of Jesus Christ for granted, but seek to experience the manifestations of his love, provision, protection, healing, and his power to save in their daily lives. I will argue, however, that it is inadequate christologically to perceive and relate to Jesus Christ merely as a problem-solver.

It is crucially important to acknowledge that the cultural, religious, and existential issues that characterize the grassroots and constructive Christologies of African Christianity are both legitimate and misguided. They are legitimate because they create some helpful contexts for undertaking constructive interpretations and appropriations of the Christ-Event. They are misguided because many theologians and lay Christians have failed to articulate these social, religious, and cultural conditions in ways that allow Jesus Christ to function both as a question and a solution to the needs of humanity. To put it differently, African Christians need to rediscover that Jesus does not come to us merely as the one who provides all our needs; he also shapes our understandings of our needs. The ideology of self-accumulation permeates the thinking of the majority of these Christians. The challenge that faces them is the task of interacting with the dialectics of God's provision and God's act of self-giving as represented in and through Jesus Christ. In the remainder of this book, I will explore the implications of these dialectics for constructing a Revealer Christology model for the Africa contexts.

PART TWO

A Revealer Christology:

Towards a New Christological Model

4

A Revealer Christology for the African Contexts

IN CHAPTERS TWO AND THREE, I EXAMINED AND CRITIQUED SOME OF the major constructive and also the grassroots (oral) Christologies of African Christianity. I contended that some theologians have been highly critical of what they consider to be the predominant representations of Jesus Christ in the teachings of some classical Western missionaries. For some of these theologians, most of the Western-informed images of Jesus Christ cannot fit properly into the cultural categories of Africa and as a result pose a serious christological dilemma for African Christianity. In order to deal with this christological dilemma, these theologians have developed some christological models that aimed to re-express and appropriate the Christ-Event in a relevant and meaningful way in and for the African contexts. At the grassroots level, as I argued in chapter three, many Christians who do not have theological training seek to experience and obtain Jesus' power to combat their existential problems.

I argued that although most of the constructive and grassroots Christologies that exist in African Christianity reflect the attempts by some theologians and many lay Christians to contextualize the Christ-Event in their contexts, many of these Christologies are inadequate because they construe Jesus Christ primarily as a solution. The major christological problem with a Christology that is merely solution-oriented is that it fails (as evidenced in some of the christological models I have examined) to account properly for the dialectic underlying the person and work of Jesus. The crucial missing element in most of the christological models I examined in chapters two and three is the failure of many theologians and lay Christians to construe Jesus simultaneously as a question and a solution. When we construe Jesus as a question and at the same time as a solution, he will no longer function merely as

143

solution to human needs or as a tool that human beings can employ and manipulate to obtain solutions to their existential problems. On the contrary, Jesus Christ will critique, remold and inform the ways human beings construe their problems and the type of solution they anticipate. Therefore, the question that informs the christological model I will be referring to as a Revealer Christology model in this book is this: If we present Jesus Christ simultaneously as the answer/solution to the existential questions/problems of African Christians and also as the questioner who critiques and reshapes their perceptions of their existential problems and the solutions to such problems, what will he and African Christians look like?[1] As I have already indicated in the introduction, this question is set against the background of the *Taylorian christological presupposition* that asks "if Jesus Christ were to appear as the answer to the questions that Africans are asking what would he look like?"[2] I argued that this latter question was appropriate when Taylor proposed it, but could no longer inspire an adequate Christology to meet the needs of many present-day Christians.

This chapter will function as the backdrop to and foundation of chapters five, six and seven. It sets out the christological context on which the Revealer Christology is built. Several consequences follow from this. First, I will reserve an extensive discussion on the christological contents of the Revealer Christology model until we get to chapters five, six and seven. Second, I will concentrate primarily on the works of African theologians. And third, although the Revealer Christology model I will construct in this book draws insights from the already existing grassroots and constructive Christologies in African Christianity, it will differ from them, providing a distinct christological outlook for interpreting and appropriating the Christ-Event in the contexts of Africa.

The key issues I explore in this chapter are the idea of revelation in African theological and christological discourses, the meaning of revealer as it is used in this book, and the theological and contextual parameters of the Revealer Christology as it is developed in this book.

---

1. I will explain the meaning of the expression Revealer Christology later in this chapter.

2. See the introduction.

Revealer Christology Model and Revelation Discourse

It is essential to explain the concept of revealer and its usage in the Revealer Christology model that is developed in this book. This is necessary because the word revealer can conjure up several theological ideas when it is connected to Christology. One such idea is revelation, a concept that has become notoriously difficult to describe in the wake of the several meanings, criticisms, fierce debates, and suspicions associated with it.[3] Since revelation as a theological concept is an integral part of the theological and christological discourse in Africa, it is proper to briefly examine it and to define its relationship to the Revealer Christology model I develop in this book.

The Idea of Revelation in African Theological Discourse

Some theological and christological discussions that exist in African Christianity have proceeded from the premise that God has revealed God's self and his purpose for God's creation (particularly for human beings) in creation and in some specific events such as the Christ-Event. These divine acts of self-revealing or self-disclosure are what many theologians have labeled *revelation*. Unsurprisingly, the meanings and scopes theologians assign to revelation vary and sometimes conflict. But for the purpose of this book, I will focus on their understandings of the correlation between a divine revelation and theological discourses. For the majority of African theologians, God has revealed himself and purposes in and through the creation.[4] Bolaji Idowu, one of the earliest African theologians, defines revelation broadly to include the possibility of a "divine self-disclosure" and the capacity of the human mind to understand it.[5] For him, the possibility of a divine self-disclosure necessitates or requires a being that possessing a cognitive capacity. Therefore, he rejects the views of Rudolf Otto and Mircea Eliade on revelation precisely because, in his thinking, they tended to "refer to the sacred

[handwritten margin notes: Divine revelat. Theologic Discourse]

---

3. Idowu, *African Traditional Religion*, 51–69. See also Gunton, *Brief Theology of Revelation*; Thiemann, *Revelation and Theology*; Niebuhr, *Meaning of Revelation*, 19–41; Pannenberg, *Jesus—God and Man*, 115–33.

4. Ezeh, *Jesus Christ the Ancestor*, 50.

5. Idowu, *African Traditional Religion*, 51.

in terms which may be construed as impersonal."[6] He insists that there is inherently a cognitive and teleological undertone to a divine revelation. In other words, God is only capable of self-disclosure if he has the cognitive capacity to do so. He argues that God's self-manifestation is always linked to some sort of purpose.

> The question then is, can one speak strictly of "the numinous" or the sacred *manifesting* or *revealing* itself unless one implies a living Being as the agent of manifestation? Manifestation or revelation presupposes an agent with a conscious will causing a situation by which the manifestation could be apprehended. Thus, it also implies purpose.[7]

For Idowu, revelation is the consequence of religion. To him, the encounter of human beings with the being who is "Wholly Other," to him, originates from the "Wholly Other who reveals himself."[8] He argues that the "created order and man's inner link with God" are the "two principal media of revelation."[9] By a "created order" he means the entire creation, as recorded in the Genesis narrative, which according to him, bears "the seal of the Maker, the seal of God's self-disclosures" in every aspect.[10] It is the Genesis idea of *Imago Dei* that Idowu refers to as "man's link with God." He defines the image of God here as the source of human cognitive faculty.

> This is to say that man is made a rational being, intelligent, equipped with will and a sense of purpose; there is something of the divine in him which makes him addressable and responsible ... and, therefore, there exists in him the possibility of his spirit being in communion with the Divine Spirit.[11]

He locates this understanding of the image of God in humans in the Nigerian indigenous anthropology. He continues:

> This same fact is expressed in several African concepts of man. For example, the Yoruba believe that whereas an arch-divinity may be commissioned to mold a man's physical parts, only the

6. Ibid., 53.

7. Ibid.

8. Ibid., 54.

9. Ibid.

10. Ibid.

11. Ibid., 55.

Deity has the eternal prerogative of putting the essence of being into man. In Igbo as well as in Yoruba, the designation of the essence of being, *ori* and *chi*, derive directly from the name of Deity: ORISE (*Ori-se*), CHUKWU (*Chi-ukwu*); and this by implication means that the essence of man's being derives directly from Deity.[12]

He argues that the revelatory manifestation of God is not limited to any given culture or race. The theological relevance of this assertion anchors on his rejection of the claim that God has revealed himself ultimately in any single religion. He writes:

> God is one, not many; and to one God belongs to the earth and all its fullness. It is this God, therefore, who reveals Himself to every people on earth and whom they have apprehended according to the degree of their spiritual perception, expressing their knowledge of Him, if not as trained philosophers or educated theologians, certainly as those who have had some practical experience of Him. It would be looking at facts through the spectacles of cultural pride and affected superiority to deny this; it would be blasphemous to say that while the loving God cared for a particular section of His world, He had nothing in a clear, unmistakable way, to say, or to do with the rest.[13]

Consequently, he contends that it is theologically inadequate to categorize God's revelation in a dualistic way that makes a distinction between "God's climactic revelation in Jesus Christ" and the manifestation of God in a "man-made religion, i.e., other religions besides Christianity."[14]

Byang Kato, an Evangelical theologian, was one of the Nigerian theologians who rejected Idowu's understanding of revelation on the grounds it moved in the direction of religious pluralism and undermined the definitive revelation of God in Jesus Christ. But he construed revelation in the intellectualist or propositional sense of post-Enlightenment Protestantism, especially in its North American categories.[15] He agrees with Idowu on the revelatory manifestation of God in his creation and especially in human beings who are created in the image

---

12. Ibid.

13. Idowu, *Olodumare*, 31.

14. Idowu, *African Traditional Religion*, 56.

15. Many Protestant theologians have classified revelation into two categories, namely general revelation and special revelation. See Henry, *God, Revelation and Authority*.

of God. However, he denies that the general revelation and the image of God in human beings are sufficient to lead people to God's salvific knowledge. He writes, "Apart from the general revelation and the fact of the vestiges of *Imago Dei*, direct revelation of God to leaders of other religions is highly improbable."[16]

After his study of the indigenous religion of the Jaba people of the northern Nigeria, Kato concludes that it is only in Jesus Christ human beings can encounter God's definitive and salvific revelation, which for him, is not existent in any other religions apart from Christianity. According to him with "the coming of Christ, all other revelations come to an end. It is most unlikely that either Jaba or any other non-Christian people have received a direct revelation from God."[17]

Yusufu Turaki and Tokunboh Adeyemo, like Kato, adopt the categories of special and general to explain God's self-disclosure in human history. Adeyemo argued that "general revelation implies that God the Creator is self-revealed in His work."[18] A general revelation ensures that human beings "may enjoy the knowledge of God without the special revelation attested in Scripture."[19] He insists, however, that this does not mean that the general revelation is "insufficient" for salvation, but rather that it is never intended to be "redemptive."[20] He writes, "technically we can say that general revelation, by its very purpose, is limited in the sense of its non-redemptiveness."[21] Adeyemo's intention, like Kato, is to safeguard the uniqueness of the incarnation and the exclusivist claim that there is no salvation outside of Jesus Christ. Again he writes:

> I uphold the biblical claim of the uniqueness of Jesus Christ as to His essence, His incarnation, His vicarious death and resurrection, and the forgiveness of sin and salvation He offers every believing sinner. Unlike *Ela* [a lesser divine being in Yorubaland who is believed to be a savior] or any other divinity of African

16. Kato, *Theological Pitfalls in Africa*, 44.

17. Ibid.

18. Adeyemo, *Salvation in African Tradition*, 19.

19. Ibid.

20. Sam Oleka agrees: "We know that general revelation does not offer man knowledge of God's love, peace and personal relationship with God as they are offered to man in Christ in the New Testament. Furthermore, it does not teach man about God's saving 'grace and truth' through Jesus Chris" (John 1:17). See Oleka, "Authority of the Bible in the African Context," 80.

21. Adeyemo, *Salvation in African Tradition*, 25.

Traditional Religion, He was not created nor was He a demigod. Rather, He is God by whom all things are made, the second person of the Trinity, and the Redeemer of mankind.[22]

Turaki agrees with both Idowu and Kato on the idea of revelation as God's self-disclosure of himself. Also they agree on the imprints of God's revelatory manifestation in human beings as God's image bearers and on other parts of creation. He writes: "Revelation goes beyond our understanding of creation and the world as a given order. Human knowledge, understanding and wisdom of creation and the world and limited, unless guided by God Himself. Man who is created in the image of God has the knowledge, somewhat, of his Maker."[23] Like Kato and Adeyemo, Turaki argues that God's general revelation in creation is marred by and "subject to the corrupting influence of sin."[24] Therefore, Turaki contends that human beings are in need of a special revelation.[25] He also argues that the Christ-Event is the ultimate and definitive act of God's revelation. The "special revelation of Jesus the Messiah crowns all of God's revelations to humanity."[26] And this is precisely the basis of God's ultimate and definitive revelation in the Christ-Event that makes Jesus "the unique savior of the whole world."[27] Framed in an evangelistic tone, Turaki contends that there is only one possible correct way to have access to God's salvation; namely, Jesus Christ. In addition, he argues that to reject Jesus Christ is theologically and existentially suicidal.

> We have to accept the fact of "conflict of claims" because of the plural nature of human composition in the world. But among these claims of salvation, there can be only one that represents God truly. All that religions can do is to present the claims of their "revelations" to the "choice" of humanity. Their Creator

22. Ibid., 29.

23. Turaki, *Unique Christ for Salvation*, 225.

24. Ibid.

25. The majority of Nigerian Evangelical theologians construe Jesus Christ and the Bible as God's special revelations. Sam Oleka, an Evangelical, gives a helpful summary of these views of Jesus Christ and the Bible. "The heart of God's revelation is Jesus Christ, the eternal Word of God. As true man and true God 'He became flesh and lived for a while among us' (Jn 1:14). . . . The other form of God's special revelation is the Bible. It is a record of God's words to His creatures (2 Tim 3:16); Christ the Incarnate Word is known through the written Word, the Bible." See Oleka, "Living God," 128.

26. Turaki, *Unique Christ for Salvation*, 226.

27. Ibid., 227.

will hold all human beings, in the final analysis, responsible for
their choice. The one who chooses damnation has only himself
[or] herself to blame. God does not stop humanity and/or Satan
from offering alternative "paths" of salvation.[28]

The concept of a revealer in the Revealer Christology model I
develop in this book differs from post-Enlightenment Protestant understandings of revelation that have informed the views of Turaki,
Adeyemo, and Kato. It also differs from Idowu's pluralistic understanding of revelation. Although an exhaustive examination of their views of
revelation falls outside the parameters of this chapter, it is important to
highlight the theological and christological problems with their understandings of revelation.

First, the classification of revelation into general and special can
be misleading and can betray the unity underlying God's revelation.
Kato, Adeyemo and Turaki, influenced by post-Enlightenment North
American Protestantism, classify creation under God's general revelation and the Bible and the Christ-Event under God's special revelation.[29]
According to Kato, the Bible is God's written revelation and Jesus Christ
is God's living revelation.[30] Idowu, Adeyemo, Kato and Turaki have all
confused God's activity such as creation with God's *revelation of himself*. The creation of God (human beings and other existing beings and
things in the universe), is not God's revelation of God's self. The creation
affirms the "facticity and universal scope of the divine working but propose no specific location."[31] Therefore, the creation is only *revelatory*
insofar as it points to the revelation of God in the Christ-Event. All
other revelatory acts of God—before and after the Christ-Event—are
only *pointers* to God's self-disclosure in and through the Christ-Event.
They witness to the revelation of God in Jesus Christ. These acts in most
cases *tell us something* about God, but do not *reveal* God's self. It is only
Jesus Christ that reveals God's self.[32] Nicholas Wolterstorff captures the
difference between telling about something and revealing something:

28. Ibid., 228.

29. What exactly constitute special revelation has become highly debatable today amidst North American Evangelical, Reformed, and Protestant theologians. See
Tiessen, *Who Can Be Saved?*, 113–22; Carson, *Gagging of God.*

30. Kato, *Biblical Christianity in Africa*, 21–22.

31. Farley, *Divine Empathy*, 252.

32. Karl Barth correctly notes that we have "not universal deity capable of being
reached conceptually, but this concrete deity—real and recognizable in the decent

Revelation is not dispelling just any sort of ignorance. Telling you that I left the keys on the counter is not, in normal circumstances, *revealing* to you the location of the keys—even though it does dispel your ignorance. Dispelling ignorance becomes *revelation* when it has, to some degree and in some way, the character of unveiling the veiled, of uncovering the covered, of exposing the obscured view. The counterpart of the revealed is the hidden.[33]

It is vital to recognize that prior to the Christ-Event God unveiled his anger, love, compassion, and sovereignty in diverse ways.[34] In other words, people did not come to know and have a relationship with God only after the Christ-Event. Keeping this in mind is important because it provides a helpful theological context for understanding the difference between the pre-Christ-Event divine manifestations and God's revelation of God's self in the Christ-Event. Theophany and other revealing or revelatory manifestations of God in history *say* something about God and God's relationship to the world. Jeffrey Niehaus has noted that the God of the Old Testament (before the Christ-Event) revealed himself to the people of Israel and did not allow them to "guess" who he was.[35] According to Niehaus, "the God of the Old Testament could appear whenever and wherever he chose."[36] And God did appear to people beginning from the Garden of Eden (the pre-Sinai theophanies) and continued to appear beyond the Sinai theophany.[37]

However, the Christ-Event is the only unique action of God (in human history) that demonstrates God's act of relating to the world, particularly human beings, as God-man. The uniqueness of the Christ-Event entails partly that all other manifestations or revelatory acts of God can attain their full potential meanings and significances only in and through Jesus's person and work. Jesus Christ construes himself in this way. For example, he says to the woman of Samaria, "Everyone who drinks this water will be thirsty again, but whoever drinks the water I

---

grounded in that sequence and peculiar to the existence of Jesus Christ." Barth, *Humanity of God*, 48.

33. Wolterstorff, *Divine Discourse*, 23–24.

34. Hebrews 1.

35. Niehaus, *God at Sinai*, 17.

36. Ibid., 18.

37. Ibid., 142, 181–86.

give him will never thirst. Indeed, the water I give him will become in him a spring of water welling up to eternal life."[38]

God has, theologically speaking, revealed himself definitively in history in the Christ-Event. Karl Barth underscored this idea of revelation when he argued:

> Revelation itself is connected with nothing different or higher or earlier than itself. Revelation as such is not relative. Revelation in fact does not differ from the Person of Jesus Christ, and again does not differ from the reconciliation that took place in him. To say revelation is to say, "The Word became flesh."[39]

For Barth, as John McDowell argues, "Christian talk of God is only properly located in the event of the revelation in Jesus Christ."[40] The Apostle John communicated a similar idea in a provocative way, "No one has ever seen God, but God the one and only, who is at the Father's side, he has made him known."[41]

Unlike Kato, Adeyemo and Turaki, Idowu pays little attention to the uniqueness of the Christ-Event in his discussion on revelation. John Parratt has argued that by "paying little attention to the place of Jesus Christ in revelation," Idowu obscures both the uniqueness of Christianity and the "unique nature of the African concept of God, for which Idowu himself pleads."[42] I will examine the relationship between the God Jesus communicates and interprets and the indigenous views of God in chapter five. It suffices to note here that some of the characteristics of God, which Jesus embodies, can upset the African indigenous understandings of God or the Supreme Being as the most powerful, untouchable and who has withdrawn from a relationship with humanity because of human sinful actions. On the contrary, Jesus Christ preaches not only the God who is powerful, but also the God who is touchable, reachable, self-giving, and vulnerable.[43]

Second, it is important to recognize that the Christ-Event does not guarantee that people will always accept God's salvific blessings. Parratt

38. John 4:13–14, *NIV*.

39. Barth, *Church Dogmatics*, 134.

40. McDowell, "Karl Barth, Emil Brunner and the Subjectivity of the Object of Christian Hope," 25–41.

41. John 1:18, *NASB*.

42. Parratt, *Reinventing Christianity*, 69.

43. See chapter five.

Neither God in Creation nor Special in [Christ] meant they will know Him

has pointed out that Idowu blurs the difference between God's existence and people's knowledge of him which is based solely on his revelation of himself.[44] Idowu puts himself into a serious theological difficulty when he confuses God's revelation with God's creation and salvation in his attempt to secure a "universal availability of God" and to undo any form of "exclusivism conceived in racial or cultural terms."[45] God's manifestations in his act of creating (the world, human beings, etc.) do not guarantee that people will know him. And although God's complete, radical, and definitive self-disclosure in the Christ-Event provides the opportunity for people to know, experience, and to enjoy a unique relationship with God, it does not guarantee that people will always accept this opportunity. The Christ-Event provides a unique opportunity for human beings to experience God's remolding, critiquing, gracious love, forgiveness, acceptance, and blessings, but it is only God who can possibly convey God's salvation to people.

The Concept of Revealer in the Revealer Christology Model

In what way can a systematic-contextual theologian interpret the Christ-Event to engage befittingly with the contemporary situation—cultural, spiritual, religious, and socio-economic—of Africa? This is not entirely a new question. In some ways, the theologians and Christian laity I have examined in this book have wrestled with and attempted to answer this question. However, the Revealer Christology model that is developed in this book aims to answer this question from a way that differs both in content and structure from the existing christological models in Africa. It differs from them in that it construes Jesus is a revealer of divinity (God, lesser spirit beings, and the spirit world) and humanity (human beings and the human world). To say that Jesus is the revealer of divinity and humanity, in the context of this book, means that he communicates and interprets divinity and humanity for the purpose of enacting a relationship between God and humanity.

Four presuppositions inform this christological contention. First, the Christ-Event is God's definitive and complete revelation of divinity and humanity. It is a mistake to construe Jesus the Christ as the revealer of God alone. Theologians are accustomed to speaking of Jesus

44. Parratt, *Reinventing Christianity*, 67.
45. Bediako, *Theology and Identity*, 282.

Part of Revealer

Christ as the revelation of God but have overlooked that he is also a revelation of humanity. This book argues that the ideas of the "Word became flesh" and "God with us," understood correctly, require we see the Christ-Event as a revelation of both divinity and humanity. It is a serious theological fault to concentrate only on the revelation of God or divinity in and through the Christ-Event and to overlook the significance of the Christ-Event for humanity.

Second, the uniqueness of the Christ-Event does not lie merely in the ontological composition of Jesus's person, but also in Jesus' meaning and significance for human beings and God, and the relationship existing between them. It would have been utterly useless if God had appeared in human history (in Jesus Christ) just for the sake of the adventure or simply to show he had the power to become human. Therefore, the Revealer Christology model that is developed in this book explores and engages with the dialectics of and connections between the person and work of Jesus Christ and his significance for many Christians who are seeking and hoping for a divine liberation, healing, and providence.

Third, the Christ-Event is a divine *manifestational act* by which God makes himself accessible to human history in the person and work of Jesus Christ for the purpose of being in a relationship with human beings.[46] This, of course, does not mean that human beings can exhaust or encapsulate the mysteries of divinity and humanity. What it means, however, is that human beings can know the meaning and significance of humanity and divinity through the Christ-Event. It is a theological mistake to see Jesus Christ as the revealer of the propositional truth of God and humanity. As a communicative or meditative act, the Christ-Event presents us with Jesus who embodies God's relationality by entering into a relationship with humanity—God's own creation. The Christ-Event also provides a unique way for human beings to experience and encounter God, other spiritual beings and their fellow human beings. The key motif underlying this unique encounter is *relationship*. The aim of the Christ-Event is not to provide human beings with a mere clear, comprehensive, intellectual, and exhaustive knowledge of

---

46. I am adopting Nicholas Wolterstorff's differentiation between a "non-manifestational revelation" and a "manifestational revelation." According to him, a "*non-manifestational* revelation is revealing that P by asserting that P, whereas a manifestational revelation is revealing that P by some means other than assertion." See Wolterstorff, *Divine Discourse,* 27

God, other spiritual beings and human beings, but rather to provide a revealer through whom human beings can have a meaningful relationship with God, and to judge their preconceptions and understandings of other spiritual beings, human beings, and the human world.

Fourth, the Christ-Event is a *hermeneutical act*. This means that Jesus Christ interprets divinity and humanity, and critiques and reforms human beings' preconceptions of God, other spirit beings and humanity. Hermeneutic is not used here in its traditional rendering—the "reflection on the principles that undergird correct textual interpretation."[47] In this book, a *hermeneutical act* refers to an interpretative framework for imagining and experiencing the mysteries of the relationship between humanity and divinity. Understood in this way, the Christ-Event is the forum in which human beings and God interact and enjoy an unprecedented relationship. Insofar as the Christ-Event also furnishes human beings with the opportunity to judge their knowledge of and relationship with God, other spiritual beings and their fellow human beings, it is an *interpretative act*. It is not sufficient to posit that Jesus Christ stands as the figure through whom African Christians can come to an adequate knowledge of the spiritual and human worlds. In order for Christians to understand the nature and goals of the Christ-Event, they must also perceive Jesus Christ hermeneutically; that is, they must construe Jesus as the revealer who questions, judges, critiques and reconstructs their previous relationship with God and with other human beings.

Jesus construed the nature, purpose, and significance of his mission in both *communicative* and *interpretative* ways. For example, when he declared that he had not come to destroy the Law or the Prophets but to fulfill them,[48] he presented himself not only as a good teacher whose aim was to make his followers understand the Hebrew Scripture correctly, but also as the one who embodied divine presence and through whom the Jewish people can have an unprecedented fellowship with God. The understanding of Jesus Christ as the revealer through whom people could know the will and purpose of God for humanity and divinity is also evident in the conversation between him and the Samaritan woman. Confused and bewildered at the words of Jesus, the Samaritan woman said to him, "I know that a Messiah . . . is coming. When he

47. Vanhoozer, *Is There a Meaning in this Text?*, 19.

48. Matthew 5:19.

comes, he will explain everything to us."[49] Before the Christ-Event, those who were associated with some forms of Judaism anticipated a Messiah who would function as the interpretative framework or a revealer of God's purpose. Jesus' response, which came in the form of *I am sayings*, sets the context for the uniqueness of his messianic work. [50] By saying to the woman "I am he,"[51] Jesus unequivocally declared himself as the anticipated Messiah. In addition, as the revealer of divinity and humanity, he functions as a hermeneutical lens through which people can know themselves and evaluate and experience a unique relationship with God and other human beings.[52]

Revealer Christology and the Issues of Christological Approaches

Should theologians worry about the beginning point of Christology? Or should they avoid the question about a point of departure and just get on with *christologizing*? Kevin Vanhoozer has noted the contemporary shift away from many modern theologians who "devoted considerable energy to prolegomena."[53] Many contemporary theologians in the West are realizing the difficulty of trying to develop a theological method before starting to do theology. Vanhoozer himself embarked on the task of developing "a new possibility for doing theology beyond prolegomena," that is, "a way of speaking of God that allows the theological matter to influence the theological method."[54]

Many theologians are still preoccupied with christological methods, assuming that the validity of any Christology lies in its well-defined methodology. The only options that seem to be available to them are

49. John 4:25.

50. Bauckham, "Monotheism and Christology in the Gospel of John," 160.

51. John 4:26.

52. Here the challenges that Jesus puts forward to the Samaritan woman are that she needs to judge her understanding of herself, her understanding of the relationship between the Jews and the Samaritans and her understanding of her relationship with God in the light of the Christ-Event.

53. Vanhoozer, *First Theology*, 15. I am indebted to John McDowell for the awareness of this paradigmatic shift in theological methodology.

54. Ibid., 16.

Christology from above and Christology from below.[55] A few examples will illustrate this observation. Ukachukwu Chris Manus situates his King Christology model in the territory of a Christology from below. In the opening words of chapter six of *Christ, the African King: New Testament Christology*, he postulates:

> The purpose of this chapter is based on the overall interest of this book; namely, the "Christology from below." Since the human condition of Jesus in this world of ours is traceable according to the best . . . historical and exegetical methods, it is therefore made the starting point of the following chapters. Scripture makes it clear that Christology takes off from the man, Jesus of Nazareth and reflects on his divine transcendence . . . [56]

Enyi Ben Udoh and Justin Ukpong also favor a Christology from below.[57] On the contrary, Turaki speaks for many theologians who use a high Christology method when he contends: "Jesus the Messiah has no origin and He is not created. He is the Eternal One with God the Father."[58] Again he writes,

> He is above the cyclical rhythm of nature as He is the Creator of nature. He transcends the powers of nature and cannot be subject to them. Furthermore, Jesus the Messiah is neither an ancestor nor "one of them." He did not originate from within human nature. He is its Creator.[59]

Some Western theologians also think of high Christology and low Christology as the only two available approaches from which a theologian can undertake a christological construction.[60] Veli-Matti Karkkainen is an example.

> There are two options, in principle, for inquiry into the person and work of Christ. Conveniently, these have been labeled, "from above" and "from below." Christology from above begins with the confession of faith in the deity of Christ expressed in

---

55. Theologians sometimes call Christology from above a *high Christology*, and Christology from below a *low Christology*.

56. Manus, *Christ, the African King*, 118.

57. Udoh, "Guest Christology," 263–64; Ukpong, "Christology and Inculturation," 43.

58. Turaki, *Unique Christ for Salvation*, 136.

59. Ibid., 138.

60. Pannenberg, *Jesus—God and Man*, 33–36.

the New Testament. Christology from below begins with an inquiry into the historical Jesus and the historical basis for belief in Christ.[61]

Since the Revealer Christology as developed in this book model falls outside of these two approaches, it will be necessary to explain the approach I use. While a methodology can be helpful in undertaking the task of a constructive Christology, it should not be a prerequisite for christologizing; it should not obstruct the actual doing of Christology, and it should not introduce an unwarranted dichotomy between the divinity and humanity of Jesus Christ. It is, therefore, misleading to ask, should a Christology begin from above or from below? Beginning a christological inquiry from either of these two approaches will lead to a reductionistic or parochial understanding of the Christ-Event. Nicholas Lash has questioned the appropriateness and usefulness of the metaphors—below and above—for a constructive Christology.[62] He argues that these metaphors are "inappropriate to the task of systematic Christology" since a "systematic reflection" on the person and work of Jesus Christ arises normally out of the "Christian confession of the humanity and divinity of Jesus Christ."[63] The major christological problem with constructing a Christology either from below or from above is that such Christology will run the risk of introducing a destructive gulf and dichotomy between the divinity and humanity of Jesus Christ. The test of any reliable Christology, therefore, is inherent in its awareness of the impossibility of successfully interpreting the Christ-Event either from below or from above. The Brazilian theologian, Leonardo Boff, has noted the dialectical nature of a christological inquiry.

> When we speak of Jesus we must always think of God and the human person, both at the same time and in conjunction. . . . The unity of God and human person in Jesus is so profound that it should be possible to discover his humanity in his divinity and his divinity in his humanity.[64]

61. Karkkainen, *Christology*, 12.

62. Lash, "Up and Down in Christology," 35. In this essay, Lash rebuts the arguments of Wolfhart Pannenberg against Christology from above.

63. Ibid.

64. Boff, *Jesus Christ Liberator*, 181.

It is inadequate to limit our christological methods to either Christology from below or Christology from above. And since these methods, when taken in isolation, deepen the gulf between divinity and humanity, the very gulf that the Christ-Event bridges, I will undertake the task of developing an alternative approach that will engage with the dialectics of divinity and humanity from the perspective of the person and work of Jesus Christ. In this book, I will employ a dialectic-holistic approach to develop a Revealer Christology model. This approach integrates the christological approaches from below and from above without taking either of these approaches as a point of departure. While points of references are helpful, it should be noted that they are not indissolubly connected with constructive Christology. In other words, we do not need to begin either from below or from above before we can successfully write a constructive Christology. The dialectic-holistic approach is grounded in the claim that in the Christ-Event we encounter a figure, Jesus the Christ, who embodies divinity and humanity. Joseph Weber rightly warns against the danger of introducing a dubious dichotomy between the humanity and divinity of Jesus Christ. He writes, "the humanity of Jesus cannot be considered apart from his divinity, because the divinity is constructive of this particular, specific man."[65] When we construct a Christology that takes its starting point either from the historical Jesus or the Incarnate *Logos* we may succeed in destroying the divine-human union embodied by Jesus Christ. Millard Erickson notes that a Christology from below moves in the direction of reason while a Christology from above moves in the direction of faith. This assumes a modern separation of faith and reason, an ideology that characterized liberal scholarship's quest to rediscover the historical Jesus (*historie*) and to distinguish him from the Jesus of faith (*geschicthe*).[66] But Erickson contends, and rightly so, that a viable Christological method would adopt "neither faith alone nor historical reason alone, but together, in an intertwined, mutually dependent, simultaneously progressing fashion."[67]

In brief, an adequate christological method should be holistic and dialectical. It should be able to accommodate both the mystery and the invitation to probe the mystery of Jesus's divinity and humanity. The

65. Weber, "Karl Barth and the Historical Jesus," 50.

66. See Kahler, *So-called Historical Jesus and the Historic, Biblical Christ.*

67. Erickson, "Christology from Above and Christology from Below," 54.

fact that the majority of the followers of Jesus even in our time continue to see him as a divine being or God requires that theologians are to take seriously the claim that God has revealed himself in Jesus Christ. Any Christology that is Christian must engage with the claim that Jesus of Nazareth embodied divinity and humanity. In what follows, I will examine the circumference of the Revealer Christology model that is developed in this book.

The Circumference of the Revealer Christology Model

Revealer Christology and Classical Christology

"How can Jesus Christ mediate and interpret divinity and humanity for the African peoples when he was a Jew and not an African?" is a serious question African theologians should not ignore. In this book, I argue that the answer to this question cannot be divorced from the classical Christian christological construal of Jesus Christ as consubstantial with divinity and humanity. J. N. D. Kelly has noted that the "problem of Christology, in the narrow sense of the word, is to define the relation of the divine and human in Christ."[68] Whereas the council of Nicaea focused primarily on the divinity of Jesus Christ, the council of Chalcedon explored and created a circumference for understanding the relationship of divinity and humanity of Jesus Christ.[69] Uchenna Ezeh has engaged in a constructive development of the Christologies of the councils of Nicaea and Chalcedon. In chapter two, we saw that he explored the cult of African ancestors and built his Ancestor Christology model on both African indigenous understanding of ancestors and the major christological formulations from Nicaea (325) to Chalcedon (451). Ezeh notes that the Christology in the Nicene Creed was formulated within the context of the Trinity.[70] For him, the Nicene Council's use of *homoousios* (of the same substance) to describe Jesus's

68. J. Kelly, *Early Christian Doctrines*, 138.

69. Grillmeier, *Christ in Christian Tradition: From the Council of Chalcedon (451) to Gregory the Great (590–604)*, 3–5. See also Anderson, *Paradox in Christian Theology*, 63–76.

70. Another way of putting it is that "The dogma of the Trinity developed as the Church's response to a question about the identity of Jesus Christ." See Pelikan, *Christian Tradition: A History of the Development of Doctrine—The Emergence of the Catholic Tradition (100–600)*, 226.

relationship with the Father implies that "in Jesus the transcendent and radically immanent God is in the world as God made man."[71] He argues that Jesus Christ as the "radically immanent God-man can be well understood from the African sense of solidarity."[72] Solidarity here refers to the African indigenous understandings of the interrelationship between the spiritual world and the human world. Using the indigenous concept of the ancestor cult, Ezeh contends that the divine-human tension, which the Nicene and Chalcedon Councils introduced, is present in the African indigenous cosmologies.

> In the African cosmology, there is this quest for unity between God and man. There exists the spiritual as well as the material world. Through the ancestors the divine and the human, the spiritual and the material worlds are held together. There is therefore this divine-human tension also in the African concept of the ancestor.[73]

Apart from Ezeh, no other African theologian that I am aware of has explored extensively the classical christological formulations of the church councils and interpreted them in light of some indigenous concepts.[74] This is not to suggest that most theologians construct their Christologies in the ways that conflict with the classical christological formulation of the divinity and humanity of Jesus Christ, but rather that they have failed to articulate clearly the relation of this classical christological formulation to their Christologies.[75]

The Revealer Christology model that is developed in this book espouses and reinterprets the classical christological confession of Jesus Christ as both divine and human for the contemporary African contexts. This means that the model builds on the christological circumference (Jesus as divine-human) created by the classical Christian councils whilst at the same time explaining and interpreting the Christ-Event in a manner that interacts meaningfully with the context of life of the people of Africa. As developed in this book, the Revealer Christology model

71. Ezeh, *Jesus Christ the Ancestor*, 201.

72. Ibid.

73. Ibid., 252.

74. See chapter two for a critique of Ezeh's Ancestor Christology model.

75. Some Nigerian theologians such as Enyi Ben Udoh and Bolaji Idowu have constructed Christologies and theologies that to some degree have denied the divinity of Jesus Christ. See chapter two.

Reveal. Christ.

know!.
1) relation.
2) true
3. judment

proposes that it is in and through the Christ-Event African Christians can (a) come to a true knowledge of God, other spiritual beings, and human beings, (b) enjoy a relationship with God and with other human beings, (c) judge their notions of divine—human relationship or the relationship between the spiritual world and the human world.

Some Western theologians have pointed out that the christological controversy of the early period of Christian history leaned more toward the deity of Jesus and not his humanity. "In the classical periods of christological controversy," John McIntyre writes, "the subject which commanded most attention was that of the deity of Christ."[76] For him, the controversy revolved around the issue of the identity of Jesus and the identity of God. He notes that the subject-matter was concerned with

> whether Jesus Christ was to be identified with God, whether he was "very God of very God," _homoousios_, of one substance with the Father; or whether he was only of similar nature to God; or as the semi-Arians maintained, as regards all the essential attributes of deity he was dissimilar to the Father; or, as Arius himself is thought to believe, he did not coexist from all eternity with the Father, but originated in time by the Father's will, though as his first and most glorious creation.[77]

Of course, that the classical theologians devoted much of their energy to defend the deity of Jesus does not mean they overlooked his humanity. In fact, it was the humanity of Jesus Christ that partly informed the defense and controversy of his divinity. Therefore, the christological controversy, and the councils and creeds that followed aimed to develop a two-nature Christology. Chalcedon, in particular, wanted to map out the christological parameters within which Christians can work out the christological equation of how the divine and human natures of Jesus relate.[78]

It is important to note that the Nicene Creed and Chalcedonian christological formulation have not resolved the christological problems that are associated with the identity of Jesus. Apart from the fact that these two important historic documents have emerged from some early Christians whose cultural, political, and religious contexts differ

76. McIntyre, _Theology after the Storm_, 61.

77. Ibid.

78. Karkkainen, _Christology_, 72.

significantly from the contemporary African contexts, and therefore require a reinterpretation, the documents cannot claim to have a final say on the Christ-Event. They were, of course, not intended to provide definitive and final christological formulations. Rather, they aimed to provide the christological parameters for measuring what is and what is not an adequate Christian interpretation of the person of Jesus Christ. In addition, it is important for a theologian to rediscover that the Christ-Event is a mystery and that no single theological explication can claim an exhaustive articulation of its meaning, purpose, and significance.

Revealer Christology and the Religious Quests of African Peoples

As I have already indicated, the Revealer Christology model as it is articulated in this book, aims to interpret the Christ-Event in the manner that engages concretely, relevantly and interactively with the experiences and the context of life of the peoples of Africa, particularly Christians. In order to achieve this enormous task, I will locate this model within the three major religious quests which are deeply rooted in the religious thinking of most Nigerian people.

The first is the quest to understand the blurry and unclear inter-relationship between the spiritual world and the world of human beings. Any serious researcher of the indigenous religions will notice that Africans are constantly searching for a way to understand the spiritual world which they believe to have a direct bearing on their existence. Although some people who have not been informed by the indigenous religions may simply discard this quest as mere superstition, what remains evident is that many people still think of their existence and subsistence on the earth in the categories of the spiritual-human inter-relation. This is so because they construe the spiritual world and the human world, not as two divisible abodes, but rather as two indivisible aspects of one abode. Emefie Ikenga-Metuh observes: "The world of the human experience is seen as one fluid, coherent unit, in which spirits, men, animals, plants . . . are engaged in continuous interaction. The invisible world of spirits and the visible world shade into and mutually influence each other."[79]

---

79. Ikenga-Metuh, *African Religions in Western Conceptual Schemes*, 3–4.

Spiritual world → vital —

There is no aspect of human life, for many Africans, which the spiritual world does not influence. Although one must be careful not to speak of African societies as a unit, many theologians and historians of religion agree that the "concept of reality and destiny are deeply rooted in the spirit world."[80] The Kenyan theologian, John Mbiti, has reminded scholars of African religions to avoid the error of trying to treat the "spiritual universe" and "physical world" separately because they "intermingle . . . so much that it is not easy or even necessary . . . to separate them."[81] The quest to understand the spiritual world and the belief in the impact of the activities of some spiritual beings on the human world have continued to shape African Christians' prayers, songs, beliefs, and interpretations of Jesus Christ. For example, when there is a poor harvest, the majority of the people attribute it to a curse from either God, or other benevolent spirits, or malevolent spirits. This belief greatly informs many Christians' understanding of God and Jesus Christ as it is evident in the salvation testimony of Ben Fubra-Manuel. According to him, becoming a Christian and personally experiencing Jesus Christ is a

> fulfilling experience because you don't know the emptiness you walk with everyday when you are not a Christian. When you come to Jesus . . . you feel complete. You don't feel superhuman. You don't feel that you are holy as you should be . . . You become, in the words of the Apostle Paul, a new creation with a new sense of values, a new way of looking at the totality of reality. Now the practical effects are wonderful because if you are complete in Jesus then you are not afraid of the many things around that people fear—the witches, the wizards, the Ogbanje, the juju—because you find completeness in Jesus.[82]

Many Africans live in constant fear of evil spirits. Sometimes they see evil people as agents of the devil. For the majority of Christians, it is only Jesus who can effectively protect people, as Fubra-Manuel has indicated, from such malevolent spirits and people. But some Christians who think that Jesus may delay in giving them spiritual protection when they need him sometimes use other means of protections such as

80. Turaki, *Unique Christ for Salvation*, 60.

81. Mbiti, *African Religions and Philosophy*, 75.

82. Fubra-Manuel, interview by author, tape recording, Aba 12 March 2006.

amulets. Others use holy water or stickers which their pastor or priests have blessed.[83]

The second quest consists in the attempts of many people to maneuver and manipulate the spiritual world to work in their favor in their struggles to achieve wellbeing. In the thinking of many Africans, it is possible to appease and manipulate gods, ancestors, and even evil spirits, to bring blessings on people.[84] This is because most people believe that some evil spirits "are subject to man if one knows how to manipulate them."[85] This quest underscores some of the understandings of the power and acts of Jesus. Amadi, a member of the Presbyterian Church, highlighted the impact of this quest on Nigerian Christians. In his response to the question "are there some Nigerian Christians that go outside of Jesus to find solution to their problems," he said:

> Yes, many, in fact, the whole of Aba. There are so many people that are looking for ways to solve their problems. But I keep on telling them that Jesus is not a talisman. You don't use him as a talisman. He is not an ordinary person. So if you are telling him to solve your problems he must make sure that you are in line with him.[86]

Amadi generalizes this phenomenon. However, the most important point to note here is that the traditional belief in the ability of human beings to control spiritual beings has crept into the Christologies of many Christians.

The traditionalists consult some powerful native doctors to prepare charms for them to control some evil spirits. Christians who object to any attempt to obtain amulets from the native doctors consider their prayer as a powerful charm and tool that is available to them for a spiritual warfare.[87] The expression *ekpere bu ogwu mu gworo*, literally, "prayer is the charm or amulet that I have prepared" is a familiar phrase among the Igbo Christian communities. On most occasions, this expression

---

83. See chapter six for an extensive discussion on how the Revealer Christology model as developed in this book interacts with Nigerian Christians' understandings of the spirit world.

84. Imasogie, *African Traditional Religion*, 38.

85. Ibid.

86. Amadi, interview by author, tape recording, Aba, April 10, 2006.

87. See chapter six for an extensive discussion on Nigerian Christians' beliefs about Jesus and demonic forces.

is used as a spiritual missile against the evil spirits or wicked people. Partly, this expression indicates a total submission, dependence and loyalty to the power of Jesus Christ. But it can also indicate the confidence of many Christians on the power of prayer in combating spiritual forces that work against the wellbeing of human beings. The primary focus here is not on prayer as enjoying God's presence or even as petitions; it is rather on the quest of the majority of Africans to maneuver the spiritual world in order to attain a peaceful and blissful existence.

Beneath the two previous quests lies the third quest; namely, the search for a medium or person that can function as a lens through which they can understand the events that happen around them. This quest is widespread in many African societies. Diane Stinton observes.

> When afflictions occur within a community, such as wrongdoing, illness, or witchcraft, African religions recognize various means to discover the reasons for the disharmony in the universe and to prescribe measures for rectifying the problem, thereby restoring the force of life. Intermediaries are those beings who function in these roles of discernment and mediating reconciliation.[88]

This quest is evident in Nigerians' use of intermediaries. For many Christians, Jesus Christ is the ultimate intermediary through whom people can approach God and seek his forgiveness and blessings. The traditionalists (and some Christians) may use intermediaries such as diviners. The Revealer Christology model that is proposed in this book presents Jesus Christ as the being who reshapes radically the content of these quests. I will examine the implications of these three quests in the remainder of this book.

Revealer Christology in Relation to Apotheosis and Quasi-Docetism

There are two major potential christological problems which can arise from the portrayal of Jesus as a figure who embodies, mediates and interprets divinity and humanity in the African contexts. These are apotheosis and quasi-docetism. I will regard these christological problems

---

88. Stinton, *Jesus of Africa*, 110.

as potential because they have not penetrated African Christian christological *discourses*.

APOTHEOSIS

In the indigenous religions, some ancestors can metamorphose into the status of a deity. It is important to recognize that in the thinking of many African peoples not every dead person becomes an ancestor. Kwesi Dickson, a notable Ghanaian theologian, warns that "the cult of the dead is not to be equated with the cult of ancestors" because "to die is not to automatically become an ancestor."[89] There are some prerequisites for becoming an ancestor, and interestingly, an individual must meet the criteria while he or she is alive in order for him to qualify as an ancestor. Omosade Awolalu and Adelumo Dopamu have noted: "West African peoples believe that only those who lead a good life, live to a ripe old age, die a good death, and are accorded full burial rites can become ancestors."[90] The Tanzanian theologian, Laurenti Magesa, has described the ancestors as "the pristine men and women who originated the lineage, clan or ethnic group" and also the people who have provided their people with their names.[91] But the criteria for becoming an ancestor differ from one African society or ethnic group to another. However, there are some requirements that appear to permeate the structures of the majority of ancestral cults in Africa. These include being above reproach, respect for ancestral traditions, prosperous life, death that comes through old age and proper burial.[92]

The requirements to become a member of this highly exalted class of ancestors are not clear. In the cosmology of Yoruba, an ethnic group in Nigeria, only kings may be deified. One example of such kings is

89. Dickson, *Theology in Africa*, 69.

90. Awolalu and Dopamu, *West African Traditional Religion*, 274.

91. Magesa, *African Religion: The Moral Traditions of Abundant Life* (Maryknoll: Orbis, 1997) 47. What is often omitted in some discussions on the requirements for becoming an ancestor is the issue of power. As we shall see in the case of Sango, the Yoruba god of thunder and lightning, it is the power he exhibited as a king, and not his lifestyle, that qualified him as an apotheosized ancestor.

92. See Ilogu, *Christian Ethics in an African Background*, 41; Ikenga-Metuh, "Ritual Death and Purification Rites among the Igbo," 3–24; Parrinder, *West African Religion: A Book of the Beliefs and Practices of Akan, Ewe, Yoruba*, 116; Cox, *Rational Ancestors*, 355; Oduyoye, "Identity Shaped by the Ancestors: Examples from Folk Talk of the Akan in Ghana," 73.

Sango, the Yoruba god of lightning and thunder.[93] Two major versions of the Sango legend have survived in Yoruba history; namely the orthodox and non-orthodox views.[94] A. L. Hethersett's *Iwe Kika Ekerin Li Ede Yoruba* helped to popularize the orthodox version of Sango legend.[95] According to the orthodox version, Sango was the fourth *Alaafin* (king) of Ọyọ. Although a powerful king, he ruled with cruelty. His cruelty and tyranny resulted in complaints from among his subjects and even among his wives. The complaints, especially from his wives, frustrated him and he decided to escape the unbearable complaints and quarrels by opting to reside in a dense forest. And it was while he was residing in the forest that he ascended into heaven.[96] According to this view, Sango continues to rule with great power in the form of thunder and lightning from heaven. The non-orthodox version, on the contrary, claims Sango committed suicide on realizing that one of his messengers who was fed up with his tyranny and cruelty conspired to kill him.[97] Adherents to the non-orthodox view maintain that the lightning and thunder that are associated with the wrath of Sango are the magical acts of some of his admirers who wanted to vindicate their respect for the controversial king.[98] For those who hold the non-orthodox version, the admirers of Sango manipulate some diabolical powers in the forms of lightning and thunder to eliminate those who insist that Sango committed suicide, a type of death that is considered to be shameful in the Ọyọ's worldview.[99]

The origin of Sango worship has continued to elicit debate among some scholars of Yoruba indigenous religion. Akinwumi Isola, for example, argues that Hethersett's account of Sango's history is a total distortion.[100] He contends that Sango worship predates Babayemi Itiolu,

93. Omari, "Candomble: A Socio-Political Examination of African Religion and Art in Brazil," 135–59.

94. Bolaji Idowu uses the term orthodox to describe a version of the legend which contends that Sango translated or ascended into heaven. I employ the expression non-orthodox to describe another version of the legend from the orthodox version. See Idowu, *Olodumare*, 90.

95. Hethersett, *Iwe Kika Ekerin Li Ede Yoruba*.

96. Idowu, *Olodumare*, 91.

97. Ibid., 90.

98. Schlitz, "Yoruba Thunder Deities and Sovereignty," 67–84.

99. Ibid., 91; See also Idowu, *African Traditional Religion*.

100. Isola, "Religious Politics and the Myth of Sango," 93–99.

the fourth Alaafin of Ọyọ, who Hethersett claimed became divinized as Sango.[101] According to Isola, Jegbe, a hunter and one of the children of Oodua established Ọyọ under the power of Sango. Therefore, Isola contends, "Since Sango was there at the foundation of Ọyọ" it is preposterous to argue that the fourth Alaafin was the king who became Sango.[102] It is important to note that Isola does not doubt that that people of Ọyọ deified their fourth Alaafin. For him, it is an important tradition in Ọyọ to deify each Alaafin. This is because Ọyọ people believe that when an Alaafin is on the throne, "he incarnates Sango, and when dead, he is deified and becomes Sango."[103]

The exact origins of Sango worship may have been lost in antiquity, but what remains clear is that many Yoruba people (and some people from other ethnic groups in Nigeria) continue to dread Sango, the god of thunder and lightning. And the majority of people continue to associate it with the fourth Alaafin of Ọyọ. My primary concern here is not to provide a historical explanation of Sango worship, but rather to articulate the potential christological problem that apotheosis poses to a Nigerian contextual Christology. It is not too difficult for many Africans to accept that the historical figure, Jesus of Nazareth, is also God because already they do believe that God or gods can be incarnated in human bodies and that some powerful heroes or kings can become gods. The potential christological problem, then, is that many may construe Jesus as a deified hero or ancestor.

Here, William Horbury's *Jewish Messianism and the Cult of Christ* helps to illuminate the potential perception of Jesus as a divinized hero.[104] Horbury argues that the early Christian devotion to Jesus "bore a close resemblance to contemporary gentile cults of heroes, sovereign deities and divinities."[105] After exploring some hymns and acclamations to Christ represented in the New Testament and in the writings of some Early Church Fathers, Horbury argues that the "praises and homage offered to Jesus ... seem to take place naturally in the series of Jewish royal and messianic praises...."[106] The main point of Horbury's contention is

101. Ibid., 97.
102. Ibid.
103. Ibid.
104. Horbury, *Jewish Messianism and the Cult of Christ*.
105. Ibid., 3.
106. Ibid., 140.

that the worship of Jesus was not novel because the worship of heroes was already part of Jewish cultic culture. Larry Hurtado concedes that the "earliest Christian reverence for Jesus seems to have drawn upon pre-Christian Jewish tradition," but insists that Horbury fails to note the differences between the Jewish people's reverence for heroes, king, martyrs and Christians' devotion to Jesus. He writes,

> Horbury seems to me to blur unhelpfully the very real differences between ancient Jewish reverence for martyrs, messiahs, or other figures and the distinctive pattern of devotion to Jesus in early Christian sources, and he fails in attempting to offer a historical explanation for the worship of Jesus. The fact is that we simply have no evidence that any figure, whether human or angelic, ever featured in the corporate and public devotional practice of Jewish circles in any way really comparable to the programmatic role of Jesus in early Christian circles.[107]

For Hurtado, the early Christian devotion to Jesus is rooted strongly in some religious or revelatory experiences.[108] He acknowledges that this devotion predicates on a "theological inference" but maintains that this theological conviction stems from the revelatory experiences of some individuals who have "encountered the risen and glorified Christ."[109]

I will not examine in detail the conversation between Horbury and Hurtado in this book. Their main objective is historical and not a theological interpretation of the Christ-Event. The concern here is to articulate a potential christological *mis*understanding of the person of Jesus Christ in African Christianity that might arise from a culture that divinizes heroes, kings, or ancestors. To construe Jesus as an apotheosized hero or ancestor, like Sango, is a misunderstanding of Jesus's understanding of himself and his apostles' perception of him as represented in the New Testament. Although there seems to be a similarity between the orthodox version of Sango ascension and the Christian understanding of the ascension of Jesus to heaven, there is a radical difference between the divinization of Sango and the Christian conception of Jesus's divinity. Thomas Morris notes that the early followers of Jesus believed that "creaturely categories" were inadequate for conceptualizing him because of the extraordinary events surrounding his life

107. Hurtado, *How on Earth Did Jesus Become a God?*, 21–22.

108. Ibid., 192.

109. Ibid.

and ministry.[110] For Jesus, as well as his early followers, the Christ-Event is a divine act of revealing or a radical reconstruction of how people previously perceived divinity and humanity.

QUASI-DOCETISM

The name Docetism derives from the Greek verb *dokeo*, meaning "to seem or appear."[111] Docetism is a form of high Christology that elevates Jesus so high that it is at the point of eclipsing his real humanity. Central to this Christology is an attempt to explain how a previously divine person can actually become a real human person.[112] This type of Christology existed in the second-century Gnosticism. "In the Gnostic Christology," as Pannenberg argues, "the divine Revealer was connected only temporarily with a human body and left it again before Jesus' death."[113] A Christology is docetic if it construes Jesus as a divine being who merely seemed or appeared to be a human being.[114] The key problem with Docetism is that it destroys the union of divinity and humanity in Jesus Christ. If the humanity of Jesus merely functioned as a garment housing a divine being, then it followed that the human experiences of Jesus, including his sufferings on a cross, were not real.[115]

The cult of masquerade in Nigeria teaches what can be described as quasi-docetic ideology: an ideology that is grounded in the assumption that a spiritual being can appear in a seemingly human form when it visits the human world to bring messages from the ancestors or from the gods. The Igbo people of south-eastern Nigeria designate this spirit-human messenger as *mmanwu* or *muo*, literally spirit or conventionally "the spirits of the ancestor" or the "spirit of the dead." The Yoruba people of western Nigeria have a similar understanding in the *Egungun* cult. They believe that *Egungun* are the spirits of the ancestors.[116] *Muo* and *Egungun* appear in the physical world concealed most times in scary

110. Morris, *Our Idea of God*, 159.

111. J. Kelly, *Early Christian Doctrines*, 141.

112. Greene, *Christology in Cultural Perspective*, 17.

113. Pannenberg, *Jesus—God and Man*, 125.

114. McGrath, *Christian Theology: An Introduction*, 356.

115. Ibid.

116. Abimbola, "Place of African Traditional Religion in Contemporary Africa," 51–58.

costumes and masks. This is perhaps the reason many Nigerians generally refer to such spirit messengers as masquerades. Those who are initiated into the cult, however, know that the person inside the costume is an ordinary human being, although he may be highly skilled in magical practices. But some who are not initiated into the cult continue to dread masquerades, thinking that they are spirit beings that appear in seemingly human bodies. This is because the masquerades can speak human languages and eat human food. Undoubtedly, the cult of masquerade is disappearing from the cultures of Nigeria. But many people (both the initiated and uninitiated) continue to dread and honor masquerades to the extent that it is still considered to be an abomination to unmask them. In fact, it is also considered a taboo to reveal the identity or mention the name of the person in the costume. And in some societies it is an abomination for a woman to see a masquerade. If this happens, the head of the cult may require an enormous amount of money and livestock from anyone who reveals the identity of the person inside the costume in order to appease the spirit of the ancestor that is believed to have appeared in a human form.

In many Nigerian societies, masquerades appear during great festivals, such as the New Yam festivals, Christmas, New Year, Easter and so on.[117] Occasionally, they appear in times of great turmoil, during which they visit several homes and deliver messages they claim to have received either from the ancestors or from the gods. Sometimes they deliver messages of comfort and pronounce blessings upon the people they visit. Other times they warn the clan of an impending catastrophe. People in return show their reverence and appreciation to them by pouring libations or presenting them with beautiful gifts. Some people may ask the masquerades to take some messages back to their gods or their ancestors. Thus, masquerades function primarily as divine messengers. They also sometimes exhibit great magical powers to convince people that they are sent by the gods or ancestors.

As a revealer of divinity, Jesus functions as a bearer of a divine message. He reveals to humanity the love, wrath, blessing, comfort and the purpose of God for his creation. The life and ministry of Jesus Christ are intended to provide us with a sufficient knowledge of God and his redemptive purpose for the creation. A Nigerian traditionalist

---

117. The reasons masquerades appear during Christmas and Easter celebrations are primarily to collect gifts and money from admirers.

may, therefore, construe Jesus in the same way he or she construes masquerades. This is because Jesus and masquerades at some levels seem to have similar functions: they are bearers of divine or spiritual messages. However, to construe Jesus as *muo* or a masquerade is a total misunderstanding of the person and function of Jesus. Two arguments can be presented to explicate this claim. Firstly, an *muo* is an ordinary human being who wears a mask and costume, who claims that the spirit of an ancestor has taken possession of him. Many people today no longer see masquerades as the spirit beings or the spirits of ancestors who appear in seemingly human forms as traditionally construed, but rather as ordinary human beings in (sometimes scary) costumes. The appearance of a young people masquerade cult in many Nigerian societies has contributed to the diminishing of the traditional understanding of some masquerades as spirit beings. As William Rea observes,

> The most often stated view of egungun is that they are beings from heaven. There are differences in attitude to this. Clearly young men regard masquerades as metaphysically more powerful than others, but generally, even if there was full belief that there was no man in the mask, it no longer applies to young men's masquerading.[118]

Unlike the masquerades who are merely men but who purport to be spirit beings or the spirits of ancestors, Jesus embodies both divinity and humanity.

Secondly, there is a difference between the functions of Jesus and the functions of masquerades. One of the helpful ways of examining this difference is to explore the relationship between women and the masquerade cult. Apart from the fact that in many Igbo societies, women cannot be masquerades, it is also striking to note that women are not even allowed to see some masquerades. The experience of Bess Read when she visited Nigeria to book *Mmanwu* festival in Enugu in 1993 highlights the gulf between women and the masquerade cult. As a researcher, Read anticipated that she would have a closer view of the masquerades. But her hope was crushed when Chief Maduakor, one of the organizers of the festival, told her that she could not see the masquerades because she was a woman. This is how she narrates her experience.

118. Rea, "Rationalizing Culture," 98–117.

> ... when Chief Maduakor, one of the organizers arrived, he in-
> formed me that the Mmanwu Festival Committee would allow
> me to book the festival, even though I was a woman and should
> have nothing to do with masquerades, but there was a condition:
> the all-male committee has also decided that only my husband
> would be allowed on the stadium floor to take pictures of the
> maskers. Despite my status as a researcher, as a woman I would
> have to watch the festival from a cool distance in the stands—
> and no arguments on this point was permitted. Surprised and
> dismayed, I handed my cameras to Benjamin [her husband] and
> was escorted to a shaded seat in the VIP section.[119]

Some feminist theologians have pointed out the christological problems with some andocentric cultures and traditions.[120] Jesus the Christ
stands opposed to the masquerades that do not associate with women.
Through his actions and preaching, Jesus critiqued some Jewish derogatory attitudes toward women, even women who were considered to be
terribly sinful.[121] Thus, unlike the masquerades that have no serious
meeting point with women, Jesus breaks down the barrier that sepa-
rates the world of men and the world of women.

To conclude this chapter, the Revealer Christology model that is
developed in this book should not be associated with quasi-docetism
or apotheosis. Both represent some *potential problems* for a contextual
African Christology because they can generate a total distortion of the
meaning, identity and significance of Jesus Christ. Central to the concept of Jesus as a revealer of divinity and humanity is the claim that he
functions as a figure through whom the Christians can have access to
a true knowledge and relationship with God and their fellow human
beings.

The purpose of this chapter, as already stated, is to construct a
background on which to build the Revealer Christology model that
will befit African contexts. So far, I have explored the major issues that
inform this model. In the following chapters, I will proceed to examine
the christological contents of the proposition that the Christ-Event interprets and mediates divinity and humanity for the purpose of enacting, sustaining, judging and rebuilding the relationship between God
and humanity, and between human beings and the spirit being that
many African Christians construe as malevolent.

119. Read, "Playing with Prohibitions," 71.

120. See chapter two for the examination of some Feminist Christologies.

121. John 4.

5

Revealing Divinity

The Significance of Jesus for God-talk in African Christianity

MANY CONTEXTUAL CHRISTOLOGIES OF AFRICAN CHRISTIANITY HAVE remained largely a one-sided process. The theologians who construct these Christologies have continued to construe a contextual Christology as an undertaking that is geared towards an explication of the Christ-Event in light of the indigenous understandings of the world and also the experiences of Africans. They see their task as primarily to present Jesus Christ in the ways that have direct bearing on the religious, cultural and socio-economic conditions of Africans. The key question they are seeking to answer is: what would Jesus look like when he is explained in the categories that synchronize with the worldviews and experiences of African peoples?[1] But the problem with doing contextual Christology in this one-sided way is that an adequate contextual Christology requires a double process that is strongly rooted in a mutual interaction between Jesus Christ and a given community. Therefore, a contextual Christology should not be a constructive process that seeks only to interpret the Christ-Event in the ways that synchronize with the worldviews and experiences of Africans. It should also be a constructive process of reinterpreting the indigenous religious beliefs and experiences Africans in the ways that synchronize with the meaning and purpose of the Christ-Event. In this sense, then, a contextual theologian needs to recognize that it is inadequate and misleading to attempt to answer the question "what would Jesus look like when he is expressed in the categories that befit their contexts?" in isolation from the question "what would the worldviews and experiences of the people look like

---

1. See the introduction and chapter two.

when they are examined in light of the Christ-Event?" The task of the theologian, therefore, includes both the explication of the Christ-Event in light of the contexts of the people and also, more importantly, the examination of their understandings of the world, and also their contexts in light of the Christ-Event. The Revealer Christology model that is developed in this book explores and engages with these two integrally and indissolubly united aspects of contextual Christology.

The overarching thesis of this book is the contention that the meaning and significance of the identity and work of Jesus the Christ is embedded in his revealing (that is, communicating, mediating and interpreting) of divinity and humanity or the spiritual world and the human world. In this chapter, I will examine the content of an aspect of this christological assertion; namely, the contention that Jesus is a revealer of divinity. The Revealer Christology model that I develop in this book does not operate from the assumption of a dichotomy between the spiritual world and the human world. Conversely, I build the model on the interrelatedness of the spiritual and the human worlds as they are construed in the indigenous traditions of Africa.

I use the word divinity in this book in a way that includes spirit beings, such as ancestors, angelic beings, Satan, evil forces or spirits, and God. There are two principal reasons for this broad definition of divinity. Firstly, any Christology that limits the Christ-Event to Jesus' interaction with God and excludes his relationship with other spiritual beings is inadequate. Such Christology overlooks some important aspects of the life of Jesus Christ. He interacted not only with God but also with other spirit beings. During his life on the earth, the ministry of Jesus extended to and was shaped by his views of God, angels, demons and Satan. Secondly, an adequate Christology needs to interpret the Christ-Event in the way that presents Jesus as the individual who can enable Christians to re-think their life's ultimate questions. These questions include: how does the spiritual world correlate to the human world? How can human beings enjoy a relationship with God? Thus, the Christology that is suitable to the African situations should be broad enough to allow Jesus to communicate, interpret and critique the relationship between humanity and God and humanity and the spirit world. I will examine God-talk in contemporary African Christianity, focusing on the indigenous ideas of the Supreme Being and his relationship with the God of Jesus Christ. I will also explicate the claim that Jesus is a revealer of God, focusing on the ways the Christ-Event provides a window upon God's manifestations in human history.

Ideas of God in African Christianity and Indigenous Religions

Where does one go to in order to gain access into the existing ideas of God in the indigenous religions of Africa? One way to pursue this difficult task is to examine the names the African peoples ascribe to God. The reason for the use of this approach is primarily because naming is a powerful tool people employ to describe the nature, character and actions of things, human beings and spiritual beings.[2] Many theologians, of course, recognize the limitation of theological languages, and the limitations of such languages in describing the Supreme Being or God. Cultures and worldviews also complicate further the limitations of theological languages. For example, when a theologian speaks of God as *he* and not as *she*, the theologian unveils immediately his or her cultural background, stylistic preference, and theological presuppositions and prejudices. In some Western theological circles, theological language has continued to pose great difficulties for theologians. Langdon Gilkey has observed that there are myriads of concepts and categories many Western Christian theologians employ when speaking about God. Broadly, these categories can be subsumed under personal—in the historical and ontic senses; and impersonal—in the ontological and metaphysical senses. Gilkey contends that there are compelling reasons to believe that these two categories have strong roots in Christian religion.[3] For many African theologians, human beings can only speak about God in an analogical sense. As the ultimate source of the world, human language cannot describe exhaustively the being and activities of God. All theological languages are human in nature, and not divine, and as such are subject to the limitation of human cognitive categories and capacities.

---

2. Idowu, "God," 24.

3. Gilkey, "God," 76–77.

Naming God: Is the Christian God the Supreme Being of African Indigenous Religions?

In the late eighteenth century, Olaudah Equiano, a Nigerian who was sold to slave traders sometime around 1756,[4] wrote about the culture and religion of the Igbo people of eastern Nigeria: "As to religion, the natives believe that there is one Creator of all things, and that he lives in the sun, and is girded round with a belt, that he may never eat or drink; but, according to some, he smokes a pipe, which is our own favorite luxury."[5]

Although Equiano did not give an extensive description of the nature and character of this being the people of Igboland believe to be the "Creator of all things," he nevertheless provided a gateway into the indigenous theology of Igbo people. Today, many Nigerian theologians and historians of religions agree that the idea of a Supreme Being permeates the religious mindset of the people. In theological discourse, the problematic issue is not whether African peoples have a concept of God. The debate rather revolves around two concurrent issues. The first is the origins of this highly exalted Spiritual Being. Some scholars have argued that the idea of a Supreme Being is foreign to the indigenous religious thought of Africa. Others have rejected this assumption and have argued that the idea of the Supreme existed in Africa before the advent of Christianity and Islam. The second debate centers on the identity of the Supreme Being, and how this being compares to the Christian God. While some argue that the Supreme Being is identical with the God of Jesus (the Christian God) others insist that the Christian God is different from the Supreme God of the indigenous religious thought. These dual issues are vital to a contextual Christology and merit a close examination.

4. Walvin, *An African's Life: The Life and Times of Olaudah Equiano, 1745–1797*, 3. Walvin has noted that Olaudah only adopted the "name Equiano in the last decade of his life, when he had become a public and published figure." Before he adopted the name Equiano, Olaudah was known as Gustavus Vassa.

5. Equiano, *Interesting Narrative and Other Writings*, 40.

THE ORIGINS OF THE SUPREME-BEING TALK IN THE INDIGENOUS RELIGIONS

According to J. Omosade Awolalu, the "existence of God is taken for granted" in Africa. This is so because the idea of God has been part of the indigenous worldviews of African peoples long before they came in contact with Islam or Christianity.[6] For him, it is "no exaggeration to say that atheism or agnosticism is foreign to an indigenous Africa."[7] Consequently, he unleashed his frustration against and disagreement with "foreign researchers into African Religion who claimed that Africans did not know God before the advent of Islam or those who asserted that Africans could not comprehend God because they were not philosophical enough to be able to do so."[8]

But it is not only non-Africans that have argued in support of the foreignness of a Supreme Being in the indigenous African thought. In *The Supreme Being as Stranger in Igbo Religious Thought*, Donatus Ibe Nwoga, a Nigerian, argued that the Europeans introduced the concept of the Supreme Being to the Igbo people of eastern Nigeria.[9] For Nwoga, some scholars have come to accept, albeit wrongly so, "that the more civilized thing to have is the Supreme Being" in the religious and theo-logical discourses of African indigenous worldviews.[10] He advances two major arguments to buttress his claim that the idea of a Supreme Being has not always been part of the Nigerian indigenous religious thought.

Nowga's first argument is that the idea of a Supreme Being arises from a monotheistic view of the world, which for him, is strange to the indigenous worldviews of the Igbo people.[11] According to him, the concept of a Supreme Being emerges from the answer of the "Judeo-Christian-Islamic religious tradition" to the "question of order and meaning" of life.[12] He contends that the idea of a Supreme Being infil-trated into the religious thinking of Nigerians after they encountered the Western missionaries. Also, he argues that the idea of a Supreme

6. Awolalu, "God: The Contemporary Discussion," xix.

7. Ibid.

8. Ibid.

9. Nwoga, *Supreme Being as Stranger in Igbo Religious Thought*.

10. Ibid., 7.

11. Ibid., 8.

12. Ibid., 9.

Being has continued to exist in the worldview of Nigerians because of the works of some theologians who have shared the monotheistic view of God.[13] For him, the indigenous religious theology or understating of the spirit world is polytheistic and not monotheistic. This is evident, according to him, in the readiness of many Nigerian people to communicate with and worship many gods.

> It is obvious however that the contemporary Igbo, while accepting the omnipotence and omnipresence, etc., of *Chukwu*, is still easily prone to seek other causes and other solutions for problems in his life. He is quite satisfied to give God his due at mass and service on Sunday and go home and give *Amadioha* his due. Is this to be explained as impatience and a return to trusted habits from the past, or as a continuation of a structure of pluralistic conceptualization of causality, a validation under pressure of the tradition of polytheism in Igbo religious thought? In other words, does the present accreditation by scholars of Supremacy to Chukwu accord with the tradition of thought and practice among the Igbo?[14]

Nwoga's response to his foregoing questions is that the Igbo people are prone to seek other gods because of the polytheistic nature of their indigenous religions.

The fact that many Nigerians are comfortable with multiple religious allegiances, or readily express their allegiances to the Supreme Being and to other gods is hardly a convincing argument against the claim that the idea of a Supreme Being has always been part of the structure of the indigenous religious worldview. Nowga's argument seems to operate with the following logic: the people whose indigenous religious worldview is monotheistic are not prone to seek other gods or sources of solution. Since the Igbo people are prone to seek other gods, it follows that their indigenous worldview is polytheistic and not monotheistic. This assumption is unwarranted. Even in the monotheistic religions, which Nwoga argues are responsible for the existence of the idea of a Supreme Being, some adherents of these religions sometimes consult other gods. For example, many Jews at different times abandoned Yahweh to worship other gods.[15] Whilst we can concede

---

13. Ibid., 31.
14. Ibid., 8.
15. Exodus 32.

that some Nigerians' belief in the existence of many gods is a possible legitimate explanation for some people's multiple religious allegiances, it can be argued that the existence of such multiple allegiances does not necessarily warrant the claim that the idea of a Supreme Being is foreign to the indigenous religions.

It is also problematic to describe the indigenous religions of Nigeria as polytheistic. If by polytheism Nwoga means the belief in the existence of independent gods, it can hardly be an adequate description of the indigenous understandings of the Supreme Being and the lesser gods who are believed to be the creatures and the messengers of the Supreme. For example, Igbo people sometimes call *Anyanwu* (sun) the son of God or the Supreme Being.[16] Bolaji Idowu and Osadolor Imasogie have cautioned against ascribing polytheism to the indigenous religions on the basis that African peoples simultaneously believe in a Supreme Being and other lesser gods.[17] Idowu describes this religious condition as "diffused monotheism" and "implicit monotheism." He writes,

> I modify this "monotheism" by the adjective "diffused," because here we have a monotheism in which there exist other powers which derive from Deity such being and authority that they can be treated, for practical purposes, almost as ends in themselves. The descriptive phrase "implicit monotheism" will serve as well as "diffused monotheism."[18]

Imasogie explores the hierarchical structure of the traditional societies, arguing that it is precisely the idea of hierarchy that underlies the indigenous concept of the pantheon of divinities.[19] On the basis of this hierarchy, Imasogie describes the simultaneous beliefs in the Supreme Being and other gods as "bureaucratic monotheism."

> In order to retain monotheism and yet preserve its peculiar expression in the Nigerian traditional religion, this writer would suggest the phrase "bureaucratic monotheism." This has the advantage of pointing to the socio-political conditions which

16. Ezeanya, "God, Spirits and the Spirit World, with Special Reference to the Igbo-Speaking People of Southern Nigeria," 37.

17. Geoffrey Parrinder is among those who have described African beliefs in the Supreme Being and other lesser divinities as polytheistic. See Parrinder, "Theistic Beliefs of the Yoruba and the Ewe Peoples of West Africa," 236–37.

18. Idowu, *African Traditional Religion*, 135–36.

19. Imasogie, *African Traditional Religion*, 23.

greatly influence the Nigerian religious expression of intrinsic monotheism which undergirds its religious experience.[20]

Whether or not polytheism and a modified version of monotheism describe adequately Nigerians' belief in the existence of gods remains problematic. But what is clear is that the indigenous religions provide for a concurrent belief in a Supreme Being and other gods. These gods, according to the indigenous worldview, own their existence to the Supreme Being.

When the peoples of Africa encountered Christian and Islamic religions that propagated the idea of an Almighty and Supreme Being who is the Creator of the world, they undoubtedly learned and borrowed some ideas from these religions.[21] However, the influence of Christianity and Islam on the indigenous idea of the Supreme Being should not be assumed, as Nwoga has done, to be an indication that the people did not have the idea of a Supreme God as part of their indigenous religious mindset. The majority of theologians and historians of religion have continued to argue, and rightly so, that the idea of the Supreme Being has always been an integral part of the indigenous religions. As Francis Anyika contends:

> It was not the Christian missionaries that brought the knowledge of the Supreme God to the Igbo of Nigeria. It was not the Europeans who engaged in secular business that brought it either. . . . The knowledge of the Supreme Being has from time immemorial been an integral part of Igbo traditional religious belief systems.[22]

The second argument that Nwoga advances in support of his claim that the idea of a Supreme Being is foreign to the indigenous understandings of the world Nigeria revolve around his view of *chi* which Nwoga claims *is* the Igbo god. He argues,

> it is my thesis that the Igbo person's experience and consciousness of transcendent power operating in his personal affairs gave rise to and is subsumed in the concept of *chi*. Around this concept of *chi* he consolidated his expectations of life and fortune. It is this *chi* that is the god of the Igbo person. Each person

20. Ibid., 25.

21. McVeigh, *God in Africa*, 36–47.

22. Anyika, "Supreme God in Igbo Traditional Religious Thought and Worship," 5–20.

has his god though it requires a certain level of maturity before a person can set up a shrine to the god. In special circumstances, however, the shrine may be set up earlier. It is to this god that each head of the family is a priest, taking care of himself and his family by appeals to his *chi* and by sacrifices to the same *chi* when the need arises. It is at the altar of this *chi* that each person reinvigorates his existence and life and fortune.[23]

For Nwoga, then, if there is any idea of a god in the indigenous Igbo worldview, it is the personalized *chi*. He argues that the expression "*Chukwu* (Big God)" is a combination of *chi* (god) and *ukwu* (big). According to him, this was the big God of the people of Aro of eastern Nigeria.

> When, however, the Aro went into the rest of Igboland to trade in slaves, they took with them, both for protection and as an additional business, the reputation of their *Chi-Ukwu* (Big Chi) thereby elevating *Ibini Ukpabi* to the status of the last arbiter, the god beyond whom there could be no surer answer to problems.[24]

He fails to properly account for the complexity of the word *chi* in Igbo religious and cultural thought. *Chi* has several meanings including "daylight," "day," "god," "spirit," "guardian spirit," and the "essence of a divine being."[25] *Chi* also could be a shortened form of *Chukwu* (Big God) and *Chineke* (God the Creator). Bartholomew Abanuka argues that the scholars who associate *chi* with the Supreme Being "confuse reality or being (being as such) with the innermost nature or essence of particular things."[26] For him, *chi* technically means real in the sense that "every particular thing can be said to be real."[27] Chi is that which can be predicated of all individual or particular things without exception. It is a general characteristic of all particular things. In this regard, chi has the same meaning as reality or being (being as such).[28]

Abanuka seems to overstretch the word *chi* beyond the level an ordinary Igbo can possibly recognize it. The problem with the philosophi-

23. Nwoga, *Supreme God as Stranger in Igbo Religious Thought*, 33.
24. Ibid., 36.
25. Abanuka, *Philosophy and the Igbo World* , 2.
26. Ibid., 3.
27. Ibid.
28. Ibid.

cal meaning he ascribes to *chi* is that it can hardly fit into the normal usage of the word, and it is doubtful if this philosophical conception is part of the original idea of *chi* in the indigenous Igbo worldview. The overarching idea of *chi,* as an existent being, and when it is not a shortened form of *Chukwu* or *Chineke*, refers to a personal god or more appropriately a "personal guardian spirit." However, for the Igbo, as Emefie Ikenga Metuh has rightly noted, it is *Chukwu* (the Supreme, Big or High God) that gives *chi* to every person. He writes: "At the moment of his conception, God assigns to each person a 'Chi,' an emanation of himself, which thereafter acts as a guardian angel of the person to whom it is assigned."[29]

Like Chukwu, Olodumare, created the universe, human beings and spirit beings. As Idowu observes,

> Someone who has made a careful book of all the material which our sources afford will have no hesitation in asserting that Olodumare is the origin and ground of all that is. That is the fact which impresses itself upon us with the force of something incontrovertible. From all the evidence which we gather from the traditions, the Yoruba have never, strictly speaking, really thought further back than Olodumare.[30]

Byang Kato, although a critic of natural revelation, nonetheless concedes the idea of a Supreme Being exists in the indigenous religion of the people of Jaba of northern Nigeria.[31] It is a mistake to see the Supreme Being as a foreign concept which Christianity and/or Islam introduced to the indigenous religions. The Supreme Being has always been part of the religious beliefs in the indigenous religions.

The other theological tension concerns the relationship between the Supreme God of the indigenous religions and the Christian idea of God. It is to this theological debate that I will now turn.

29. Ikenga-Metuh, *African Religions in Western Conceptual Scheme*, 27.

30. Idowu, *Olodumare*, 18.

31. Kato, *Theological Pitfalls in Africa*, 38.

THE SUPREME BEING OF THE INDIGENOUS RELIGIONS AND THE CHRISTIAN GOD

The debate on whether or not the God of Christianity is the same God of some other world religions is not only restricted to African theological discourses. In some Western societies too, such discussions have exerted heavy influence on the debate on Christian relation to other religions. For example, John Hick likens a rediscovering of the centrality of God in the religious pluralism debate to the Copernican revolution.[32] The question I seek to explore here is: "is the God of Christianity the same as the Supreme Being of the African Indigenous Religions?" This question is unduly broad and can be misleading. This is partly because the nature and the content of the comparison can vary from one theologian to another. What does the word same mean in this context? Does it mean exact correspondence? Or does it mean a seeming correspondence? In the latter sense, the task of the theologian will be to find some similarities between the indigenous ideas of God (Supreme Being) and the Christian views of God. Some theologians have engaged in this task.[33] In the former sense, the theologian has the burden to demonstrate whether or not the indigenous ideas of the Supreme Being adequately represent what Christianity teaches about God. But the problem with this task is that many Christian communities hardly agree on the same set of propositions or beliefs about God. And even when they have such common propositions or beliefs they have interpreted them differently and sometimes contradictorily.[34]

The idea of God, so long as God stands as the creator of the world and as its providential ruler, exists in Christianity and the African Indigenous Religions. Therefore, we are compelled to grant that the God of Christianity is the God of the indigenous religions, however wrongly and inadequately the traditionalists have construed him. Undoubtedly, Christianity and Islam have in some ways influenced the indigenous ideas of God. But a close examination reveals that the indigenous religions share some of the Christian views of God. According to the indig-

32. Hick, *God and the Universe of Faiths: Essays in the Philosophy of Religion.*

33. See Dairo, "God and Inculturation Theology in Africa," 227–36; Enuwosa, "Exploring the Nature of God in the New Testament for Meaningful Development in Nigeria," 212–26.

34. A good summary of some different understandings of God is Karkkainen, *Doctrine of God.*

enous religions, the world is a direct consequence of God's creative act. The world is believed to be open-ended, allowing the lesser beings of the spiritual world and the Supreme Being to interfere and inform the lives of humans, animals, and all other things that exist in the human world. In some ways, as we will see later in this chapter, Christianity also teaches divine providence.

But the relationship between the Christian God and the Supreme God of the indigenous religions or other religions cannot be restricted to the notions of correspondence or sameness. This is because limiting the discourses of God (in the context of religious pluralism) only to an ontological resemblance or sameness can lead to an abstract metaphysical construction that obstructs the theologian from exploring the unique understandings the Christ-Event provides to the identity, acts, and character of God. The indigenous views of God and African Christians' views of God must be subjected to a re-evaluation in the light of the Christ-Event.

Viewed from a christological perspective, the Christ-Event provides the framework for engaging the mystery of God. This mystery interestingly permeates the thinking of Christians and adherents of the indigenous religions. For them, God is a mysterious being whose origin and identity partly escape human beings. As Abanuka comments:

> One of the enduring difficulties in the discussions about God is that he is not to be conceived like other particular things, let us say a tree or a mountain, which stands out there. It is normal for one to say that he has seen or touched a certain tree or mountain. One could also say that he has seen God or touched a certain man. However, when one says that he has seen God or touched him, his hearers will, of course, raise their eyebrows—a sign that they will not understand the statement, "I have touched God," in the sense in which one usually understands the statement, "I have touched a tree." Our concepts of material or sensible things differ from our ideas of immaterial or non-sensible beings, particularly God.[35]

He attempts to unpack the complexity that informs the images of God in the indigenous religions. This complexity equally shrouds the African Christians' understandings of God. As I have argued throughout this book, the indigenous views of the world have a great influence

---

35. Abanuka, *Philosophy and the Igbo World*, 1.

on Christians' understandings of God more than Jesus's view of God. This is understandable since the indigenous cultures, religions, and tradition are part of the matrix from which many Christians develop their worldview. In chapter three, we saw that the majority of Christians desert Jesus Christ to find solutions to their problems when he is too slow, at least in their thinking, to solve their problems. I examined some of the causes of this desertion. Here it is important to highlight one of the possible causes of this phenomenon which arises from an indigenous religious thought. Nwoga correctly argues that the relationship between the majority of Igbo people and their gods is contractual.[36] The consequence of this type of relationship is that the majority of the Igbo people are willing to serve their gods on the condition the gods function and act when the people want them to do so. Many people abandon the gods that fail to respond to their needs, and immediately replace them with other gods. This understanding of the human-divine relationship undoubtedly has permeated the knowledge of God in African Christianity.

God-talk is notoriously difficult. The Christ-Event does not provide us with an easy escape out of this theological difficulty. In fact, if a theologian approaches the Christ-Event with the intent to exhaustively grasp God, the Christology of the theologian is doomed to failure. This is because it is doubtful if the intent of Jesus Christ is to provide people with an exhaustive knowledge of God. But if such is not the intent of Jesus, what exactly is the purpose of the Christ-Event?

The Christ-Event and God-Talk: Understanding the Relationship between Jesus Christ and God

Every christological construction that seeks to understand the person and work of Jesus Christ ought to answer the question: what is the meaning and purpose of the Christ-Event? This is because we can only know and appropriate in our conditions the person and work of Jesus Christ by reconstructing and articulating the meaning and significance of the Christ-Event. Jesus Christ frequently spoke about his person and activities in light of his mission or what the Father has sent him to do.[37]

---

36. Nwoga, *Supreme God as Stranger in Igbo Religious Thought*, 30.

37. John 17:3–5.

A crucial question here is what is the task of Christology? In chapters two and three, I explored some of the major Christologies that exist in African Christianity. We saw that the Neo-missionary Christology construes the task of contextual Christology as delineating the superiority of Jesus Christ over some of the Christologies of Western missionaries, and also over African indigenous religions and cultures. The culture-oriented theologians see the task of Christology as rediscovering the values of the indigenous religions and cultures and using them as resources for interpreting the Christ-Event. The liberation-oriented theologians and some of the grassroots Christologies emerging from the Nigerian Christian laity tend to move away from an abstract construction of the personhood of Jesus Christ. Many Christians seek for the practical implication of what Jesus Christ has done, and the responsibility of the Christian communities to participate in and to extend his work in the world. This understanding of the task of Christology is gaining prominence among some Western contextual theologians. To cite one example, Graham Ward contends that Christology should be driven by the question "where is the Christ?" and not by the question "who is the Christ?" or "what is the Christ?" For him,

> The Christological enquiry . . . does not begin with the identity of the Christ, what in dogmatics is the nature as distinct from the work of Christ; it begins with an analysis of the operations whereby Christ is made known to us. And in being made known we participate in him.[38]

The task of Christology should be intrinsically connected to the meaning and purpose of the Christ-Event. Daniel Migliore observes: "While the traditional distinction of person and work is used in Christology for convenience, it can be seriously misleading. We cannot speak meaningfully of anyone's identity, and certainly not of Jesus's identity, apart from that person's life act."[39] The interpretation and explication of the meaning and purpose of the Christ-Event is precisely the task of Christology. The person and work of Jesus Christ provide a window upon the meaning and significance of the Christ-Event for humanity and divinity. Since we do not have a direct access into the mind of Jesus Christ, we are left with the option of an indirect access

---

38. Ward, *Christ and Culture*, 1.

39. Migliore, *Faith Seeking Understanding*, 168.

through a careful interpretation of his words and actions. The task of Christology, therefore, is to discover the meanings and significances of the actions, words, and the entire lifestyle of Jesus Christ both for our contexts and beyond our contexts. The failure to approach the meaning and the purpose of the Christ-Event from a holistic perspective is the principal reason many of the existing Christologies in contemporary African Christianity have created a problematic ditch between the work and person of Jesus Christ. Some theologians have attempted to build a bridge over this ditch by constructing some christological models which primarily reflect what they think of Jesus Christ and what they want him to do for their communities, but failing to create enough space for the Christ-Event itself to inform and critique their Christologies.[40] In what follows, I will examine the christological content of the claim that Jesus Christ is a revealer of God.

What then should be the task of an African contextual Christology? I argue that the task of the Christology involves two related activities. First, the Christology should explicate the nature and purpose of the Christ-Event in the manner that allows Jesus Christ to interact with the histories and experiences of the peoples of Africa, and in the manner that allows him to function as the medium through which they can experience a *unique* knowledge of and relationship with God, other spiritual beings and their fellow human beings.[41] Second, the Christology should also inquire into and examine the ways the indigenous religions and contemporary experiences of African peoples provide a widow upon the task of interpreting and appropriating the Christ-Event in the twenty-first century. Understood in this way, rather than becoming an obstruction, an adequate African Christology must be able to interpret the Christ-Event in a manner that allows Jesus to effectively engage with and judge the changing spiritual, religious, socio-economic, and cultural exigencies of African peoples. It must also examine how Africans can embody the context of Jesus's liberating presence.

Until now, I have only made a broad christological assertion-that Jesus reveals divinity—but have not articulated the content of this christological statement. What does it mean, in the Revealer Christology model as developed in this book, to say that Jesus Christ reveals divin-

40. See chapter two.

41. As the God Incarnate, Jesus Christ in an unprecedented way mediates between God and humanity.

ity? Or since this chapter concentrates primarily on God, what does it mean to say that Jesus is a revealer of God? The remainder of this chapter will be an explication of this christological query. Suffice to state here that in the Revealer Christology model I am proposing, the contention that Jesus reveals God entails that the Christ-Event communicates and interprets in an unprecedented way the identity (characteristics, purpose, activities) of God and *judges* and *reinterprets* human beings' previous knowledge of the identity of God. This understanding of Jesus Christ arises from the contention that the Christ-Event is the decisive act of God in history to reveal himself. This revelation of God's self is complete and remains the parameters and the standard for judging any other manifestations of God in history.

Jesus the Revealer of God's Mysteriousness and Relationality

Who is the God who has revealed himself in the Christ-Event? If this question is to become relevant to the African contexts, we must approach it both from the christological parameter which the councils of Nicaea and Chalcedon have created, and the context of life of Africans.[42] A move in this direction is Uchenna Eze's Ancestor Christology.[43] When we approach the question who is the God Jesus reveals? from the perspective of the Christ-Event, we are compelled to contend that God has a divine face and a human face. Or to put it in another way, God is both divine and human. The paradox of the God-man suggests that Jesus the Christ possesses consubstantiality with human beings and consubstantiality with God: Jesus the Christ is true God and true man.[44] This christological tension is what underlies the Nicene and Chalcedonian christological formulations and confessions. An African *Christian Christology* ought to engage with the classical confession of Jesus Christ as truly human and truly God. Whist a theologian needs not employ the highly sophisticated language of Chalcedon or Nicaea, he or she will need to interact with the classical christological claim that Jesus is both consubstantial with humanity and divinity. Ezeh recognizes this when

42. See chapter four.

43. Ezeh, *Jesus Christ the Ancestor*. For a critical examination and critique of Ezeh's ancestor Christology, see chapter two.

44. Grillmeier, *Christ in Christian Tradition: From the Council of Chalcedon (451) to Gregory the Great (590–604)*, 4.

he argues that his ancestor christological model seeks to "maintain that the incarnate state of the Son of God, as 'true God and true man'" demonstrates that Jesus is ancestor par excellence.[45]

The mystery of the divinity and humanity of Jesus Christ denotes that God has not shied away from revealing himself to and initiating a relationship with human beings. God acts and speaks; he is self-revealing. Since God is really *other*,[46] the possibility of undoing his otherness (so that human beings can know and experience him) solely depends on his self-disclosure. To put this in a common theological expression: it is impossible to know God without God unveiling himself. As Rowan Williams contends,

> In spite of everything, we go on saying "God." And since God is not the name of any particular thing available for inspection, it seems that we must as believers assume that we talk about God on the basis of "revelation"—of what has been shown to us by God's will and action.[47]

God controls and chooses "how to communicate with his creation and creatures" and to ensure that the process of such communication is in "accordance with the good pleasure of his will."[48] In Christian thought, Jesus-talk is related to God-talk, and precisely to God's self-disclosure. In this sense, Jesus Christ is the revelation of God in human history or is the human face of God. It is precisely on this ground that he is the revealer of God. It is in and through Jesus Christ that human beings can encounter God's embodied presence, relationality and mysteriousness. And it is in and through Jesus Christ that we can examine and judge our previously held ideas of God's mysteriousness and also his relationship with other spirit beings as well as human beings.

At this point it is necessary to highlight once again what appears to be a christological wishful thinking—an assumption that is devoid of any substantial content when it is closely examined. This is the assumption that Jesus Christ, as the one in whom God has manifested himself, is the easy route to escape the difficulties and mystery of God-talk. God, for the people who think in this way, is too abstract and totally escapes

45. Ezeh, *Jesus Christ the Ancestor*, 252.

46. Evans, *Historical Jesus and the Jesus of Faith*, 180.

47. Williams, *On Christian Theology*, 131.

48. Turaki, *Unique Christ for Salvation*, 218.

the finite human mind as opposed to Jesus who had human properties. This is one of the reasons many Christians perhaps switch to God-talk when they discuss Jesus and vice versa.[49] This switching is also not totally unconnected with the indigenous understanding of the complexity and transcendence of the Supreme Being and the need to approach him through the lesser divinities and the ancestors.

Two major problems with this assumption are noteworthy. First, the Christ-Event does not aim to bring a clearer picture or to explain exhaustively the mystery of God. As Rowan Williams has reminded us:

> The potential strain upon our normal framework of talk about God, the degree of possible ambiguity and conflict, is unique. Jesus is God's "revelation" in a decisive sense not because he makes a dimly apprehended God clear to us, but because he challenges and queries an unusually clear sense of God . . . not because he makes things plainer—on the "veil-lifting" model of revelation—but because he makes things darker.[50]

It follows that the Christ-Event aims to communicate and interpret for human beings God's initiative to involve God's self in a radical relationship with human beings, and also to judge their preconceived knowledge (whether or not they think of such knowledge as dim or clear, sufficient or insufficient) of God. Second, using Christology as an easy escape route from the complexity of God-talk is problematic because it may lead to an underestimation of the mystery of the Christ-Event. Those who assume that the Christ-Event is an easy way out of the mystery of God have forgotten too quickly that insofar as the Christ-Event is the revelation of God's self, it still remains an event that is largely beyond human comprehension. In fact, depending on how one approaches it, Jesus-talk can be more difficult than God-talk. For example, it may be more difficult to articulate how God has localized God's being and presence in Jesus Christ than to construe God simply as the Being who has not localized his presence in a single event, but rather in various events, cultures, and communities.[51] In addition, we can speak of the Christ-Event as consisting in a dual mystery. Since God is a mystery and humanity (as I will argue in chapter seven) is equally a mystery, it follows that the mystery of the Christ-Event sometimes can

49. In some cases, this switching arises from a trinitarian view of God.

50. Williams, *On Christian Theology*, 138.

51. See Idowu, *Olodumare*, 31.

be more difficult to express than the mystery of God, for the mystery of Jesus Christ embodies, coalesces, communicates and interprets the mystery of divinity and humanity. The Christ-Event, for the Apostle Paul, remains a mystery that will continue to perturb all inquirers into the "unreachable riches of Christ."[52]

Some African theologians have attempted to explain the mystery of God in diverse ways. Idowu appeals to the universal revelatory actions of God. For him, these actions include God's self-manifestations in the act of creating or bringing into existence the world and its inhabitants.[53] The major theological difficulty with the appeal to God's manifestations of himself in the act of creating is that it may provide some indications of the handiwork of God but will lack the capacity to lead human beings to a relationship with God. Kato appeals to the Scripture as the ultimate source from which people can know God.[54] The problem with restricting the knowledge of God to the Bible, as Kato and others have done, is that it leads people to conceive the Bible as *God's revelation* rather than as a witness or expression of God's revelation. But some others (theologians and the laity) have continued to seek for a true knowledge of God in the "saving presence of the God-man, Jesus Christ."[55] This latter approach is central to the Revealer Christology model I develop in this book.

How do we understand the claim that Jesus reveals God? This *faith* question attracts another that is more difficult to answer; namely, how is it that Jesus is a revealer of God? Specifically from a Christian position, the answer to this latter question is rooted strongly in faith. In this context, faith means "a commitment to and conversion to what the event of Jesus concretely enacts," to use the language of Rowan Williams.[56] Daniel Migliore also emphasizes the importance of faith in Christological discourse when he contends that the "*knowledge of Jesus Christ is not simply 'academic' or historical knowledge; it is faith knowledge. Faith in Christ is not just knowing* about *him but trusting* in *him and being ready to follow him as the way, the truth and life.*"[57]

52. Ephesians 3:8.

53. Idowu, "God," 17–29.

54. See Kato, *Theological Pitfalls in Africa*.

55. Imasogie, *Guidelines for Christian Theology in Africa*, 15.

56. Williams, *On Christian Theology*, 170.

57. Migliore, *Faith Seeking Understanding*, 167. Italics are in the original.

Faith here does not mean believing what is not true or believing something that lacks warrant. It refers to an activity that is rooted in human cognitive faculty, involving the will, and propelled by the Holy Spirit.[58] To say then that confessing Jesus as a revealer of God or that he is true God is a statement of faith means that although such confessions are not rid of serious intellectual content, they arise primarily from a deep conviction in people propelled by God. When understood in this way, faith should not obstruct serious exploration of what it means to confess Jesus as true God or the revealer of God. On the contrary, it would inspire further inquiry into the God-human relation through the perspective of the Christ-Event.[59]

At the heart of the Christian faith is the claim that Jesus is the central and the ultimate point of mediation through which human beings can know, relate to and encounter God. And as Roger Haight points out, this claim is so rudimentary that "when asked about the nature and reality of God, the Christian can respond God is like Jesus."[60] This claim, of course, does not mean that a "Christian's knowledge and encounter with God come exclusively through Jesus Christ," but that he "supplies the central symbol and norm for understanding God."[61] Although it is fundamentally a statement of faith, the claim that Jesus is a revealer of God, however, is not based on arbitrary assumptions. It is based on a substantial historical event of Jesus Christ. Therefore, it is helpful to answer the question "how is it that Jesus Christ is a revealer of God?" not in isolation from the question how does Jesus Christ reveal God?

Many Christians, who are informed by the indigenous religious thought, seek to understand God's being and ways and how he relates to the human world. Although in most cases, they prefer to talk about Jesus, ancestors, or the lesser gods at the time of crises: it is the quest to know the identity and work of God that largely underpins their theological questions. In this book, a revealer is defined to include both *communicative* and *interpretative acts.*[62] As both the *communicative and interpretative acts*, the Christ-Event provides us with the opportunity

58. Plantinga, *Warranted Christian Belief*, 246–48.

59. The phrase *fides quaerens intellectum* ("faith seeks understanding") should inform serious inquiry into the significance of Jesus Christ for God-talk.

60. Haight, *Jesus—Symbol of God*, 88.

61. Ibid.

62. See chapter four.

to encounter God in and through Jesus Christ. The entirety of the life, words and actions of Jesus Christ reveal (and corresponds with the purpose and actions of) God. The writer of the Epistle to the Hebrews makes this point:

> In the past, God spoke to our forefathers through the prophets at many times and in various ways, but in these last days he has spoken to us by his Son, whom he appointed heir of all things, and through whom he made the universe. The Son is the radiance of God's glory and the exact representations of his being. . . .[63]

In addition, the communicative and interpretative acts which are embedded in the Christ-Event provide the framework for understanding the significance of the person and work of Jesus Christ. In other words, by revealing God and other spiritual beings, Jesus Christ reveals also his own identity and work.[64]

Returning to the issue of how Jesus reveals God's mystery and relationality, it is helpful to examine how he expresses his relationship with God (the Father). This is important because in the indigenous African religions, God is somewhat a remote Supreme Being who relates to his created world indirectly through the *lesser gods* he created. Some theologians and historians of religion have reacted against the claim that the Supreme Being is not worshipped, insisting that he remains the object of worship even when some worshipers do not mention him explicitly when they pour libations and offer sacrifices. According to Stephen Ezeanya, during sacrifices

> God may be mentioned and his help invoked explicitly. Sometimes he is not mentioned at all; but whether he is mentioned or not, he is generally believed to be the "ultimate recipient of offerings to lesser gods, who may be explicitly referred to as intermediaries."[65]

When this understanding of the Supreme Being is examined in light of the Christ-Event, at least one point of difference and conflict emerges. Whereas the peoples of Africa can have a *direct* experience of

---

63. Hebrews 1:1–3, *NIV*.

64. I will return to this contention later to examine its theological and christological implications.

65. Ezeanya, "God, Spirits and the Spirit World," 37.

and relationship with God in and through Jesus Christ, they can only have an *indirect* relationship with God (as he is construed in the indigenous religions) for he remains too far away to reach directly. But in Jesus Christ God has come close to humans even to the point of becoming one of them. Consequently, they can relate to God directly through Jesus Christ.

Jesus presents a complex picture of God. There are numerous biblical passages that give us some clues as to how he construes his relationship with God. Here, I will examine some of his sayings which John recorded in his Gospel. In John 14:7–9, he recorded a saying of Jesus that appeared to be theologically outrageous, at least in the ears of his immediate hearers. Jesus said to Thomas, one of his disciples, "If you really knew me, you would know my Father as well. From now on you do know him and have seen him." Amazed at these words, Philip, another disciple of Jesus, asked him to show them the Father. In response Jesus said: "Anyone who has seen me has seen the Father." Undoubtedly, Jesus is here referring to God as his Father. But what exactly did he mean by such seemingly outrageous statements? Certainly, he did not mean to express the non-corporeal ontological nature of God. If Jesus taught that "God is Spirit"[66] it followed that he did not intend the statement "anyone who has seen me has seen the Father" to mean that God the Father was corporeal.[67] Since Jesus was truly human, he was corporeal. And if he wanted the statement to mean the ontological being of God the Father who is Spirit he would have expected his disciples to think of the Father as a corporeal being. Certainly that did not seem to be the case. In fact, if the Christ-Event tells us anything at all that is unique, it is that we are doomed to failure if we want to know what "God is in himself" for all that we have access to "is the narrative of God with us."[68] But this does not mean that our knowledge of God with us (in and through Jesus Christ) is insufficient or unable to bring us to a close relationship and experience of God.

Since God the Father is not corporeal and Jesus is corporeal, yet Jesus claims that to encounter him is to encounter God the Father, we

66. John 4:24, *NIV*.

67. Note that the issue here is not whether or not God could become corporeal. But rather whether God (the Father) is corporeal in the sense we can speak of Jesus's corporeality.

68. Williams, *On Christian Theology*, 159.

are faced with a most serious theological and christological problem. From the perspective of Jesus, then, the expression God undergoes a radical change in meaning: *God* is a term that refers to at least more than one being. God as a name or an expression becomes even more complex when we also take into account the fact that Jesus speaks of his entire life and ministry as connected intrinsically with another being he describes as the Spirit of God or Holy Spirit. For example, in one occasion he said to his accusers: "But if I drive out demons by the Spirit of God, then the kingdom of God has come upon you."[69] It seems, then, Jesus unveils that God relates to humanity as the Father, the Son of the Father (Jesus himself) and the Spirit of the God.

The idea of Trinity, like any other theological language, must be approached with caution. For example, when theologians speak of the Trinity they enter into a complex discussion on the essence of God. But it is important to note that when theologians discuss the essence of God and describe him with the language of Trinity they are speaking particularly of "how they have come to know him."[70] The theological implication of this subjective knowledge of God is that it may not completely capture the essence of God even though it is grounded in God's self-revelation. Whilst God's self-revelation ensures that human beings can encounter, experience and know him, it does not guarantee that human beings will always explain his being and activities correctly, exhaustively, and in an intellectually reasonable way.[71]

Some African theologians have not shied away completely from a serious engagement with the doctrine of Trinity. However, although they use the terminology Trinity and speak of God in the trinitarian categories, they have not engaged in an in-depth discussion of the doctrine. In spite of the absence of an exhaustive discussion on Trinity in the writings of many African theologians, the concept of the Triune God continues to undergird most of the African contextual theologies and Christologies. For example, Imasogie has argued:

> Christian theology cannot be universal . . . until every cultural group has brought its peculiar perception of God through Christ. It is only when the Word becomes flesh in every cultural

69. Matthew 12:28, *NIV*.

70. Gunton, *Becoming and Being*, 146.

71. The earliest heresies (for example, the subordinationist view of Jesus Christ) show that some Christian theologians have explained the Trinity in different ways.

human situation that the "unsearchable riches" of God in Christ can be approximated, as much as it is humanly possible under the mediation of the Holy Spirit.[72]

I will not undertake an exhaustive discussion on the Trinity since it is not the primary concern of this book. It is, however, inadequate to discuss the God of the Christ-Event without approaching it from a trinitarian perspective. This is primarily because the trinitarian category introduces us to the mystery and relationality of God.

Kevin Vanhoozer has summarized the idea of Trinity in the history of Christian thought as consisting in "economic Trinity," that is, the activity of "One God who relates to the world through Spirit and Son," and "ontological Trinity," that is, "the belief in the eternality of the triune God."[73] In *The Trinity*, Karl Rahner warns against the danger of separating the Christian teachings on the One God and the Triune God or privileging the one over the three persons that form the Godhead.[74] He argues that for too long Western theologians, following St. Augustine, have leaned unduly towards the idea of One God and have paid very little attention to the idea of the Triune God or the three persons of the Godhead. Drayton Benner has argued recently that Rahner's explication of his axiomatic unity between economic Trinity and immanent Trinity led him into some difficulties that he could have avoided if he had "adhered to Augustine's view of a close but differentiated relationship between immanent Trinity and the economic Trinity."[75] Rahner may have accused St. Augustine of some of the theological crime that he did not commit, as Drayton has argued. But we must acknowledge that Rahner has brought into light a theological truth that has been undermined and ignored; namely, the relationality that undergirds the persons of the Godhead.

The ontology of substance or the metaphysical idea of the Trinity, which goes back to Tertullian who first constructed Trinitarian terminology,[76] "conveys more the sense of God as an independent, stand-alone being," according to Carl Raschke," than the sense of the "One who

---

72. Imasogie, *Guidelines for Christian Theology in Africa*, 86.

73. Vanhoozer, *First Theology*, 54.

74. Rahner, *Trinity*, 15–21.

75. Benner, "Augustine and Karl Rahner," 25–38.

76. McGrath, *Christian Theology: An Introduction*, 321.

is genuinely triune."[77] Raschke goes on to indict "Western Trinitarian doctrine" with the error of "giving lip service to the orthodox portrait of God as truly and paradoxically three-in-one [but] tended to give subtle preference to the aseity or in-himselfness of God, leaving critics of early Christianity to wonder whether the church really meant what it is said."[78]

Rahner's *The Trinity* has been largely responsible for the desire of contemporary theologians to move away from an abstract construction of the ontological category of the Trinity and to focus on the develop- ment of relationality in the Godhead. The emphasis of this understand- ing of the Trinity has been on *persons* rather than on the *substance* of the Trinity.[79] Jesus emphasized and intended his hearers to know about the relationship that exists among the Father, the Holy Spirit, and him- self which is geared towards a common goal: to provide humans be- ings with the opportunity to enjoy a relationship with God. As Clark Pinnock notes:

> By the power of the Spirit, Jesus announced of a God who wills human wholeness. Therefore he went not to the righteous but to the sick and the outcast, to gather them under God's wings. By the Spirit he set people free from entrapment. He brought them hope and liberated their relationships. Demonic powers were driven out, and creaturely life was restored. All these hap- pened because the energies of the life-giving Spirit were at work in Jesus.[80]

The key difficulty for theologians who explicate the doctrine of the Trinity is how to bring together the ideas of substance and relationality (*perichoresis*) that are characteristic of the Godhead. Perhaps the nature of the mystery of the Trinity should force them to hold the two charac- teristics together. They must be willing to recognize that the oneness of the Trinity entails both the shared consubstantiality and relationality of the three divine persons—the Father, Jesus Christ, and the Holy Spirit.

Returning to Christology, which is the primary focus of this book, it is important to note that although Jesus claims to enjoy an unprec- edented relationship with God the Father (even in the sense of possess-

77. Raschke, *The Next Reformation*, 152.

78. Ibid.

79. See LaCugna, *God for Us*; Grenz and Franke, *Beyond Foundationalism*, 192.

80. Pinnock, *Flame of Love*, 88–89.

ing all the qualities of God), his primary task was not to prove to his contemporaries and disciples that he was God. It was rather to express the unique relationship that exists between them and the significance of that relationship for human beings.[81] In addition, his intention is to help his followers and contemporaries to know and acknowledge that he was the one who embodied the true knowledge, identity and character of God. Therefore, the sayings of Jesus which indicate his unique relationship with God such as "No one knows who the Son is except the Father, and no one knows who the Father is except the Son . . ."[82] and "I am in the Father and the Father is in me"[83] suggest he intends to communicate that his identity and work equally reveal the identity and work of God, the Father.

By revealing the identity, character and mission of God the Father, Jesus also reveals his own identity, character and mission. But we are to understand this dual revealing to have arisen from a shared sense of origin, objective and relationship. Jesus Christ represented himself as the one whose mission and identity were consistent with the identity and work of the Father and the Holy Spirit. Therefore, to encounter the identity and work of Jesus Christ is to encounter the identity and common purpose of the three beings that make up the Godhead as construed in some classical Christian doctrines.

In Christian theology, the mystery of God is also expressed by stating that he is partly knowable and partly unknowable. The meaning Christian theologians ascribe to this grand theological statement varies from one theologian to another. Even outside of the Christianity, for instance, some adherents of the indigenous religions will normally concede the ways of God or the gods are sometimes unknown to human beings. It is noteworthy that when some lay Christians or adherents to the indigenous religions admit that the ways of God or the gods are sometimes unknown they do so from a practical vantage point and not from mere abstract academic perspective. In other words, the issue of God's mystery arises normally from the context of real life issues or experiences and not from an abstract construction. It is usually during the time of great loss of life, or job, an unanswered prayer, and in great times of difficulties that most Africans, who seek for the help of

81. See John 7:3; 9:4 and Luke 4:43.

82. Luke 10:22.

83. John 14:11, *NIV*.

God or the gods, will acknowledge in desperation that the ways of God are sometimes too complex for human beings to fathom. It is noteworthy that Jesus also discussed the mystery of God in practical contexts and not in abstract academic contexts. In the majority of occasions in which Jesus engaged in discussion about God, it was a practical concern which aimed at the transformation of human lives that drove the conversation.[84]

By revealing the mystery of God's nature, character, and purpose, Jesus Christ also reveals the mystery of God's own being, character, and purpose. Interestingly, the mystery of the identity of Jesus has been subsumed under the debate of the relationship between his human and divine natures. When some of the proponents of the earliest christological heresies attempted to articulate the relationship between the human and divine natures of Jesus Christ in precise terms, the result was a distortion of the balance that held together the unity and uniqueness of each of the natures.[85] The Chalcedonian council (in agreement with the Nicene Creed) responded to this imbalance by proposing that Jesus is truly God and truly man.[86] The New Testament writers also did not seem to bother themselves with the issue of explaining in precise ways how the human and divine natures of Jesus related to each other. The major danger of trying to discover and explain in precise terms the relationship between the humanity and divinity of Jesus Christ is that such project will encounter stalemate and can lead to some avoidable confusions and heresies. In addition, such endeavor fails to acknowledge the purpose of the Christ-Event. In the person and work of Jesus

---

84. Mark 2:23–28; 10:24–27; John 4:4–26; 14:5–14.

85. Arianism was the view that denied the full divinity of Jesus Christ. Docetism, on the contrary, was the view that denied the full humanity of Jesus Christ. The Nestorians denied the doctrine of *theotokos* and effectively introduced a dangerous dichotomy between the two natures of Jesus Christ. Eutychianism and monophysitism unduly subsumed the two natures of Jesus Christ and construed him as neither God nor human but a *tertium quid* (or a third thing). Adoptionism taught that Jesus, as human, was the Son of God by adoption. Theopaschitism is the view that teaches that it is impossible for Jesus to suffer because of the union of the divine and human natures of Jesus. For a good summary of these heresies, see Quash and Ward, *Heresies and How to Avoid Them*.

86. Although the Chalcedonian council did not explain the way in which the hypostatic union (of the two natures—human and divine—of Jesus) originate and relate to each other, it drew parameters on which to measure how the union cannot be expressed.

Christ, God has in an unprecedented way undone his otherness for the purpose of uniting with and relating to human beings. The divine undoing of divine otherness is also a divine invitation to human beings to enjoy and learn from God who has created them. This invitation equally entails a rethinking on the part of human beings their understanding of themselves, their world and the spiritual world. The consequences of this re-thinking will become evident as I explore God's acts of self-giving and self-dispossessing as demonstrated in the Christ-Event.

Jesus the Revealer of God's Life of Self-giving

The Christ-Event shows that God has *given* himself as a gift to humanity. This is a christological assertion that upsets the notion of a powerful, self-gaining and self-promoting God that is prevalent in African Christianity. It also upsets the Africans indigenous notions of a remote and unforgiving Supreme Being who has withdrawn himself from direct communication with human beings because they violated his law.[87] The apostle Paul expressed God's self-giving and self-dispossessing in Philippians 2:6–11. In this passage, Paul incorporated into his letter a classical Christian christological ode.[88] This hymn, however, introduces a christological tension when it uses the Greek verb *kenoo* (to empty) to describe Jesus's act of self-giving.

> Who, being in very nature God, did not consider equality with God something to be grasped, but made himself nothing, taking the very nature of a servant, being made in human likeness. And being found in appearance as a man, he humbled himself and became obedient to death— even death on a cross![89]

According to Kato, this "moving hymn on the humiliation and exaltation of Jesus Christ the Lord . . . should motivate us to make the Gospel relevant in every situation everywhere, without comprising it."[90] The need

---

87. Adeyemo has argued that African "Christians need to transmit the message that Africa's broken rope between heaven and earth has been once and for all re-established in Christ. Africa's God, who, as they say, withdrew from men to the heavens, has now come down to man [in the person of Jesus Christ] so as to bring man back to God." See Adeyemo, *Salvation in African Tradition*, 96.

88. Hawthorne, *Philippians*, 100.

89. Philippians 2:6–8, *NIV*.

90. Kato, *Biblical Christianity in Africa*, 24.

to contextualize the Christ-Event in Africa underlies Kato's contention. However, he does not go on to explicate how this christological hymn can function as a motivation for contextual theology or Christology.

Philippians 2:6–11 provides a window upon the earliest Christians' devotion to Jesus Christ.[91] More importantly, it provides the context for explicating the self-giving of God's self to humanity. Biblical scholars, philosophical and systematic theologians (particularly in the West) have wrestled with the theological and christological problem this hymn has created. Systematic and philosophical theologians have concentrated primarily on the theological and christological import of *kenoo*. The concentration on the meaning of this Greek verb has resulted sometimes in abstract christological constructions that hardly have any bearing on the context of Philippians 2. Some of these christological constructions are exemplified in some kenotic theories.[92] For Francis Hall, a kenotic theory teaches that the

> Divine Logos, in order to take up our nature upon Him and submit in reality to its earthly conditions and limitations, abandoned what was His before He became incarnate. In particular, it is alleged most commonly, that He abandoned what kenoticists call His relative or His metaphysical attributes, of omnipotence, omnipresence and omniscience, so as to be dependent upon the aid of the Spirit, wholly circumscribed by space, and deprived of knowledge.[93]

The question of what did Jesus empty himself is what has informed the kenotic theory that Hall is describing. However, there something is wrong with this line of questioning.[94] It presumes that the Second

91. Hurtado, *How on Earth Did Jesus Become a God?*, 84.

92. This theory developed in the seventeenth century and revolved around the controversy between "Lutheran theologians based at the universities of Giessen and Tubingen." McGrath has summarized the key issues of the controversy as follows: "The gospel makes no reference to Christ making use of all his divine attributes (such as omniscience) during his period on earth. How is this to be explained? Two options seemed to present themselves to these Lutheran writers as appropriately orthodox solutions: either Christ used his divine powers in secret, or he abstained from using them altogether. The first option, which came to be known as *krypsis*, was vigorously defended by Tubingen; the second, which came to be known as *kenosis*, was defended with equal vigor by Giessen." See McGrath, *Christian Theology*, 377.

93. Hall, *Kenotic Theory*, 1.

94. It is both exegetically and theological flawed and misleading. For a helpful survey and critique of the predominant views on the meanings and the ethical, christologi-

Person of the Trinity needed to empty himself of something before he could become a true human being. In other words, the incarnation necessarily required the Son of God to empty himself of his divine attributes such as omniscience. Consequently, the question assumes that self-emptying entails self-limiting.[95] But is this understanding inherent in the christological ode of Philippians 2?[96]

The expression *heauton* ekeno[set macron over *o*]sen (emptied himself) in verse 7 should not be understood in isolation from other important expressions in the text such as *en morphē theou* (in the form of God) in verse 6, *ouch hegēsato* (did not regard) in verse 6, *etapeinōsen heauton* (humbled himself) in verse 8, and *morphēn doulou labōn* (taking the form of a slave) in verse 7.[97] When we locate the expression emptied himself within the broader context of the passage, it is clear that Paul does not intend the expression emptied himself to be understood in a literal sense, but rather in a metaphorical or poetic sense. In other words, the expression emptied himself does not entail a literal emptying or relinquishing of something. Gerald Hawthorne has argued that *heauton ekenōsen* "is a poetic hymnlike way of saying that Christ poured out himself, putting himself totally at the disposal of people (cf. 1 John 3:16), that Christ became poor that he might make many rich (2 Cor 8:9; cf. also Eph 1:23; 4:10)."[98] According to Larry Hurtado, emptied himself in the context of Philippians 2 involves "taking a slave-form and being born in human likeness—that is, as a human."[99] Thus, the force of the emptying in the passage of Philippians 2 does not lie in *what is relinquished,* but rather on *what is taken on.* "Here the humble

---

cal and theological import of *kenoo* and *en morphē theou* among biblical scholars, see Park, *Submission within the Godhead and the Church in the Epistles to the Philippians,* 17–31; Hawthorne, *Philippians,* 111–14; Hurtado, *How on Earth Did Jesus Become a God?,* 97–104.

95. According to Charles Gore, Jesus's "supernatural knowledge" is rooted in "supernatural illumination" which is "analogous to that vouchsafed to prophets and apostles." For Gore, Jesus's knowledge is "not necessarily Divine consciousness." Therefore, Jesus, in Gore's thinking, lived in "apparent limitations of knowledge." See Gore, *Incarnation of the Son of God,* 147. This book was Gore's Bampton Lectures at Oxford University in 1891.

96. Theologically, if Jesus at any point in time (and in all possible worlds) emptied or relinquished himself of his divine properties he ceased at that point to be truly divine.

97. Hurtado, *How on Earth Did Jesus Become a God?,* 95.

98. Hawthorne, *Philippians,* 117.

99. Hurtado, *How on Earth Did Jesus Become a God?,* 96.

initiative of the Son is to the fore: in the incarnation he took on the form of a slave and would end his life on the cross."[100] Therefore, *self-emptying* does not mean in this context self-limitation.[101] On the contrary, it is clear from the context of Philippians 2 that self-dispossession, self-sacrificing, self-humbling, self-denying, and self-giving are the underlying force of the incarnation and the cross-event.[102]

Some theologians, such as Paul Knitter, have moved away from the understanding of self-emptying of Jesus Christ as self-limitation to the concept of self-opening. He writes: "Self-emptying, we are realizing, is self-opening to, self-relating to others. Without others, without those who are different (as different as creatures are from the Creator), kenosis is meaningless and, ultimately, impossible."[103] Knitter's concern here is not Christology. It is rather the relationship of Christianity to other religions and how the relationship impacts the attitudes of Christians toward the people of other religions. According to him, "*kenosis* calls all Christians to a greater openness" to truly respect "the otherness of the other."[104] Since my interest here is Christology, and not theology of religions, I will focus on the implication of self-emptying for Jesus-talk and God-talk.

The incarnation demonstrates God's willingness to give God's self as a gift to humanity. By becoming human, by refusing to exploit for his own advantage his equality with God, by becoming willing to die on the cross, and by deciding to humble himself to become a human being, the Second Person of the Trinity reveals the depth of the Triune God's willingness to give God's self to humanity in order to be in fellowship with human beings.[105] In the incarnation, then, God made his *unapproachable mystery* an *approachable mystery*. Whilst the Christ-Event remains a mystery, it nonetheless provides humanity with the opportunity to experience God's act of self-giving. The opposite consequence of this self-giving is self-gaining and self-accumulating. The God that

---

100. O'Collins, *Incarnation*, 2.

101. I will return to the christological implication of this claim later in this chapter when I examine the incarnation.

102. Hawthorne, *Philippians*, 104, 106.

103. Knitter, "What about Them? Christians and Non–Christians," 311–12.

104. Ibid., 312.

105. Philippians 2:6–11; Galatians 4:4–5.

Jesus reveals is the God of self-giving. This God is not the God who is preoccupied with power, wealth and who is unapproachable.

The prevalent idea of God in African Christianity is that of a Being who solves problems. As I argued in chapters two and three, most of the culture-oriented and the liberation-oriented Christologies existing in Africa assume that Jesus is the chief problem-solver who saves and liberates African peoples from the bondage of Western imperialism, colonization, theological and cultural hegemony. At the grassroots level, most Christians see Jesus Christ primarily as the one who liberates the oppressed from their oppressors and from their destitute condition, and who enriches and empowers people to fight against their oppressors (both spiritual beings and human beings). Whist some of them emphasize the redemptive power of God to restore sinful human beings to fellowship with God, the concerns of others are to experience divine breakthroughs in business, health, studies, and wealth. The neo-missionary and the missionary Christologies present normally Jesus as the Savior. But we are to be suspicious of the expression Savior as it is used in some of these Christologies because they present Jesus (and consequently God) as the most powerful, the invulnerable, unchangeable, the untouchable, and as the one who reserves the power to send people to hell and to save people from hell, the most powerful being who blesses and ensures that people who believe in him enjoy a total wellbeing.[106]

The key issue here that needs exploring is the assumption that God is as powerful as he can possibly be and that he has empowered Christians to overcome their physical, spiritual, emotional and socio-economic problems. Chinedu Akunne in his *Having Power with God* contends:

> Power is an essential virtue in our Christian life because with-out it, we cannot . . . overcome all the vile of the devil in our life and in the world. It is required for us to be a witness for Christ, move in his strength, might and glory to his name. It aids us in overcoming our weaknesses, identifying ourselves as God's sons' and daughters (John 1:12). Power enables us to have access to God in knowing and possessing all that God has given us as a birthright. Power enthrones us to prince-ship, to be powerful and to prevail as God's own.[107]

---

106. See Adeyemo, *Salvation in African Tradition.*
107. Akunne, *Having Power with God*, 11–12.

Adeboye essentially makes this same point when he writes:

> If you have lost the power that God has given you, there must be
> a reason. You must retrace your steps. How did it happen? One
> thing we must not forget is that God never changes. Therefore,
> if there is any [change], it comes from us. The Bible tells us that
> the gifts and calling of God are without repentance. This means
> that once God gives you a particular gift or He gives you a share
> of His power, He has given it to you forever. He has no intention
> of taking it away from you, but you can throw it away.[108]

The contentions of Adeboye and Akunne are representative of how
the majority of Christians connect God and power. Many Christian
theologians as well as the laity assume that God is the most powerful.
He is so powerful that he can make an impossibility to be possible.[109]
Since God is very powerful, he is untouchable and has also made those
who believe in him to become untouchables to the evil people and evil
spirits. What African Christians need to recognize is that it is misleading
for them to construe Jesus merely as the "the powerful wonder-worker
who manifested God," and to assume, as the Corinthians Christians
did, they are "simply continuing the power of Jesus in their own lives
through pneumatic gifts and miraculous feats."[110] The concepts of powerful Christians and a powerful God are indicative of the unwillingness
of many Christians to become self-dispossessing and self-giving.[111]

The God who has reveals God' self in the Christ-Event does not
always come as the most powerful and untouchable, but sometimes as
the most vulnerable and powerless because God has chosen the path of
self-giving and self-dispossessing. In *Christ on Trial*, Rowan Williams
reminds us of the unusual threat Jesus posed to the judges who presided
over his case—a threat that is submersed in powerlessness. He writes,

> It is not surprising, therefore that in all the Gospel narratives
> of the trial, Jesus' declaration of the gulf between his world
> and that of his judges provokes insult and abuse. He is beaten,

108. Adeboye, *God the Holy Spirit*, 27. Adeboye is perhaps the most influential leaders of the Pentecostal movement in contemporary Nigeria.

109. There is a popular song about Jesus and God in Nigeria which says: "Jehovah
Jireh, O mere impossibility possible, *O mere* impossibility possible." A literal translation
of the song is "Jehovah the provider; he has made an impossibility to be possible; He has
made an impossibility to be possible."

110. Placher, *Narratives of a Vulnerable God*, 11.

111. See McDowell, *Gospel According to Star Wars*, 23.

flogged and crowned with thorns precisely because he is powerless, because he does not compete for the same space that his
judges and captors are defending, he is a deeper rival than any
direct rival.[112]

Viewed from the Christ-Event, the God Christianity should pro-
claim is the God who is self-giving; self-sacrificing, self-dispossessing,
and not the God who is self-promoting, self-accumulating and self-
gaining.

The incarnation, God's self-manifestation and self-expressiveness
in Jesus Christ, is God's unprecedented self-manifestation in human
history. In the indigenous religions, as we have seen, God is remote and
people can encounter him indirectly through the ancestors. Conversely,
the Christian God in and through Christ-Event has in some ways undone
his otherness, and therefore making himself reachable and approachable
directly through Jesus Christ who shares consubstantiality with God.
The Christian God has brought himself to human level in the Christ-
Event. Of course, this does not mean that the God of Christianity is now
only human; the God classical Christianity professes is a mystery, but
this God has revealed himself in the human person—Jesus Christ. As
Kato observes:

> The incarnation itself is a form of contextualization. The Son
> of God condescended to pitch His tent among us to make it
> possible for us to be redeemed (John 1:14). The unapproach-
> able Yahweh, whom no man has seen and lived, has become the
> Object of sight and touch through the incarnation (John 14:9;
> 1 John 1:1).[113]

The Christian God has come to the levels of humanity, by becoming human, in order to have a relationship with human beings. This is a theological consequence of God's self-revelation in Jesus of Nazareth. Paul's
imagery of the unapproachable light in 1 Timothy 6:16 attests to the
dialectics of the complexity and revelation of God. As John McDowell
argues:

> 1 Timothy describes God as dwelling "in unapproachable light,
> whom no one has ever seen or can see" (1 Timothy 6:16). Yet
> this Light itself nonetheless illuminates all things. All creation,

112. Williams, *Christ on Trial*, 69.
113. Kato, *Biblical Christianity in Africa*, 24.

all being, is therefore properly known in the light of God's self-revelation, and this act continually purifies and makes holy our sight and hearing (cf. 1 John 1:7).[114]

In Jesus Christ, we encounter the very presence of God. Adeyemo argues that the Christian God "is the God who became flesh and dwelt among us (John 1:14). This is the crown of God's revelation to man; God revealed not through His works and attributes, but in His in very essence."[115]

The Christ-Event reveals not only God's being, but also his affection, vulnerability, love and self-giving. This brings us to the issue of incarnation: "The Word became flesh and lived among us."[116] As long as Christians continue to confess God's self-revelation, the incarnation will remain a doctrine that is at the heart of Christianity. This doctrine is one of the key teachings that distinguish Christianity from other religions. It is a doctrine that provokes people to think of Christianity as exclusivist, scandalous and oppressive. In a sense, these indictments are legitimate for what Christians mean when they confess with some New Testament writers the incarnation, to use the words of Sallie McFague, God is "embodied in one place and one place only: in the man Jesus of Nazareth. He and he alone is 'the image of the invisible God' (Col. 1:15)."[117] It is not surprising, then, that the doctrine of the incarnation has attracted several fierce criticisms.[118] In chapter four, we saw that African indigenous religions provide for the possibility of spiritual beings to become human and to appear in human forms. This is perhaps one of the reasons many Christians do not find it too difficult to believe that God has manifested God's self in Jesus Christ, or that in the Christ-Event we encounter a union of divinity and humanity. Therefore, it is not necessary to devote much time to interact with some Western writers who have continued to deny the claim that Jesus Christ is fully human and God. However, suffice to say that this classical conception of the identity of Jesus Christ has remained crucially important for understanding God-human and God-world relations in Christianity.

114. McDowell, *Gospel According to Star Wars*, 35.

115. Adeyemo, *Salvation in African Tradition*, 28.

116. John 1:14.

117. McFague, *Body of God*, 159.

118. See for example Hick, *The Metaphor of God Incarnate*.

It is important to note that Jesus and the writers of the New Testament have not provided, and perhaps did not aim to furnish us, with detailed information and the tools to test the process God employed in embodying God's presence in Jesus Christ. Even the story of the virgin birth of Jesus Christ does not tell us exactly how God has become human in the person of Jesus of Nazareth.[119] The only thing Matthew and Luke tell us is that the Holy Spirit was involved in the whole process.[120] How then can we comprehend this divine activity? Should we seek to get beyond the New Testament testimonies to find out exactly how this divine activity has occurred? African theologians have not showed any interest in engaging in such enormous task. Cornelius Olowola, one of the contemporary leading theologians in Evangelical Church of West Africa, focuses on the importance of the virgin birth for Jesus Christ, and not on the process of the virgin birth. According to him, the virgin birth "affirms the genuine humanity of Christ," "underscores the fact that Christ did not inherit a sin nature," and "underscores [Jesus'] unique person and points powerfully to the messianic redemption" which he came "to accomplish by the same supernatural power of God."[121] It is vital to state that any attempt to discover and explain exhaustively the process of the virgin birth, like the quest to separate the *Jesus of history* from the *Jesus of faith* is doomed to failure. This is because, like God-talk, an exhaustive knowledge of the process of the incarnation escapes human comprehension.

However, we need to be careful in speaking of the importance of the virgin birth for the humanity and ministry of Jesus Christ in the ways that Olowola has done. We need to avoid the temptation of elevating the humanity of Jesus to the point where he could no longer be recognizable as truly human. The incarnation, properly understood, requires that Jesus is truly human: the eternal Son of God took on the

---

119. Matthew 1:18–25; Luke 1:26–38. The story of the Virgin Birth does not suggest that the Second Person of Trinity became a Son of the Father during or after the Birth. It only informs us about God's action of becoming a human being. Wolfhart Pannenberg is therefore misleading to argue that "the legend of Jesus' virgin birth stands in an irreconcilable contradiction to the Christology of the incarnation of the pre-existent Son of God in Paul and John." See *Jesus—God and Man*, 143.

120. It is important to note that the involvement of the Holy Spirit in the process of the Christ-Event did not end with the conception of Jesus Christ. The Holy Spirit was actively involved throughout the life and ministry of Jesus here on the earth.

121. Olowola, "Person and Work of Christ," 160.

resources and prerogative of humanity while at the same time retaining his divine resources and prerogative.[122] Jesus Christ was truly human because he had all the properties that define and characterize humanity. Jesus had human body and human mind. He went through human developmental stages; he was a historical figure, a true human being. "Jesus grew in wisdom and stature and in favor with God and men."[123] But the other side of the story, to use the words of John Milbank, is that the New Testament writers compel us to see Jesus not as an ordinary man, but as the "foreordained figure: the Messiah, the Son of Man, the Son of God, or the *Logos* who has appeared in the world at the right time to accomplish human salvation."[124] A theological way to put this puzzling narrative (of the union of divinity and humanity in Jesus) is that Jesus Christ is *ontologically* a human being and a divine being.[125]

The exact ways in which the humanity and divinity indissolubly united, interacted and related in Jesus Christ will remain a mystery and a daunting puzzle for theologians. Human beings do not yet have the properties that can enable them to comprehend the entirety of divine activities; and it is doubtful if such capacity is designed by God to be part of the characteristic of true humanity. If we chose to stay within the boundaries that the New Testament has drawn, our task should be to discover the meaning and significance of the Christ-Event, and not to discover the exact content and procedures God employed in becoming a human being. We can also add that it is a fallacy to assume that the authenticity of a Christology depends on its ability to explain exhaustively the details of God's embodiment in Jesus of Christ. Rather than speculate about the details of the procedures of God' self-revelation in Jesus Christ, our primal task is to examine rigorously and articulate what God intends to say by revealing himself in a way human beings can recognize.

What comes out vividly from God's self-revelation in the Christ-Event, as I have argued persistently in this chapter, is God's act of self-

---

122. Morris, *Our Idea of God*, 169.

123. Luke 2:52, *NIV*.

124. Milbank, *Word Made Strange*, 146.

125. The functional understanding of the divinity of Jesus Christ states that "Jesus was God in the sense of being the locus of divine action." In other words, ontologically, Jesus was not God, but was an extraordinary human being because his "life became the place where could act decisively to redeem the human race." See Evans, *Historical Christ and the Jesus of Faith*, 118.

giving. The Triune God has given himself in order to unite humanity to God's relational life. Writing on the divine relationship which humanity experiences through Jesus Christ, Kathryn Tanner argues:

> The Spirit radiates the humanity of Jesus with the Father's own gifts of light, life and love; and shines through him, not simply back to the Father, but through his humanity to us, thereby communicating to us the gifts received by Jesus from the Father. In this way, the gifts of the Father indwell us in and through the gift of the Spirit itself shining through the glorified humanity of the Son.[126]

By becoming human, God gave himself, through the eternal Son, to humanity. This *act of revealing* entails self-giving, self-surrendering, and as the God who willing condescends very low to become a human being in order to have a relationship with his human creatures. By incarnating in Jesus of Nazareth, the Christ, God makes himself available for human beings to distort, insult and profane. The incarnation is the ground on which God-human relation reaches its full potential. Some African theologians such as Ezeh, Bediako, and Nyamiti have argued that although the incarnation is a particular event, it has a universal soteriological consequence.[127] Their contention, however, is set within the broad context of the compatibility of Christianity and African indigenous religions, particularly from the perspective of the ancestral cult.[128] Although we are to become suspicious of the ancestor christological model, as I have already argued, these theologians correctly note that the incarnation is the ground on which God relates to the whole humanity. It costs (in the sense of self-giving) God, not a prophet, but rather God's self, to enact a unique relationship in which humanity can enjoy divine love, friendship and fellowship. Whilst the ancestor christological model can strike a familiar chord in the ears of some African peoples who are aware of the indigenous understanding of the mediatory function of the ancestors, this model is christologically weak

---

126. Tanner, *Jesus, Humanity, and the Trinity*, 53.

127. See chapter seven for an extensive discussion on the salvific consequences of the Christ-Event.

128. Bediako, *Jesus and the Gospel in Africa*, 24–33; Ezeh, *Jesus Christ the Ancestor*, 198–203, 248–66; Nyamiti, *Christ as Our Ancestor*, 35–52.

because it fails to adequately account for the self-giving of God's self in the incarnation of Jesus Christ.[129]

To conclude this chapter, it is important to emphasize that the Christ-Event provides some radical and unique interpretations of God. It portrays God in the ways which can make Christians and the devotees of the indigenous religions to become uncomfortable, for it does not present, communicate and interpret God as the untouchable, the most powerful, the self-accumulating, and utterly transcendent. The Christ-Event contradicts any Christology that is merely solution-oriented. Conversely, it interprets and communicates God as the self-dispossessing, self-giving, self-sacrificing, vulnerable and immanent. Jesus Christ has made God reachable, touchable, and recognizable. As S. Oyin Abogunrin notes,

> The Christian understanding of history is that of a God who reveals Himself and acts in history. The God about whom Jesus spoke is the God who stoops down to seek out and to save man. . . . Biblical concept of God is that of a God who not only seeks and saves, but expresses Himself in the incarnation by coming to dwell among men in some tangible way. Otherwise, God will remain unknowable.[130]

Although we may not fathom the details of the incarnation, we know that it introduces a radical and a paradoxical picture of God—God is not only transcendent but ontologically immanent; God is not only sovereign and powerful, God is also powerless and vulnerable; and God is not only the *other* and unique in God's self, God is also self-giving. These understandings of God are grounded in the Christ-Event. These representations upset any construal of Jesus and God merely in the categories of the powerful and remote, as in the indigenous religions. Through the Christ-Event, God has made himself available to humanity by giving incarnating in Jesus of Nazareth, the Christ. Consequently, to know Jesus Christ is to know God. This *knowledge of the divine* is not merely in a cognitive sense, but involves "real, personal encounter with the risen Christ."[131] Unlike in the indigenous religions where God only relates to the world through the lesser divinities, classical Christianity

129. See chapter two for a critical examination of the ancestor christological model.

130. Abogunrin, *In Search for the Original Jesus*, 33.

131. Thompson, "Arianism," 23.

has continued to teach with the Apostles Paul and John, and some other writers of the New Testament that Jesus Christ is essentially God and that he is the human face of God.[132] It is equally important to note here that the incarnation is not the process of *human beings becoming God* (apotheosis), but rather *God becoming human*. This means that the incarnation cannot be equated with the indigenous concepts of the ancestor cult and apotheosis.[133] The relationship between Jesus Christ and some lesser spirit beings as construed in the indigenous religions and Christianity is a crucially important issue that an African Christology cannot overlook. This is the issue I examine in the next chapter.

132. John 1:1, 14; Philippians 2:6–11.

133. See chapter four for a detailed discussion on apotheosis.

6

The Malevolent Spirits in the Christologies of African Christianity

IN CONTEMPORARY AFRICAN CHRISTIANITY, THE BELIEF IN DEMONS, evil spirits and Satan, particularly at the grassroots level, shapes the ways many Christians relate to and perceive the person and work of Jesus Christ. Any serious researcher of African Christianity will notice that many Christians talk about the power of Jesus Christ to defeat and destroy the works of the evil spirits, demons and Satan in their prayers, preaching, songs, and books. In this chapter, I will focus on the beings the majority of Africans perceive as malevolent or malign spirits. The spirits are viewed in this way because many Christians construe them most times as the messengers and sources of misfortunes and evil.[1] Given that many Christians locate some of their discussions on the person of Jesus Christ and the manifestation of his power in their lives within the context of the spirit beings they consider to be evil and wicked, any christological model seeking to be relevant to them needs to engage with the Christians' beliefs in the existence and activities of the malevolent spirit beings. The Christology should also engage constructively with Jesus's attitudes toward Satan and demons and the import of his attitudes and conversation with these spirit beings for interacting with and critiquing the African Christians' perceptions of such spirit beings.

Many theologians, as we see will later in this chapter, have continued to highlight the malevolent spirit beings in their works. What is lacking, however, is a constructive Christology that questions and seeks to discover and interact with the cultural, religious, and theological

---

1. See chapter five for discussion on the complex relationship between benevolent and malevolent spirits as construed in some African indigenous cosmologies.

presuppositions that underlie many African Christians' beliefs and attitudes toward the malevolent spirit beings.[2] The key questions I explore in this chapter are: how can the Christ-Event provide a christological context for interacting with the African Christians' perceptions of the influence of the malevolent spirit beings on the human world? And in what ways can the Christians' understandings of Satan and demons contribute to the task of contextualizing the meaning and significance of Jesus Christ? I will examine some Christians' perceptions of the identity of the malevolent spirits and the implications of their understandings of such spirits, focusing primarily on the Nigerian contexts.

The arguments I examine in this chapter are: (a) the key factors that underlie most Christians' perceptions of Jesus Christ and how he relates to them and to the spirit beings they construe as malevolent are a solution-driven mindset and the indigenous view of the interrelatedness of the spirit and human worlds; (b) the Christians' preoccupation with the activities of the malevolent spirits is partly responsible for their failure to explore the contributions of humanity to the continuous existence of demonic activities that have become part of the structures of many social and ecclesiastical systems in Africa; and (c) Jesus's conversations with demons and evil spirits provide a background for examining African Christians' understandings of the identity and functions of the malevolent spirits and for stimulating in them the desire and courage to become actively involved in the dismantling of all demonic systems, cultures, and ideologies which promote injustice, oppression, poverty, subjugation and dehumanization.

This chapter is divided into two major sections. In the first section, I will examine and critique some of the understandings of the identities of the malevolent spirits in African Christianity and indigenous cosmologies. In the second section, I will probe some of the ways many

---

2. Allan Anderson has argued that many African theologians "have downplayed the importance of the spirit word" and consequently have failed to deal constructively with the persistent physical and spiritual needs of the African peoples. See A. Anderson, "African Initiated Churches of the Spirit and Pneumatology," 178–86). In this chapter, I will probe some of the factors that inform spirit–talk and the views of the activities of the malevolent spirits in Nigerian Christianity. For example, why do many Christians shout the name of Jesus Christ and begin to pray to him for deliverance during a turbulent flight, when they are sick, and when their businesses are not progressing? And why do some Christians sometimes claim to have a spiritual attack or an attack from an evil spirit when they are sick? How is it that they think in such categories? These are some of the questions that will shape my discussions in this chapter.

Christians respond to what they believe to be the activities of the malevolent spirits in their lives and their communities.

The Christ-Event and the Identity of the Malevolent Spirits

I suggested in chapter five that one of the helpful ways to understand
the highly populated pantheon of the spiritual world in the indigenous
cosmologies is to categorize them into benevolent and malevolent. In
spite of the deficiency of this classification (for example, some spirits
which are generally believed to be benevolent can sometimes bring
misfortunes in the form of punishments as in the case of the ancestors),
it remains one of the effective ways of examining the impact of the belief in the activities of evil spirits on the African Christians' perceptions
of the identity and work of Jesus Christ.

The indigenous religions generally regard the Supreme Being as
benevolent and somewhat remote. Consequently, many traditionalists
(those who adhere to the indigenous religions) do not offer sacrifice
regularly to him. Instead, they offer sacrifices regularly to several gods
and ancestors because they believe that these beings are ontologically
and relationally closer to human beings. This does not mean that the
indigenous religions teach that the Supreme Being has abandoned human affairs.[3] Mircea Eliade's notion of a sky God who is *too good* and
distant to need any direct worship is problematic and does not represent the complexities shrouding the indigenous understandings of the
relationship between the Supreme Being and the human world.[4] Some
African scholars have criticized Eliade's concept of a remote sky God,
describing it as a distortion of the predominant African indigenous
views of the transcendence and immanence of the Supreme Being. For
example, Bolaji Idowu argues that the reason many African peoples
do not sacrifice regularly to the Supreme Being must be explained in
the context of the indigenous cultural etiquette of approaching a king
through an intermediary. The Supreme Being is the almighty king and
cannot be approached directly. He can only be approached through
intermediaries—some lesser spirit beings—created for the mediatory

3. Isichei, "Ibo and Christian Beliefs," 121–34. See chapter five for an extensive discussion on the idea of the Supreme Being in Nigeria and some other African societies.

4. See Eliade, *Patterns in Comparative Religion*.

purposes.[5] Justin Ukpong accepts the mediatorial explanation of the irregularity of sacrifice to the Supreme Being but adds that this explanation needs to be located within the indigenous African "social etiquette" which teaches that a "king should not be approached or seen often" and not just to be approached indirectly through an intermediary.[6] Many African Christians, however, do not think of the malevolent spirit beings primarily as God's messengers. They do not construe the malign spirits as the messengers who can bring God's good news for his people. On the contrary, many Christians see the malevolent spirits as the enemies of God and his people. Consequently, some of the Christians consider themselves to be at war with the evil spirits and Satan.

A Christology designed for African Christians that hopes to be relevant to the people should not overlook and underestimate the malevolent spirits. The Kenyan theologian, John Mbiti, has cautioned scholars who undertake the task of interpreting and appropriating Jesus Christ in Africa to be aware that the

> greatest need among African peoples, is to see, to know, and to experience Jesus Christ as the victor over the powers and forces from which Africa knows no means of deliverance. It is for this reason that they show special interest in the Temptation of Jesus and his victory over the devil through the power of the Holy Spirit. They know that the devil is not just an academic problem but a reality, manifesting his power through ways such as unwanted spirit possessions, sickness, madness, fights, murders, and so on.[7]

Mbiti's caution is appropriate because many African peoples have continued to believe in and to wage spiritual war against the malevolent spirits. To cite one example, on 6 June 2003, the officials of Ghana Airways invited a London-based Ghanaian preacher to Accra to "lead a healing and deliverance service aimed at exorcizing evil spirits from the affairs of the airline and releasing it from its predicaments."[8] The action of the officials of Ghana Airways will not strike most African Christians as strange and weird. This is because they believe the malign

---

5. Idowu, *African Traditional Religion*, 65.

6. Ukpong, "Problem of God and Sacrifice in African Traditional Religion," 201.

7. Mbiti, "Some African Concepts of Christology," 55.

8. Asamoah-Gyadu, "'Christ is the Answer: What is the Question?' A Ghana Airways Prayer Vigil and Its Implications for Religion, Evil and Public Space," 93–117.

spirits haunt human beings and the human world, and that exorcism and the prayers aimed at liberating humanity from the snares of such spirits are appropriate and effective.

This belief is rooted partly in the indigenous cosmology which assumes that the spiritual and human worlds interpenetrate and also that the spirit beings can influence the lives and experiences of human beings.[9] It is also rooted in the assumption that Jesus Christ is a solution to the needs of human beings. But as I have consistently argued in this book, it is a distortion to perceive Jesus primarily as solution, especially when he is construed in the ways which suggest he is merely a tool for human beings to use to solve their problems.[10]

Some theologians have attempted to convince some Western scholars that the Africans' belief in the impact of the malevolent spirit beings on the lives of people cannot be dismissed as mere superstition.[11] According to Oyin Abogunrin, the African views of the world are similar to the biblical worldview, particularly the first-century Palestine in which Jesus lived and ministered. He argues that many Africans still live in the world of the New Testament—a world in which people believed in demons and a host of unseen supernatural powers.[12] The primary concern of Abogunrin is to show that no adequate African Christology can afford to ignore Jesus's interaction with some spiritual forces during his earthly ministry and the significance of such encounter for Africans. He insists that when we present in the categories which underestimate his supernatural activities, he will "be meaningless and irrelevant in the African context."[13]

It should be noted that Rudolf Bultmann's notion of demythologization is partly responsible for the decline in the discussions on demons

---

9. A. Anderson, "African Initiated Churches of the Spirit and Pneumatology,"179. See also Abanuka, *Philosophy and the Igbo World*, 63–82; Imasogie, *African Traditional Religion*, 67–78.

10. I will return to this issue later in this chapter.

11. Some Asian scholars have also criticized some Westerners for their dismissal of demonic possession as superstitious and as a characteristic of non-civilization. See Selvanayagam, "When Demons Speak the Truth! An Asian Reading of a New Testament Story of Exorcism," 33–40.

12. Abogunrin, *In Search for the Original Jesus*, 39.

13. Ibid, 43.

and Satan among some biblical scholars.[14] Walter Wink has described the marginalized status of angelology and demonology in the West.

> Angels, spirits, principalities, powers, gods, Satan—these, along with all other spiritual realities, are the unmentionables of [the Western] culture. The dominant materialistic worldview has absolutely no place for them. These archaic relics of superstitions pass as unspeakable because modern secularism simply has no categories, no vocabulary, no presuppositions by which to discern what it was in the actual experiences of people that brought these words to speech.[15]

Since my primary focus in this chapter is the African contexts, and not the western contexts, I will not interact with the complex discussions on demonology in the writings of some Western theologians. However, it is important to point out that Wink raises a serious challenge for any Western scholar who dismisses without a critical reflection on the demonic systems which promote injustice and oppression in the world.[16]

Returning to the African contexts, I have argued that the majority of Christians continue to take Satan and evil spirits seriously in their exposition of the Christian gospel message and in their daily lives. And even beyond Africa, as Afe Adogame has noted, some Nigerian Christians living in Europe have continued to believe in the existence and influence of demonic and evil forces on their lives.[17] But what are the factors that propel these Christians to think in this category? We are to recognize that there are complex factors which are responsible for this state of affairs. In this book, I argue that a major factor is the indigenous understandings of the interrelatedness of the spiritual and human worlds.

It is difficult to ascertain the extent to which the biblical teachings on demons and evils spirits have shaped African Christians' the understandings of the existence, identity and activities of malign spirits.

14. Bultmann wrote: "No-one can use the electric light and the radio or the discoveries of modern medicine and at the same time believe in the New Testament world of spirits and miracles." See Bultmann, *Kerygma and Myth*, 5.

15. Wink, *Unmasking the Powers*; Dow, "Case for the Existence of Demons," 199–209.

16. I have mentioned Wink here to highlight the difference in the ways people in the West and African peoples react to demon-talk.

17. Adogame, "African Instituted Churches in Europe: Continuity and Transformation," 235–36.

This difficulty stems from the fact that many Christians have borrowed some ideas from the indigenous religions as well as from the biblical teachings on Satan, demons and evil spirits. Therefore, it can be argued that the understandings of the existence of bad or evil spirits among Christians derive from the amalgamation of the indigenous religions and the biblical teaching on such spirit beings. It is necessary, then, to examine both the indigenous views and the biblical ideas of the malevolent spirit beings.

Many Christians see Satan as the head of the satanic forces that include demons or evil spirits, and people who belong to occult groups.[18] Therefore, it will be helpful to examine the identity of Satan first before examining demons and other members of the satanic family as construed by most African Christians.

Naming the Diabolic: Satan and Evil Spirits as construed in African Christianity

Is Satan God's Eternal Rival?

Most Christians perceive and treat Satan as a powerful opponent of God whose mission is to compete with God. Some treat Satan in the ways which suggest he is an eternal enemy of God who has the capacity to destroy permanently the good works of God when he is not constantly checked and bound. On the contrary, I will argue that this understanding of Satan can lead to a dangerous dualism that is strange to Jesus's understanding of God's activities in the world in which evil exists. I will also contend that although Satan is a powerful spirit being who has the capacity to distort God's sovereign rule over the world, he is not an eternal rival of God.

How exactly should we speak of and describe Satan?[19] Theologians disagree on whether or not Satan should be described in a personal or an impersonal way. In the *Fair Face of Evil*, Nigel Wright is wary of speaking of Satan as a personal being for fear of exalting him to the

---

18. In this book, Satan is used as a proper name for the spirit being that Jesus construes as a distorter of God's rule. I will also use the name Satan interchangeably with the Devil (*ho diabolos*).

19. For an examination of the historical development of Satan-talk from the Old Testament time to contemporary era, see Kelly, *Satan: A Biography*.

detriment of God.[20] According to Wink, speaking of Satan as a "literal "person" . . . who materializes in human form as a seducer and fiend" is a "Christian fantasy."[21] On the contrary he argues:

> The Satan of the Bible is more akin to an archetypal reality, a visionary or imaginal presence or event experienced within. But it is more than inner, because the social sedimentation of human choices for evil has formed a veritable layer of sludge that spans the world. Satan is both an outer and an inner reality.[22]

For Wink, it is unnecessary to assume that Satan will often "reveal himself . . . in individual cases," for Satan has the capacity to infiltrate the structures and ideologies of all human societies.[23] Wink raises an important issue which I will explore later in this chapter. It suffices to note here that many Christians seem to concentrate on the spiritual attacks and spiritual forces but ignore the demonic indigenous traditions and other oppressive systems that are dehumanizing. For example, whereas many Christians are ready and willing to pray to bind demons and evil spirits, many of them fail to work to dismantle the indigenous views that promote oppression. What African Christians need to recognize is that Satan and demonic forces are subtler than possessing and tormenting a few individuals. Also they need to learn from Jesus and work to dismantle and criticize all forms of demonic systems that promote subjugation and oppression of human beings.

Many Christians in Africa construe Satan as a fallen angel and therefore address him as a personal spirit being. This understanding of Satan, as we will see later, derives from their interpretations of some Old Testament passages. In addition, their understanding of Satan as a personal being stems from some indigenous views of the malevolent spirits. The New Testament perceptions of Satan are not entirely strange to the indigenous worldview of Nigeria. The words *Ekwensu* (Igbo) and *Esu* (Yoruba) are used for Satan in the Igbo and Yoruba Bible. In the indigenous thought of Igbo and Yoruba, *Ekwensu* and *Esu* are believed to be evil spirits.[24] According to Idowu, *Esu* is "capable of promoting

20. Wright, *Fair Face of Evil.*

21. Wink, *Unmasking the Powers*, 25.

22. Ibid.

23. Ibid., 28.

24. Ezeanya, "God, Spirits and the Spirit World: With Special Reference to the Igbo–Speaking People of Southern Nigeria," 30.

good and evil with what appears to be unrestrained license."[25] For him, *Esu* is "certainly not the Devil of the New Testament acquaintance, who is the opposition to the plan of God's salvation to man."[26] He, however, equates *Esu* with Satan, the tempter of Job, who he considers to be one of the "ministers of God and has the office of trying men's sincerity and putting their religion to proof."[27] Idowu concludes that *Esu* is a minister of *Olodumare* (the Supreme God).

> What we gather from our sources is that *Esu* is primarily a 'special relations officer' between heaven and earth, the inspector-general who reports regularly to Olodumare on the deeds of the divinities and men, and checks and makes report on the correctness of worship in general and sacrifices in particular.[28]

Again he writes,

> There is an unmistakable element of evil in *Esu* and for that reason he has been predominantly associated with things [that are] evil. There are those who say that the primary function of *Esu* in this world is to spoil things. But even so, we cannot call him the Devil—not in the New Testament sense of that name. What element of "evil" there is in *Esu* can be found also to some degree in most of the other divinities. The most that we can gather from the evidence of our oral traditions is that he takes mischief-making as his "hobby" just as any person corrupted by power which seems uncontrolled may find sadistic relish in throwing his weight about in unsympathetic, callous ways.[29]

Idowu sees the indigenous religions of Africa as God-given and, as the Ghanaian theologian, Kwame Bediako notes, he consequently argues that there is continuity in the concept of God "from the African pre-Christian past into the present Christian experience."[30] This understanding of God's activities in the indigenous religions influenced Idowu's interpretations and application of the Christian teachings and Scripture to the African context. That he equates *Esu* with Satan in Job's narrative is indicative of his intention to demonstrate the similarity and

25. Idowu, *Olodumare*, 50.

26. Ibid., 80.

27. Ibid.

28. Ibid.

29. Ibid., 83.

30. Bediako, *Theology and Identity*, 281.

compatibility of the Old Testament world and also the Nigerian indigenous understandings of the spiritual and human worlds.

In order for Esu to be the "inspector-general" of Olodumare it is required that the Yoruba people view Olodumare as a king operating in a celestial court in which *Esu* has an established role.[31] In the indigenous Yoruba religion, as Imasogie notes, "*Olodumare* appoints the divinities, each to a particular department of nature over which he is the ruler and governor."[32] According to Idowu, *Olodumare* is the "King with unique and incomparable majesty."[33] In both Yoruba and Igbo cosmologies, these mysterious beings are military figures. This explains why Idowu describes him as the "inspector-general" of *Olodumare*. In some societies in Igboland, for example, in Asaba, the festival of *Ekwensu* is connected with the display of wealth and military prowess.[34] He is never considered to be the opponent of the Supreme Being. But whether or not *Esu* is the Satan who tried Job and destroyed his health and material possession is of very little significance. What is important to note, however, is that in the Yoruba worldview, *Esu* like *Ekwensu* in the Igbo indigenous religion is a mysterious and dreaded spirit. Also, the majority of Igbo and Yoruba Christians perceive *Ekwensu* and *Esu* as the biblical Satan.

However, it should be noted that (largely because of the translation of Satan as *Ekwensu* and *Esu* in Igbo and Yoruba Bibles) many Nigerian Christians have adopted the rendering of *Esu* and *Ekwensu* as Satan or devil, who they regard as the chief destroyer of human happiness and the antagonist of God. According to Precious Uzobike, a member of Christian Pentecostal Mission, Satan is the devil that causes Christians to "be spiritually sick." For her, this is a dangerous state for a Christian

---

31. Kirsten Nielson has argued against the view that the kinship or royal council was the underlying imagery of Job's prologue. Arguing for the image of a father, she asserts: "In contrast to earlier research, I believe that the author [of Job] does not depict an image of the heavenly council but the image of a father and his sons. But if these scene is not official meeting between the king and his functionaries but a meeting within the family; it is indeed not unreasonable that one of the sons should yield to his jealousy towards this absent—but in spirit always present—favorite son and attempt to discredit him, so as to be able later to supersede him in his positions." See Nielson, *Satan: The Prodigal Son?*, 87.

32. Imasogie, *African Traditional Religion*, 24.

33. Idowu, *Olodumare*, 40.

34. Isichei, "Ibo and Christian Belief," 124–25.

to be because Satan exploits it and "attacks the Christian" and can afflict the Christian with "physical sickness such as barrenness, incurable diseases, stroke [and] epilepsy."[35] Most Christians construe Satan as the enemy of God, and consequently the enemy of Christians. As a result, they consider themselves to be at war with Satan and his cohorts. But for some, it is God, and not Satan or human beings that initiated this war. Chinedu Ihesiaba represents the Christians who view the relationship between God and Satan in this way. He writes,

> God had earlier than now; long ago, declared . . . war against Satan—the Devil and his co-workers. Seeing that Satan had seduced and destroyed man . . . God therefore declared war between man and Satan—the archenemy of God and man. "I will put enmity between you and the woman, between her offspring and your offspring. Her offspring will crush your head and you will bit his heel" (Gen 3:15).[36]

Since Satan is the "archenemy of God," for Ihesiaba, he is undoubtedly the one that is responsible for the existence and multiplicity of sins in the world:

> Satan introduced many tricks and wiles of which most of them [belong to the category] of possession of human body and soul. . . . He enslaves man and forces man to be under his authority and demonic operation whereby he inflicts sickness and other ailments of his victim. Through all these wiles and tricks, he compels man to do . . . evil things which God forbids [such] as gay, lesbianism, worship of false strife, division, heresy, etc.[37]

A deceitful tactic of Satan, according to Jude Nwachukwu, a Roman Catholic priest, is to solve some problems for people (including Christians) who seek his help. This is a misplaced desire. The solution-driven mindset (which I have criticized in this book) is partly responsible for this understanding of Satan. Also this mindset has propelled some Christians to seek for Jesus's power over Satan and demonic forces. Nwachukwu goes on to contend that Satan solves the problems of people with the intention to deceive and compel them to mistrust God's providence. In an interview he said:

---

35. Uzobike, interview by author, tape recording, Aba 24 May 2006.

36. Ihesiaba, *Exorcism and Healing Prayer*, 63.

37. Ibid., 65

> [In order] to get one hundred people, the Devil can save one life, or claim to save the life of one person. The person will become the agent [of the Devil] getting more people for him. So this is the problem we face here in Nigeria. We don't have patience with Christ and we don't believe. If we have faith and run to Christ with our problem Christ will solve it.[38]

Nwachukwu is responding to the question "do some Nigerian Christians go outside of Jesus Christ to find solution when he seems not to solve them?"[39] He is certainly not a lone voice. Many Christians in Nigeria see Satan as a deceiver precisely because, in their thinking, he solves problems for people and hopes to compel them to believe that he has the power to solve problems more quickly than Jesus. An ECWA member, Benedict Ufomadu observes: "We have seen that in the native doctors' place, Satan answers people quickly and immediately. When someone comes to him, he saves and does for the one what the person wants so that the person can believe in him."[40]

Joshua Balogun agrees but contends that the gifts of Satan bring more sorrow than joy. Balogun has written that prior to his conversion to Christianity, he was a member of "14 secret cults," was once a leader of six of the secret cults, a dedicated Muslim, a wizard and a native doctor. After his conversion to Christianity in 1988, he soon became a very popular evangelist partly because he told the stories of his experience in occultism and how Jesus Christ delivered him. In his *Redeemed from the Clutches of Satan*, based on his experience as one who was formerly a native doctor, Balogun wrote:

> You see, I want to point out to my readers how ticklish Satan is. He will eat so deep into the hearts of men that they will never be satisfied. They will forget who they are, their parents, homes, and above all, their religion. . . . Many wealthy business tycoons . . . would be so debased and bewitched by Satan that they will come down to a little village of about six houses to a witchdoctor . . . prostrate before his idols to seek for more power. Oh what a calamity! This dirty trickster of a doctor would prepare concussions from dead human flesh and bones, give them to eat and will charge them heavily for this evil power they had gotten.

38. Nwachukwu, interview by author, tape recording, Aba 22 June, 2006.

39. See chapter three for the discussion on Nigerian Christians' attitude towards seeking solution outside of Jesus Christ.

40. Ufomadu, interview by author, tape recording, Aba, 28 May 2006.

> Sorry to say, most of these [people who get such powers] always
> die mysterious death. As their wealth came, so it would also go
> away. Satan is merciless.[41]

In the thinking of Balogun, native doctors are agents of Satan.
They help to perpetuate Satan's malicious activities by temporarily providing people with wealth, protection and power. Ihesiaba has warned
that Satan is warring ferociously because he knows that "he will soon
be chained in hell."[42] He also argued that Christians are to be on the
watch for Satan is "roaming around the earth . . . seeking someone he
may mislead, one whom he may devour."[43] Enoch Adeboye has warned
Christians against the subtlety of Satan. "The devil can never speak the
truth," writes Adeboye, "but you have to be very careful because the
devil knows the Bible and can quote it."[44] The point Adeboye is trying to
make is that Christians need to be vigilant because Satan has the ability
to deceive and to compel them to think that "God . . . is speaking" to
them.[45]

Many African theologians see Satan as a personal malevolent spirit
being. John Mbiti, a Kenyan theologian, speaks of Satan as a personal
spirit being who is an arch-enemy of Jesus Christ. He writes,

> From the temptations to the cross, Jesus is fighting against [the]
> powers of evil, Satan being the arch-enemy of the Gospel (Matt
> 4:1–11). His healing of diseases and other infirmities, his casting
> out of demons, and even his raising of the dead, are acts which
> constitute the eschatological overthrow of evil powers by the
> Messiah . . .[46]

Byang Kato has noted that the Jaba people of northern Nigeria see
Satan as a real and personal being.[47] In many Christian communities in
Nigeria, Satan remains a significant and dreaded spirit who is capable
of ruining and destroying the happiness of people by bringing sickness
and other forms of horrendous misfortunes upon people. Many theolo-

41. Balogun, *Redeemed from the Clutches of Satan*, 12.

42. Ihesiaba, *Exorcism and Healing Prayer*, 66.

43. Ibid.

44. Adeboye, *God the Holy Spirit*, 19.

45. Ibid.

46. Mbiti, *New Testament Eschatology in an African Background*, 140.

47. Kato, *Theological Pitfalls in Africa*, 37.

gians as well as the Christian laity have continued to view Satan as the antagonist and the chief opponent or the leader of the opposition group that fights and competes with God and Christians. Efe Ehioghae speaks for many Christians when he argues that the New Testament presents Satan "as the leader of the spiritual forces that are marshaled against God and his saints."[48] This view of Satan is widespread in many African Christian communities. Undoubtedly, Mbiti represents many African theologians who consider Satan to be occupying "the leading position in the New Testament demonology."[49] For Mbiti, in order to arrest the activities of the satanic forces, it is necessary to first of all capture Satan. And for him, "this is precisely what Jesus has done in his ministry, and most effectively [on] the cross."[50] Many Christians have continued to construe Satan as a powerful leader of an opposition force who is fighting to mislead many people so as to bring such people under God's judgment. I will argue, however, that viewing Satan as rival of God and the leader of the opposition group that competes and fights against God is misleading and inadequate. On the contrary, in the following section, I will propose that Satan is a distorter of God's rule but not an equal and eternal being that competes with God.

SATAN AS A DISTORTER OF GOD'S RULE

Satan is not an eternal opposite being that competes with God. Even if we see him as a fallen angel, he remains a creature of God and therefore is not an eternal rival of God. Such dualism is hardly traceable to Jesus Christ. Although Jesus directed some of his preaching, teaching and criticism against satanic and demonic forces, he maintained that God is the sole ruler of the creation. It is God that has authority over the creation, and he has given this authority to the Son, Jesus the Christ.[51] I will argue that it is misleading to view Satan as an opponent of God in the ways that suggests he is an eternal competitor of God. The Christ-Event demonstrates that Satan is a distorter of God's rule and not an eternal rival of God.

---

48. Ehioghae, "Concept of God and Evil: A Christian Perspective," 432.

49. Mbiti, *New Testament Eschatology in an African Background*, 141.

50. Ibid.

51. Matthew 28:18.

The New Testament authors do not present their discussions on angels, demons and Satan systematically. Jesus's discussion on Satan is not systematic in nature. "Jesus certainly took for granted the reality of Satan," writes I. Howard Marshall, "and sometimes spoke about him in a poetic manner . . ."[52] Perhaps Jesus needed not to undertake a systematic teaching on Satan, demons and the demoniac because such spirit beings were very familiar in his immediate Jewish context. But what is central in his conversations with Satan and demons is his attempt to deconstruct, probe and reshape some of the predominant views of these spirit beings in his culture. In addition, it is important to recognize that Jesus's ministry, broadly speaking, seeks to critique and dismantle all forms of worldviews that arrogate to human beings or spirit beings the authority and sovereignty that belong to God alone. It also seeks to dismantle the cultures and beliefs systems that perpetuate dehumanization and oppression.

The identity of Satan is expressed in his actions as the *chief distorter* of God's rule and as the accuser of the people of God.[53] The debate on whether or not Satan is a personal independent spirit being does not bother the majority of African Christians. It should also be noted that Jesus does not discuss the mode of being of Satan but rather the activities of Satan. When approached from the perspective of the Christ-Event, it is more adequate to see Satan as a distorter of God's rule rather than as an eternal and equal opponent of God. Commenting on Mark 1:21–28, Morna Hooker writes: "Satan was in no sense regarded as God's equal, but as one who had rebelled against his authority, who for the moment was allowed his way, but who ultimately would be crushed."[54]

The danger of construing Satan as an antagonist or an opponent of God is that some people will assign to him a status of an eternal rival—a position he does not (and is never intended to) occupy. If Satan is the eternal rival of God, it follows that God sets his acts against Satan and relates to him in that capacity. This understanding of Satan will introduce a form of dualism which is strange to Jesus's understanding of the God-creature relationship. Understood correctly, from the vantage point of the life and ministry of Jesus Christ, Satan's task is to counterfeit

52. Marshall, *Gospel of Luke*, 168.

53. The use of masculine pronoun *his* here is not suggestive that Satan is male. As a spirit being, Satan must be presumed to be genderless.

54. Hooker, *Gospel According to St. Mark*, 61–62.

and distort God's rule. Therefore, Satan is not a leader of an opposition group which competes with God's leadership. But although he cannot oppose God's rule as God's equal rival, it is important to recognize that Satan has the capability of distorting God's rule partly by arrogating to himself the status of an alternative ruler of the world. This is evident in the temptation of Jesus Christ at the beginning of his ministry. It could be argued that Satan desires for people to view him as the eternal opponent of God. By asking Jesus to "bow down and worship him" as a requirement for gaining earthly possessions, Satan aimed at distorting the sovereign lordship of God and wanted Jesus to see him as an alternative to and an antagonist of God.

We are to see Satan's claim of having an authority over the kingdoms of the world as untruthful.[55] Contemporaries of Jesus Christ, including the writers of the synoptic gospels, may well have believed that the "entire populations of humans . . . have long been under Satan's authority," and that the majority of them are "willingly giving him glory and obeying his command."[56] Jesus, however, counteracts this belief. Throughout his earthly life, Jesus Christ demonstrated through some of his teaching and miraculous works that it is to him, and not Satan, that God has given a sovereign authority over the creation. We need to recall that as Jesus neared the end of his life on earth, he told his disciples "All authority in heaven and on earth has been given to me."[57] Interestingly, he made this claim whilst commissioning his disciples to carry on with his ministry of restoration and reconciliation of humanity.[58] This ministry of Jesus and its extension and continuation through the followers of Jesus Christ are aimed at reversing and exposing Satan's distortion of God's rule or kingdom.

Even in the Old Testament, the predominant view is that God is the sole owner and ruler of God's world. There is no indication that God has relinquished or given to Satan the authority to rule over God's creation. Therefore, Satan's claim of having authority over the kingdoms of the world cannot be true if we understand the claim to mean that he has a sole authority over the world. Marshall makes this point vividly:

55. Mathew 4:8–10; Luke 4:5–7.

56. Garrett, *Demise of the Devil*, 40.

57. Mathew 28:18, *NIV*.

58. See chapter seven for an examination of the restoration and reconciliation ministry of Jesus Christ and how it affects humanity.

> Whereas in the OT this realm and authority lie in the hands
> of God, here the devil claims that it has been given to him and
> that consequently he has the right of disposal (cf. Mk16:14; Jn
> 12:31; 14:30; 16:11; 1 John 5:19; Rev 13:2). Ultimately, however,
> the devil's claim was not true, nor was his word to be trusted.[59]

The responses of Jesus to Satan's requests during the temptation also indicate he was aware of the intention of Satan to distort the rule of God and also his intention to coerce him to believe that there was an eternal alternative opposition's rule to God's rule. Jesus reminded Satan that it was God alone who was the sole owner and ruler of the world, and therefore the only Being that was worthy of worship: "It is written: 'worship the Lord your God and serve him only.'"[60] Commenting on this response, Marshall notes: "God alone is to be worshipped, so that there can be no question of the Son of God offering worship and service to the devil, even for such an apparently great reward."[61]

As we have already seen, many African Christians tend to see the relationship between Satan and God in a dualistic sense. On the contrary, I contend that an appropriate way to construe Satan, when viewed from the perspective of the Christ Event, is to see him as a distorter of God's rule and not an eternal rival of God. Satan could have achieved his aim to arrogate to himself the position of the leader of the opposition group that competes with and fights against God if he succeeded in coercing Jesus to think of him in such way. It follows that African Christians and all people who think of Satan as the eternal antagonist of God have failed to learn from Jesus's attitude towards Satan. Such people gratify the desire of Satan to be seen as a powerful opposition leader against the leadership of God. Leon-Joseph Suenens has warned of the theological fallacy in construing Satan as the antagonist of God.

> The . . . dualistic Manichean speculations cautions us against
> all theories that present the Devil as a kind of Counter-Power,
> and Antagonist directly opposed to God, vying with him as an
> equal opponent in a battle. For we must take care not to envis-
> age Satan as an Antigod, thus making God and the Devil two
> contending absolutes: the Principle of Good grappling with the
> Principle of Evil. God is the one and only Absolute, sovereign

---

59. Marshall, *Gospel of Luke*, 172.

60. Luke 4: 8, *NIV*.

61. Marshall, *Gospel of Luke*, 172.

and transcendent; whereas the Devil, a creature of God and originally good in his ontological reality, plays in Creation the role of a destructive, negative and subordinate parasite. He is the father of lies, of perversion.[62]

There is consensus among the majority of African theologians that the rule of God or the kingdom of God is the central theme in the ministry of Jesus Christ.[63] It should not be surprising then that Jesus talked about his experience and conversation with Satan in the ways that were designed to bring his readers to the knowledge of God's rule.[64] Against the popular views prevalent among "many religious Jews" who believed the world was "under the tyranny of Satan and evil," as Larry Hurtado notes, "Jesus' message signifies that God has began to establish his rule" in the world. [65] The intent of Satan was to distract, distort, and coerce Jesus into losing focus on the very mission he has come to accomplish: to enact and announce the approaching of God's rule and the "accompanying convictions about his role as its herald, indeed, its dramatic vehicle."[66] To say that Jesus announced the approaching rule of God is not to suggest that prior to the Christ-Event God's rule was absent from the world. It is rather, as Mbiti argues: "what in Judaism was yet to come has arrived in the person and work of Jesus Christ."[67]

Theologians disagree on the exact nature, content and character and even the meaning of the kingdom. Ukachukwu Manus argues that the nature of the kingdom of God is a mystery.[68] Walter Burghardt has reminded Christians of the progressive nature of the kingdom of God. In his thinking, the kingdom of God will "slowly but surely grow in grace and unity until the end of time when a dream divine will be realized and . . . Christ the King" will present to his Father a kingdom in which peace and justice reigns.[69] Whatever meanings we ascribe to Jesus's un-

---

62. Suenens, *Renewal and the Powers of Darkness*, 7.

63. See Mbiti, *New Testament Eschatology in an African Background*, 40–44; Manus, *Christ, the Africa King*, 147–67.

64. It seems Jesus believed that Satan is a personal spirit being and not an abstract desire within human beings.

65. Hurtado, *Mark—New International Biblical Commentary*, 22.

66. Ibid.

67. Mbiti, *New Testament Eschatology in an African Background*, 42.

68. Manus, *Christ, the African King*, 151.

69. Burghardt, "A Just King, a Just Kingdom," 9.

derstanding of the kingdom of God, it is important to acknowledge he wanted his hearers to know that God, through the Christ-Event, has enacted and engaged in a new relationship with humanity of which God remains the sole ruler. Although Satan distorts God's rule by promoting and perpetuating evil in the world, Jesus counteracts Satan's distortion of God's rule by criticizing oppressive systems and healing the spiritual, physical and physiological wounds that Satan inflicts on people.

Satanic Forces as Tempters and Accusers of God's People

While Satan is not an eternal antagonist of God, I argue he is an accuser of God's people and also a distorter of God's rule. Satan has the power to compete with, distort, and influence people. Jesus makes this clear when he says to some of his listeners: "You belong to your father, the devil, and you want to carry out your father's desires."[70] Jesus goes on to define the desire of the devil as consisting in distorting God's truth that he mediates.[71] According to Russell, "Possession is one of the most common means Satan uses to obstruct the Kingdom of God."[72] The majority of African indigenous views of the world do not give a pneumatological explanation of the origin of evil.[73] Many of them view human beings as solely responsible for their alienation from God. No fallen angels or any lesser spirit beings tempted and compelled them to disobey or distrust God.[74]

But according to the Genesis creation and fall stories, the Serpent represents a mysterious source of temptation that compelled Adam and

70. John 8: 44, *NIV*.

71. "He was a murder from the beginning, not holding to the truth, for there is no truth in him. When he lies, he speaks his native language, for he is liar and the father of lies. Yet because I tell you the truth, you do not believe me!" John 8: 44–45, *NIV*.

72. Russell, *Devil*, 237.

73. The expression pneumatological is used here in a broad sense (not in the narrow theological sense of the theology of the Holy Spirit) to describe angels because of their nature as spiritual beings.

74. There are numerous Nigerian and African myths about human beings' alienation from God. These myths are hardly popular today probably because of the influence of Christianity and Islam in Nigeria. Since this chapter is not dealing on human relationship with God, it will be unnecessary to discuss these myths here. I will , however, return to this topic in chapter seven. The basic texts that discuss these myths include Imasogie, *African Traditional Religion*, 32–33; Mbiti, *African Religions and Philosophy*, 97–99.

Eve mistrust God. Some Christian theologians (due to the influence of the New Testament teachings on Satan) have interpreted the myth of the Serpent in the *Genesis-Fall* narrative as symbolic of a creaturely enemy of God, namely, Satan. However, the Old Testament represents Satan as a member of the heavenly cohort and not as an independently existing evil being. He is responsible for testing and coercing people to do evil. Wink notes, after examining 1 Chronicles 21:1, Zechariah 3:1–5 and Job 1–2, that in all these passages, "Satan manifests no power independent of God. Even when Satan slays, it is not Satan who does so, but God who slays through Satan. . . . God alone is supreme; Satan is not evil, or demonic, or fallen, or God's enemy."[75] For him, the notion of Satan as an adversary must be understood in the context of a "faithful, if overzealous, servant of God, entrusted with quality control and testing."[76]

"I call Jesus 'the healer of multiple diseases' and the 'One who softens what is hard'. Anytime I call him, wonders happen in the town of Satan."[77] This was the response of Shedrach Okonkwo, a member of Christ Holy Church, when he was asked about his favorite name for Jesus. When I asked to him explain what he means by "*obodo Ekwensu*," literally, the "town or village of Satan," he said: "Satan has his agents, I mean, his demons, witches, wizards, and evil spirits" who help him to torment Christians.[78] Many Africans believe that the world is filled up with spirit beings some of which are co-workers or agents of Satan. For them, the primary function of the malevolent spirits is to "make conditions difficult for a person to fulfill his destiny."[79] These spirits are innumerable and are capable of possessing an individual either as a result of an inducement from the individuals or by the desire of the spirits to force themselves upon people, sometimes altering their consciousness.[80]

---

75. Wink, *Unmasking the Powers*, 14.

76. Ibid.

77. Okonkwo, interview by the researcher, tape recording 25 June 2006.

78. Ibid.

79. Imasogie, *African Traditional Religion*, 51.

80. Crapanzano has described spirit possessing as "any altered or unusual state of consciousness and allied behavior that is indigenously understood in terms of the influence of an alien spirit, demon, or deity. The possessed act as though another personality—a spirit or soul—has entered their body and taken control. Dramatic changes in physiognomy, voice and manner usually occur." See Crapanzano, "Spirit Possession," 12. See also Cox, "Spirit Mediums in Zimbabwe: Religious Experience in and on behalf of the Community," 190–207.

For many Christians, demons and evil spirits (including spirits from the dead wicked people) aim to cause human beings unhappiness by executing Satan's wicked desires. As Ihesiaba has argued:

> Satan has legions of spirits who rebelled against God with him. They are sometimes called bad angels, demons, evil spirit, etc. These spirits work under Satan and they operate on his side. These are fallen angels deceived by Satan to work or carry out his evil acts against man. They are referred to as the agents of Satan and they are evil. Their duty is to possess a human body and torment it. They do the work and the will of their master— the Devil.[81]

Anyone familiar with the history of contemporary African Christianity will notice that there are numerous stories and testimonies by people who are delivered from demonic possessions. Some of these people have gone ahead to become renowned evangelists or founders of churches. What is noteworthy about such testimonies of deliverance from demonic and satanic influences and attacks is that the truthfulness or untruthfulness of a given account does not destroy Christians' belief in the existence of Satan and demons. Many of them continue to believe that demons parade everywhere and are constantly seeking the downfall of the people of God.

Most Christians hardly bother with the speculation about the origins of demons. They seem to be certain about demons' association with Satan. Demons are believed to be fallen angels who followed Satan in disobeying God. The key biblical text that some of them employ to support this view is Ezekiel 28:11–19—the prophecy against the king of Tyre. According to Ihesiaba, "Lucifer was created good and perfect without blame," but after he "exalted himself and . . . prided himself against his maker" he "was thrown out of the presence of God."[82] Since Satan is created, Ihesiaba argues, he is therefore not omniscient.[83] To make up for limited knowledge, Satan relies on his demons to monitor Christians.[84] Ihesiaba challenges Christians to be careful not to attribute

---

81. Ihesiaba, *Exorcism and Prayer*, 33.
82. Ibid., 32.
83. Ibid.
84. Ibid., 33.

omnipotence to Satan for he also "has limited power [and] therefore cannot be everywhere."[85]

Another thing that is noteworthy is the abode of Satan and evil spirits. On this Ihesiaba has written: "After being thrown out of heaven, down to earth and seas, [Satan] now roams about the face of the earth, seas and the sky, from these areas he and his agents relentlessly carry out their functions of destruction."[86]

In the Nigerian indigenous religions, the abode of the demons and evil spirits (or spirits in general) is ambivalent. The Igbo believe that the spirits live beneath the earth.[87] Idowu notes that the spirits of the dead who have not been accorded proper burial ceremonies, like the spirit of wicked people who are dead, become "wanderers of a place of no abode."[88] The indigenous religions, as Imasogie observes, teach that evil spirits hover around "everywhere and are particularly active at night."[89] Some Nigerians believe that traditional healers can invoke some evil spirits and "send them to destroy their enemies."[90] Evil spirits are also believed to have the power, when not bridled, to "make conditions difficult for a person to fulfill his destiny."[91] The belief that evil spirits and demons operate at night explains perhaps why some Christians organize night vigils or all night prayer services. Most of them believe that Satan and his demons have their meetings and execute their evil plans in the night. These Christian devote most of their time praying and pronouncing judgment on Satan and his agents during the night vigils. Most of them use Scriptural passages as their spiritual munitions to wage war against evil spirits.

In African Christianity, theological discussions on the influence of the malevolent spirit beings on the human world have followed two opposite directions. The first view dismisses the belief in the impact of the malevolent spirits on people's daily lives as mere superstitions and

---

85. Ibid.

86. Ibid., 34.

87. Kalu, "Church Presence in Africa: A Historical Analysis of the Evangelization Process," 15.

88. Idowu, *African Traditional Religion*, 187.

89. Imasogie, *African Traditional Religion*, 38.

90. Ibid.

91. Ibid., 51.

as a consequence a fear.[92] According to Kato, the "dominating fears and superstitions concerning the spirit world are so dreadful" that what the Jaba people and all African peoples are in need of is "an instantaneous *Superstitio* and complete cure . . ."[93] Kato's objective is to discredit some of the traditional beliefs about the spirit beings.[94] For example, he considered the Jaba people's traditional belief about the domain of Satan as superstitious. He narrated a story that he believed indicated that the "backbone of the superstition [about Satan] was broken" when the missionaries of the Sudan Interior Mission built their station around one of the purported domains of Satan.

> The Spirits are always associated with "Kuno," Satan. Jaba have never doubted the existence or activities of Satan. He is a real person to them. Iron smelting is an old trade in Jaba land. . . . Legends are told of the hearths being old mansions of Satan. Before the advent of missions, it was taboo to dig up any of the furnace hearths. People firmly believed that if a person dug out the hearth, he would become mad. When the Sudan Interior Mission built their station near one of the forbidden sites, and later had the occasion to dig up the "Satan house," the local people at Kwoi expected them to become mad. As this did not happen, the backbone of the superstition was broken. Very few people still believe in this "Satan house." But the belief in Satan as a person persists.[95]

I will return to critique this view after I articulate the second which is undoubtedly the most popular in Africa. For many Christians, the effects of the works of the malevolent spirit beings permeate and influence every aspect of the lives of human beings. Many of these Christians believe that every event in the human world is a result of an action or decision of some spirit beings. They construe their health, wealth, wellbeing, poverty, spiritual life, and every aspect of their lives against the background of the belief in the power and influence of the

92. For a radical version of this view see Lewis, *Religion in Context*, 39. For criticism against the hysterical explanation of the exorcism of Jesus Christ, see Instone-Brewer, "Jesus and the Psychiatrists," 133–48; Crislip, "Sin of Sloth or the Illness of Demons?," 143–69.

93. Kato, *Theological Pitfalls in Africa*, 38.

94. Kato does not seem to deny the existence of all the lesser spiritual beings whether malevolent or benevolent as it is construed in the traditional religion.

95. Kato, *Theological Pitfalls in Africa*, 37.

spiritual beings.[96] They see their lives most of the times as battlefields on which bad and good spiritual beings engage in warfare.[97] Consequently, many see Christianity or the local churches as spiritual battlefields. As the bishop of Church of God Mission, B. C. Edohasim has noted:

> Christianity is warfare. . . . The battleground of the devil is not in the political arena, but the church. There are people in the church who do not know that there is a warfare going on. Ironically, some may not know that the devil can turn an elder against the pastor, a deacon against the deaconess or the congregation against the church authority.[98]

Many Christians think of their existence, not only in relation to God, but also in relation to the lesser spirit beings, particularly the evil spirits. The issues of spiritual warfare that Paul speaks of in Ephesians 6 preoccupy the hearts of most of these Christians so much that they constantly see themselves to be at battle with demons, Satan, and evil spirits. According to Edohasim, the moment a "person opens his soul to receive Christ as the Savior," Jesus evicts Satan from the person's spirit. However, Satan "does not give up the battle." He continues to fight to regain control over the person.[99] When a Christian is ill, barren, poor, and non-prosperous, he or she has an already-made answer to the source of these conditions he or she construes as misfortunes: Satan and his host of demons and evils spirits. This mindset propels some Christians to pray to God for deliverance and to obtain a divine power to cast out the demons that are responsible for the majority of their misfortunes. This mindset equally sets the stage for Jesus Christ to battle against Satan and his demons with the intention to free his followers from their snares. Since many Christians believe that there is no aspect of their

96. Many Nigerian Christians, devotees of the indigenous religions and Muslims continue to interpret the daily events in their lives from the perspective of the spirit-human interrelation. See Danfulani, "Factors Contributing to the Survival of the Bori Cult in Northern Nigeria," 412–47.

97. This view underestimates the roles of human beings in the perpetuation of demonic activities in the world and the responsibility of human beings in dismantling the demonic activities in their societies. The danger is that many Christians continue to look for the source of evil in the spirit world but ignore that some of their actions and beliefs that promote racism, sexism, poverty, dehumanization, and injustice are evil and demonic.

98. Edohasim, *Don't Be Talked out of Your Miracle*, 23.

99. Ibid., 45.

lives which Satan and his cohort cannot influence, they are compelled to surrender to Jesus Christ who they believe is able to confront and defeat Satan and his legion.

The foregoing two views on the operation of the malevolent spirits are misleading and are incapable of generating an adequate and relevant Christology that probes and critiques African Christians' understandings of the spirit world and the spirit beings. However, the construal of Africans' belief in demon possession as mere anachronistic and superstitious risks a distortion and underestimation of the importance of Jesus's understanding of his life and ministry in relation to the complex malign, dehumanizing and oppressive activities of demons and evil spirits. As O'Collins notes,

> During his ministry Jesus presented his activity in the service of the present coming kingdom of God as a victorious conflict with satanic powers (e.g., Mark 3:27). He taught his followers to pray for deliverance "from the evil one" (Matthew 6:13; Mark 14:38; Like 11:4). Jesus knew his redemptive work to involve liberation from sin, evil and a misuse of the law and to bring the gift of life in abundance.[100]

Jesus's teaching, preaching, exorcism and other miraculous healings indicate, as Roy Yates has noted, "his Messianic assault on the powers of evil."[101] The inability of many African contextual theologians to provide some constructive Christologies that engage with the beliefs in demons and other malevolent spirits is partly responsible for the readiness of many Christians to consult some diabolic and occult sources when they encounter persistent misfortunes. Prior to the advent of Western Christian missionaries, the indigenous religions "had provisions for spiritual healing, casting out of inimical spirits . . . and material prosperity."[102] The indigenous ways of dealing with evil spirits vary depending on the prescriptions of a diviner or a native doctor. When a person suspects the activity of an evil spirit or wicked people, the normal thing to do is to consult a diviner to find out what and who is responsible for the misfortune.[103] Many Christians visit prophets and prophetesses to seek knowledge about the sources of their problems.

100. O'Collins, *Jesus Our Redeemer*, 116–17.

101. Yates, "Jesus and the Demonic in the Synoptic Gospel," 39–57.

102. Folarin, "Contemporary State of the Prosperity Gospel in Nigeria," 70.

103. Imasogie, *African Traditional Religion*, 38.

The credibility of these diviners, native doctors, prophets and prophetesses is not the concern of this book. What is of interest here is the willingness of many Christians to consult such people in order to discover the causes of and the possible solutions to their misfortunes. Some diviners sometimes may require the person to "make sacrifices to appease the evil spirits."[104] Imasogie notes that whilst the sacrifices "may not be expensive," they "are irksome."[105]

Some churches which belong to the category of African Independent or Indigenous Churches (AICs) and most Pentecostal churches rose quickly to fame in Africa partly because they provided a practical Christian response and procedures for dismantling and exorcising evil spirits from the lives of people. But the view that sees misfortunes in human life as a consequence of the actions of the malevolent spirits can become an escapist notion that diminishes human responsibility and overemphasizes the activities of the malevolent spirits.[106]

From the perspective of the Christ-Event, Satan has the power to influence the people of God. One example is the apostle Peter. Jesus rebuked Peter for speaking and acting under the influence of Satan. On hearing Jesus's prediction of his death, Peter "took him aside and rebuked him."[107] Jesus responded immediately with a sharp warning: "Get behind me, Satan! You are a stumbling block to me; you do not have in mind the things of God, but the things of men."[108] One of the key ideologies Jesus aims to dismantle here is the idea of self-accumulation. In some African contexts, this idea is subsumed in the desire of many Christians to seek solution from Jesus Christ. Peter seems to desire for Jesus to complete his ministry without experiencing the suffering and humiliation of the cross. Although, as I will argue in the next chapter, the cross of Jesus Christ exposes the wickedness and evil actions of humanity, Jesus's stern rebuke demonstrates that he considers Peter's easy escape mindset (crown without the cross) to be in contradiction with the acts of self-giving and self-sacrificing which are central to the Christ-Event. What many Christians who have allowed the solution-

104. Ibid.

105. Ibid.

106. It is also an attempt to render Christian spirituality a matter of management and technique.

107. Matthew 16:22, *NIV*.

108. Ibid., 16:23.

oriented mindset to shape their Christologies have overlooked is that Jesus Christ preaches self-giving and not self-accumulation. In some cases, when Christians pray to Jesus to deliver them from the attacks of the evil spirits so that they can bear children, make profit in their businesses, enjoy good health and so on, they do so because they want to enjoy and to accumulate the things that they consider to be essential to living a fulfilled life. The Christ-Event shakes this mindset to its foundation. African Christians need to rediscover that Jesus is simultaneously a question and a solution to their needs. Jesus is not simply there to solve the problems of human beings; he seeks to inform and remold their understandings of their problems, needs and aspirations.

It is noteworthy that the demonic activities against the rule of God do not always have to come in the form of possessing a few people. Satan and his demonic cohort can be subtler than living within people and even in the case of using the possessed people to bring about some good such as healing the sick or foretelling the future.[109] Since ushering in the kingdom of God, Jesus has given his followers the power and grace to expose and criticize injustice, and dismantle oppression.[110] It follows that the individuals, groups of people and/or governments that have promoted oppression and injustice are under demonic influence. Manus has argued that the numerous accounts of the

> healing miracles by Jesus and his disciples, the victory over the powers of demons, especially the vanquishing of the oppressive, destructive anti-social forces which pontificated as Legion (Mt 5:9) and the condemnation of all vices arising from wealth and its inordinate pursuit described with the Semitic imagery, *Mammon*, riches (Lk 16:13), represent Jesus as the harbinger of God's sovereignty so eagerly awaited by many.[111]

It is surprising that Manus who is articulating a New Testament Christology for the African context, does not go on to situate his foregoing contention within the concrete experiences of African peoples. However, he has provided us with a helpful context for expressing the extent of the activities of Satan. It can be argued that the most effective way Satan and his cohorts have perpetuated their activities in Africa is by infiltrating the ecclesiastical and political systems. Anyone, for ex-

---

109. Acts 16:16–40.

110. Luke 4.

111. Manus, *Christ, the African King*, 152.

ample, who is familiar with Nigerian history, will notice that the majority of the people have continued to experience injustice and oppression. These manifestations of demonic influence can be seen in the lives of many people who are living in abject poverty whilst a few individuals steal and siphon the country's resources. The sad consequence is that the majority who are poor cannot get justice when they have an encounter with the few powerful rich individuals. The time is really overdue; Nigerian Christians as well as other African Christians must learn to extend their responses against the demonic activities to all systems that promote injustice, dehumanization, subjugations and oppression. They need to use the power that Jesus has given them to tear down the structures of oppression in their societies. In this way they will continue with Jesus's work against satanic and demonic activities.

Dealing with the Malevolent Spirits: The Christ-Event in relation to the activities of Satan and Demonic Forces

Jesus Christ and People of God as Restrainers of Satan and Demonic Forces

Jesus Christ understood his ministry to include restraining the powers, distortions, and influences of satanic forces. And he achieved this by refusing to succumb to the temptations of Satan, by rebuking demons that lived within people and tormented their lives, by exposing and condemning social and ecclesial systems that promoted injustice, and by solving the spiritual and physical problems of the people that encountered him. Knowing that the goal of Satan is to distort God's rule or the kingdom of God by deceiving people and coercing them to believe that he is an equal competitor of God, Jesus, through his ministry and life, initiated the process of curbing the activities of Satan and his cohort. It is interesting to note that Jesus has equally given authority to "his apostles to expand his attack upon demonic power."[112] All followers of Jesus must oppose demonic activities. Like Jesus and the apostles, Christians have the authority to restrain demonic activities against God's rule on earth by following Jesus and the apostles in rebuking demons from people and combating demonic activities in their communities and societies.

---

112. Hurtado, *Mark*, 26.

But in what ways are Christians to understand the approaches Jesus employed in dealing with demonic forces? And what are the implications of such approaches for contemporary African Christians? These questions introduce us to the critical issue of how Christians respond to satanic forces and activities.

COHABITING WITH THE MALEVOLENT SPIRITS

It has become customary for Christians to assert that Jesus Christ *defeated* Satan and demonic forces. Commenting on Luke 8:26–30, Robert Stein argues:

> Jesus defeated the demons, a legion in number (8:30) and with superhuman power to break chains (8:29). The supernaturally powerful demons, however, could only "beg" (8:28) Jesus, for they had not ability to counter the power of the "Son of the Most High God."[113]

James Dunn and Graham Twelftree have argued that "Jesus saw his exorcisms as the defeat of Satan."[114] Ihesiaba speaks for many Christians who believe that Jesus has defeated Satan and all evil powers. He encourages Christians to remember that "Jesus is [their] victory; he conquered death and all the powers of the enemy."[115] Onah Odey has equally argued that salvation is described in the Bible as "God and Christ breaking the gates of brass, iron, death, and hell." He goes on to contend that this view of God and Christ "represent the defeat of the power of Satan and his cohorts which the Bible calls principalities, powers, rulers of darkness, wickedness in high places, prince of the air and demons."[116]

We are to become, however, cautious of the language of defeat when examining the relationship between Jesus and Satan and all malevolent spirits. This is because the language of defeat conjures up the image of bringing something to an end or rendering something ineffective. In this sense, it can be assumed that Jesus has made Satan and demons ineffective or that he has brought their activities or their distortion of God's rule to an end. This is certainly not the case. Satan

113. Stein, *Luke—The New America Commentary*, 259.

114. Dunn and Twelftree, "Demon-Possession and Exorcism in the New Testament," 219.

115. Ihesiaba, *Exorcism and Healing Prayers*, 67–68.

116. Odey, "Superstitious Beliefs and Practices," 145–46.

and demons continue to manifest in people's lives, possessing and using them to extend their distortion and perversion of God's rule. When approached from the context of the *already-not yet* tension that underlies Jesus's proclamation of the Kingdom of God, an appropriate term for describing Jesus's assault on satanic forces, beginning from the time of his ministry and continuing to the present time, is restraining. The language of defeat seems to belong to the not-yet aspect of the a*lready-not-yet* tension. In other words, defeat seems belong to the end of a process. By enacting a new relationship between God and human beings, Jesus began the ongoing process of restraining the powers and activities of Satan and demons. However, this process is ongoing and will only come to completion at the return of Jesus Christ.[117] One of the implications of this ongoing restraining of satanic forces is that Christians who are living in the human world cannot escape such spirit beings. Since Jesus has *not yet* eradicated the activities of Satan and other malevolent spirits, Christians have no option but to continue to live in the world in which satanic forces can influence. This should only make them continue to use the authority Jesus has given to them to restrain, rebuke, and exorcise satanic forces.

CONFRONTING THE MALEVOLENT SPIRITS: SILENCING, REBUKING, AND EXORCISM

Many Christians have not only learned to cope with the malevolent spirits (because in their thinking they cannot escape them) but also to confront them. This state of affairs, of course, is not unique them. Before the advents of Christianity and Islam, African peoples had formulated ways to deal with, appease, exorcise, and confront the spirit beings they believe to be malevolent. Two beliefs undergirded this state of affairs. The first is the belief that, using the right technique and appropriate power and approach, human beings can transform (or sometimes confuse) a malevolent spirit, making the spirit become benevolent, or at least stopping the spirit from causing misfortunes.[118] The second is the belief that the most effective and safe way to deal with a malign spirit is to confront the spirit by rebuking, binding and exorcising the

---

117. See Revelation 20:7–10.

118. Turaki, *Unique Christ for Salvation*, 61; see also Mbiti, *African Religions and Philosophy*, 79–83.

spirit from the lives of people. These two beliefs have informed many Christians' attitudes toward the malevolent spirits.[119]

Before exploring how these Christians respond to the activities of Satan and malevolent spirits, I will highlight some of the encounters Jesus had with some evil spirits. This will help to create a useful christological milieu to examine the attitudes of Nigerian Christians toward the malevolent spirits. The writers of the synoptic Gospels record some of Jesus's confrontations with the malevolent spirits. Jesus rebuked, silenced, and exorcised demons from people. "'Be quiet!' said Jesus sternly, 'come out of him.'"[120] Mark's intent here is to show that Jesus has authority over evil spirits.[121] In addition, Mark aims to show the irony that some "demons know [Jesus], but the people cannot perceive his real significance."[122] However, it is clear from the narratives of Jesus's encounters with demons that he demonstrated his authority over them by rebuking and expulsing them from people. Interestingly, Mark shows that Jesus's authority derives from God and not from Beelzebub.[123] That Mark recorded some occasions when Jesus withdrew from the crowd to pray to God is an indication that God is the source of Jesus's authority. As Hurtado argues, "Mark's account shows the source of Jesus' power against illness and demons and also provides in Jesus' behavior an example for his readers in Jesus' earnest and dedicated pursuit of God in prayer."[124]

Many pastors and Christians in African now mimic the steps of Jesus for dealing with demonic forces. Some have published books on the practical steps to deal with Satan and demons.[125] Ihesiaba's list of the steps to take in dealing with Satan and demons is long and include praying "in the name of the Father, and of the Son and of the Holy Spirit," confessing sins, inviting the Saints to assist in the process, inviting angels, singing praises to God, and inviting the blessed Virgin Mary. At a glance one can sense the Roman Catholic background of Ihesiaba.

119. Luke, however, warns against merely using the name of Jesus for exorcism without having a relationship with him. See Acts 19:11–21.

120. Mark 1:25, *NIV*. See also Luke 4:41.

121. Mark 1:27.

122. Hurtado, *Mark*, 29.

123. Mark 3:20–30.

124. Hurtado, *Mark*, 29.

125. A good example is Atado, *Welcome Jesus, Bye Bye Satan*.

But like the majority of Christians, irrespective of their denominations, Ihesiaba instructs his readers to rebuke, bind, destroy, and silence Satan and demons and to break down their strongholds. He writes:

> Rebuke and bind any spirit that will hinder the prayers, healing, deliverance, exorcism, etc. The enemy, the devil, is within and around; in the air, sea, or land. Therefore arrest and destroy him and his handworks. Declare war at his kingdom, destroy his weapons, let there be fire in his operation room, or wherever he may be operating from. Remember that 'whatever you bind on earth shall be considered bound in heaven (Matt. 18:18).[126]

It is misleading to read Jesus's confrontation with Satan and evil spirits as a prescriptive way or as a set of rules for his apostles and Christians to follow in dealing with Satan and demonic forces. For example, when Jesus silenced some evil spirits by not allowing them to speak it was not merely because he wanted to demonstrate that he had power to silence demons. The silencing of demons should rather be understood in the context of the theme of the messianic secret that Mark was developing.[127] Therefore, Christians cannot consider Jesus's silencing of demons as a model for confronting evil spirits. It is a mistake to assume that Jesus has prescribed rules, methods and principles on how to restrain satanic forces as Ihesiaba has suggested.[128]

There are several problems with emulating or mimicking Jesus's style of exorcism but two are noteworthy. First, the exorcist may become the centre of attraction. People may praise him rather than Jesus Christ who is the source of power for restraining the activities of Satan. In Africa today, many Christians move frequently from one church to another in pursuit of a pastor or prophet they believe to be a specialist in healing and exorcising demons and evil spirits from people and businesses, and in breaking ancestral curses.[129] Second, there is an ontological difference between Christians and Jesus Christ. He is divine and human, but Christians are only human. As the one who is consubstan-

---

126. Ihesiaba, *Exorcism and Healing Prayers* 124.

127. Mark 1:24–25, 34; 3:11–12; cf. 8:29–30; 9:9. See Hooker, "'Who Can This Be?' The Christology of Mark's Gospel," 98.

128. Ihesiaba, *Exorcism and Healing Prayers*, 77–86.

129. The irony is that some of these preachers have been exposed as members of several occult societies. Joshua Balogun in *Redeemed from the Clutches of Satan* testifies that some Nigerian well-known preachers came to him to obtain powers when he was a renowned native doctor before his conversion to Christianity.

tial with God, Jesus embodies divine deliverance which surpasses mere restoration of the physical or mental conditions. His healings included the spiritual condition of the people. He was not able only to expulse demons from people; he was also able to cure everything that separated them from God.[130] He criticized and rebuked the people who dehumanized and relegated the poor and vulnerable to the periphery of the society. Thus, the ability of Jesus to deliver people from their physical and mental sufferings and also his ability to bring them into a relationship with God are the key elements that distinguish Jesus from other exorcists of his time.[131]

The most penetrating lesson Christians are to learn from Jesus's encounter with Satan and evil spirits is that remaining and constantly drawing strength and encouragement from Jesus is the ground from which his followers can successfully contribute to the ongoing restraining and dismantling of the activities of Satan and other malevolent spirit beings. Jesus rebuffed the Jews who claimed that "he manipulated demons to bring himself glory."[132] The key issue is the source of the power by which Jesus accomplished his exorcism. He refuted the accusation that he maneuvered or appeased Beelzebub in order to achieve deliverance or healing. Unlike the "diabolical power of magicians," Jesus argued that his power is "rather a triumph of God" over Satan and evil spirits.[133] Demons aim to promote activities that are opposed to the characteristics of the Kingdom of God. To use the words of C. F. D. Moule, demons have infiltrated into human society and have continued to promote evil practices such as "broken homes and false relationships and setting up tensions where there should be harmonious co-operation."[134] Since Jesus aimed to promote the characteristics of the Kingdom of God—the way of life that reflects God's rule—he was in conflict with Satan and demonic forces that induced people to exhibit contrary characteristics.[135] The challenge for Christians is to detach their allegiance from the indigenous traditions which teach that human beings can ma-

130. Stein, *Luke—The New America Commentary*, 258.

131. Dunn and Twelftree, "Demon-Possession and Exorcism in the New Testament," 220.

132. Hurtado, *Mark*, 28.

133. Garrett, *Demise of the Devil*, 45.

134. Moule, *Gospel According to Mark*.

135. See Matthew 12:8.

neuver and induce malevolent spirits to bring good fortune. Also, they must re-think and allow Jesus Christ to critique their solution-oriented mindset which has shaped their Christologies. African Christians need to become aware that dehumanization and oppression carried out both in the church and in the society at large are demonic and must be criticized and overturned. This implies that Christians should be ready and willing to work with other Africans who are not Christians in tearing down all forms of satanic activities.

In conclusion, I have explored the significant place of the identity and activities of the malevolent spirits in contextualizing the significance of the person and work of Jesus Christ. I also explored how the relationship between Jesus and the malevolent spirits can provide a helpful context for examining and critiquing some African Christians' interpretation and appropriations of the Christ-Event. The solution-oriented mindset and the indigenous understandings of the interrelatedness of the spirit and human worlds are the two major ideologies that are largely responsible for Christians' perceptions of the identity and work of the malevolent spirit beings and their understandings of Jesus's power over such spirit beings. And as I have argued throughout this chapter, a Christology that underestimates the encounter between Jesus and the malevolent spirit beings is in danger of eclipsing an important element that helps us to define the person and work of Jesus Christ. An adequate African contextual Christology needs to construe Jesus as the person who questions and reconstructs African Christians' understandings of the malevolent spirits.

If Jesus Christ is the enactor of God's rule, satanic and demonic forces are the distorters of God's rule. From the onset of Jesus's ministerial life, Satan (like in the Garden of Eden in Genesis) tempted him with the intention to seduce him and coerce him to distrust God and ultimately to distort God's rule on the earth. "The devil's aim," Marshall argues, "is evidently to persuade Jesus to disobey, dishonor and distrust God."[136] The Christ-Event dismantles the strongholds of Satan and demons. Jesus is the one who victoriously restrains and will ultimately put to an end the activities of Satan and evil spirits that have continued to torment humanity.

---

136. Marshall, "Christology of Luke's Gospel and Acts," 124.

> For just as a conqueror invades a territory, proclaims himself
> as king to the existing inhabitants, and demands that they now
> serve him—emphasizing that he is the ruler by various shows of
> strength, including the defeat of any rebels who oppose him—
> so Jesus proclaims the arrival of God's rule in what was Satan's
> territory, sets free Satan's captives, and attacks Satan's allies.[137]

The attack on and the restraining of Satan is ongoing. Jesus's restraining
of the activities of satanic forces will continue through his followers for
he has given them the authority to do so. "Calling the Twelve to him, he
sent them out two by two and gave them authority over evil spirits."[138]
There is no doubt this authority extends beyond the twelve initial followers of Jesus to include those who will believe in Jesus through their
message.[139]

137. Ibid., 125.
138. Mark 6:7.
139. John 17:20.

7

Revealing Humanity

The Significance of Jesus for Rethinking the Understandings of Human Beings in Africa

IN CHAPTERS FIVE AND SIX, I EXAMINED THE UNDERSTANDINGS OF GOD and the malevolent spirit beings as construed by the majority of African Christians, focusing on some ways in which such understandings can provide some helpful contexts for engaging with and interpreting the mystery of the Christ-Event. I argued that Jesus Christ mediates and interprets divinity and humanity. In this chapter, I will probe some of the predominant understandings of humanity in African Christianity as reflected in the writings of some key theologians.[1]

Humanity is a mystery. In a sense, it can be argued that humanity-talk can be more difficult than God-talk. This is because we can assume that God, as a self-existent being, is capable of knowing God's self exhaustively and completely.[2] Also, although we can talk about God and associate him with some categories that are available to us, he remains a mystery and cannot be reduced to our categories.[3] Humanity, when it is defined to include the beginning, existence, action, and future destiny of human beings remains a great puzzle. The mystery of humanity is responsible partly for the confusion in present-day culture and theology regarding the essential constitution of the meaning and properties

---

1. The majority of African theologians have discussed their theological anthropologies in their broad theological works.

2. Some North American Evangelical theologians have debated vigorously God's knowledge. The debate has centered on open-theism and classical theism. See Sanders, *God Who Risks*; Ware, *God's Greater Glory*; Ware, *God's Lesser Glory*; Pinnock, *Most Moved Mover*.

3. Fubura-Manuel, *Greater Purpose*, 24.

of human beings.[4] Throughout the history of Christianity, theologians have wrestled with the issue of the meaning, purpose and nature of human beings. And as David Kelsey has pointed out, theologians have pursued these issues, not from a distinctively anthropological spectrum, but from several theological themes such as creation, revelation and sin.[5]

Shaped by their conditions, many African Christian theologians have continued to explain human beings in relation to God.[6] Some others have discussed the meaning of humanity from the indigenous views of human beings.[7] My overarching task in this chapter is to explore the meaning, identity and hope of humanity from the perspective of Christology. I will argue that in order for African Christians to come to a true knowledge and experience of what God desires for humanity, they are to constantly engage with the mystery of Jesus Christ. The Christ-Event invites them to re-think the indigenous views of humanity and human beings' relationship with God in light of the identity and mission of Jesus Christ. As I will argue later, the indigenous views of humanity partly shapes many African Christians' understandings and beliefs of who they are, what they are to expect from Jesus and how they are to relate to God. An adequate African contextual Christology, therefore, should interact with and probe the indigenous perceptions of humanity. It is not sufficient for Christians to seek to know the meaning and destiny of humanity only from their preconceived ideas of humanity. On the contrary, they are to simultaneously explore what it is to be essentially human from their history and experience and in and through the Christ-Event. This implies that a Christian theological anthropology should be christocentric. The Tanzanian theologian, Andrea NgWeshemi, makes this point when he writes: "the history of the man Jesus of Nazareth contributes constitutively toward the answer to the question concerning the essential nature of human beings. He is the image of what is human to which Christian commitment to the human can refer for guidance."[8]

4. McIntyre, *Theology after the Storm*, 66.

5. Kelsey, "Human Being," 141–67.

6. See Ezeh, *Jesus Christ the Ancestor*.

7. See Imasogie, *African Traditional Religion*.

8. Ng'Weshemi, *Rediscovering the Human*, 103.

But how should Christians construe humanity from the Christ-Event? I have argued throughout this book that the grand purpose of the Christ-Event is the enactment of a relationship between God and humanity. This enactment exposes two things. First, it demonstrates God's deep desire to be in a loving relationship and covenant partnership with human beings. Second, it exposes human beings' flight away from God and the serious consequences of their rejection of God's offer of relationship. Jesus Christ critiques and sometimes radically reshapes people's preconceptions of humanity and divinity as part of achieving God's purpose of the Christ-Event. Therefore, in order for Christians to understand and appreciate who they are as human beings, and how they are to relate to God and the spirit beings, they need to rethink humanity in light of the Christ-Event. This presupposes that the Christ-Event mediates and interprets humanity in the ways which are recognizable to human beings. The question that this presupposition attracts is: what is humanity from the perspective of the Christ-Event? I will argue that the Christ-Event shows that human beings express God's relationality, are fallen creatures of God, and are restorable creatures of God. I will examine these presuppositions, locating them within African Christianity, although focusing on Nigeria.

This chapter is divided into two major sections. I examine in the first section the theological meaning of the claim that humanity expresses God's relationality and its implications for the African Christian context. In the second section, I examine and critique some indigenous views of humanity's separation from and restoration to God. I will also examine some key theologians' interpretations of the fall and restoration of humanity.

Humanity as the Expression of God's Relationality

The Christian and the African indigenous views of human beings as the creatures of God presuppose God's relationality. In chapter five, I argued that the classical Christian concept of the Trinity entails God's relationality. God exists as a relational being and as a community—as the Father, the Son and the Holy Spirit. Since God, as the indigenous religions and Christianity claim, has created human beings, it follows, theologically speaking, that God has equally exhibited and demonstrated his relationality by creating and relating to the beings who are ontologically different from him. The relationality of God towards humanity presupposes that human beings are both *dependent creatures* and *precious creatures*. These views of humanity, however, pose problems for some theologians who explain the meaning of humanity primarily in terms of human beings' sins against God. The views also pose a problem for many Christians who relate to Jesus and God in the ways which suggest that God exists primarily for the purpose of solving the problems of humanity. In what follows, I will explore how these understandings of God and humanity shape many of the existing Christologies in Africa Christianity.

Human Beings as God's Dependant Creatures

There are several myths regarding the origin of human beings in the indigenous cosmologies. These myths are usually terse.[9] Writing specifically about the Yoruba myth of creation, Osadolor Imasogie observes that it is not "clear as to where the first people were created. It would appear that they were created in heaven" and afterwards "sent down to inhabit the earth" by the Supreme Being.[10] Like in the indigenous cosmologies of Nigeria, in spite of the equivocal nature of the myths of creation, the majority of the indigenous cosmologies of Africa teach that the Supreme Being is the source of all that is in existence, including human beings and the lesser spirits.[11] In the thinking of the Kenyan theologian, John Mbiti, the majority of African peoples "place the creation of man towards or at the end of God's original work of creation."[12] According to him, African peoples also believe that human beings came into existence in pairs as "husband and wife, male and female." However varying the indigenous accounts of creation are, Mbiti argues, the belief that "God is the originator of man" exists in the majority of the creation myths.[13]

9. Some of these myths are not compelling. For example, some teach that the Supreme Being sent chameleon on several occasions to the earth after creating it to see if it was both solid and habitable before he created and sent human beings down from heaven to live on it. Imasogie, *African Traditional Religion*, 31.

10. Ibid.

11. Ng'Weshemi, *Rediscovering the Human*, 23.

12. Mbiti, *African Religions and Philosophy*, 93.

13. Ibid.

With the advent of Islam and Christianity, the myriad of African creation myths have suffered a huge blow: they have been progressively disappearing and rapidly giving way to the Christian and Islamic concepts and theologies of creation. But what have remained somewhat intact are the beliefs that the Supreme Being created human beings and that human beings are the most important living creatures in the human world. As the most important creatures in the physical world, human beings, in the indigenous thought, are at the centre of existence. Mbiti is one of the earliest African theologians who articulated the idea that the indigenous religions believe that human beings are "at the very centre of existence."[14] He goes on to argue that African peoples' belief about the centrality of human beings in the world has become a hermeneutical framework through which they explain their roles in the world.

> African peoples see everything else in its relation to this central position of man. God is the explanation of man's origin and sustenance: it is as if God exists for the sake of man. The spirits are ontologically in the mode between God and man: they describe or explain the destiny of man's afterlife.[15]

This indigenous understanding of human beings has made some theologians dub African indigenous religions as anthropocentric. "African ontology," writes Tokunboh Adeyemo, "is basically anthropocentric. Man is at the very centre of existence and everything else is seen in its relation to the central position of man."[16] Uchenna Ezeh shares a similar view. He writes,

> In the African universe, man occupies a pride of place. Basically the African traditional religion is anthropological. Man being the centre of the universe, he is the bridge between the spiritual beings and the material beings. . . . Man is the epicenter in the created order, and understands himself, his role, and prospects in the scheme of things in the world as such.[17]

Again he argues that for the African people, life

> revolves around man and his overall welfare and not primarily God and the deities. . . . There is no worship of God for its sake.

14. Ibid., 92.
15. Ibid.
16. Adeyemo, *Salvation in African Tradition*, 56.
17. Ezeh, *Jesus Christ the Ancestor*, 50–51.

The result is that when the African makes contacts with God either through prayers, sacrifices, divination or fortune-telling the overriding concern is to advance the overall human wellbeing, as well as to ensure protection from all dangers.[18]

Although the indigenous thought of Africa teaches the centrality of human beings in the world, it does not see human beings as competitors of God. It is also important to distinguish the idea that human beings are the crown of creation from the understanding of humanity as the centre on which all other creatures, spirit beings, including God, revolves. It is vital to note that the majority of the indigenous African cosmologies teach that God created human beings and that human beings can only discover and achieve their full potential in relation to God and other spirit beings. As Emefie Ikenga-Metuh notes, "Man comes from God. He has a definite mission to fulfill in God's plan and he will eventually go back to God."[19] A form of Christian eschatology may have influenced Ikenga-Metuh's contention. In the indigenous cosmologies, the goal of human beings is to join the ancestors after their death and not go back to God. However, Metuh correctly argues that the view "which sees the African religion as purely anthropocentric and God on the periphery in the African worldview" is greatly mistaken.[20] The anthropocentric reading of the African indigenous ideas of human beings needs to be guarded cautiously so as to preserve the notion of human dependence on the spirit beings such as ancestors, gods and the Supreme Being. But it is vital to acknowledge that although the indigenous cosmologies construe human beings as lower in status than the ancestors, the lesser spirit beings and the Supreme Being, and therefore dependent on them, they equally perceive human beings to be at the centre of creation in the ways which suggest that God exists to serve humanity. I will argue that this view of humanity occupies a central role in the world can generate and promote idolatry.[21] Three arguments can be presented to buttress this contention.

18. Ibid., 51.

19. Ikenga-Metuh, *African Religions in Western Conceptual Scheme*, 95.

20. Ikenga-Metuh, *God and Man in African Religion*, 54.

21. I will adopt Sam Oleka's definition of idolatry as "anything in the life of an individual or group that claims or is given the loyalty which belongs to God alone." See Oleka, "Living God," 131.

First, the understanding of humans as the being who are the *centre of existence* (when it is understood to mean that God exists to serve human beings) subtly enthrones human beings to the status that is due only to God. Mbiti's popular phrase "it is as if God exists for the sake of man" captures the subtlety underlying the indigenous African quest to enthrone human beings to the status of glory while dethroning God. It can be argued that African peoples' view of humans as the beings who are the centre of existence magnifies the significance of human beings and subtly diminishes, dethrones and distorts God's significance in the world. In this sense, then, the African peoples' belief in the centrality of human beings in the world poses a serious threat to God's glory and centrality in the world. Yusufu Turaki, one of the Nigerian leading Evangelical theologians, contends that any attempt by human beings to arrogate to themselves the status of glory and centrality is sin against God. He writes: "Man's worship of self is a very serious crisis of false identity . . . Since man has lost his original identity in God his creator, he must instead create a false one upon which to rest and anchor his self-made identity."[22] I will examine some Nigerian theologians' perceptions of sin and humanity later in this chapter. Here, it suffices to note that although we can trace humanity's desire for autonomy and flight away from God back to the Genesis theories of humanity's separation from God, we are to recognize that the issue of human beings' desire to dethrone God, and also to enthrone humanity as the centre of existence are informed by complex factors. These include the ever-changing worldviews of human communities, the ongoing cross-cultural interactions among peoples of different cultures, and several social conditions.

But how does a Revealer Christology model, as developed in this book, engage with the indigenous views of humanity? To put it differently, how does Jesus Christ, as the one who mediates and interprets humanity and divinity, interact with the indigenous cosmologies which present humanity as the glory of existence in a way that suggests God exists to guarantee the wellbeing of human beings? In this book, I have argued that to construe Jesus Christ or God as primarily a problem-solver is to distort the relationship that God enacts through the Christ-Event. We are to bear in mind that Jesus upheld the glory of God throughout his ministry. Even in his miraculous work, which could have placed him at the very centre of existence, Jesus usually

---

22. Turaki, *Unique Christ for Salvation*, 151.

introduced God-talk with the intention of leading people to focus on God as the very source and centre of existence. Expressions such as "No one is good—except God alone," for example, indicate not only Jesus's solidarity with humanity, but also his desire to refocus the attention of his contemporaries on the centrality of God as the creator and as the one who sustains the entire creation.[23] An adequate African Christian theological anthropology, therefore, should be suspicious and critical of any view of humanity that underestimates and eclipses the glory and centrality of God in the world.

The second argument which can be advanced in support of the contention that viewing humans as the beings who are the centre of existence can become idolatrous is that this view of humanity is largely responsible for the readiness of many Africans to use God, the lesser spirit beings and even their fellow human beings as tools to achieve wellbeing. To be human, according to the indigenous worldviews of Africa, entails enjoying life which requires possessing wealth and good health. Many people consult native doctors, sorcerers and medicine people to inquire about their conditions so as to make appropriate sacrifice in order to, negatively, protect themselves against any misfortune, and positively, to gain and accumulate more wealth and to experience good health. The practice of consulting mediums, diviners and native doctors for the purpose of knowing the causes of misfortunes is widespread in many African societies.[24] The key issue to note here is that the practice of consulting some intermediaries is driven by the assumption that human beings are at the centre of existence and, therefore, possess the right to draw insights and resources both from the human and spirit worlds to sustain their central place in the world.

The practice of using God, other spirit beings, and even human beings as tools to achieve wellbeing by some people is rooted in a dubious relationship. The missing gene in this practice is a relationship that is not rooted in selfishness. People choose the gods they believe can help them to achieve their goals and drop the ones that seem powerless to help them to achieve their goals.[25] What immediately comes to mind here is Jesus's stern rebuke of the people who followed him simply because of the things they could gain from him.

23. Mark 10:17–18, *NIV*.

24. Mbiti, *African Religions and Philosophy*, 166–93. See chapter six.

25. Nwoga, *Supreme Being as Stranger in Igbo Religious Thought*, 8–9.

> I tell you the truth, you are looking for me, not because you saw miraculous signs but because you ate the loaves and had your fill. Do not work for food that spoils, but for food that endures to eternal life, which the Son of Man will give you. On him God the Father has placed his seal of approval.[26]

Contrary to building a relationship on selfish motives, Jesus enacts a relationship that is rooted in God's unselfish, self-dispossessing, and self-giving in and through the Christ-Event.[27] He challenges and encourages his contemporaries to seek a relationship with God on the basis of self-giving.[28] This is one of the christological implications of the Christ-Event many theologians have not explored. Some, however, have discussed the theme of self-giving only when they discuss the cross-event. Turaki, for example, writes, the "greatest offer of Jesus to humanity is his offer of himself to humanity on the cross . . ."[29] In chapter five, I argued that God's acts of self-giving are demonstrated in the Christ-Event and not only on the cross. The incarnation, death, and the entire life of Jesus Christ seek to dismantle self-accumulation and solution-oriented mindsets. African Christians need to rediscover and explore the implications of God's self-giving as manifested in the Christ-Event. One of such implications which relates directly to this book is that God's self-giving upsets the deep quests of many Africans for solutions to their spiritual and other needs, especially when such quests obstruct God's criticism.

The third argument is that some African Christians abandon Jesus Christ to consult and worship other gods when Jesus, in their thinking, appears not to be solving their problems. This manner of relating to Jesus is idolatrous. For Jesus Christ, serving two masters or worshiping God and other gods is an act of idolatry.[30] By consulting other gods for solutions to their problems, the Christians who engage in such practice bestow upon creaturely images, idols, and demonic forces the reverence that is due to God alone. The apostle Paul con-

26. John 6:32–33, *NIV.*

27. See chapter five for discussion on the nature of God's self-giving as manifested in and through the Christ-Event.

28. John 3:16; Philippians 2:5–8.

29. Turaki, *Unique Christ for Salvation,* 161.

30. See Matthew 6:24.

sidered such acts as misplaced and nefarious. In his Epistles to the Christians in Rome, Paul wrote:

> For although they knew God, they neither glorified him as God nor gave thanks to him, but their thinking became futile and their foolish hearts were darkened. Although they claimed to be wise, they became fools and exchanged the glory of the immortal God for images made to look like mortal man and birds and animals and reptiles....[31]

Any human act that misplaces God's sovereignty over God's creation and bestows upon human beings or things the reverence that is due to God alone is idolatrous. This is the main consequence of the indigenous construal of human beings as occupying the central spot in the world. It is an assault on and attempt to suppress God's glory. One of the aims of the Revealer Christology model that is developed in this book is to explore, from the perspective of the Christ-Event, the implications of God's self-giving for understanding what he intends for and requires from humanity. I will return to this issue later in the chapter. In what follows, I will explore other theological and anthropological implications of the claim that God is the Creator of human beings.

Human Beings as God's Precious Creatures

Some African theologians explain humanity primarily from the perspective of humanity's sin against God. But I will argue that this theological anthropology has overshadowed some biblical representations of human beings as precious, beautiful and wonderful creatures of God who are made in God's image and likeness.[32] The majority of African theologians hardly examine the implication of God's estimation of human beings as precious creatures. Even when this status of human beings is hinted at in discussions of *imago Dei*, some theologians run quickly through its theological consequence in order to get to what they consider to be the most important starting point for a Christian

31. Romans 1:21–25, *NIV*.

32. Genesis 1:26. Some earlier Christian theologians made a distinction between image and likeness. But the majority of contemporary theologians argue that image and likeness "represent the kind of repetition characteristic of ancient Hebrew style." See Placher, "What's Wrong with Us? Human Nature and Human Sin," 134.

theological anthropology; namely, the fallen condition and sinfulness of human beings. Turaki, for example, poses the question: "what are the biblical definition, condition and relationship of man to his Creator?"[33] His response to this question illuminates the sin-driven theological anthropology of some theologians. He writes:

> The state of man in relation to his Creator has been described in Genesis.... In this book, we see man's falling away from the "origin" and the "beginning of man's alienation from God." The fall of man into sin through disobedience to his Creator brought ruin to man and the entire humanity and creation.[34]

According to Turaki, the sinful condition of human beings places them in a lost state. He warns that the theologies of many African theologians will remain weak if they continue to ignore the seriousness of the sinfulness of humanity.

> African theology seems not to have this powerful definition of the sinful state of humanity. It is not critical enough about "African culture and traditional religion."... The Bible has clearly defined the fallen and sinful state of humanity. The mission and evangelism agenda is almost absent in African theology and this is because African theology has a very weak theology of the fall, sin and redemption.[35]

We need to make a distinction between underestimating the influence of sin in discussing human beings' relationship with God and overemphasizing human sinful acts or sinfulness to the point of underemphasizing the preciousness of human beings as God's image bearers. Turaki's concern about some theologians who underestimate the influence of human sins and sinfulness in order to construct the theologies of salvation, religions, and God that synchronize with the African indigenous worldviews is legitimate. He is not the first to register this concern. Some of his Evangelical predecessors such as Kato and Adeyemo have accused some African theologians such as John Mbiti and Bolaji Idowu of constructing weak theological anthropologies. Kato argued persistently that the "Christian message of total deliverance from the original and practical sins of the individual is what African people

---

33. Turaki, *Unique Christian for Salvation*, 220.

34. Ibid.

35. Ibid., 223.

... need."[36] But Kato, Turaki, and others who have underemphasized the preciousness of human beings in order to construct their anthropology, Christology and soteriology commit essentially an opposite error.

It is important to articulate some of the consequences of underestimating and underemphasizing the preciousness of human beings as God's image bearers. In both Christianity and the indigenous religions, human beings are believed to be the creatures of God. As human beings, we exist because God is and has made a decision to bring us into existence. A helpful way to understand the connection between God and humanity is to construe human beings as the consequence of God's gracious act of giving.[37] When we construe humanity in this way, we will exercise more caution when speaking of human beings as enemies of God and totally depraved. As God's gifts, human beings are precious creatures and companions of God. But even as God's precious gifts, human beings can distort what and who God intends them to be by mistrusting and disobeying God.[38] However sinful human beings are, it is important to acknowledge that God has never ceased to love them and to extend fellowship and relationship to them. This, of course, includes judging them for their sins. In both pre-Fall and post-Fall, human beings have remained God's image bearers who have continued to attract God's mercy, love and relationship.[39]

The view of human beings as the enemies of God is demeaning and responsible partly for the emphasis on the divinity of Jesus Christ and the underestimation of his humanity in African Christologies. As we saw in chapter three, many Nigerian lay Christians see Jesus Christ as God, the Son of God and the Messiah, and rarely see him as one of them, a human being. Some theologians have also continued to explain the person of Jesus Christ predominantly in terms of his divinity. What African theologians and lay Christians need to rediscover is the dialectic that underlies the divinity and humanity of Jesus Christ. A Christology that discusses the person of Jesus Christ predominantly only in terms of his divinity to the exclusion of his humanity or vice versa is inad-

36. Kato, *Theological Pitfalls in Africa*, 43.

37. Jones, "What's Wrong with Us? Human Natures and Human Sin," 143–44.

38. Genesis 3.

39. I will explore the theological ideas of the *Fall* under *Human Beings as Fallen Friends of God* later in the chapter.

equate.[40] Such a Christology underestimates the mystery of the unity of humanity and divinity in Jesus Christ as articulated in the Nicene and Chalcedonian councils.[41] In addition, such a Christology needs to rethink the mystery and the import of the incarnation and God's grace in the relationship he provides for humanity through Jesus Christ.

Christians are not (supposed to be) deists primarily because they claim that God has maintained a relationship with the creation. Through creating and relating to human beings, God elevates the status of human beings to that of precious creatures. As a result of these divine acts, human beings have formed a community with God in and through Jesus Christ. That God chooses to reveal God's self in human history as a human being (in Jesus the Christ) demonstrates, not only God's interest in human beings as God's gifts and creatures, but also God's love for humanity. It follows, then, that any action, perception, and theological view that devalues and demeans human beings is in direct conflict with God's perception of human beings. As the precious creatures and gifts of God, human beings express the glory of God. In human beings, then, we can expect to experience the splendor, awesomeness and the grandeur of God's gifts. The Christ-Event needs to be located within this context of God's love and willingness to be in a relationship with human beings in spite of their sinfulness.

It is noteworthy that the indigenous African views of the world see human beings as part of the Supreme God's comprehensive story, in which human beings exist in a communal relation with fellow human beings, with God and with other spirit beings. As Peter Paris observes, "the community is a sacred phenomenon created by the Supreme God, protected by the divinities and governed by the ancestral spirits. Thus a full participation in the community is a fundamental requirement of all human beings."[42] The notion of human beings as the product of community-making is a distinctive characteristic of the indigenous African anthropologies.[43] In these anthropologies, human beings are

---

40. Philippians 2:6–7; Hebrews 1:1–3; John 1:14.

41. See chapter five for discussions on the Christologies of the Nicene and Chalcedonian councils.

42. Paris, *Spirituality of African Peoples*, 51.

43. Some African theologians have used the concept of community to develop the doctrine of the Trinity, church and the communion of the saints. See Nyamiti, *Christ As Our Ancestor*, 103–26.

believed to be created to be in a community, and unless they belong
to a community, they will never attain their full potentials. Based on
his study of the Bantu peoples, the Bashi of central Kivu of Congo, the
Rwanda and the Barundi, Vincent Mulago argued that African peoples
exist as a community. For him, the community includes the living, the
ancestors and God. He argues: "A relationship of being and life between
each individual and his descendants, his family, his brothers and sisters
in the clan, his antecedents, and also with God, the ultimate sources of
all life."[44]

Before Mulago, Placide Tempels argued, "For the Bantu, man never
appears in fact as an isolated individual, as an independent entity."[45] The
point that Mulago attempts to make is that in the indigenous views of
the world an individual exists only because the community exists. "The
life of the individual is grasped at it is shared."[46] This sense of communality has withstood various threats, especially the Western notion
of individualism. By comparison, the sense of individualism in the West
is opposed to the community-oriented societies of Africa. The writings
of the Greek theologian, John Zizioulas, have uncovered and criticized
the individualistic nature of some Western cultures. In *Communion and
Otherness: Further Studies in Personhood and the Church,* Zizioulas provokingly postulates:

> Is it not true that, by definition, the other is my enemy and my
> "original sin," to recall the words of French philosopher, J. P.
> Sartre? Our Western culture seems to subscribe to this view in
> many ways. Individualism is present in the very foundation of
> this culture. Ever since Boethius in the fifth century identifies
> the person with the individual . . . and St Augustine at about the
> same time emphasized the importance of . . . self-consciousness
> in the understanding of personhood, Western thought has nev-
> er ceased to build itself and its culture on this basis.[47]

In the thinking of Zizioulas, the greatest threat to Western individualism is the other.

> Communion with the other is not spontaneous; it is built upon
> fences which protect us from the dangers implicit in the other's

44. Mulago, "Vital Participation," 138.
45. Tempels, *Bantu Philosophy,* 72.
46. Ibid., 139.
47. Zizioulas, *Communion and Otherness,* 1.

> presence. We accept the other only in so far as he or she does not threaten our privacy or in so far as he or she is useful for our individual happiness.[48]

I have referenced Zizioulas here only to highlight a major difference in the ways most Western societies and African societies construe the place of the individual in the community.[49] But since my focus in this book is Africa, I will not engage in an in-depth comparative analysis of the concepts of community in the Western and African societies.

Returning to the idea of community in African societies, it is important to keep in mind the notions of communality and relationality which inform the perceptions of human beings in the indigenous Africa. Keith Ferdinando notes that a "human being in Africa is not just a multiple self but also a social self who is not to be identified simply in terms of his own individuality. It is this which sharply distinguishes African thought about human nature from much of that found in the West."[50] Contrary to the Western notion of "I think therefore I am," many African peoples posit "I am because we are."[51] As John Pobee argues: "If Descartes' *cogito ergo sum* represents the Western person's understanding of reality, i.e., individualism, *homo Africanus* would rather say *cognatus sum, ergo sum*, i.e., 'I am because I am related to others by blood.'"[52] In other words, for many African peoples, the identity of an individual is embodied in, protected and defined by the community. The individual person derives his or her identity by belonging to his or her community, both the living and the dead. As Mbiti observes,

> In traditional life, the individual does not and cannot exist alone except corporately. He owes his existence to other people, including those of past generations and his contemporaries. He is simply part of the whole. The community must therefore make, create or produce the individual; for the individual depends on the corporate group.[53]

---

48. Ibid.

49. This is not to suggest that the practice of individualism does not exist in Nigerian and African societies or that the sense of community does not exist in some Western societies.

50. Ferdinando, *Triumph of Christ in African Perspective*, 23.

51. Mbiti, *African Religions and Philosophy*, 108–9.

52. Pobee, "Health, Healing, and Religion," 59–60.

53. Mbiti, *African Religions and Philosophy*, 108.

The cult of the ancestors is a visible phenomenon in the indig-enous African cosmologies which expresses peoples' strong belief in the "continuity between the dead and the living."[54] Imasogie has noted that the rites of passage are "very crucial in the African traditional set-up" because they are means of sustaining "active interaction between human and the spiritual communities."[55] In Nigeria, like in many other African societies, typically when a child is born, the family of the child organizes for him or her several rites of passage with the intent to introduce and incorporate him or her into the community that com-prises of both the living and the dead. The ancestors, particularly the family ancestors, are expected by many African peoples to continue to provide and protect for their children from the spirit world.[56] Death does not amputate an individual from his community. And in order for human beings to attend their life potentials they must "maintain a vital relationship with nature, God, the deities, ancestors, the tribe, the clan, [and] the extended family."[57]

There are some issues concerning the indigenous African notion of community that merit a close examination. The definition of human beings in relation to their community provides a helpful insight for con-structing a Christian ecclesiology. Although individuals make up the church, no single individual can constitute the church. The language of unity that permeates the New Testament ecclesiology only makes sense within the context of a community.[58] An individual Christian can reach his or her spiritual potential only within the community to which he or she belongs. It is unchristian to define a Christian in relation to the individual person; it should rather be in relation to the community of believers. Zizioulas has contended that the notion of a community is inherent in and indissolubly connected with the concept of a person. According to him, it is "demonic to attribute one's own identity to one-self or to an a-personal something."[59] He maintains that a "person is

54. Imasogie, *African Traditional Religion*, 37.

55. Ibid.,55.

56. Ibid.

57. Sidhom, "The Theological Estimate of Man," 102.

58. For example, see Ephesians 4:1–13; Romans 12:3–14.

59. Zizioulas, *Communion and Otherness*, 141–42.

always a gift from someone." Thus, for him, the "notion of self-existence is a substantialist notion, not a personal one."[60]

Some proponents of the ancestor christological models have continued to maintain that the notion of human beings as the product of community-making is also a helpful context for interpreting the Christ-Event from the African perspective.[61] Some have argued that the notion of communality, as it is construed in many African societies, is similar to the idea of "corporate personality" in ancient Israel in which the acts of the individual affected the community to which he or she belongs.[62] But the concentration has been, to use the words of Ng'Weshemi, on how Jesus "participates decisively in the cultural, socio-economic and political life of African brothers and sisters" as the senior Ancestor.[63] For him, since the Christ-Event occurred in human history, Jesus's significance must be understood within the community of people, for it is in the context of the community that he can share "the anxiety, needs, thoughts, and hopes of fellow members and work for the transformation of the community. . . ."[64]

Africans' resilience to the ideologies that threaten their views of community may not be unconnected with the benefits which come with such community-oriented structures. For example, in many rural societies in Nigeria, the family, clans, and kindred continue to share the burdens of each other and the joy of each other. For instance, the Nigerian marriage customs provide an opportunity for the clans to share in the blessings of the bride's and the groom's families. The usually expensive ceremonies are normally geared towards the satisfaction of the requirements stipulated and preserved by the elders of the clan. But a significant issue that is noteworthy is that the Nigerian people's perception and stratification of human beings into categories has their root in the notion of communality. In the indigenous cosmologies, a child is a true human being on the basis of a successful completion

---

60. Ibid. It is important to read Zizioulas' understandings of community or relationality and personhood from the context of his argument on the relationality of the persons of the Trinity. See Zizioulas, *Being as Communion*, 15–17.

61. Ng'Weshemi, *Rediscovering the Human*, 151.

62. This is essentially the contention of South Africa scholar Bonganjalo Goba in his essay "Corporate Personality," 65–73.

63. Ng'Weshemi, *Rediscovering the Human*, 151.

64. Ibid.

of the required rites of passage and not on the grounds of the socio-economic circumstances that he or she is born. [65] This way of perceiving a newborn is widespread in many African societies. Benjamin Ray observes, "Newborn infants are remade into new beings with new social roles" during the "middle or liminal phase of transition" in African concepts of rites of passage.[66] During this transition stage, "newborn infants are made into human persons, children are made into adults, men and women are made into husband and wife, deceased people are made into revered ancestors, princes are made into kings."[67] Ng'Weshemi has also argued, "For Africans, one is not human simply by birth. Rather, one becomes human through a progressive process of integration in society."[68] According to Imasogie, "The new-born child is looked upon . . . as a stranger to the family into which he is born as well as to . . . human community."[69]

It is vital to keep in mind that this understanding of human beings is rooted in the notion of a communal relationship.

> Individuals obtain their basic identity by belonging to the community. The underlying thinking here is that an individual is never born whole and fully human. It is the family, clan, and community to which one belongs that enables one to become a mature person. One is prepared and led into adulthood in order to accomplish and live the fullness of life without disruption and to become a vital, upright, responsible and well humanized individual member of one's community in particular, and human kind in general.[70]

Laurenti Magesa links Africans' understanding of true or full humanity to the rite of marriage, especially the marriages that produce children. He argues that marriage is the "means to attain full humanity." He writes: "The expansion of the community circle results in togetherness as those involved actualize their full humanity. But what truly completes the

65. Imasogie, *African Traditional Religion*, 52–62.

66. Ray, *African Religions*, 91.

67. Ibid.

68. Ng'Weshemi, *Rediscovering the Human*, 15.

69. Imasogie, *African Traditional Religion*, 53.

70. Ng'Weshemi, *Rediscovering the Human*, 18.

humanization of a person in this world is the mystical union with the ancestors, which is achieved only through the generation of children."[71]

Defining human beings in terms of what they have achieved through the rites of birth, puberty, and marriage is oppressive. These rites of passage generate into taboos when people fail to observe them or wrongly practice them. This underscores the "thin layer of difference between taboo and custom."[72] If the individuals who have not undergone the rites of birth and puberty are not considered to be fully human, the rites are oppressive and can generate serious identity crises. The casualties of this oppressive system are sometimes some Christian converts who refuse to perform some of the initiatory rites for their children on the grounds that they are unchristian practices. Chinua Achebe in *Things Fall Apart* describes the social standing of such Christian converts during the days of the classical Western missionary.[73] Many who have undergone the rites regard the individuals who refuse to undergo the rites as inferior and subhuman. In addition, sometimes they cannot share from some of the things that belong to the community such as land or even marry someone from their community.

When examined in light of the Christ-Event—a divine act demonstrating God's liberating and undoing of all forms of dehumanization and oppression—African perceptions of true human beings in terms of their observance of rites of passage is wanting. This implies that people who are disabled, couples who are unable to bear children, and people who die quite young without undergoing any of the major rites of passage such as marriage should no longer be seen as objects of wrath or people under the curse of the ancestors or other spirit beings.

From the perspective of the ancestral cult, these classes of people are not truly human and cannot belong completely to the community which is maintained by the ancestors. Marriage is a very important rite because it is through it that couples can bear legitimate children and consequently perpetuate and keep alive the traditions and lineage of the ancestors. Individuals who die without being married are normally classified as premature death and sometimes as evil children for they are not going to contribute to the propagation of their ancestry. The

71. Magesa, *African Religion*, 128.

72. Ilogu, "African Traditional Religious Systems of Social Control: A Nigerian Example," 143.

73. Achebe, *Things Fall Apart*.

issue that immediately comes to mind is Jesus Christ, an individual who died without getting married and having any children.[74] Within the indigenous Africa cultures, Jesus belongs to the category of evil children and his death can be seen as premature, and ultimately irrelevant. Ng'Weshemi seems to be aware of how the death of Jesus as unmarried person poses a difficulty for the ancestor Christology. However, he dismisses it, albeit in a non compelling way, by arguing that Jesus Christ "can be excused in light of the other essential and distinctive deeds he performs and situations he goes through for the sake of fellow community members and which no other human beings have ever accomplished."[75]

In contrast to African indigenous construal of authentic, true and real humanity in terms of the observations of the traditional rites of passage or what they have achieved, the new community that Jesus Christ enacts defines human beings, not in terms of what they have achieved, but in terms of what God has done for them—creating and relating to them. The Christ-Event upsets, critiques, and condemns any understanding of humanity which is inherently oppressive. The Sermon on the Mount, for example, expresses Jesus's criticism of the systems and cultural values which perpetuate the sufferings of the poor and the vulnerable. Since in the indigenous thought of Nigeria, as we have seen from the arguments of some theologians, a human being becomes truly human only when he or she undergoes the required rites of passage, it stands in need of a re-examination in the light of the Christ-Event, for it is oppressive. Human beings are precious because they are God's creatures and also because of what God has done for them in and through Jesus Christ.

Human Beings as Fallible and Restorable Creatures of God

Something has happened to the relationship between God and human beings—so the indigenous religions and Christianity claim. This claim is represented in the myths or religious narratives. Since myths tell something much deeper about the community that creates or believes

74. We can also add the Nigerian Catholic priest who takes the vows of celibacy.

75. Ng'Weshemi, *Rediscovering the Human*, 152.

in them, a critical examiner should look beyond the symbolic representations to excavate from the deeper structural level what the myths and religions narratives essentially communicate. I argue that in both the indigenous myths of creation and the African Christians' interpretations of the Genesis 3 narrative, what is at stake is a broken relationship between God and humanity. But what has really happened? What are the consequences? Is it possible for human beings and God to have a good relationship again? I will explore and respond to these questions in the remainder of this chapter.

Humanity in a Broken Relationship with God

The word fallen in this book refers to humanity's potentiality to sin as well as human beings' acts of distorting, disobeying and refusing God's offer of relationship. In the indigenous religions, God and human beings at some earliest time enjoyed a friendly relationship. Edwin Smith observes, it "appears to be a very widespread notion in Africa that at the beginning God and man lived together on the earth . . ."[76] This relationship was broken due to some human actions. Several myths of creations have variously explained the human actions that were responsible for the broken relationship. On this, Smith notes, "owing to misconduct of some sort on the part of the man or more frequently, of a woman—God deserted the earth and went to live in the sky."[77] Imasogie has summarized three surviving versions of the myths which specify the actions that purportedly caused the breaking down of the relationship between God and human beings. The first version teaches that the relationship was broken as result of a man's disobedience that was inspired by greed. The myth states that God established a "rule regulating the getting of food from the sky" that prohibited human beings from taking more food than they needed. But a greedy man broke the rule "and consequently, the sky receded . . . and the easy access to heaven was sealed up."[78] The second version states that "God became bored with constant bickering among men and the necessity of spending much of his time reconciling them." Therefore, he "decided to move farther away from men."[79] The

76. Smith, "Whole Subject in Perspective: An Introductory Survey," 7.
77. Ibid.
78. Imasogie, *African Traditional Religion*, 32.
79. Ibid.

third version teaches that "a woman defiled the sky by touching it during her monthly period."[80] Since the action "was something that was expressly forbidden," God withdrew the privilege of free communication between heaven and earth."[81]

Some African theologians have contended that some of the indigenous myths regarding the broken relationship between God and humanity correlate to the Genesis narrative of the Fall which has informed the traditional Christian explanation of the broken relationship between God and God's creation. Charles Nyamiti, the Tanzanian theologian, for example, postulates that the belief in the broken relationship between God and human beings constitutes "an interesting parallelism between Christianity and . . . African traditional religions,"[82] and also can "serve as a useful point of departure for explicating the doctrine of Redemption."[83] It is difficult to determine the extent to which the traditional Christian teachings on Adam's sin have influenced some of the indigenous myths of the broken relationship between God and human beings. What is important to highlight here, however, is that these indigenous myths neither intend to present theories of the origin of evil nor to describe the cause of human evil actions as some classical theologians have construed *human sin nature* as a consequence of the fall. The myths rather intend to explain the remoteness of the Supreme Being. They aim to explain why the Supreme Being "enters [the human world and human affairs] less frequently than might be expected . . ."[84] Equally important to note is that, according to the indigenous religions, human beings "sought in vain for a return to a golden age of spiritual happiness and unhampered interaction" with God.[85] Since then, human beings can only relate to God through some lesser gods or divinities and ancestors.[86]

[handwritten: Indig. Creation Myths] [handwritten: Not a systematic understanding of evil]

80. Ibid.

81. Ibid., 32–33.

82. Nyamiti, *Christ as Our Ancestor*, 34.

83. Ibid., 35.

84. Smith, "Whole Subject in Perspective: An Introductory Survey," 7.

85. Imasogie, *African Traditional Religion*, 33.

86. It is primarily on the basis of the belief that human beings can relate to God through the ancestors that some African theologians have proposed and constructed their ancestor christological models. See Nyamiti, *Christ as Our Ancestor*, 35.

Many Christians (both the laity and theologians) have continued to employ Genesis 3 as the authentic narrative that provides the context for explaining the strained and broken relationship between God and humanity. Adeyemo represents many Christians when asserts:

> Prior to the historical fall of Adam, in whom all men fall as one, an unbroken link of fellowship and communion existed between man and God. . . . The accounts of Genesis and the rest of the Scriptures make it plain that man did not continue in the state of purity and blessed communion with God. Man rebelled against God by yielding to Satan. And the separation that took place then affected and still does affect that many may claim to know of God.[87]

He goes on to state that in "any sound doctrine of salvation the question of sin is paramount."[88] He contends that in the Yoruba's indigenous thought, sin is "an act not as a nature, forgiveness consists of community acceptance after the prescribed penalty" has been met.[89] He considers the indigenous Yoruba's conceptions of sin and forgiveness as inadequate on the grounds that they do not explain the presence of sin nature in human beings and that they do not account properly for human beings' sins against God.[90] Kato essentially viewed the Jaba people's concepts of sin in the same way: "Sin [for the Jaba people] boils down to only social ills." He insists that "sin against the society is only a minor manifestation of the basic sin of rebellion against God."[91] After examining some of the indigenous myths regarding the destroyed relationship between God and human beings, Adeyemo notes the following difference between the indigenous and Christian biblical views of sin.

> While the traditional religions [of Africa] place emphasis on the acts of sin and the consequences, the Bible places emphasis on the sin nature of every man. The biblical revelation concerning sin as a nature lies embedded in sacred history. In Genesis three the origin of sin in the human race goes back to the fall of Adam and Eve in the [garden of] Eden. All mankind was in Adam seminally. Through this seminal relationship all man-

87. Adeyemo, *Salvation in African Tradition*, 25.

88. Ibid., 51.

89. Ibid., 56.

90. Ibid.

91. Kato, *Theological Pitfalls in Africa*, 42.

kind sinned against God and the sin nature has since then been
passed on from generation to all born of a man. . . . Biblically
man is a sinner not because he sins, but man sins because he is
a sinner by nature. The emphasis is not on the act or the exter-
nal manifestation, but rather on the internal, the intrinsic nature
and the essential condition of man.[92]

Adeyemo's contention provides us with a helpful background to
examine the concepts of sin in African Christianity. The majority of lay
Christians will respond to the question "who is Jesus to you?" by saying
Jesus is my savior.[93] In most cases, this answer arises from what they
have been taught or what they have read from the Bible about the sin
of Adam and Eve and how the sin has affected the entire humanity.
Although the majority of these Christians lack the sophistication that
is needed in explicating the connection between the sin of Adam and
Eve and the entire humanity, they continue to believe that it is because
of the sin of Adam and Eve and the impact of the sin upon humanity
that God has acted in and through the Christ-Event. Jesus Christ came,
according to Thompson Onyenechehi, "to do the work of salvation for
mankind" and "to save mankind from the consequences of sin as we are
taught in Genesis 3."[94] Adeyemo, following Kato, argues that because of
the sin of Adam and Eve the entire humanity became totally depraved.
For him a total depravity entails that "God's image is distorted in every
part of man, but not obliterated."[95]

It is vital to recognize that the biblical writers describe sin and its
consequence in different ways. This means that it is impossible to encapsulate sin in one terminology such as total depravity or original sin.
What Adeyemo is wrestling with is the question 'how is it that the sin
of Adam and Eve has a consequence upon humanity?' For him, human
beings were "seminally in Adam" and when he sinned against God, humanity equally sinned. Adeyemo here follows St. Augustine's concepts
of the original sin and universal guilt.[96] Some scholars today argue that

92. Adeyemo, *Salvation in African Tradition*, 59–60. St. Augustine has influenced
Adeyemo's view of the transmission of the sin of Adam and Eve to their posterity. I will
return to discuss the theological implications of this view of the Fall.

93. See chapter three for an extensive discussion on Nigerian grassroots Christologies.

94. Onyenechehie, interview by author, tape recording, March 10, 2006.

95. Adeyemo, *Salvation in African Tradition*, 26.

96. I will return to examine Adeyemo's view of sin later in this chapter. See

Augustine mistranslation of the Greek *eph ho* as "in whom" led him to argue that sin is seminally transmitted.[97] Philip Hefner notes that Augustine "elaborated the concepts of Adam's fall, the transmission of Adam's sin and its consequences through conception," that is, "specifically, sin is carried by a man's semen."[98]

The key biblical text here is Romans 5:12. The apostle Paul seems to think of humanity as originating from one ancestor; namely, Adam:

> The God who made the world and everything in it is the Lord of heaven and earth and does not live in temples built by hands. . . . From one man he made every nation of men, that they should inhabit the whole earth; and he determined the times set for them and the exact places where they should live.[99]

It should not be surprising then that he considers Adam's sin "to spread throughout the human race from its first beginning" and that all persons have contributed "their own share of it."[100] From the perspective of Romans 1 and 2, it is clear that Paul sees human beings as utterly sinful and enemies of God. In Romans 5, however, he provides the context for his views of human beings as sinful and enemies of God. Although human beings have from the beginning disobeyed God, because of his love, God has in the Christ-Event (gospel) provided the remedy for human sins which is qualitatively greater than the source (Adam) of the sins of humanity.

> But the gift is not like the trespass. For if the many died by the trespass of the one man, how much more did God's grace and the gift that came by the grace of the one man, Jesus Christ, overflow to the many! Again, the gift of God is not like the result of the one man's sin: The judgment followed one sin and brought condemnation, but the gift followed many trespasses and brought justification. For if, by the trespass of the one man, death reigned through that one man, how much more will those who receive God's abundant provision of grace and of the gift of righteousness reign in life through the one man, Jesus Christ.[101]

Augustine, *The City of God*, trans. Gerald G. Walsh and Grace Monahan (New York: Fathers of the Church, 1952) 380.

97. Tiessen, *Who Can Be Saved?*, 75.

98. Hefner, *Human Factor*, 126.

99. Acts 17:24–26, *NIV*.

100. Wright, *The Climax of the Covenant*, 39.

101. Romans 5:15–17, *NIV*; see also 8:1–4.

On the issue of original sin which Adeyemo has raised, it is vital to probe into the meaning of this theological expression and to test its relevance and meaningfulness for the African contexts. It is vital to keep in mind that the concept of *original sin* may not be wholly adequate for explaining the broken relationship between God and humanity in Africa. The word *original* in the expression *original sin* is ambivalent. Does the word mean *first* in which case *original sin* means the *first sin*? Or does *original* refer to *origin* in which case *original sin* will mean the *origin of human sin*?[102] Kato seems to use the expression original sin in both senses. According to him, "Man's fundamental dilemma is alienation from God. The historical account of Genesis chapter three gives the root cause of all sufferings here and in the life to come."[103] Gregory Olikenyi also sees the story of Adam's and Eve's disobedience as indicating the etiology of sin:

> At the very point in time in creation, all humanity was intended to find fulfillment in God. But sin entered the world with its drastic consequences—such as guilt, sickness, and death—which affected the entire cosmos (cf. Gen 3:17–19; Rom 5:12–14); all humanity, as a result, forfeited it divine destiny (cf. Rom 3:23).[104]

Since, as I have already noted, the African indigenous myths of humanity's alienation from God do not intend to communicate the beginning point of human's sin, but rather to communicate the remoteness of God,[105] it is doubtful if the concept of the original sin, as Kato and Adeyemo use it, can communicate the Christian teachings on the sinful human condition effectively to the peoples of Africa. In addition, the view that the Genesis 3 narrative aims to provide an etiological context of sin is highly debatable. Hefner has noted that another possible way of reading the Genesis narrative is to see it as a description of the present

---

102. The theological expression original sin, if it is understood as the first sin, presupposes a state of original righteousness. Theologians have also disagreed on whether "the concept of original righteousness refers to an actual historical period when human beings were sinless and from which they have fallen." See Hefner, *The Human Factor*, 127.

103. Kato, *Biblical Christianity in Africa*, 17.

104. Olikenyi, *African Hospitality*, 62.

105. Some scholars have queried the myths to discover if they intended to exonerate God's remoteness (since it was the disobedience or sinful acts of human beings that caused it) or to "show "divine capriciousness and unfairness." See McVeigh, *God in Africa*, 137–39.

sinful state of human beings.[106] He proposes a third way of understanding the presence of sin in humanity, which seems to be influenced by his desire to bridge the gulf between the two foregoing views and to avert the possible extremity of the two views.[107]

However one understands the Genesis 3 narrative, it is important to note that in the mind of the author, the relationship between God and humanity has been affected for the worse. Although we read of several other evil or sinful acts in Genesis after the story of the disobedience of Adam and Eve, we have to wait until the New Testament era, specifically in the writings of Paul, to see a direct connection between the Genesis story of the *Fall* and the presence of sin in humanity. Whether or not we describe the inability of human beings not to sin as the consequence of a sinful nature in humanity, as many theologians have done,[108] what is evident is that human beings have continued to act and live in the ways which hurt the relationship that exists between them and God: this is the present sinful condition of humanity.

Jesus the Christ acknowledges the sinful condition of humanity, but it seems that he locates this within the broader context of a new relationship which God has enacted through him. He mediates and interprets, as the revealer of divinity and humanity, what God expects from and intends humanity to be. It is striking that Jesus does not make any direct reference to the Genesis story of the disobedience of Adam and Eve in his teachings on the sinful human condition. Although we are to be very careful in erecting theological presuppositions on the ground of silence, it is not out of place to postulate that perhaps Jesus has avoided referencing the story of the Fall in Genesis because his concern is to articulate the actual human sinful condition and not to trace, as the apostle Paul does, the primordial source of human sinful condition. In contrast to the Genesis 3 narrative, which focuses on *human disobedience or mistrust*, in the thinking of Jesus Christ, the actual human sinful condition lies in the *rejection of the new relationship* God has specifically located in and through the Christ-Event. This does not mean that Jesus's view of the human sinful condition and that of the author of

---

106. Hefner, *Human Factor*, 127.

107. Ibid., 139.

108. These theologians have been influenced by the apostle Paul (see Romans 7 and 8.) and perhaps St. Augustine's concepts of *non-posse non-peccare* (not able not to sin).

Genesis 3 are mutually exclusive.[109] By disobeying God's instruction not to eat from a particular tree, Adam and Eve ultimately rejected God's fellowship since enjoying divine fellowship entails obedience to divine command.

The novelty of Jesus's understanding of God-human relation lies in the fact that he preaches that God is ready to judge and deal with humanity's disobedience and also to offer them a new fellowship through the Christ-Event. From the perspective of the Christ-Event, then, what hinders human beings from having a relationship with the God of Jesus Christ is the rejection of Jesus's invitation to all people to accept his vision of the kingdom of God. Jesus and his gospel are not mutually exclusive. In fact, quite the opposite, rejecting Jesus means rejecting the good news he embodied and preached and vice versa. Therefore, it is not possible for anyone who rejects Jesus's invitation to embrace his vision of the kingdom of God to become part of the kingdom of God.[110]

Jesus's announcement of the kingdom of God, which was the "very centre of his mission and message,"[111] is intrinsically related to God's initiative to reconcile with human beings, to re-establish himself as the ruler, not only of the world in which the Jews lived, but also as the ruler of the whole world. Jesus's announcement of the kingdom of God surprised and disturbed many Jews, not because it was a novel idea, but because the picture of the kingdom of God he painted, to use the words of N. T. Wright, "did not look like what they had expected."[112] It challenged Israel's core understandings of humanity, divinity, and God-world relation: in the kingdom of God, oppression and dehumanization have no place, God's judgment will not fall upon the Gentiles nations alone as the Jews anticipated, but upon both the Jews and the Gentiles,

---

109. Some theologians associate the seed of the woman in 3:15 with Jesus Christ, and the snake bite with death to Jesus death on the cross, the crushing of the snakes head with Jesus victorious resurrection from the dead. See Turaki, *Unique Christ for Salvation*, 163–64.

110. The soteriological implications of this christological claim are to be understood within the parameters of people who live after the Christ-Event, have had the opportunity to have an encounter with the gospel of Jesus either through divine or human agency, and are cognitively capable of understanding the gospel.

111. Wright and Borg, *Meaning of Jesus: Two Versions*, 33. See also Manus, *Christ, the African King*, 147–49; Mbiti, *New Testament Eschatology in an African Perspective*, 42–44.

112. Wright, *Meaning of Jesus*, 35.

God's love will reign, Jews and Gentiles will share from the same table of fellowship; oppression will not be tolerated, and the Jews are "to abandon alternative kingdom visions" and join in Jesus's kingdom visions.[113]

When human beings refuse to acknowledge and accept the new relationship that God provides and offers to them, they expose their self-centeredness, rebelliousness, and disobedience to God. Jesus unveils this in his encounter with Nicodemus, as John records:

> For God so loved the world that he gave his one and only Son, that whoever believes in him shall not perish but have eternal life. For God did not send his Son into the world to condemn the world, but to save the world through him. Whoever believes in him is not condemned, but whoever does not believe stands condemned already because he has not believed in the name of God's one and only Son. This is the verdict: Light has come into the world, but men loved darkness instead of light because their deeds were evil.[114]

In this popular passage, Jesus presents in a most penetrating way the condition of humanity in relation to God. People who are not part of the new relationship that God has enacted through Jesus Christ are perishing and are *ede kekritai*, "already condemned." But the primary task of Jesus is not to condemn human beings, but rather to introduce them to God in the way that radically upsets, challenges, and critiques what human beings consider to be truly human; namely, to become autonomous and ultimately free from God's relationship. "For God did not send his Son into the world to condemn the world, but to save the world through him."[115]

Misery, oppression, poverty, alienation, otherness, and sickness that are prevalent in Africa; and not only in Africa but around the globe, are some consequences of rejecting, and failing to accept the unique relationship God is offering to human beings through Jesus Christ. According to Nyamiti, the Fall brings "unhappy consequences" which includes bodily diseases, death, evil possessions.[116] Kato agrees: "The nature of man's fundamental dilemma does not lie in mere physical suffering. It does not lie primarily in horizontal relationships with his

---

113. Ibid., 40.

114. John 3: 16–21, *NIV*.

115. Ibid.

116. Nyamiti, *Christ As Our Ancestor*, 55.

fellow man. All human tragedies, be they sickness, poverty, or exploitation, are merely symptoms of the root cause, which the Bible calls sin."[117] But for Jesus, God's self-revelation in the Christ-Event demonstrates God's desire to provide and sustain a new relationship with fallen humanity. How are we to understand this relationship? This is the question I examine below.

Enacting a New Relationship

God became human in Jesus Christ in order to bring human beings back to what God intended them to be. This is a dominant reading of the Christ-Event. But what does this perception of Jesus Christ mean for African Christians? The Christ-Event introduces a new hope for humanity: it gives humanity a hope to enjoy a fellowship with God in and through Jesus Christ. This divine fellowship is multifaceted. Although it is grounded primarily on God's offer of relationship to human beings, it is an interpersonal relationship that includes God-world relation, God-human relation, human-human relation and human-world relation. In other words, the relationship that Jesus Christ enacts and sustains connects divinity and humanity. As I have already argued, when examined in light of the Christ-Event, sin in relation to God means repudiating and rejecting God's fellowship. Terrance Tiessen has noted that although "the story of the tragic Fall of humankind into sin comes very early in the biblical narrative," the "rest of the story is a wonderful account of God's work of grace to restore sinful human beings to fellowship with himself" and also to "renew the whole cosmos."[118]

The majority of Christians see Jesus Christ as the one who can bring about the restoration of the fallen humanity. Clear as it may seem, there is still something strange about this claim. What does it mean to posit that Jesus is the bringer or enactor of the new God-human relationship? Theologically, the claim that Jesus is the savior of the world means very little without explication just as the claim there is no salvation outside of Jesus Christ equally means very little (in the pluralist context of Africa) without explication. The latter claim fits more properly into the area of theology of religion and falls outside the parameters of this book.[119]

117. Kato, *Biblical Christianity in Africa*, 16.

118. Tiessen, *Who Can Be Saved?*, 83.

119. But the key theological question is: Is Jesus Christ both ontologically and epis-

My concern here is the former question. What does it mean to say that Jesus is the savior of the world or the one through whom humanity can be reconciled and restored to a divine fellowship? This is a broad question and needs to be unpacked. A helpful way to explore this question is to ask another question which fits more properly into the task of this book; namely, how is it that the fallen human beings are also restorable to God's loving fellowship? The answer to this question is inherently connected with the Christ-Event: the incarnation, teaching and preaching, death on the cross, resurrection, and the ascension are all part of God's acts of initiating and sustaining a loving fellowship and covenant partnership with humanity. Therefore, Jesus Christ stands at the centre of Christianity precisely because he is the one who enacts the God-human relationship which is at the centre of the Christian faith. The restoration of fallen humanity to God is "only a possibility on the account of the life, death, and resurrection of Jesus Christ."[120] Ng'Weshemi makes a similar point. If "we want to discover the true and essential nature of human beings," he argues, "we have to look at Christ in whom what is fallen has been restored."[121] Again he writes,

> Jesus stood for life, but true life result from his work as he liberates humanity from the impediments that make it difficult for them to live a full and meaningful life. Evil or sin, disease, imperfection, alienation, estrangement or segregation, exploitation, oppression, and finally death are the antitheses of life. And Jesus worked toward renewal and restoration of the original creation, and perfection of human beings to wholeness.[122]

The Ghanaian theologian, Kwame Bediako concurs,

> Jesus Christ, himself the image of the Father, by becoming one like us, has shared our human heritage. It is within this human heritage that he finds us and speaks to us in terms of its ques-

---

temologically necessary for salvation? Ontological necessity raises the issue of whether or not people have experienced divine salvation, even before the Christ-Event, without the second Person of the Trinity. Epistemological necessity raises the issue of whether or not people can experience God's relationship only on the basis of their hearing the gospel being preached and explicitly express their faith in Jesus. A helpful introduction to these issues is Okholm and Phillips, eds., *Four Views on Salvation in a Pluralistic World.*

120. McGrath, "Particularist View: A Post-Enlightenment Approach," 171.

121. Ng'Weshemi, *Rediscovering the Human*, 108.

122. Ibid., 112.

tions and puzzles. He challenges us to turn to him and participate in the new humanity for which he has come, died, been raised and glorified.[123]

There is a common tendency among many African theologians to concentrate on and overemphasize the cross-event and to underemphasize some other aspects of the Christ-Event when exploring the process of humanity's restoration to God. This is, however, unwarranted.

The *incarnation* indicates God's willingness to identify with human beings even in their sinful condition with the intent to critique their sinfulness and to provide them with the hope of restoration. In chapter five, I examined the incarnation and therefore need not rehearse what I have already said about this event. What I need to do here is to locate this event in God's overall acts of enacting, through Jesus Christ, a new relationship that will bring God and human beings into a covenant partnership. Before the advent of Jesus Christ, God related to human beings in some ways which sustained the radical ontological difference between humanity and divinity. Although God spoke with human beings and communicated to them through various means such as fire, violent wind, miraculous acts, angels, and so on, he remained distanced ontologically from them: God had not yet become consubstantial with human beings. But in and through the Christ-Event, God became consubstantial with human beings.

At least two interrelated reasons can be advanced to explain the purpose of the incarnation. First, the sinfulness of humanity renders human beings incapable of enacting any effective and lasting relationship with God. Human beings are sinful and corrupt and as such cannot if unaided produce the righteousness which God requires for keeping a relationship with humanity. Thus, it is partly on the ground that human beings cannot on their own restore themselves back to fellowship with God that he has incarnated in the person of Jesus the Christ.[124] Most Christians readily say that Jesus came to save them from sins—the sin of Adam, the sins of their forbears and their own sins. In the thinking of many of these Christians, God sent Jesus Christ because human beings cannot save themselves from their sins and yet they are desperately in

---

123. Bediako, *Jesus and the Gospel in Africa*, 24.

124. O'Collins, *Jesus Our Redeemer*, 81.

need of a relationship with God. Elizabeth Adeyemi Olusola, a member of ECWA, speaks for many when she says:

> Jesus is my Savior. He came to this world to save us [who are] sinners. As the Bible says, those who believe in him will live forever, even when [they] die in this world, [they] are going to see him [and] to rejoice with him. And I believe that God is my Savior.[125]

Ben Fubara-Manuel who is a member of the Presbyterian Church of Nigeria agrees with Olusola but expresses his understanding of Jesus Christ and God's offer of relationship to humans in a more sophisticated way.

> When I say that Jesus is my Savior, I think first of all in terms of the one who gives me the sense of connection to God. I know that I am not lost, that I don't exist alone, but that I have a connection to the almighty God. For me, not to be saved is to lose this connection. To be saved is to have it back.[126]

Some Nigerian theologians have explored the extent sin has damaged the image of God in human beings. For Kato, sin has "distorted the image of God" in human beings but has not "destroyed [the image] in the sense of being eradicated," for if it were so, human beings "would be deprived of morality, a will to decide, and ability to make rational choices."[127] Although he does not explain explicitly what constitutes the image of God in human beings, it seems that he favors the view that sees the *imago Dei* as consisting in human *cognitive faculty* that enables human beings to make moral judgment and to reason. Turaki describes the image of God as "man's differentia, which marks him out from the rest of all created things" and which is "the basis of his sacredness and the sanctity . . . of life."[128] Idowu, like Kato and Turaki, sees *imago Dei* in humanity as divine substances which God has deposited in all human beings. According to him, "there is something of the divine in man which makes him addressable and responsible" and therefore indicates that "there exists in him the possibility of his spirit being in community

125. Olusola, interview by author, tape recording, Aba, 2 June 2006.

126. Fubara-Manuel, interview by author, tape recording, Aba, 12 March 2006.

127. Kato, *Biblical Christianity in Africa*, 18.

128. Turaki, *Unique Christ for Salvation*, 219.

with the Divine Spirit."[129] Adeyemo also describes the image of God in humanity in a cognitive sense. Like Kato and Turaki, he contends that sin has distorted the image of God in human beings and has made them susceptible to the temptation and incapable of worshiping God truly.[130]

> The cognitive view of the image of God in humanity is widespread in African theological anthropologies. The major problem with the cognitive understanding of the *imago Dei*, as evidenced in the argument of Idowu, is that it leads to construing the specific feature of the image of God in terms of a "divine deposit" or "divine input" in human beings. What has influenced Idowu here is the Yoruba indigenous concept of *ori* which he defines as "essence of personality, the personality-soul in a man [that] derives from *Olodumare*."[131]

The Igbo concept of *chi* (here construed in the sense of a guardian angel) is similar to *ori*. According to Uchenna Ezeh, *chi* is the "spark of God which God gives each person at conception."[132] In the Igbo worldview, this spark of God in human beings is called *chi*. In chapter five, we saw that *chi* in this context functions as a guardian spirit which controls the destiny of a person. Some scholars have argued that when a person dies his or her "*chi* goes back to God to give an account of his [or her] work on earth."[133] But when the individual reincarnates God may give the person a different *chi*, especially if the previous chose a bad fortune for the person.[134]

It is becoming predominant among some Western theologians to construe the image of God in terms of relation. For example, Robert Jenson has written: "In Genesis, the specific relation to God is *as such* the peculiarity attributed to humanity. If we are to seek in the human creature some feature to be called the image of God, this can only be our location in this relation."[135] A few African theologians are beginning

129. Idowu, *African Traditional Religion*, 55.

130. Adeyemo, *Salvation in African Tradition*, 26.

131. Idowu, *Olodumare: God in Yoruba Belief*, 171.

132. Ezeh, *Jesus Christ the Ancestor*, 56.

133. Ibid., 57.

134. Ibid. See also Ikenga-Metuh, *African Religions in Western Conceptual Scheme*, 111.

135. Jenson, *Systematic Theology*, 58.

to interpret the image of God in humanity in a relational sense.[136] This understanding of *Imago Dei* fits properly the indigenous African sense of community. My interest here, however, lies in the effect of sin on humanity. Many Christian theologians today will not disagree that sin affects every aspect of human life. In most cases, this is only understood in a soteriological or moral sense. The sinfulness of humanity makes it equally impossible for human beings to comprehend and appreciate God's relationship. Human beings require a divine quickening and kindling, usually associated with the Holy Spirit, before they can rediscover their sinfulness and their status before God as his fallen creatures. This means also that human beings need a divine relational stirring to enable them to recognize a divine relational offering of restoration.[137]

Second, the incarnation expresses the extent of God's love and desire to identify with humanity. The extent of this divine desire to be in solidarity with humanity is evident when we take account of the fact that human beings are fallen. As Turaki notes,

> The greatest revelation of Jesus Christ the Messiah to humanity is his revelation of God as Father who seeks after the lost man. God is not seen as "withdrawn," austere, authoritarian and whose disposition is only to judge man, the sinner. God is revealed in Christ's loving, gracious, compassionate, forgiving and faithful.[138]

Without the incarnation human beings may never know the depth and width of God's love for them, how much he desires to identify with them in their sinful and lowly condition, and how much he surrenders and disposes in order to bring them into a divine loving relationship. By becoming human, God demonstrates that the sinfulness and the sinful acts of human beings are not able to deter him permanently from having a relationship with them. Thus, although sin hurts God, and he hates it, yet his love is very deep and continues to propel him to seek to have a relationship with human beings. The author of Isaiah presents this picture about God when he quotes him as saying: "'Come now, let

---

136. See Kapolyo, *Human Condition*, 46–53.

137. I explored the Christian concept of the Trinity and its implication for Christology in chapter five. Here, although our focus is on Christology and humanity, it is vital to recognize that the Father, Son and the Holy Spirit *is* (in a Trinitarian sense) involved in the process of God's restoration of fallen humanity.

138. Turaki, *Unique Christ for Salvation*, 150.

us reason together,' says the LORD. 'Though your sins are like scarlet, they shall be as white as snow; though your sins are red a crimson, they shall be like wool.'"[139] Jesus Christ also teaches that God has not allowed the sins of human beings to steer him away from having a relationship with them. Quite the opposite, it is the sinfulness and sins of human beings that inspire God all the more to seek a relationship with them by sending his Son to enact the relationship. Responding to the Pharisees who thought that it was comprehensively wrong for Jesus to dine with the people who were considered to be religiously and socially sinners, Jesus said: "'It is not the healthy who need a doctor, but the sick. But go and learn what this means: 'I desire mercy, not sacrifice.' For I have not come to call the righteous, but sinners."[140] Through the incarnation God reopens the wound caused by human sins but does not look away; instead, he identifies with sinful and fallen humanity for the purpose healing and restoring them to what he intends for them to be.

The *miracles and teachings* of Jesus Christ, particularly about the kingdom of God, unveils God's gift to and expectations of human beings in order for them to participate in and benefit from the divine kingdom. Regarding the connection between Jesus's miraculous works and salvation he embodies, O'Collins writes:

> Matthew, Mark, and Luke ... recall not only that Jesus worked miracles but also that his miraculous deeds were powerful signs of the kingdom, inextricably bound up with his proclamation of divine salvation. His healings and exorcisms were compassionate gestures, the first fruits of the presence of the kingdom which manifested God's merciful rule already in operative in and through his person.[141]

O'Collins correctly notes that the miraculous healings of Jesus Christ expresses God's restoration. By healing people of their infirmities, Jesus shows that the relationship he enacts involves dealing with human sufferings. We must expand the language of suffering here to include the spiritual, emotional, physical, social, and psychological aspects of human life.[142] By healing people of their sufferings, Jesus communicates that

---

139. Isaiah 1:18, *NIV.*

140. Matthew 9:12, *NIV.*

141. O'Collins, *Jesus Our Redeemer*, 95.

142. Some Nigerian theologians have argued that the difference between the salvation of a biblical Christianity and the idea of salvation in the indigenous religions

God's restoration of humanity is not merely a futurist phenomenon. It is rather a two-phased phenomenon which includes the immediate and the future. Whilst God's complete and total restoration of humanity is a future event that belongs to the Second-Coming event, evidently, God has already started restoring human beings into what God intends them to be through the miraculous work of Jesus Christ. Some feminist theologians have reminded us of the "social healing" Jesus has introduced by erasing the oppressive barriers that separate males and females. In the judgment of Anne Nasimiyu-Wasike, for example,

> Jesus' attitude toward women is clearly reflected in miracle stories, parables and discourses. All four Gospels portray Jesus in several incidents as showing concern for women, not just for their well-being but for their being as persons. He gave them their true worth and dignity. Jesus' approach to women was revolutionary. He treated women and men as equals; this was new, given the contemporary cultural view of his time.[143]

The teaching of Jesus Christ revolved around his vision of the kingdom of God. In the Sermon on the Mount, he discussed several issues which differed radically from some of his contemporaries' understanding of God-human relation. For Cornelius Olowola, Jesus expressed the requirements for entering into the kingdom of God in the Sermon on the Mount. He argues that, although Jesus presents these requirements in the ways that require human action, they are nevertheless unattainable without a divine help. He writes,

> It is clear from the impossible demand of this holiness that grace and mercy alone offers any hope of entering into the kingdom. Thus, Christ taught the nocturnal Nicodemus that the entry into the kingdom was possible only to those who those regenerated by the Holy Spirit (John 3).[144]

---

of Nigeria is that whilst the former teaches that salvation entails experiencing God's restoration, the latter teaches that "to be saved primarily means to be accepted" by the community of the living members of the community and the ancestors. Adeyemo, *Salvation in African Tradition*, 93–96. See also Ferdinando, *Triumph of Christ in African Perspective*, 389–92.

143. Nasimiyu-Wasike, "Christology and African Woman's Experience," 73.

144. Olowola, "Person and Work of Jesus Christ," 162–63.

Olowola seems to open up the classical debate on the relationship between *divine Grace* and *human freewill*,[145] or to use the contemporary theological expression, the debate on synergism and monergism.[146] Many African Christians, depending on their denominational and personal theological positions, may disagree on whether or not God only saves those whom he has effectually called. Roughly speaking, Christians of Pentecostal and Wesleyan backgrounds may insist that God saves only those who have in their own free will accepted his offer of salvation. Some Christians who see themselves as Evangelicals (especially those who have been influenced by Calvinism) may argue that people are only capable of accepting God's offer of salvation because he has given them a special quickening or calling. Whereas this debate may be prominent among theological students, it is hardly a serious issue at the grassroots level. Also, the *synergistic* and *monergistic* debate has not yet occupied an important place in contemporary African theological scholarship.

In the West, however, particularly among some North American theologians, this debate is intense and has continued to shape soteriological discourses. For example, Tiessen has argued that "all of the [soteriological] positions can be categorized as either monergistic or synergistic understandings."[147] He goes on to contend that "between these two [positions] there is no middle ground."[148] Tiessen's contention is theologically careless and fails to acknowledge the difficulty of subsuming theological positions under *neat* categories. The expression synergism and monergism are in fact misleading because both positions can (and should) intersect. Timothy Ware, one of the leading Orthodox theologians, has reminded us that it is possible to hold the essential elements of monergism and synergism together.

> The West, since the time of Augustine and the Pelagian controversy, has discussed this question of grace and free will in somewhat different terms; and many brought up in the Augustinian

145. The debate centered on St. Augustine of Hippo and Pelagius. The complexity of this debate explains why these two theologians have been variously interpreted.

146. Contemporary theologians associate (roughly) *synergism* with Arminian and Wesleyan traditions and *monergism* with Calvinistic and Evangelical traditions. Tiessen, *Who Can Be Saved?*, 17–20, 66–70.

147. Ibid., 18.

148. Ibid.

tradition—particularly Calvinists—have viewed the Orthodox idea of "synergy" with some suspicion ... God knocks, but waits for us to open the door—He does not break it down. The grace of God invites all but compels none ... But it must not be imagined that because a person accepts and guards God's grace, he thereby earns "merit." God's gifts are always free gifts, and we humans can never have nay claims upon our Maker. But while we cannot "merit" salvation, we must certainly work for it, since faith without works is dead (James ii, 17).[149]

Ware may be accused of a simplistic explanation of a highly complex issue. However, what his contention indicates is the possibility of holding together the key essential elements of synergism and monergism. Jesus Christ teaches that salvation is a gift from God and that human beings have the responsibility to accept or reject the gift.[150] Consequently, the soteriology or Christology that underestimates the gracious salvific gift of God and the responsibility of human beings to accept or reject the gift is inadequate and distorts Jesus's vision of the kingdom of God.

The Revealer Christology model that I have proposed in this book argues that a Christian anthropology and Christology that aim to be relevant to what humanity means to the majority of contemporary Africans must be ready to go beyond the classical debates on sin to grapple with and criticize the actual dehumanizing conditions many people experience. Bernard Ukwuegbu is undoubtedly correct when he argues that Christians "who follow Jesus Christ [in] doing good, criticizing human [oppressive] structures, and changing society for the better" understand truly the practical implications of their faith in Jesus Christ.[151] Perhaps the major sins that concern the majority of Africans today are the maltreatment of many widows by some of their husbands' relatives, poverty that is caused by and rooted in greediness, and ethnic and religious conflicts which are driven by some people's selfish ambitions. Jesus's vision of the kingdom of God is critical of these sins.

The *cross-event* graphically exposes paradoxically both the extent of human sinfulness and God's sovereignty in orchestrating and including the sinful acts of human beings into his own process of restoring the

---

149. Ware, *Orthodox Church*, 222.

150. John 1:12; 3:16; Mark 1:14.

151. Ukwuegbu, *Confrontational Evangelization*, 49.

fallen humanity. That the Christ-Event provides the possibility for human beings to be reconciled to God is hardly a debated issue in African Christianity. For Kato, "to seek salvation elsewhere than through the shed blood of Jesus Christ is heretical."[152] According to Turaki,

> Reconciliation between God and man (Rom 5:8–11; 2 Cor 5:18; Col 1:19–22) is rooted in the redemptive work of Christ on the cross. The enmity and the wrath of God and judgment upon man as a result of the fall has been abolished by the cross of Christ and the result is that man now has access to God, peace, and forgiveness of God upon repentance and belief in Jesus Christ the Messiah (Rom 5:8–11; 5:1, 2; 8:1).[153]

Many theologians are preoccupied with the redemptive solution the cross-event provides. What is noteworthy, which is often overlooked, is that the cross-event exposes humanity's selfishness and violence. Most theologians have become so accustomed to speaking of the death of Jesus Christ as *God's sacrificial act* that they have overlooked the anthropological implication of the cross-event. Commenting on the difference between the sacrificial death of Jesus Christ and the ritual sacrifices in African indigenous religions, Adeyemo asserts:

> [The] ritualistic approaches to God have failed to satisfy the deepest longings and aspirations of man. The constant reaching upward to a distant and perhaps indifferent deity has produced alternative approaches. The Christian approach is to affirm that God for all time has performed a full and final ritual of sacrifice that has opened up complete and constant union with Him. This is the gracious sacrifice of Jesus Christ on the cross . . .[154]

According to Gunton, the "feeling of the rightness or even necessity of a sacrificial dimension to our existence runs very deep in human experience."[155] Gunton uses the word sacrifice in a metaphorical sense. He notes that the use of the word sacrifice to describe the death of Jesus Christ is propelled by the desire to show what is "now the only one sacrifice that really matters."[156] We have seen that Adeyemo makes a similar point. For him, the death of Jesus Christ is the "full and final ritual of

---

152. Kato, *Biblical Christianity in Africa*, 22.

153. Turaki, *Unique Christ for Salvation*, 168.

154. Adeyemo, "Idea of Salvation in Contemporary World Religions," 201.

155. Gunton, *Actuality of Atonement*, 120.

156. Ibid., 123.

sacrifice."[157] The difference between Gunton and Adeyemo lies in their understanding of the use of sacrifice. Whilst Gunton uses the word in a metaphorical sense, Adeyemo uses it a literal sense.

My primary concern here is to explore the contribution the cross-event makes in God's activities of restoring human beings into a divine fellowship. The concept of sacrifice is present in the indigenous religions.[158] In Adeyemo's understanding, the death of Jesus Christ expresses God's punitive act: God punishes and sacrifices Jesus Christ in order to save and reconcile humanity to himself.[159] Olowola shares this view but seems to suggest that it was Jesus Christ who sacrificed his own life. "As God's specially appointed Priest," Olowola argues, "Christ displayed the love and mercy of God by interceding and by sacrificing his own life on behalf of a fallen world."[160] For Adeyemo and Olowola, however, the death of Jesus Christ guarantees a hope for the restoration of sinful humanity into a "spiritual fellowship and moral harmony with God."[161] Jesus accepted his death neither as a fate nor as a deserved punishment for his revolutionary teachings. His death, properly understood, demonstrates his self-giving of himself (which is in accordance with God's purpose) for the restoration of fallen humanity. Thus, the idea that the death of Jesus Christ was God's act of punishing Jesus Christ on behalf of humanity is theologically misleading because it fails to properly account for Jesus's willful act of giving himself as a gift. Gunton warns that if we are to avoid the "suggestions that the sacrifice of Jesus is in some way a punitive substitution, in which God punishes him for our sins," we must pay attention to the fact that the death of Jesus Christ "is not the imposed death of the beast, but the voluntary self-giving of a man."[162] Jesus's self-giving is striking when it is located within the Jewish context where people offer sacrifice to God. In this reversal of roles, instead of human beings offering sacrifice to God, God gives himself in the

---

157. Adeyemo, "Idea of Salvation in Contemporary World Religions," 201.

158. Offering sacrifices to appease an angry ancestor is a common religious practice among those who adhere to the indigenous religions. See Adeyemo, *Salvation in African Tradition*, 33–41.

159. Adeyemo, "Idea of Salvation in Contemporary World Religions," 201, 208.

160. Olowola, "Person and Work of Jesus Christ," 166.

161. Ibid., 167.

162. Gunton, *Actuality of Atonement*, 124–25.

death of Jesus Christ. For Gunton, sacrifice, when understood in the sense of God's self-giving, "remains a matchless conceptual expression of the theological significance of all that Jesus began and continued among us."[163]

The view that God punished his Son by sending him to the cross to die on behalf of sinful humanity, or that Jesus Christ' sacrifices himself on behalf of a sinful humanity, can sometimes blur and overshadow the fact that the execution of Jesus Christ on the cross demonstrates the width, depth, and height of human sinfulness and wickedness. Richard Mouw puts it this way: "In the death on the cross God also took our violent impulses upon himself, mysteriously absorbing them into his very being in order to transform them into the power of reconciling love; and then he offers that love back to us as a gift of sovereign grace."[164] The death of Jesus on the cross exposes the wickedness, violence and determination of human beings to remain independent and estranged from God. It is vital to point out that the word *sacrifice* needs to be carefully explained if it is not to obstruct an effective interpretation and appropriation of the Christ-Event in Africa.[165] Human sacrifice was part of the religious rituals of a few indigenous Nigerian societies. But this is hardly practiced today and many contemporary Nigerians largely consider it an evil act.[166] The notion that a Father punitively executes his Son for the sake of having a fellowship with others will come across to many Nigerians (even in the indigenous societies where human sacrifices were practiced) as a taboo rather than as an act of *unselfish love* for others. Even the concept of a once-for-all understanding of the death of Jesus Christ will simply not do as a way of explaining the bad omen and taboo that the imagery of a divine Father ordering the death of his Son for the purpose of saving others conjures up.

The punitive sacrificial view of the cross-event can hinder people from seeing the execution of Jesus Christ as the climax of human repudiation of God's fellowship. The paradox of the cross-event lies in the fact that God orchestrated the evil act of human beings (that is, the execution of Jesus Christ) into his purpose of restoring and extend-

163. Ibid., 127.

164. Mouw, "Violence and the Atonement," 171.

165. In the West, some theologians have accused Christianity of promoting violence on the grounds of the doctrine of the atonement.

166. See Idowu, *Olodumare*, 147.

ing his loving fellowship to the sinful and wicked humanity. The death of Jesus Christ therefore (1) exposes the extent of the wickedness and sinfulness of human beings—even to the point of killing the one who knew no sin, (2) expresses the susceptibility of human beings to the influence of satanic forces even to the point of teaming up with them to distort God's rule and to repudiate his offer of relationship to humanity, (3) demonstrates God's willingness to risk the life of his Son in order to enact a relationship with human beings,[167] and (4) demonstrates God's power to bring out something good from human wickedness. The key paradox here is that although God comes to us as the *powerless* and *voiceless*, by allowing Jesus Christ to be executed by human beings, he, at the same time, criticizes and condemns the wickedness, self-possession, and oppressive acts of violence of human beings. The resurrection of Jesus Christ illuminates this paradox. Ukachukwu Manus has written: "in raising him, God confirms his presence, his love and power in the person of Jesus Christ."[168] The resurrection of Jesus Christ from the dead has demonstrated God's sovereignty over the wickedness of humanity and his willingness to give humanity a new hope even at the cost of giving himself to humanity.

In conclusion, the overarching theme of this chapter is that God's self-giving, demonstrated in the Christ-Event, has mediated and interpreted humanity in a way that upsets some of the understandings of humanity in the indigenous anthropologies. One example of the views of humanity which conflict with God's intention for humanity is the construal of humans as the beings who are the centre of existence. The Christ-Event also exposes the danger of the act of using God and human beings as tools to achieve wellbeing. Therefore, the Christologies which are rooted primarily in the quest to gain solution from God but overlooks how God in Jesus Christ shakes and criticizes their understandings of solution is wanting. I have argued throughout this book that such a solution-driven mindset is rooted partly in the indigenous anthropology. To perceive humans as the beings who are the centre of existence is idolatrous. It distorts Jesus's perception of human beings as creatures who are to continually negotiate their being, identity, purpose and destiny (within their contexts) in light of the Christ-Event. Since humanity exists because God is, it is therefore important for Christians

167. Luke 20:9–19.

168. Manus, *Christ, the African King*, 210.

to continue to explore afresh the implications of God's purpose for humanity (which is hidden in the mystery of the Christ-Event) and to criticize and dismantle every form of dehumanization that confronts the peoples of Africa.

Conclusion

THE PERCEPTIONS OF DIVINITY AND HUMANITY IN CONTEMPORARY African Christianity require a fresh examination in light of the meaning, purpose and significance of the Christ-Event. In this book, I have argued that the majority of the existing grassroots and constructive Christologies are solution-oriented.[1] Whilst hardship, fear of the malevolent spirits, and the desire to achieve wellbeing have induced many lay Christians to see Jesus Christ primarily as a solution, the quests to secede from Western cultural and theological hegemony and also to decide for African Christianity what qualifies as an authentic Christology have compelled many theologians to construe Jesus Christ as a solution to the problems of dehumanization and imperialist Christologies. These Christologies are indicative of the endeavor of some Christians' yearning to concretely and relevantly interpret and appropriate the Christ-Event to befit their conditions.[2] But whereas these Christologies reflect originality and novelty, and contribute to the development of christological discourses in Africa, they are somewhat inadequate because the majority of them lack the capacity to generate the self-criticism, mutuality and dialectical conversations that are needed for interpreting and appropriating Jesus Christ in a specific human context, whilst at the same time maintaining the uniqueness of the Christ-Event as the locus

1. What is striking about the solution-oriented Christologies of many lay Christians is that many of these Christians "believe that there are certain issues in life which can only be solved by the corresponding spiritual forces and some cannot be handled by Christianity, no matter what." See Turaki, *Unique Christ for Salvation*, 110.

2. Justin Ukpong sees contextualization as "making the Christian message [to] penetrate the fabric of a society." Again he argues, an "authentic contextualization is the fruit of a genuine encounter between the Christian message and the local context. It is a cultural response to the challenge of the Good News." Ukpong, "Contextualization: A Historical Survey," 286. Ferdinand Nwaigbo similarly sees contextualization as the task of a people "applying the Gospel message analytically to their own culture and of carrying it out holistically within the cultural, religious and historical framework of that shapes a particular environment (*the con-text*) in which the local churches are founded." Nwaigbo, "Twenty-five Years of Contextualization," 291.

of God's revelation. To achieve this, Christians must begin to ask a new set of christological questions. These questions should have the capacity to inspire the Christologies that perceive Jesus Christ both as a question and a solution. I proposed and constructed a Revealer Christology model on one of such new questions; namely, if we present Jesus Christ as both the question and solution to African Christians' perceptions of their needs and the solutions to their needs, what will he look like and what will they look like? I proposed this question as an alternative to the question: "if Jesus is presented as the solution to the wants and the questions that Christians are asking, what would he look like?"[3] The latter question, or a variation of it, is largely responsible for the existing Christologies in African Christianity. The former question that I have proposed arises from the contention that the uniqueness of the Christ-Event lies not only in what God achieves *vocally* but also in what God achieves *silently* in and through the person, life and work of Jesus Christ. In the context of this book, part of what God achieves *vocally* is the answer or solution (such as miraculous healing and providence) he provides. The silence act of God refers to what God stimulates *non-vocally* (that is, what God has hidden) in the solutions that Jesus provides to the needs of humanity; namely, questioning and self-criticism.[4] When Jesus, for example, *vocally* answers the prayer of the Christian couples who are seeking to have children by blessing them with children of their own, part of what Jesus does *silently* is to stimulate the couples to engage in self-critical reflection. It is the responsibility of such couples to undertake the rigorous and humbling task of discovering the questions Jesus is asking in the solutions he has provided. The couples must rethink the solution-oriented mindset that permeates African Christianity and the indigenous religions which are largely responsible for some of the dehumanizing treatments many African couples who are unable to have children, particularly women, receive from the people who are able to have children. Here what African Christians need to rediscover is what God has hidden and revealed about humanity in the Christ-Event.[5]

3. See the introduction of this book for the impact of John Taylor's christological questions on African contextual Christologies.

4. I am indebted to Luther's *theologia crucis* (theology of the cross).

5. For discussions on the roles of children in some Nigerian Christians' understandings of the meaning of humanity, see chapter three.

The grassroots and constructive Christologies I examined throughout this book have concentrated on how Jesus functions as a solution, but have ignored that it is christologically problematic to see Jesus as a solution without at the same time and in the same relation construe him as the one who questions Christians' understandings of their needs and the solutions they anticipate. According to Clement Ogbonnaya, "the moment God becomes a shepherd to you, you will never lack anything" since God will "make you to lie down in green pastures."[6] Driven by the same desire for solution, Enoch Adeboye, one of the leading Pentecostal pastors in Nigeria, has written: "if you are ill and you come to Jesus Christ, your medical bills will become history, in Jesus name."[7] Fintan Ufomadu says this about Jesus: "Jesus came and died because of my sin. Instead of me going to hell, I will go to heaven by the faith I have in him and by my belief that he died for me on the cross and saved me from going to hell."[8] The understandings of Jesus Christ that Ogbonnaya, Ufomadu and Adeboye have projected are that of a problem-solver. These understandings of Jesus are also widespread among theologians, although most of them have concentrated on the tasks of expressing Jesus with and within the indigenous religious and cultural categories and constructing the Christologies and theologies that deconstruct the images of Jesus in the teachings of the classical Western missionaries.[9] Their predominant task is to prove that Jesus Christ ought to be contextualized to suit a given culture. According to Osadolor Imasogie,

> There is always a search for living and relevant symbols that
> mediate the saving presence of God in Jesus Christ. . . . He does
> not become real to people merely on the basis of what an ear-
> lier generation and culture has said, as important as this is. He
> becomes real only on the basis of the authentic discernment by
> every generation. When this discernment occurs the new gen-
> eration discovers, to its joy, that the Christ thus disclosed is the

---

6. Ogbonnaya, *I Am Too Big to Be Poor*, 6.

7. Adeboye, *God the Holy Spirit*, 3.

8. Ufomadu, Interview by author, tape recording, Aba, 28 May 2006.

9. See chapter two. The challenge for a African theologian is to construct a Christology that has the capacity to *break away* from merely criticizing and deconstructing Western missionaries' theological hegemony to constructing the Christologies that engage with the contemporary issues that confront many Christians.

same as eternal Christ known by the earlier generation and culture in their own situation.[10]

Throughout this book I have explored the christological problems with construing Jesus Christ merely as a solution—either as a solution to the existential needs or as a solution to a theological oppressive hegemony. One of the key problems with a solution-oriented Christology is that it overlooks the capacity of the Christ-Event to question, critique, upset, and reconstruct the ways many Christians construe their problems and the solutions that they hope to get from Jesus Christ. A solution-oriented Christology needs to be critiqued and reworked to create a forum for Jesus to function, not only as a solution, but also as a problem or a question, if the Christology hopes to be both relevant to its contexts but at the same time represent faithfully the purpose and significance of the person and work of Jesus Christ.

I have proposed a Revealer Christology as an alternative christological model to the existing Christologies in Africa. This model argues that Jesus Christ mediates and interprets humanity and divinity for the purpose of enacting and sustaining a relationship between God and God's creatures, particularly human beings. It is precisely on this ground that Jesus Christ operates as a revealer of divinity and humanity. But what can a Revealer Christology do for African Christianity? What is the warrant for developing a Revealer Christology model when there are already existing christological models in Africa? The two helpful ways to respond to these questions are to articulate the contextual and christological warrants for the Revealer Christology for Africa.

The Contextual Warrant of the Revealer Christology Model

The Revealer Christology model I have developed in this book exposes and bridges the unnecessary dichotomy existing between the grassroots and constructive Christologies of African Christianity. This model has interacted constructively with the issues propelling and informing most grassroots and constructive Christologies. This dichotomy, as I argued in chapter three, is not simply an academic/non-academic divide. It is rather a dichotomy that operates at a deeper level, sometimes gener-

10. Imasogie, *Guidelines for Christian Theology in Africa*, 18.

ating some conflicting and competing agenda. For example, whereas many theologians attend to the need to produce a *contextualized Jesus* by dressing him up in the indigenous metaphors, the majority of lay Christians seek to experience a Jesus who has the power to solve their existential problems. This dichotomy is dubious and disastrous for African Christianity. This will become evident when we recognize that the concerns of lay Christians and theologians ought to mutually inform and shape their interpretations and appropriations of Jesus in their context.[11]

It is also noteworthy that the gulf between lay Christians and theologians has deepened with the rise of churches with founding pastors who have no formal theological training.[12] Many lay Christians today readily quote and recite the words of prophecy, comments, or sayings of their pastors and preachers (who are usually not trained in theology) which they hear in preaching or read in books. None of the interviewees made a single reference to the writings of the African theologians who can be considered heavy weights in theological scholarship. Is it because these Christians have lost faith in their theologians? If the answer is in the affirmative, is the reason because the theologians have remained far too academic and have continued to speak languages and discuss issues that escape many Christians who do not have a formal theological training? It may not be entirely true that the reason many Christians who have not studied theology avoid or fail to take theologians seriously is because they cannot understand and connect with the issues that the theologians are discussing. However, the fact that most theologians are discussing some issues which escape the majority of Christians is largely responsible for this state of affairs.

11. In addition, this dichotomy raises an important ecclesiastical question: how could African Christian churches develop without theologians who take seriously the questions the laity is asking? Many African theologians have for too long devoted their time to answer the christological questions some classical Western missionaries have consciously or unconsciously inspired or the questions their peers are asking, but have neglected the questions the Christian laity is asking about Jesus. It is deplorable that most of the constructive Christologies purportedly written for an African context have remained strange to the christological needs and questions of many lay Christians.

12. This is not to suggest that all contemporary African theologians have ignored totally the questions that lay Christians are asking. The Circle of Concerned Women, for example, is a theological association that encourages African female theologians to engage with some grassroots issues. See chapter two for an examination of some key African feminist Christologies.

The dichotomy between theologians and the laity is real, but unwarranted. Some Christians consider theology (and a theologian) to be a deadly virus that gradually destroys the faith of Christians. In the thinking of some of these Christians, blessed is the Christian who has not met a theologian for he or she will see God. This thinking, of course, needs to be criticized and corrected. But can this be done if theologians continue to deepen the gulf by talking in the language that escapes the majority of Christians who are not theologians? Two things in particular are noteworthy in appraising the dichotomy between grassroots and constructive Christologies. First, a Christian community without theologians will be in danger of depending on foreign theologies to continue to exist. A dangerous corollary of this unnecessary dependence is that the Christian community cannot be genuinely contextual and innovative in its interpretation and appropriation of the Christ-Event. Also, the foreign theologies may be largely unsuitable for the African contexts. Second, the theologians who fail to take seriously the questions their community is asking will risk constructing abstract theoretical concepts that are misguided and irrelevant to their communities, however clever and sophisticated they may appear to be. Such theologies would hardly last. They will fall to the wayside because they cannot adapt to the rapid cultural, religious and socio-economic challenges of their communities.

The Revealer Christology model that is developed in this book has initiated a process of bridging the gap between theologians and the Christians who do not have a formal theological training by interacting with the questions they are asking. I have queried and conversed constructively with the major issues that have stimulated Jesus-talk among Christians. I have interacted extensively with the spirit world as construed by Christians and have also constructed a christological response to the issue of the malevolent spirits, a topic many theologians have ignored.[13]

Christianity and the indigenous religions concede God's activity in the world, albeit in some competing ways. This view of God and the world influences Christians' perceptions of their identity and their relationship with God, the lesser spirit beings, and humanity. The indigenous religions of many African societies teach that there is a continuum

---

13. See chapter six.

and interconnectedness between the spiritual and human worlds. Keith Ferdinando observes,

> Within African traditional religion the invisible and visible worlds are not seen as two separate spheres but as different dimensions of a single indivisible reality, which act and react upon one another. While the invisible world remains to some degree mysterious, human fortunes are held to be significantly determined by the activities and attitudes of the spirits which inhabit them.[14]

Ferdinando captures the attitude of many African peoples towards the spiritual world. There is a strong belief that the events which occur in the human world most likely resulted from an action that has taken place in the invisible or spiritual world. Imasogie notes: "The African sees life as a mystery to be lived out on a mysterious planet ruled by spiritual forces of good and evil. There is no event without spiritual/metaphysical cause; hence, man must look beyond physical events to their spiritual etiology."[15] Yusufu Turaki makes the same point when he writes,

> The spiritual world or the realm of the supernatural is, in a sense, a battleground of spirits and powers that use their mystical powers to influence the course of human life. These mystical powers can be designated as positive or negative, good or evil and they bring blessings or curses. If man only knew how to master and control the realm of the supernatural, the world would be a much happier place.[16]

The belief in the interrelationship between the worlds of spirit beings and human beings has influenced many people's quest to understand and maneuver the activities of the spirit beings in order to achieve wellbeing. Turaki correctly notes that the "human quest to control or influence" the spiritual world has resulted in a "variety of specialists such as medicine men or women, rainmakers, mediums, diviners, sorcerers, magicians and witches."[17] For example, the couples who fear that they are barren will normally consult some diviners to find out if some spirits, ancestors, gods, or humans are responsible for their barrenness, and

14. Ferdinando, *Triumph of Christ in Africa Perspective*, 27.

15. Imasogie, *African Traditional Religion*, 67.

16. Turaki, *Unique Christ for Salvation*, 61.

17. Ibid.

also to discover what may be required to appease, pacify or maneuver the causes of the barrenness. The desire of African peoples (including Christians) to penetrate, understand and maneuver the spiritual world provides a window upon their beliefs and aspirations. I have developed a Revealer Christology model in this book to inquire into and engage constructively with this phenomenon by construing Jesus Christ as the God-man who mediates and interprets divinity and humanity with the intent to create and uphold a relationship between God and human beings. To construe Jesus Christ in this way will provide a relevant context to engage with the knowledge of God, the spirit world, and humanity that the majority of Africans seek to gain from diviners, magicians and mediums.

Another contribution the Revealer Christology model as developed in this book makes to the development of Christology in Africa and beyond is that it has been designed to provide a helpful context or platform for African contextual Christologies to interact with the Christologies emerging from other parts of Africa and non-African societies. One of the dangers that a contextual Christology must seek to avoid is to become irrelevant to the development of the Christologies that exist outside of its context. The Christian theologian who undertakes the task of developing a contextual Christology is to be ready to confront this problem by drawing upon the Christologies already existing in other parts of the world. A contextual Christology is parochial if it is designed from and intended only to serve its local audience. Some contextual Christologies emerging from many parts of the sub-Saharan Africa are parochial in their structures and contents. This is because those who construct them write from the backgrounds of anti-Western Christologies and pro-African Christologies, demonstrating very little or no attempt at all to create a linking road between their Christologies and the Christologies that are coming out from the churches in the West, and even sometimes in Asia, Latin America, and the Oceanic region. One example is the disassociation of African theology from Black American liberation theology. Ernest Mbefo praises John Mbiti as the savior who redeemed African theologians from doing theology in light of Black theology which was championed by some African American theologians such as James Cone. Mbefo writes,

> It was Mbiti that demolished the alliance that was developing
> between American black theology and African theology when

he warned: "Black Theology cannot and will not become African Theology" because the two theologies have different historical and social backgrounds. They "emerged from quite different historical and contemporary situations." African liberation theology should rather concern itself with what the theological community identifies as "anthropological poverty," namely the abuse and misuse of the African person in his historical contact with other races.[18]

What Mbefo, Mbiti and others whose share their view fail to acknowledge is that although Black American liberation theology and Black theology as developed in South Africa have different historical contexts, they project a similar Christology: they both critique injustice and oppression by presenting Jesus as a model or an archetype of liberation.[19]

The need to avoid parochialism in doing contextual Christology cannot be ignored. Sometimes it is easy to get stuck in searching through the religious, cultural, and socio-economic contexts of a local community to find resources for Christology. But the theologian who aims to construct a contextual Christology that is relevant in the twenty-first century Christianity must look beyond his or her local context when interpreting the Christ-Event. A contextual Christology that is parochial will deprive other Christian communities of the unique contributions it can offer to the ongoing quests to discover and appropriate the meaning and significance of Jesus in the contemporary world.[20] On the one hand, Asian, African and other non-Western theologians who write contextual theologies are no doubt helping some Western theologians to become aware that no theology escapes contextualization. Of course, the postmodern philosophy, which promotes heterogeneous plurality and incredulity towards metanarratives and the dichotomy of centre/margin, may have compelled some Western theologians to rethink their approach to theology.[21] But it is the non-Western theolo-

---

18. Mbefo, *Christian Theology and African Heritage*, 54.

19. See chapter two for discussion on liberation and Black theologies.

20. Kwame Bediako, following Andrew Walls, hopes that the indigenous religions of Africa may someday "point the way into the Christian future and the future of Christian theology." If this expectation happens, Bediako argues that "the African contribution [to Christian theology] will have been an important one." See Bediako, *Jesus and the Gospel in Africa*, 60.

21. See Lyotard, *Postmodern Condition*; Tracy, *On Naming the Present*; Greene, *Christology in Cultural Perspective*; Carl Raschke, *Next Reformation*.

gians that have championed contextual theologies and have cautioned against imposing a christological proposition on a foreign context. On the other hand, a parochial Christology will risk missing the process of refining that usually comes from interacting with similar or opposing Christologies that exist outside of its context. To avoid the dangers of parochialism, it is necessary that an African contextual Christology is open to dialogue and interaction with the Christologies emerging from World Christianity. This is one of the reasons I interacted with some theologians outside of Africa in this book.

The Christological Warrant of the Revealer Christology Model

The key question here is: does the Revealer Christology model as developed in this book interact adequately with and interpret the Christ-Event? It is important to recognize that diverse models, such as, Son of God, Son of Man, Christ, priest, and prophet are used in the Bible to describe Jesus of Nazareth. The vital question for a contextual theologian to answer is: do these models describe exhaustively the mystery of the person and work of Jesus of Nazareth? A careful study of the history of Christian Christology shows that the majority of theologians have answered this question in the negative. In some classical Christian traditions, we encounter models such as the Second Person of the Trinity, the logos, and so on. African Christologies have produced models like the Chief Ancestor, the Life Giver, the Healer, Guest, etc. If every Christology is contextual in so far as it arises from some specific contexts, it follows that we are bound to have multiple christological models. The changing face of human contexts demands that theologians respond with contextually-driven interpretations of the Christ-Event to match the contours of the changing human needs.

The challenge for an African theologian who constructs a contextual Christology is not to confine what he or she says about Jesus Christ to the biblical representations of him. It is rather to construct a Christology that truly represents the meaning and significance of Jesus Christ as well as thoroughly situating it within the context which inspires his or her Christology. The problem that is facing the majority of African Christians today (although not entirely unconnected with the classical presentation of Jesus Christ by Western missionaries) is not Western theological hegemony. It is also not the problem of how to explain Christianity as a *foreign religion* to the indigenous peoples of Africa by using a local category. It is an error to assume that the peoples of Africa cannot truly experience Jesus Christ unless he is described with a local metaphor, for example, as an ancestor. Some theologians who construct culture-oriented Christologies are guilty of this error. It is important to point out here that ironically this assumption is suggestive of a derogatory view of African peoples as incapable of understanding the complex teaching of Christianity about Jesus Christ if he is not explicated with a local metaphor.[22] The primary issue that confronts African Christianity today is the perception of Jesus Christ merely as a solution to peoples' problems. This understanding of Jesus, as I have consistently argued in this book, is problematic because the majority of lay Christians and theologians have excluded the role of Jesus in critiquing how they perceive their problems and the solution to the problems. Consequently, many Christians abandon Jesus to consult other possible solutions when they feel that Jesus is either incapable or unready to solve a particular problem.[23] Others simply use Jesus as a tool to achieve their agenda of liberation, which ironically are driven by oppressive ambitions and ego.[24] Therefore, the Christology that will benefit contemporary African Christianity must be able to inspire a contextualization and counter-contextualization process in which Christians can begin to construe Jesus Christ as the divine and human being who questions their perceptions of their problems and solutions as well as redefines and solves their problems. A major pragmatic implication of this claim is that Christians need to evaluate who they are and their understandings of wellbeing in light of the Christ-Event. They are to explore the meanings and significances of the Christ-Event from and within the indigenous worldview, their Christian traditions and religious and social experiences. This, however, does not mean that they are to ascribe to and impose on Jesus the meanings that compete with his understanding of his identity as the Son of God and his mission

22. I am not suggesting here that it is inadequate to explain Jesus Christ with a local religious or cultural category, but that one does not need to limit oneself to such categories.

23. As I have argued in this book, most of these problems are rooted in the quest to understand and maneuver some spirit beings for the purpose of achieve wellbeing.

24. For example, some African feminist theologians are highly suspicious of the theologies that are written by African male theologians. See chapter two.

as the enactor of God's new relationship with humanity.[25] An adequate *African contextual Christology* occurs when African Christians (laity and theologians) approach, interpret and appropriate the Christ-Event from their own history and experience and at the same time invite Jesus Christ to probe, shape, interpret their perceptions of humanity, and God and to mediate and interpret God and his desire for humanity.

I have argued that a befitting way to approach and explicate the Christ-Event for African Christianity is the construe Jesus Christ as the Revealer of divinity and humanity. A Revealer in this context is the individual who possesses the ability to mediate and interpret humanity and divinity. Thus, I have explored the Revealer Christology model within the expanding circumference of the Nicene and Chalcedonian confession of Jesus Christ as consubstantial with both divinity and humanity. Most of the existing Revealer Christologies focus on revelation and therefore concentrate on Jesus-divinity with little or no attempt to discuss Jesus-humanity.[26] But in this book I have argued that an adequate Revealer Christology ought to be constructed to represent Jesus Christ as the one who mediates and interprets humanity and divinity. We cannot adequately represent the Christ-Event if we overemphasize Jesus Christ as a revealer of divinity and ignore that he is also a revealer of humanity. Therefore, an adequate Revealer Christology (especially designed for the African contexts) will construe Jesus as simultaneously revealing (that is, mediating and interpreting) divinity and humanity for the purpose of creating and sustaining the God-human relation.

Constructing a Revealer Christology on the understanding that Jesus is simultaneously a revealer of divinity and humanity will help Christians to guard against creating a false dichotomy between the person of Jesus Christ (ontological Christology) and his work (functional Christology). An adequate Christology should hold the person and work of Jesus together as the two features of the Christ-Event, and should discuss them as the two indispensable aspects of an entity. Some of the acts of Jesus, such as miraculous healings, and some of his claims unveil his mysterious identity.[27] It is the ontology of Jesus Christ (as the

25. See chapters five and seven for discussions on the identity and mission of Jesus Christ.

26. A recent example is Mark D. Thompson, "Uniqueness of Christ as the Revealer of God," 90–110.

27. For example, by saying to the paralyzed man "your sins are forgiven" (Mk 2:10;

being who embodies both humanity and divinity) that sets his work apart from that of his contemporaries. Any Christology that divorces the work of Jesus Christ from his identity risks underestimating the theological significance that is inherent in his miraculous works. And the Christology that concentrates only on the person of Jesus Christ and overlooks his agency will distort the relevance and the meaning of the Christ-Event. Within a short period of three and half years Jesus of Nazareth succeeded in impressing himself upon his followers that he enjoyed an unprecedented relationship with Yahweh, that he was the anticipated Messiah. Consequently, the disciples of Jesus Christ began to revere him as a divine figure who was also one of them—a human being. This radical understanding of Jesus as the Christ has shaped the content of the New Testament writings and informed the thinking of the earliest Christian communities.

However bizarre the notion that Jesus was indeed the Messiah may have appeared to their contemporaries, the earliest Christian communities interpreted his work and person in relation to his unique relationship with God. Therefore, instead of construing the miracles of Jesus as the act of a highly skilled magician, the earliest Christians interpreted them as the work of a man who embodied the presence and power of God. An adequate Revealer Christology will supply a contextual critique of the Christologies which only concentrate on discovering how the work of Jesus can function as a model of liberation or solution to the problems Africans face. Whilst it is important to locate the meaning of the Christ-Event within the experience of a given community, we must recognize that if the ontological and functional questions about Jesus are not adequately addressed, we will risk a distortion of his universality and particularity, and his divinity and humanity. In this book, I have developed a Revealer Christology model to account for the contexts of African Christianity as well as the meaning, purpose and significance of God's manifestations of himself in the Christ-Event.

Luke 5:24), Jesus unveils that he is different from the prophetic figures of his day. The sin of blasphemy which the "Pharisees and the teachers of the law" accused Jesus of also demonstrates that his contemporaries knew that he was making a claim that only one who is God or at least enjoys an unprecedented relationship with God could make.

Appendix 1

Pre-set Questions for Semi-Structured Individual Interviews

Who is Jesus Christ to you?

Where do you get your knowledge about Jesus Christ?

Are there some experiences in your life that you think have any connection with Jesus Christ?

In your experience, does Jesus solve problems?

In your experience, are there some Nigerian Christians who go outside of Jesus Christ to look for solution to their problems?

If Jesus were to tell you to make a request what would you ask him for?

Appendix 2

Interviews with the Members of the Roman Catholic Church (St. Ambrose), Umuoba Road, Aba

James Olayinka: May 3, 2006

Chidi Maduka: May 3, 2006

Bridget Udoma: June 20, 2006

Ndidi Aharanya: June 20, 2006

Promise Chidindu Ahamefuna: June 20, 2006

Jude Nwachukwu (Priest): June 22, 2006

Christina Ezebike: June 22, 2006

Ogechi Nnanna: June 22, 2006

Tobechukwu Ihedinaobi: June 22, 2006

Teresa Akunne: June 22, 2006

Interviews with the Members of The Presbyterian Church of Nigeria, Ogbor Hill, Aba

Dr. Amadi: April 10, 2006

Peter: March 14, 2006

Queen Mamoh: May 18, 2006

Mrs. Comfort: June 18, 2006

Ukweni O. Ukweni: June 18, 2006

Ejim Okonkwo: June 18, 2006

Ben Fubura Manuel (Pastor): March 12, 2006

Sister Favor: June 18, 2006

Florence Nnenna Eze: June 18, 2006

Kinsley Unuegbu: July 5, 2006

Interviews with the Members of ECWA English Church/ECWA Church Umuokea, Aba

Moses Attah: February 29, 2006

Iliya Habu: February 29, 2006

Chioma: March 8, 2006

Blessing Oparauche: March 8, 2006

Mary Asonye: March 22, 2006

Thompson Onyenechehie (Pastor): March 10, 2006

Benedict Ufomadu: May 28, 2006

Elizabeth Adeyemi Olusola: June 2, 2006

Humble Douglas: June 17, 2006

Dosemu Bola: June 28, 2006

Interviews with the Members of Christ Holy Church (Odoziobodo); No. 3, Aba

Favor Okpara: June 25, 2006

Veronica Okeke: June 25, 2006

Shedrach Chukwuemeka Okonkwo: June 25, 2006

Blessing Madu: June 25, 2006

Kate Agu: June 25, 2006

Favor Okafor: July 9, 2006

Emanuel Ahamba: July 9, 2006

Chukwuemeka: July 9, 2006

David Umeike (Pastor): July 9, 2006

Chidozie Okoye: July 9, 2006

Interviews with the Members of Christian Pentecostal Mission, Ngwa Road Aba

Faith Ukaegbu: May 6, 2006

Emeka Nnabuko: May 10, 2006

Chukwuemeka Azunwa: May 17, 2006

Alex Iwuchiwueze: May 17, 2006

John Okpara (Pastor): May 24, 2006

Precious Uzobuike: May 24, 2006

Ernest Mbefo: May 24, 2006

Faith Iwuchukwu: May 24, 2006

Blessing Madubuko: May 24, 2006

Gloria Eze: May 24, 2006

Bibliography

Abanuka, Bartholomew. "Ancestors and the Idea of Ultimate Reality and Meaning in the Igbo Worldview: A Further Contribution to URAM Igbo Studies." *Ultimate Reality and Meaning* 13 (1990) 134–44.

———. *Philosophy and the Igbo World*. Onitsha: Spiritan, 2004.

Abimbola, Wande. "The Place of African Traditional Religion in Contemporary Africa: The Yoruba Example." In *African Traditional Religions in Contemporary Society*, edited by Jacob K. Olupona, 51–58. St. Paul: Paragon, 1991.

Abogunrin, Oyin S. *In Search of the Original Jesus*. Ibadan: University of Ibadan, 2003.

Abonyi, Clifford. *Satan, You're a Liar.* Nsukka: Fulladu, 1993.

Achebe, Chinua. *Things Fall Apart*. London: Heinemann, 1958.

Achunike, Hilary C. *The Influence of Pentecostalism on Catholic Priests and Seminarians in Nigeria*. Lagos: Charles & Patrick, 2004.

Adamo, David Tuesday. "The Use of Psalms in African Indigenous Churches in Nigeria." In *The Bible in Africa: Transactions, Trajectories, and Trends*, edited by Gerald O. West and Musa W. Dube, 336–49. Leiden: Brill, 2000.

Adeboye, Enoch A. *God the Holy Spirit: Be a Conductor of His Power*. Largo: Christian Living, 2002.

Adegbola, Adeolu. "A Christian Interpretation of the African Revolution." In *Christ and the Younger Churches: Theological Contributions from Asia, Africa, and Latin America*, edited by Georg F. Vicedom. London: SPCK, 1972.

Adeyemo, Tokunboh. "The Idea of Salvation in Contemporary World Religions." In *Issues in African Christian Theology*, edited by Samuel Ngewa, Mark Shaw, and Tite Tienou, 198–209. Nairobi: EAEP, 1998.

———. *Salvation in African Tradition*. Nairobi: Evangel, 1978.

Adiele, Shed N. "Historical Background to the Advent of Christianity in Eastern States of Nigeria." In *The Niger Mission: Origin, Growth, and Impact 1857–1995*, edited by Shed N. Adiele, 1–19. Aba: ISAECO, 1996.

Adogame, Afe. "African Instituted Churches in Europe: Continuity and Transformation." In *African Identities and World Christianity in the Twentieth Century*, edited by Klaus Koschorke, 225–44. Wiesbaden: Harrassowitz, 2005.

———. *Celestial Church of Christ: The Politics of Cultural Identity in a West African Prophetic-Charismatic Movement*. Frankfurt: Lang, 1999.

———. "The Use of European Traditions in Book of Religion in Africa: West African Perspective." In *European Traditions in the Book of Religion in Africa*, edited by Frieder Ludwig and Afe Adogame, 375–81. Wiesbaden: Harrassowtz, 2004.

Aguwa, Jude C. "Taboos and Purification of Ritual Pollutions in Igbo Traditional Society: Analysis and Symbolism." *Anthropos* 88.4–6 (1993) 539–46.

Ajayi, J. F. Ade. *Christian Missions in Nigeria, 1841–1891: The Making of a New Elite.* Ibadan History Series. London: Longmans, 1965.

Akinade, Akintunde E. "Who Do You Say That I Am?—An Assessment of Some Christological Constructs in Africa." *Asia Journal of Theology* 9 (1995) 181–200.

Akunne, Paul Chinedu. *Having Power with God.* Lagos: Ikechbenjamin, 2004.

Alasuutari, Pertti. *Researching Culture: Qualitative Method and Cultural Studies.* London: Sage, 1995.

Alberigo, Giuseppe, and Alphonse N. Mushete, editors. *Towards the African Synod.* London: SCM, 1991.

Amoah, Elizabeth, and Mercy Oduyoye. "The Christ for African Women." In *With Passion and Compassion: Third World Women Doing Theology,* edited by Virginia Fabella and Mercy Oduyoye, 35–46. Maryknoll, NY: Orbis, 1988.

———. "Christology and Popular Religions: An African Constructive Statement." *Voices from the Third World* 22.2 (1999) 82–86.

Aniako, Chike. "Ancestral Legitimation in Igbo Art." *West African Religion* 18 (1979) 13–30.

Anijielo, Anthony Chukwuma. "A Pastoral Perspective of the Socio-Cultural Challenges of Nigerian Priests and the Church in the Twenty-First Century." In *Witnessing Christ in Contemporary Nigeria,* edited by Anacletus Nnamdi Odoemene, 1–20. Port Harcourt: IHBC-CIWA, 2005.

Anyawu, H. Onyema. "Why Igbo Abandoned Their Gods." *African Theological Journal* 14.2 (1985) 91–99.

Anyika, F. "The Supreme God in Igbo Traditional Religious Thought and Worship." *Communio Viatorum* 32.1–2 (1989) 5–20.

Anderson, Allan. "African Initiated Churches of the Spirit and Pneumatology." *Word & World* 23.2 (2003) 178–86.

Anderson, James. *Paradox in Christian Theology: An Analysis of Its Presence, Character, and Epistemic Status.* Carlisle, UK: Paternoster, 2007.

Apel, Dean. "Towards a Sumburu Christology." *Currents in Theology and Mission* 23.5 (1996) 356–67.

Appiah-Kubi, Kofi. "Christology." In *A Reader in African Christian Theology,* edited by John Parratt, 69–81. London: SPCK, 1987.

Asamoah-Gyadu, J. Kwabena. "'Christ is the Answer: What is the Question?' A Ghana Airways Prayer Vigil and Its Implications for Religion, Evil and Public Space." *Journal of African Religion* 35 (2005) 93–117.

Atado, Joe Chuks. *Welcome Jesus Bye Bye Satan: Spiritual Pills to Overcome Your Problems.* n.p.: The Feast of Our Lady of Sorrows, 1990.

Athaus-Reid, Marcella. "'Pussy, Queen of Pirates': Acker, Isherwood and the Debates on the Body of Feminist Theology." In *Embodying Feminist Liberation Theologies,* edited by Beverley Clark, 157–67. London: Continuum, 2004.

Aune, David E. *Revelation 5–16.* Word Biblical Commentary. Vol. 52B. Nashville: Nelson, 1998.

———. "Stories of Jesus in the Apocalypse of John." In *Contours of Christology in the New Testament,* edited by Richard N. Longenecker, 292–319. Grand Rapids: Eerdmans, 2005.

Awolalu, J. Omosade. "The Concept of Death and Hereafter in Yoruba Traditional Religion." *West African Religion* 18 (1979) 57–59.

———. "Sin and Its Removal in African Traditional Religion." *Journal of American Academy of Religion* 44 (1976) 275–87.

Awolalu, Omosade J. A. "God: The Contemporary Discussion." In *God: The Contemporary Discussion*, edited, E. Ade Odumuyina, xv–xxvii. Ago-Iwoye: NASR, Olabisi Onabanjo University, 2005.

Awolalu, Omosade J. Awolalu, and Adelumo P. Dopamu. *West African Traditional Religion*. Ibadan: Onibonoje, 1979.

Ayegboyin, Deji. "Li Oruko Jesu: Aladura Grass-root Christology." *Journal of Africa Christian Thought* 8 (2005) 11–21.

Ayres, Lewis. *Nicaea and Its Legacies; An Approach to Fourth-Century Trinitarian Theology*. Oxford: Oxford University Press, 2004.

Azikiwe, Nnamdi. "The Future of Pan-Africanism." In *Ideologies of Liberation in Black Africa, 1856–1970: Documents on Modern African Political Thought from the Colonial Times to the Present*, edited by J. Ayo Langley, 302–27. London: Collins, 1979.

———. "Monotheism and Christology in the Gospel of John." In *Contours of Christology in the New Testament*, edited by Richard N. Longenecker, 148–66. Grand Rapids: Eerdmans, 2005.

Baeta, C. G, editor. *Christian and African Culture*. Accra: Christian Council of the Gold Coast, 1955.

Bahemuka, Judith M. "The Hidden Christ in African Traditional Religion." In *Jesus in African Christianity: Experimentation and Diversity in African Christology*, edited by J. N. K. Mugambi and Laurenti Magesa, 1–15. Nairobi: African Initiatives, 1989.

Baker, Mark D., and Joel B. Green. *Recovering the Scandal of the Cross: Atonement in New Testament and Contemporary Contexts*. Carlisle, UK: Paternoster, 2000.

Balogun, Joshua Olajide. *Redeemed from the Clutches of Satan*. Lagos: Noade, 1990.

Barth, Karl. *Church Dogmatics*. Vol. 1, part 1: *The Doctrine of the Word of God*. Edinburgh: T. & T. Clark, 1936.

———. *The Humanity of God*. London: Collins, 1961.

Bauckham, Richard et al., editors. *Jesus 2000*. Oxford: Lion, 1989.

Baur, John. *2000 Years of Christianity in Africa: An African History 62–1992*. Nairobi: Paulines, 1994.

Bediako, Kwame. "Biblical Christologies in the Context of African Traditional Religions." In *Sharing Jesus in the Two Third World: Evangelical Christologies from the Contexts of Poverty, Powerlessness and Religious Pluralism*, edited by Vinay Samuel and Chris Sugden, 115–75. Bangalore: Partnership in Mission–Asia, 1983.

———. *Christianity in Africa: The Renewal of a Non-Western Religion*. Edinburgh: University of Edinburgh Press, 1990.

———. "The Doctrine of Christ and the Significance of Vernacular Terminology." *International Bulletin of Missionary Research* 22.3 (1998) 110–11.

———. *Jesus and the Gospel in Africa: History and Experience*. Maryknoll, NY: Orbis, 2004.

———. "Jesus in African Culture." *Evangelical Review of Theology* 17 (1993) 54–64.

———. *Theology and Identity: The Impact of Culture upon Christian Thought in the Second Century and in Modern Africa*. Yaoundé: Regnum,1992.

———. "Understanding Theology in the 20th Century." In *Issues in African Christian Theology*, edited by Samuel Ngewa, Mark Shaw, and Tite Tienou, 56–72. Nairobi: EAEP, 1998.

Beek, van Walter, and Dennis L. Thomson, editors. *Religion in Africa*. London: Heinemann, 1994.

Benner, Drayton C. "Augustine and Karl Rahner on the Relationship between the Immanent Trinity and the Economic Trinity." *International Journal of Systematic Theology* 9 (2007) 24–38.

Boersma, Hans. *Violence, Hospitality and the Cross: Reappropriating the Atonement Tradition*. Grand Rapids: Baker, 2004.

Boesak, Allan Aubrey. *Black Theology Black Power*. London: Mowbrays, 1976.

Boff, Leonardo. *Jesus Christ Liberator*. Translated by Patrick Hughes. London: SPCK, 1992.

Boff, Leonardo, and Clodovis Boff. *Introducing Liberation Theology*. Liberation and Theology 1. Translated by Paul Burns. Tunbridge Wells, UK: Burns & Oates, 1986.

Bogdan, Robert C., and Sari Knopp Biklen, *Qualitative Research for Education: An Introduction to Theory and Methods*. Boston: Ally & Bacon, 1982.

Bonino, José Míguez. *Room to Be People*. Philadelphia: Fortress, 1979.

Borg, Marcus J., and N. T. Wright. *The Meaning of Jesus: Two Visions*. London: SPCK, 1999.

Bosch, David J. "Currents and Crosscurrents in South African Black Theology." *Journal of Religion in Africa* 6 (1974) 1–22.

Boyd, James. "Hearing the Good News: The Message of the Kingdom in Mark." *Word & World* 26 (2006) 30–37.

Brewer, David Instone. "Jesus and the Psychiatrists." In *The Unseen World: Christian Reflections on Angels, Demons and the Heavenly Realm*, edited by Anthony N. S. Lane, 133–48. Grand Rapids: Baker, 1996.

Brummer, Vincent. *Atonement, Christology and the Trinity: Making Sense of Christian Doctrine*. Aldershot: Ashgate, 2005.

Bujo, Benezet. *African Christian Morality at the Age of Inculturation*. Nairobi: Paulines, 1990.

———. *African Theology in Its Social Context*. Translated by John O'Donohue. Maryknoll, NY: Orbis, 1992.

———. "Nos anceres, ces saints inconnus." *Bulleting de Theologie Africanine* 1 (1979) 165–78.

Bultmann, Rudolf. *Kerygma and Myth*. Edited by H. W. Bartsch. London: SPCK, 1953.

Burghardt, Walter J. "A Just King, a Just Kingdom." *Living Pulpit* 15 (2006) 8–9.

Cadorette, Curt et al., editors. *Liberation Theology: An Introductory Reader*. Maryknoll, NY: Orbis: 1992.

Campagne, Fabian Alejandro. "Witchcraft and the Sense-of-the-Impossible in Early Modern Spain: Some Reflections Based on the Literature of Superstition (ca. 1500–1800)." *Harvard Theological Review* 96 (2003) 25–62.

Capps, Donald. "Jesus as Power Tactician." *Journal for the Study of the Historical Jesus* 2.2 (2004) 158–89.

Carson, D. A. *The Gagging of God: Christianity Confronts Pluralism*. Grand Rapids: Zondervan, 1996.

Carvalho, Emilio J. M. de. "What Do the Africans Say Jesus Is?" *Africa Theological Journal* 10.2 (1981) 17–25.

Clark, Walter H. et al, *Religious Experience: Its Nature and Function in the Human Psyche.* Springfield, IL: Thomas, 1973.

Cleage, Albert. *Black Messiah.* New York: Sheed & Ward, 1968.

Cole, Victor. "Africanising the Faith: Another Look at Contextualisation." In *Issues in African Christian Theology*, edited by Samuel Ngewa, Mark Shaw, and Tite Tienou, 12–23. Nairobi: EAEP, 1998.

Cone, James H. *Black Theology and Black Power.* New York: Seabury, 1969.

———. "Cross-fertilization: A Statement from the U.S. Minorities." In *Third World Theologies: Commonalities and Divergences*, edited by K. C. Abraham, 129–31. Maryknoll, NY: Orbis, 1994.

———. *God of the Oppressed.* New York: Seabury, 1975.

———. *Risks of Faith: The Emergence of Black Theology of Liberation, 1968–1998.* Boston: Beacon, 1999.

Constas, Nicholas P. "The Last Temptation of Satan: Divine Deception in Greek Patristic Interpretations of the Passion Narrative." *Harvard Theological Review* 97.2 (2004) 139–63.

Cott, Nancy F. *The Grounding of Modern Feminism.* New Haven: Yale University Press, 1987.

Cousar, Charles B. *A Theology of the Cross: The Death of Jesus in the Pauline Letters.* Minneapolis: Fortress, 1990.

Cox, James. "Methodological Considerations Relevant to Understanding African Indigenous Religions." In *The Book of Religions in Africa: Past, Present, and Prospects*, edited by James Cox and Jacob Olupona, 155–71. Cambridge: Roots & Branches, 1996.

———. *Rational Ancestors: Scientific Rationality and African Indigenous Religions.* Cardiff: Cardiff Academic Press, 1998.

———. "Spirit Mediums in Zimbabwe: Religious Experience in and on Behalf of the Community." *Studies in World Christianity* 6.2 (2000) 190–207.

Cracknell, Kenneth. *Justice, Courtesy and Love: Theologians and Missionaries Encountering World Religions 1846–1914.* London: Epworth, 1995.

Crapanzano, Vincent. "Spirit Possession." In *The Encyclopaedia of Religion*, vol. 14, edited by Mircea Eliade, 12–19. London: Collier Macmillan, 1987.

Crislip, Andrew. "The Sin of Sloth or the Illness of the Demons? The Demon of Acedia in Early Christian Monasticism." *Harvard Theological Review* 98.2 (2005) 143–69.

Crossan, John Dominic. "Why Is Historical Jesus Research Necessary?" In *Jesus Two Thousand Years Later*, edited by James H. Charlesworth and Walter P. Weaver, 7–37. Harrisburg, PA: Trinity, 2000.

Dairo, A. Olalekan. "God and Inculturation Theology in Africa." In *God: The Contemporary Discussion*, edited by E. Ade Odumuyina, 227–36. Ago-Iwoye: NASR, Olabisi Onabanjo University, 2005.

Daneel, Marthinus L. "Towards a Theologia Africana: The Contribution of Independent Churches to African Theology." *Missionalia* 12 (1984) 64–89.

Danfulani, Umar Habilar Dadem. "Factors Contributing to the Survival of the Bori Cult in Northern Nigeria." *Numen* 46.4 (1996) 412–47.

Davies, Margaret. *Matthew Readings.* Sheffield: JSOT Press, 1993.

Davies, Stevan L. *Jesus the Healer: Possession, Trance, and the Origins of Christianity*. London: SCM, 1995.

Daly, M. *Beyond God the Father: Toward a Philosophy of Women's Liberation*. Boston: Beacon, 1973.

De Gruchy, John. "Salvation as Healing and Humanization." In *Christ in Our Place: The Humanity of God in Christ for the Reconciliation of the World*, edited by Trevor Hart and Daniel Thimell, 32–47. Exeter: Paternoster, 1989.

Dedji, Valentin. *Reconstruction and Renewal in African Christian Theology*. Nairobi: Action, 2003.

Dembski, William A. *The Case for Angels*. Carlisle, UK: Paternoster, 2002.

Dickson, Kwesi A. *Theology in Africa*. London: Darton, Longman, & Todd, 1984.

Dorries, David W. *Edward Irving's Incarnational Christology*. Fairfax, VA: Xulon, 2002.

Dow, Graham. "The Case for the Existence of Demons." *Churchman* 94.3 (1980) 199–209.

Dulles, Avery. *Models of Revelation*. Maryknoll, NY: Orbis, 1983.

Dunn, James D. G., and Graham H. Twelftree. "Demon-Possession and Exorcism in the New Testament." *Churchman* 94.3 (1980) 210–25.

Edet, N. Rosemary. "Christianity and Africa Women's Rituals." In *The Will to Arise: Women, Tradition, and the Church in Africa*, edited by Mercy Amba Oduyoye and Musimbi R. A. Kanyoro, 25–39. Maryknoll, NY: Orbis, 1992.

Edet, Rosemary, and Bette Jacenta Ekeya. "Church Women of Africa: A Theological Community." In *With Passion and Compassion: Third World Women Doing Theology—Reflections from the Women's Commission of the Ecumenical Association of Third World Theologians*, edited by Virginia Fabella and Mercy Amba Oduyoye, 3–13. Maryknoll, NY: Orbis, 1988.

Edohasim, B. C. *Don't Be Talked Out of Your Miracle*. Aba: Fraternal, 1999.

Ehioghae, Efe M. "The Concept of God and Evil: A Christian Perspective." In *God: The Contemporary Discussion*, edited by E. Ade Odumuyina, 431–43. Ago-Iwoye: NASR, Olabisi Onabanjo University, 2005.

Ela, Jean-Marc. *African Cry*. Translated by Robert R. Barr. Maryknoll, NY: Orbis, 1986.

———. "Christianity and Liberation in Africa." In *Paths of African Theology*, edited by Rosino Gibellini, 136–53. Maryknoll, NY: Orbis, 1994.

———. "The Memory of the African People and the Cross of Christ." In *The Scandal of a Crucified World: Perspectives on the Cross of Christ*, translated and edited by Yacob Tesfai, 17–35. Maryknoll, NY: Orbis, 1994.

———. *My Faith as an African*. Translated by John Pairman Brown and Susan Perry. Maryknoll, NY: Orbis, 1988.

Eliade, Mircea. *Patterns in Comparative Religion*. London: Sheed & Ward, 1958.

Enuwosa, J. "Exploring the Nature of God in the New Testament for Meaningful Development in Nigeria." In *God: The Contemporary Discussion*, edited by E. Ade Odumuyina, 212–26. Ago-Iwoye: NASR, Olabisi Onabanjo University, 2005.

Equiano, Olaudah. *The Interesting Narrative and Other Writings*. Edited by Vincent Carretta. New York: Penguin, 1995.

Erickson, Millard J. "Christology from Above and Christology from Below: A Study of Contrasting Methodologies." In *Perspectives on Evangelical Theology: Papers from the Thirtieth Annual Meeting of the Evangelical Society,* edited by Kenneth S. Kantzer and Stanley N. Gundry, 43–55. Grand Rapids: Baker, 1979.

Eto, Victoria. *How I Served Satan.* Warri: Shallom Christian Mission, 1988.

Etuk, Udo. "New Trends in Traditional Divination." *Africa Theological Journal* 13.2 (1984) 83–91.

Evans, C. Stephen. *The Historical Christ and the Jesus of Faith: The Incarnational Narrative as History.* Oxford: Clarendon, 1996.

Ezeanya, Stephen N. "God, Spirits and the Spirit World, with Special Reference to the Igbo-Speaking People of Southern Nigeria." In *Biblical Revelation and African Beliefs,* edited by Kwesi A. Dickson and Paul Ellingworth. London: Lutterworth, 1969.

Ezeh, Uchenna A. *Jesus Christ the Ancestor: African Contextual Christology in the Light of the Major Dogmatic Christological Definitions of the Church from the Council of Nicaea (325) to Chalcedon (451).* Oxford: Lang, 2003.

Farley, Edward. *Divine Empathy: A Theology of God.* Minneapolis: Fortress, 1996.

Farquhar, J. N. *The Crown of Hinduism.* New Delhi: Oriental, 1971.

Ferdinando, Keith. "The Legacy of Byang Kato." *International Bulletin of Missionary Research* 28.4 (2004) 169–74.

———. "Screwtape Revisited: Demonology Western, African, and Biblical." In *The Unseen World: Christian Reflections on Angels, Demons, and the Heavenly Realm,* edited by Anthony N. S. Lane, 103–32. Grand Rapids: Baker, 1996.

———. *The Triumph of Christ in African Perspective: A Book of Demonology and Redemption in the African Context.* Carlisle: Paternoster, 1999.

Fiorenza, E. S. *In Memory of Her: A Feminist Theological Reconstruction of Christian Origins.* London: SCM, 1983.

———. *Jesus: Miriam's Child, Sophia's Prophet: Critical Issues in Feminist Christology.* London: SCM, 1995.

Flick, Uwe. *Designing Qualitative Research.* London: Sage, 2007.

Folarin, George O. "Contemporary State of the Prosperity Gospel in Nigeria." *The Asia Journal of Theology* 21 (2007) 69–95.

France, R. T. *The Gospel according to Matthew: An Introduction and Commentary.* Leicester, UK: InterVarsity, 1985.

Fubura-Manuel, B. F. *The Greater Purpose: The Sovereignty of God in the Context of Mission.* Lagos: Aidie, 2004.

Garrett, Susan R. *The Demise of the Devil: Magic and the Demonic in Luke's Writings.* Minneapolis: Fortress, 1989.

Gibellini, Rosino, editor. *Paths of African Theology.* Maryknoll, NY: Orbis, 1994.

Giblin, Marie. "Jesus Christ in Liberation Theologies." In *Liberation Theology: An Introductory Reader,* edited by Curt Cadorette et al., 77–87. Maryknoll, NY: Orbis, 1994.

Giddings, Paula. *When and Where I Enter: The Impact of Black Women on Race and Sex in America.* New York: Morrow, 1984.

Gifford, Paul. *African Christianity: Its Public Role.* London: Hurst, 1998.

Gilkey, Langdon. "God." In *Christian Theology: An Introduction to its Traditions and Tasks,* edited by Peter Hodgson and Robert King, 88–113. London: SPCK, 1983.

Goba, Bonganjalo. "Corporate Personality: Ancient Israel and Africa." In *Challenge to Black Theology in South Africa,* edited by Basil Moore, 65–73. Atlanta: John Knox, 1974.

Goldenberg, Naomi. *The Changing of the Gods: Feminism and the End of the Traditional Religions*. Boston: Beacon, 1979.

Goldingay, John. *Models for Scripture*. Grand Rapids: Eerdmans, 1994.

Gore, Charles. *The Incarnation of the Son of God*. London: Murray, 1909.

Grant, Jacquelyn. "Womanist Theology: Black Women's Experience as a Source for Doing Theology, with Special Reference to Christology." In *Black Theology: A Documentary History*, vol. 2: 1980–1992, edited by James H. Cone and Gayraud S. Wilmore, 273–89. Maryknoll, NY: Orbis, 1993.

Greene, Colin. *Christology in Cultural Perspective: Marking the Horizons*. Carlisle, UK: Paternoster, 2003.

Grenz. Stanley J., and John R. Franke. *Beyond Foundationalism: Shaping Theology in a Postmodern Context*. Louisville: Westminster, 2001.

Grillmeier, Aloys. *Christ in Christian Tradition: From the Council of Chalcedon (451) to Gregory the Great (590–604)*. Translated by Pauline Allen and John Cawte. London: Mowbray, 1965.

Gunton, Colin E. *The Actuality of Atonement: A Book of Metaphor, Rationality and the Christian Tradition*. Edinburgh: T. & T. Clark, 1988.

———. *Becoming and Being: The Doctrine of God in Charles Hartshorne and Karl Barth*. London: SCM, 1978.

———. *A Brief Theology of Revelation*. Edinburgh: T. & T. Clark, 1995.

———. *Enlightenment and Alienation: An Essay Towards a Trinitarian Theology*. Basingstoke: Marshall, Morgan & Scott, 1985.

———. *Intellect and Action: Elucidations on Christian Theology and the Life of Faith*. Edinburgh: T. & T. Clark, 2000.

———. *The One, The Three, and the Many: God, Creation, the Culture of Modernity— The Bampton Lectures 1992*. Cambridge: Cambridge University Press, 1993.

Gutierrez, G. *The Power of the Poor in History: Selected Writings*. Translated by Robert R. Barr. London: SCM, 1983.

———. "The Task and Content of Liberation Theology." In *The Cambridge Companion to Liberation Theology*, edited by Christopher Rowland, 19–38. New York: Cambridge University Press, 2007.

———. *Theology of Liberation*. Maryknoll, NY: Orbis, 1988.

Haight, Roger. *Dynamics of Theology*. Maryknoll, NY: Orbis, 2001.

———. *Jesus—Symbol of God*. Maryknoll, NY: Orbis, 2001.

———. "Liberation Theology." In *The Dictionary of Theology*, edited by Joseph A. Komonchak, Mary Collins, and Dermot A. Lane, 570–76. Dublin: Gilland & Macmillan, 1987.

Hall, David D. "A World of Wonders: The Mentality of the Supernatural in the Seventeenth-Century New England." In *Religion and American Culture*, 2nd ed., edited by David G. Hackett, 27–51. New York: Routledge, 2003.

Hall, Douglas John. *Professing the Faith: Christian Theology in a North American Context*. Minneapolis: Fortress, 1993.

Hall, Francis J. *Kenotic Theory: Considered with Particular Reference to Its Anglican Forms and Arguments*. New York: Longmans & Green, 1898.

Hammond, Dorothy, and Atla Jablow. *The Myth of Africa*. New York: Library of Social Science, 1977.

Hampson, Daphne. "Feminism and Christology." In *Oxford Readings in Feminism: Feminism and Theology*, edited by Janet Martin Soskice and Diana Lipton, 287–301. Oxford: Oxford University Press, 2003.

Hastings, Adrian. *A History of African Christianity 1950–1975*. Cambridge: Cambridge University Press, 1979.

Hawthorne, Gerald. *Philippians, World Biblical Commentary*. Vol. 43. Rev. ed. Nashville: Nelson Reference & Electronic, 2004.

Hefner, Philip. *The Human Factor: Evolution, Culture, and Religion*. Minneapolis: Fortress, 1993.

Hegel, G. W. F. *The Philosophy of History*. Translated by J. Sibree. New York: Dover, 1956.

Hennelly, Alfred T. *Liberation Theologies: The Global Pursuit of Justice*. Mystic, CT: Twenty-Third, 1997.

Henry, Carl F. H. *God, Revelation, and Authority*. Waco: Word, 1976.

Hesselgrave, David J., and Edward Rommen, *Contextualization: Meanings, Methods, and Models*. Leicester: Apollos, 1989.

Hethersett, A. L. *Iwe Kika Ekerin Li Ede Yoruba*. Lagos: CMS, 1911.

Hick, John. *God and the Universe of Faiths: Essays in the Philosophy of Religion*. London: Macmillan, 1973.

———. *The Metaphor of God Incarnate*. London: SCM, 1993.

Hinga, Teresa M. "Christology and Various African Contexts." *Quarterly Review* 14 (1994–1995) 345–57.

———. "Jesus Christ and the Liberation of Women in Africa." In *The Will to Arise: Women, Tradition and the Church of Africa*, edited by Mercy A. Oduyoye and Musimbi R. A. Kanyoro. Maryknoll, NY: Orbis, 2001.

Hooker, Morna D. *The Gospel According to St. Mark—Black's New Testament Commentary*. London: A. & C. Black, 1991.

———. "'Who Can This Be?' The Christology of Mark's Gospel." In *Contours of Christology in the New Testament*, edited by Richard N. Longenecker, 79–99. Grand Rapids: Eerdmans, 2005.

Horbury, William. *Jewish Messianism and the Cult of Christ*. London: SCM, 1998.

Hurtado, Larry W. *How on Earth Did Jesus Become a God? Historical Questions about Earliest Devotion to Jesus*. Grand Rapids: Eerdmans, 2005.

———. *Lord Jesus Christ: Devotion to Jesus Christ in Earliest Christianity*. Grand Rapids: Eerdmans, 2003.

———. *Mark—New International Biblical Commentary*. Carlisle, UK: Paternoster, 1983.

Idowu, Bolaji E. *African Traditional Religion: A Definition*. London: SCM, 1973.

———. "God." In *Biblical Revelation and African Beliefs*, edited by Kwesi A. Dickson and Paul Ellingworth, 17–29. London: Lutterworth, 1969.

———. "Introduction." In *Biblical Revelation and African Beliefs*, edited by Kwesi A. Dickson and Paul Ellingworth, 9–16. London. Lutterworth, 1969.

———. *Olodumare: God in Yoruba Belief*. London: Longmans, 1962.

———. "The Predicament of the Church." In *Christianity in Tropical Africa: Studies Presented and Discussed at the Seventh International African Seminar, University of Ghana, April 1965*, edited by C. G. Baeta, 417–37. Oxford: Oxford University Press, 1968.

———. *Towards an Indigenous Church*. Oxford: Oxford University Press, 1965.

Ihesiaba, Fidelis Chinedu. *Exorcism and Healing Prayers. Key to Victory—Healing Techniques, Deliverance, Curse-breaking, Liberation, and Act of Piety.* Aba: CARITAS, 2005.

Ikenga-Metuh, Emefie. *African Religions in Western Conceptual Schemes: The Problem of Interpretation.* Ibadan: Claverianum, 1985.

———. *God and Man in African Religion: A Case Book of the Igbo of Nigeria.* 2nd ed. Enugu: SNAAP, 1999.

———. "Ritual Death and Purification Rites among the Igbo." *Journal of Religion in Africa* 15 (1985) 3–24.

Ilogu, Edmund. "African Traditional Religious Systems of Social Control: A Nigerian Example." In *African Creative Expressions of the Divine*, edited by Kortright Davis and Elias Farajaje-Jones, 142–57. Washington, DC: Howard University School of Divinity, 1991.

———. *Christian Ethics in African Background: A Book of Interaction of Christianity and Ibo Culture.* Leiden: Brill, 1974.

Imasogie, Osadolor. *African Traditional Religion.* 2nd ed. Ibadan: University, 1985.

———. *Guidelines for Christian Theology in Africa.* Achimota, Ghana: African Christian, 1983.

———. "The Paradox of Transcendence and Immanence of God in African Religions: A Socio-historical Explanation." *Religion* 15 (1985) 373–85.

Instone-Brewer, David. "Jesus and the Psychiatrists." In *The Unseen World: Christian Reflections on Angels, Demons, and the Heavenly Realm*, edited by Anthony S. N. Lane, 133–48. Grand Rapids: Baker, 1996.

Isherwood, Lisa. *Introducing Feminist Christologies.* Sheffield: Sheffield Academic Press, 2001.

———. *Liberating Christ.* Ohio: Pilgrim, 1999.

Isichei, Elizabeth. *A History of Christianity in Africa: From Antiquity to the Present.* Grand Rapids: Eerdmans, 1995.

———. "Ibo and Christian Beliefs: Some Aspects of a Theological Encounter." *African Affairs* 68.271 (1969) 121–34.

Isola, Akinwumi. "Religious Politics and the Myth of Sango." In *African Traditional Religions in Contemporary Society*, edited by Jacob K. Olupona, 93–99. St. Paul: Paragon, 1991.

Ita, Esesien. *The Christian: From Cradle to Glory.* Calabar: Osko, 2004.

James, William. *The Varieties of Religious Experience: A Book in Human Nature.* Reprint; New York: University Books, 1963.

Jantzen, Grace M. "Contours of a Queer Theology." In *Oxford Readings in Feminism: Feminism and Theology*, edited by Janet Martin Soskice and Diana Lipton, 344–55. Oxford: Oxford University, 2001.

Jenkins, David. *What is Man?* London: SCM, 1970.

Jenkins, Philip. *The Next Christendom: The Coming of Global Christianity.* New York: Oxford University Press, 2002.

Jenson, Robert W. *Systematic Theology.* Vol. 2: *The Works of God.* Oxford: Oxford University Press, 1991.

Jewett, Paul K. *God, Creation and Revelation: A Neo-Evangelical Theology.* Grand Rapids: Eerdmans, 1991.

Johnston, Geoffrey. *Of God and Maxim Guns: Presbyterianism in Nigeria 1846–1966.* Waterloo, Ontario: Wilfrid Laurier University Press, 1988.

Jones, Serene. *Feminist Theory and Christian Theology: Cartographies of Grave.* Minneapolis: Fortress, 2000.

———. "What's Wrong with Us? Human Natures and Human Sin." In *Essentials of Christian Theology,* edited by William C. Placher, 141–58. Louisville: Westminster, 2003.

Jonge, Marinus de. *God's Final Envoy: Early Christology and Jesus' Own View of His Mission.* Grand Rapids: Eerdmans, 1998.

Kahler, Martin. *The So-called Historical Jesus and the Historic, Biblical Christ.* Philadelphia: Fortress, 1964.

Kalu, Ogbu U. "Church Presence in Africa: A Historical Analysis of the Evangelization Process." In *African Theology en route: Papers from the Pan-African Conference of Third World Theologians, December 17–23, 1977, Accra, Ghana,* edited by Kofi Appiah-Kubi and Sergio Torres, 13–22. Maryknoll, NY: Orbis, 1979.

———. "Color and Conversion: The White Missionary Factor in the Christianization of Igboland." *Missiology: An International Review* 18 (1990) 67–74.

———. "Ethiopianism in African Christianity." In *African Christianity: An African Story,* edited by Ogbu U. Kalu, 227–43. Pretoria: University of Pretoria Press, 2005.

———. "Introduction: The Shape and Flow of African Historiography." In *African Christianity: An African Story,* edited by O. U. Kalu, J. W. Hofmeyr, and P. J. Maritz, 1–23. Pretoria: University of Pretoria, 2005.

Kant, Immanuel. "An Answer to the Question: What is Enlightenment?" In *Kant's Philosophical Writings.* Edited by Hans Reiss. Translated by H. B. Nisbet. Cambridge: Cambridge University Press, 1970.

Kapolyo, Joe M. *Human Condition: Christian Perspectives through African Eyes.* Leicester: InterVarsity, 2005.

Karkkainen, Veli-Matti. *Christology: A Global Introduction, an Ecumenical, International, and Contextual Perspective.* Grand Rapid: Baker, 2003.

———. *The Doctrine of God: A Global Introduction.* Grand Rapids: Baker Academic, 2004.

Kasper, Walter. *Jesus the Christ.* London: Burns & Oates, 1976.

Kato, Byang. *African Cultural Revolution and Christian Faith.* Jos, Nigeria: Challenge, 1975.

———. *Biblical Christianity in Africa.* Achimota, Ghana, West Africa: African Christian, 1985.

———. "An Evaluation of Black Theology." *Bibliotheca sacra* 133.531 (1976) 243–52.

———. *Theological Pitfalls in Africa.* Kishmu, Kenya: Evangel, 1975.

Kelly, Henry Ansgar. *The Devil at Baptism: Ritual, Theology, and Drama.* Ithaca: Cornell University Press, 1985.

Kelly, J. N. D. *Early Christian Doctrines.* London: A. & C. Black, 1958.

Kelly, Joseph F. *Satan: A Biography.* New York: Cambridge University Press, 2006.

Kelsey, David H. "Human Being." In *Christian Theology: An Introduction to its Traditions and Tasks,* edited by Peter Hodgson and Robert King, 141–67. London: SPCK, 1983.

King, Fergus. "Angels and Ancestors: A Basis for Christology." *Mission Studies* 11 (1994) 11–14.

Knitter, Paul F. "What about Them? Christians and Non-Christians." In *Essentials of Christian Theology*, edited by William C. Placher, 297–318. Louisville: Westminster, 2003.

Koester, Craig R. *Symbolism in the Fourth Gospel: Meaning, Mystery, Community*. Minneapolis: Fortress, 1995.

Kvale, Steinar. *Doing Interviews*. London: Sage, 2007.

LaCugna, Catherine Mowry. *God for Us: The Trinity and Christian Life*. San Francisco: HaperCollins, 1991.

Laryea, Philip T. "Mother Tongue Theology: Reflections on Images of Jesus in the Poetry of Afua Kuma." *Journal of African Christian Thought* 3 (2000) 50–60.

Lash, Nicholas. "Up and Down in Christology." In *New Studies in Theology*, edited by Stephen Sykes and Derek Holmes, 31–46. London: Duckworth, 1980.

Lewis, I. M. *Religion in Context: Cults and Charisma*. 2nd ed. Cambridge: Cambridge University Press, 1985.

Lumbala, Francois, Kabasele. "Africans Celebrate Jesus Christ." In *Paths of African Theology*, edited by Rosino Gibellini, 78–94. Maryknoll, NY: Orbis, 1994.

———. "Christ as Ancestor and Elder Brother." In *Faces of Jesus in Africa*, edited by Robert Schreiter, 116–27. London: SCM, 1991.

Luz, Ulrich. *Matthew 1–7: A Commentary*. Translated by Wilhelm C. Linss. Minneapolis: Augsburg, 1989.

Lyotard, Jean-Francois. *The Postmodern Condition: A Report on Knowledge*. Translated by G. Bennington and B. Massumi. Manchester: Manchester University Press, 1984.

Macquarrie, John. *Christology Revisited*. London: SCM, 1998.

Magesa, Lautenti. "Christ the Liberator and Africa Today." In *Jesus in African Christianity: Experimentation and Diversity in African Christology*, edited by J. N. K. Mugambi and Laurenti Magesa, 79–92. Nairobi: African Initiatives, 1989.

Mana, Ka. *Christians and Churches of Africa: Salvation in Christ and Building a New African Society*. Maryknoll, NY: Orbis, 2004.

Manus, Chris Ukachukwu. "African Christologies: The Centre-Piece of African Christian Theology." *Zeitschrift Fur Missionwissenschaft und Religionswissenschaft* 82 (1998) 3–23.

———. *Christ, the African King: New Testament Christology*. Frankfurt: Peter Lang, 1993.

———. "The Concept of Death and the After-Life in the Old Testament and Igbo Traditional Religion: Some Reflections for Contemporary Missiology." *Missions Studies* 3.2 (1986) 41–56.

———. "Jesus Kristi Oba: A Christology of 'Christ the King' among the Indigenous Christian Churches in Yorubaland, Nigeria." *Asia Journal of Theology* 5 (1991) 311–30.

———. "King-Christology: The Result of a Critical Book of Matt. 28:16–20 as an Example of Contextual Exegesis in Africa." *Scriptura* 39 (1991) 25–42.

Marshall, Catherine, and Gretchen B. Rossman. *Designing Qualitative Research*. London: Sage, 1989.

Marshall, I. Howard. "The Christology of Luke's Gospel and Acts." In *Contours of Christology in the New Testament*, edited by Richard N. Longenecker, 122–47. Grand Rapids: Eerdmans, 2005.

————. "Culture and the New Testament." In *Down to Earth: Studies in Christianity and Culture*, edited by John R. W. Stott and Robert T. Coote, 17–31. Grand Rapids: Eerdmans, 1980.

————. *The Gospel of Luke: A Commentary on the Greek Text—The New International Greek Testament Commentary*. Carlisle: Paternoster, 1978.

Martey, Emmanuel. *African Theology: Inculturation and Liberation*. Maryknoll, NY: Orbis, 1993.

Mbefo Luke N. *Christian Theology and African Heritage*. Onitsha: Spiritan, 1996.

Mbiti, John S. *African Religion and Philosophy*. London: Heinemann, 1969.

————. *Bible and Theology in Africa*. Nairobi: Oxford University Press, 1986.

————. *New Testament Eschatology in an African Background: A Book of the Encounter between New Testament Theology and African Traditional Concepts*. Oxford: Oxford University Press, 1971.

————. *The Prayers of African Religion*. London: SPCK, 1975.

————. "Some African Concepts of Christology." In *Christ and the Younger Churches*, edited by G. F. Vicedom, 51–62. London: SPCK, 1972.

McCarthy, Caritas "Christology from a Contemporary Perspective." In *Pluralism and Oppression: Theology in World Perspective*, vol. 34, edited by Paul F. Knitter, 29–47. Langham, MD: United Press of America, 1991.

McCloskey, "God and Evil." *The Philosophical Quarterly* 10 (1969) 97.

McDermott, Gerald R. *Can Evangelicals Learn from World Religions? Jesus, Revelation, and Religious Traditions*. Downers Grove, IL: InterVarsity, 2000.

McDowell, John C. *The Gospel According to Star Wars: Faith, Hope, and the Force*. Louisville: Westminster, 2007.

————. "Karl Barth, Emil Brunner, and the Subjectivity of the Object of Christian Hope." *IJST* 8 (2006) 25–41.

McFague, Sallie. *The Body of God: An Ecological Theology*. London: SCM, 1993.

McGrath, Alister. *Christian Theology: An Introduction*. 3rd ed. Oxford: Blackwell, 2001.

————. *The Making of Modern German Christology: 1750–1990*. 2nd ed. Grand Rapids: Zondervan, 1994.

————. *A Passion for Truth: The Intellectual Coherence of Evangelicalism*. Leicester. Apollo, 1996.

————. "A Patricularist View: A Post-Enlightenment Approach." In *Four Views of Salvation in a Pluralistic World*, edited by Dennis L. Okholm and Timothy R. Philips, 151–80. Grand Rapids: Zondervan, 1995.

McIntyre, John. *The Shape of Christology: Studies in the Doctrine of the Person of Christ*. Edinburgh: T. & T. Clark, 1998.

————. *Theology after the Storm: Reflections on the Upheavals in Modern Theology and Culture*. Grand Rapids: Eerdmans, 1997.

McVeigh, Malcolm J. *God in Africa: Conceptions of God in African Traditional Religion and Christianity*. Cape Cod: Stark, 1974.

Metzger, Paul Louis. *The Word of Christ and the World of Culture: Sacred and Secular through the Theology of Karl Barth*. Grand Rapids: Eerdmans, 2003.

Migliore, Daniel L. *Faith Seeking Understanding: An Introduction to Christian Theology*. 2nd ed. Grand Rapids: Eerdmans, 2004.

Milbank, John. *The Word Made Strange: Theology, Language, Culture*. Oxford: Blackwell, 1997.

Moloney, Francis J. "Jesus Christ: The Question to Cultures." *Pacifica* 1 (1998) 15–43.

Moloney, Raymond. "African Christology." *Theological Studies* 48 (1987) 505–15.

Moltmann, Jürgen. *The Crucified God: The Cross of Christ as the Foundation and Criticism of Christian Theology.* London: SCM, 1974.

———. *Experience in Theology: Ways and Forms of Christian Theology.* London: SCM, 2000.

———. *The Way of Christ: Christology in Messianic Dimensions.* London: SCM, 1990.

Montgomery, John Warwick. *The Suicide of Christian Theology.* Minnesota: Bethany Fellowship, 1970.

Moore, Basil, editor. *Black Theology: The South African Voice.* London: Hurst, 1973.

Morris, Brian. *Religion and Anthropology: A Critical Introduction.* Cambridge: Cambridge University Press, 2006.

Morris, Thomas V. *Our Idea of God: Introduction to Philosophical Theology.* Vancouver: Regent, 2002.

Mosala, Itumeleng. "The Use of the Bible in Black Theology in South Africa." In *The Unquestionable Right To Be Free: Essays in Black Theology,* edited by I. Mosala and Buti Tlhagale, 175–99. Maryknoll, NY: Orbis, 1986.

Moule, C. F. D. *The Gospel According to Mark.* The Cambridge Bible Commentary on the New English Bible. Cambridge: University Press, 1965.

———. *The Origin of Christology.* Cambridge: Cambridge University Press, 1977.

Mouw, Richard J. "Violence and the Atonement." In *Must Christianity be Violent? Reflection on History, Practice and Theology,* edited by Kenneth R. Chase and Alan Jacobs, 159–82. Grand Rapids: Brazos, 2003.

Mudimbe, V. *The Invention of Africa: Gnosis, Philosophy and the Order of Knowledge.* Bloomington: Indiana University Press, 1988.

Mugabe, Henry Johannes. "Christology in an African Context." *Review and Expositor* 88 (1991) 343–55.

Mugambi, J. N. K. *African Christian Theology: An Introduction.* Nairobi: East African Education, 1989.

———. *From Liberation to Reconstruction of Africa: African Theology after the Cold War.* Nairobi: AACC, 1997.

Mulago, Vincent. "Vital Participation." In *Biblical Revelation and African Beliefs,* edited by Kwesi A. Dickson and Paul Ellingworth, 137–58. London: Lutterworth, 1969.

Mushete, A. Ngindu. "An Overview of African Theology." *Paths of African Theology,* edited by Rosino Gibellini, 9–26. Maryknoll, NY: Orbis, 1994.

Musto, Ronald G. *Liberation Theologies: A Research Guide.* London: Garland, 1991.

Nash, Ronald H. *Faith and Reason: Searching for a Rational Faith.* Grand Rapids: Zondervan, 1988.

Newbigin, Lesslie. *Foolishness to the Greeks: The Gospel and Western Culture.* Grand Rapids: Eerdmans, 1986.

Ng'Weshemi, Andrea M. *Rediscovering the Human: The Quest for a Christo-Theological Anthropology in Africa.* Frankfurt: Lang, 2002.

Ngewa, Samuel. "The Validity of Meaning and African Christian Theology." In *Issues in African Christian Theology,* edited by Samuel Ngewa, Mark Shaw, and Tite Tienou, 48–55. Nairobi: EAEP, 1998.

Nicholls, Bruce J. "Towards a Theology of Gospel and Culture." In *Down to Earth: Studies in Christianity and Culture*, edited by John R. W. Stott and Robert T. Coote, 49–62. Grand Rapids: Eerdmans, 1980.

Nicolson, Ronald. *A Black Future? Jesus and Salvation in South Africa*. Philadelphia: Trinity, 1990.

Niebuhr, H. Richard. *Christ and Culture*. London: Faber & Faber, 1952.

———. *The Meaning of Revelation*. New York: Macmillan, 1941.

Niehaus, Jeffrey J. *God at Sinai: Covenant and Theophany in the Bible and Ancient Near East*. Carlisle, UK: Paternoster, 1995.

Nielsen, Kirsten. *Satan: The Prodigal Son? A Family Problem in the Bible*. Sheffield: Sheffield, 1998.

Njoku, Chukwudi. "The Missionary Factor in African Christianity, 1884–1914." In *African Christianity: An African Story*, edited by Ogbu U. Kalu, 191–223. Pretoria: University of Pretoria Press, 2005.

Nkrumah, Kwame. *Africa Must Unite*. London: Heinemann, 1963.

———. *Neo-colonialism: The Last State of Imperialism*. London: Nelson, 1965.

Nkwoka, A. O. "The Role of the Bible in the Igbo Christianity of Nigeria." In *The Bible in Africa: Transactions, Trajectories, and Trends*, edited by Gerald O. West and Musa W. Dube, 326–35. Leiden: Brill, 2000.

Noll, Stephen F. "Thinking about Angels." In *The Unseen World: Christian Reflections on Angels, Demons and the Heavenly Realm*, edited by Anthony N. S. Lane, 1–27. Grand Rapids: Baker, 1996.

Nolland, John. *The Gospel of Mathew: A Commentary on the Greek Text*. Grand Rapids: Eerdmans, 2005.

Nwachukwu, Daisy N. "The Christian Widow in African Culture." In *The Will to Arise: Women, Tradition, and the Church in Africa,* edited by Mercy Amber Oduyoye and Musimbi Kanyoro, 54–73. Maryknoll, NY: Orbis, 1992.

Nwaigbo, Ferdinand. "Twenty-five Years of Contextualization in the Catholic Institute of West Africa (CIWA)." *AFER* 48.4 D (2006) 289–311.

Nwoga, Donatus Ibe. *The Supreme God as Stranger in Igbo Religious Thought*. Ahiazu: Hawk, 1984.

Nyamiti, Charles. "African Christologies Today." In *Faces of Jesus in Africa*, edited by Robert J. Schreiter, 3–23. London: SCM, 1992.

———. *Christ as Our Ancestor: Christology from an African Perspective*. Gweru: Mambo, 1984.

———. "Contemporary African Christologies: Assessment and Practical Suggestions." In *Paths of African Theology*, edited by Rosino Gibellini, 62–77. Maryknoll, NY: Orbis, 1994.

Nyende, Peter T. N. "Jesus the Greatest Ancestor: A Typology-Based Theological Interpretation of Hebrews' Christology in Africa." PhD diss., University of Edinburgh.

O'Collins, Gerald. *Incarnation: New Century Theology*. London: Continuum, 2002.

———. *Introducing Catholic Theology: Interpreting Jesus*. London: Chapman, 1983.

———. *Jesus Our Redeemer: A Christian Approach to Salvation*. Oxford: Oxford University Press, 2007.

Odey, Onah Augustine. "Superstitious Beliefs and Practices: A Challenge to the Gospel." *Uyo Journal of Humanities* 7 (2002) 145–64.

Odoemene, Nnamdi Anacletus, editor. *Witnessing Christ in Contemporary Nigerian Christianity*. Port Harcourt: IHBC–CIWA, 2005.

O'Donovan, Wilbur. *Biblical Christianity in Modern Africa*. Carlisle, UK: Paternoster, 2000.

Oduyoye, Mercy Amba. "An African Woman's Christ." *Voices from the Third World* 11.2 (1998) 17–29.

————. *Beads and Strands: Reflections of an African Woman Christianity in Africa*. Maryknoll, NY: Orbis, 2004.

————. "Christian Feminism and African Culture: The 'Hearth' of the Matter." In *The Future of Liberation Theology: Essays in Honor of Gustavo Gutiérrez*, edited by Marc H. Ellis and Otto Maduro, 441–49. Maryknoll, NY: Orbis, 1989.

————. "Feminism: A Pre-condition for a Christian Anthropology." *African Theological Journal* 11.3 (1982) 193–208.

————. "Feminist Theology in an African Perspective." In *Paths of African Theology*, edited Rosino Gibellini, 166–81. Maryknoll, NY: Orbis, 1994.

————. "Gender and Theology in Africa Today," available from http://www.thecirclecawt.org/focus_areas?mode=content&id=17292&refto=2629ecirclecawt.org; Internet; accessed 4 August 2006.

————. *Hearing and Knowing: Theological Reflections on Christianity in Africa*. Maryknoll, NY: Orbis, 1986.

————. "Identity Shaped by the Ancestors: Examples from Folk Talk of the Akan in Ghana." In *The Bright Side of Life*, edited by Ellevan Wolde, 73–83. London: SCM, 2000.

————. "Jesus Christ." In *The Cambridge Companion to Feminist Theology*, edited by Susan Frank Parsons, 151–70. Cambridge: Cambridge University Press, 2002.

————. "The Value of African Religious Beliefs and Practices for Christian Theology." In *African Theology en route: Papers from the Pan-African Conference of Third World Theologians, December 17–23, 1977, Accra, Ghana*, edited by Kofi Appiah-Kubi and Sergio Torres, 109–16. Maryknoll, NY: Orbis, 1979.

————. "Women and Ritual in Africa." In *The Will to Arise: Women, Tradition, and the Church in Africa*, edited by Mercy Amba Oduyoye and Musimbi R. A. Kanyoro, 9–24. Maryknoll, NY: Orbis, 1992.

Ogbu, U. Kalu. "The Shape and Flow of African Church Historiography." In *African Christianity: An African Story*, edited by O.U. Kalu, J. Hofmeyr, and P. J Maritz, 1–23. Pretoria: University of Pretoria, 2005.

Ogbonnaya, Clement A. *I Am Too Big to Be Poor*. Aba: Footprint Communications, 2004.

Ogunboye, Ben, and Lois Fuller. "The Human Soul in Yoruba/Igbo Tradition and Bible." *African Journal of Evangelical Theology* 19 (2000) 75–86.

Okeke, George E. "Ancestor Worship among the Igbo." *Communio Viatorum* 27.3 (1984) 137–52.

Okholm, Dennis L., and Timothy R. Philips, editors. *Four Views of Salvation in a Pluralistic World*. Grand Rapids: Zondervan, 1995.

Okolo, Okolo, Chukwudum Barnabas. "The Church and the Nigerian Woman." *AFER* 27.6 (1985) 366–74.

Okorie, A. M. "The Self-Revelation of Jesus in the 'I AM' Saying of John's Gospel." *Currents in Theology and Mission* 28.5 (2001) 487–90.

Okure, Teresa. "Jesus and Mary Magdalene." In *Oxford Readings in Feminism: Feminism and Theology*, edited by Janet Martin Soskice and Diana Lipton, 312–26. Oxford: Oxford University Press, 2003.

———. "The Will to Arise: Reflections on Luke 8:40–56." In *The Will to Arise: Women, Tradition, and the Church in Africa*, edited by Mercy Amba Oduyoye and Musimbi R. A. Kanyoro, 221–30. Maryknoll, NY: Orbis, 1992.

Oleka, Sam. "The Authority of the Bible in the African Context." In *Issues in African Theology*, edited Samuel Ngewa, Mark Shaw, and Tite Tienou, 73–103. Nairobi: EAEP, 1998.

———. "The Living God: Some Reflections on Acts 17 and African Traditional Religions." In *Issues in African Christian Theology*, edited by Samuel Ngewa, Mark Shaw and Tite Tienou, 126–32. Nairobi: EAEP, 1998.

Olikenyi, Gregory Ikechukwu. *African Hospitality: A Model for the Communication of the Gospel in the African Cultural Context*. Steyler Verlag: Nettetal, 2001.

Olowola, Cornelius. "The Person and Work of Christ" In *Issues in African Christian Theology*, edited by Samuel Ngewa, Mark Shaw, and Tite Tienou, 155–74. Nairobi: EAEP, 1998.

Omari, Mikelle Smith. "Candomble: A Socio-Political Examination of African Religion and Art in Brazil." In *Religion in Africa*, edited by James Currey, 135–59. Portsmouth: Heinemann, 1994.

Onaiyekan, John. "Christological Trends in Contemporary Africa." In *Constructive Christian Theology in the Worldwide Church*, edited by William R. Barr. Grand Rapids: Eerdmans, 1997.

Onwurah, Emeka. "New Yam Festival in Igbo Land." *Journal of Dharma* 15 O–D (1990) 314–23.

———. "Priesthood in the Traditional Religion of the Igbos of Nigeria." *Journal of Dharma* 15 (1990) 45–54.

Opefeyemiti, Ayo. "Iwure: Medium of Communicating the Desires of Men to Gods in Yoruba Land." *Journal of Religion of Africa* 18 (1988) 27–41.

Owanikin, Modupe. "The Priesthood of Church Women in the Nigerian Context." In *The Will to Arise: Women, Tradition, and the Church in Africa*, edited by Mercy Amba Oduyoye and Musimbi R. A. Kanyoro, 206–19. Maryknoll, NY: Orbis, 1992.

Page, Jesse. *The Black Bishop: Samuel Ajayi Crowther*. New York: Fleming, 1908.

Pannenberg, Wolfhart. *Jesus—God and Man*. Translated by Lewis L Wilkins and Daune A. Priebe. London: SCM, 1968.

Parekh, Bhikhu. *Rethinking Multiculturalism: Cultural Diversity and Political Theory*. Hampshire: Palgrave, 2000.

Paris, Peter J. *The Spirituality of African Peoples: The Search for a Common Moral Discourse*. Minneapolis: Augsburg, 1995.

Park, M. Sydney. *Submission within the Godhead and the Church in the Epistles to the Philippians: An Exegetical and Theological Examination of the Concept of Salvation in Philippians 2 and 3*. London: T. & T. Clark, 2007.

Parratt, John. *Reinventing Christianity: African Theology Today*. Grand Rapids: Eerdmans, 1995.

Parrinder, Geoffrey. "Theistic Beliefs of the Yoruba and the Ewe Peoples of West Africa." In *African Ideas of God: A Symposium*, edited by Edwin W. Smith. London: Edinburgh House, 1950.

————. *West African Religion: A Study of the Beliefs and Practices of Akan, Ewe, Yoruba, Ibo, and Kindred Peoples*. London: Epworth, 1969.

Parsons, Susan Frank. "Accounting for Hope: Feminist Theology as Fundamental Theology." In *Challenging Women's Orthodoxies in the Context of Faith*, edited by Susan Frank Parsons, 1–20. Aldershot: Ashgate, 2000.

Pelikan, Jaroslav. *The Christian Tradition: A History of the Development of Doctrine—The Emergence of the Catholic Tradition (100–600)*. Vol. 1. Chicago: University of Chicago Press, 1971.

————. *Jesus Through the Centuries: His Place in the History of Culture*. New Haven: Yale University Press, 1985.

Pemberto, Carrie, "Harmony in Africa: Healing the Divided Continental Self—Mercy Amba Oduyoye, Feminist and Theologian." In *Challenging Women's Orthodoxies in the Context of Faith*, edited by Susan F. Parsons, 89–108. Aldershot: Ashgate, 2003.

————. *Jesus Through the Centuries: His Place in the History of Culture*. New Haven: Yale University Press, 1987.

Pinnock, Cark H. *Flame of Love: A Theology of the Holy Spirit*. Downers Grove, IL: InterVarsity, 1996.

————. *Most Moved Mover: A Theology of God's Openness*. Grand Rapids: Baker, 2001.

Placher, William C. *Narratives of a Vulnerable God: Christ, Theology and Scripture*. Louisville: Westminster, 1994.

————. "What's Wrong with Us? Human Nature and Human Sin." In *Essentials of Christian Theology*, edited by William C. Placher, 133–41. Louisville: Westminster, 2003.

Plantinga, Alvin. *God and Other Minds*. Ithaca: Cornell University Press, 1967.

————. *Warranted Christian Belief*. New York: Oxford University Press, 2000.

Platvoet, Jan. G., and Jacob K. Olupona. "Perspectives on the Book of Religions in Sub-Saharan Africa." In *The Book of Religions in Africa: Past, Present, and Prospects*, edited by James Cox and Jacob Olupona, 7–36. Cambridge: Roots & Branches, 1996.

————. *Triune God: An Essay in Postliberal Theology*. Louisville: Westminster, 2007.

Pobee, John S. "Health, Healing, and Religion: An African View." *International Review of Mission* 90.356–57 (2001) 55–64.

————. *Toward an African Theology*. Nashville: Abingdon, 1979.

————. *West Africa: Christ Would Be an African Too*. Geneva: WCC, 1996.

Pope-Levison, John R., and Priscilla Pope-Levison. "Jesus in Africa." *SEDOS Bulletin* 29 (1997) 276–77.

Pui-lan, Kwok. *Introducing Asian Feminist Theology*. Sheffield: Sheffield Academic, 2000.

————. *Postcolonial Imagination and Feminist Christology*. London: SCM, 2005.

Quash, Ben, and Michael Ward, editors. *Heresies and How to Avoid Them: Why it Matters What Christians Believe*. London: SPCK, 2007.

Rad, Gerhard Von. *Old Testament Theology: The Theology of Israel's Historical Traditions*. Vol. Translated by D. M. G. Stalker. London: SCM, 1975.

Rahner, Karl. *The Trinity*. Translated by Joseph Donceel. London: Burns & Oates, 1970.

Rapley, Tim. *Doing Conversation, Discourse and Document Analysis*. London: Sage, 2007.

Raschke, Carl. *The Next Reformation: Why Evangelicals Must Embrace Postmodernity*. Grand Rapids: Baker, 2004.

Ray, Benjamin C. *African Religions: Symbols, Ritual, and Community*. Englewood Cliff: Prentice-hall, 1976.

Rea, William R. "Rationalizing Culture: Youths, Elites, and Masquerade Politics." *Africa* 68 (1998) 98–117.

Read, Bess. "Playing with Prohibitions: Women, Agency, and Masquerades." *African Arts* 31.2 (1998) 71.

Reuther, Rosemary Radford. "Can Christology be Liberated from Patriarchy?" In *Reconstructing the Christ Symbol*, edited by M. Stevens, 7–29. New York: Paulist, 1993.

Roberts, James Deotis. *Black Theology in Dialogue*. Philadelphia: Westminster, 1987.

———. *Black Theology Today: Liberation and Contextualization*. New York: Mellen, 1983.

Robinson, John A. T. *The Human Face of God*. London: SCM, 1973.

Robson, John. "Address by Rev. J. Robson, D. D., to Rev. H. M. Waddell, on the Occasion of his leaving for Africa. Delivered in Wellington Street Church on the evening of Tuesday, the 8th of December 1845." In *Missionary Record of the United Presbyterian Church*, Vol. 1 & 2. Edinburgh: William Oliphant, 1847.

Ross, Kenneth R. "Current Christological Trends in Northern Malawi." *Journal of Religion in Africa* 27 (1997) 160–76.

Rowland, Christopher. "Introduction: The Theology of Liberation." In *The Cambridge Companion to Liberation Theology*, edited by Christopher Rowland, 1–16. Cambridge: Cambridge University Press, 1999.

Russell, Jeffrey Burton. *The Devil: Perceptions from Antiquity to Primitive Christianity*. Ithaca: Cornell University Press, 1977.

Said, Edward W. *Culture and Imperialism*. London: Chato & Windus, 1993.

Sanders, E. P. "How Do We Know What We Know about Jesus?" In *Jesus Two Thousand Years Later*, edited by James H. Charlesworth and Walter P. Weaver, 38–61. Harrisburg: Trinity, 2000.

Sanders, John. *The God Who Risks: A Theology of Providence*. Downers Grove: InterVarsity, 1998.

Sanneh, Lamin. *Encountering the West: Christianity and the Global Cultural Process—The African Dimension*. London: Marshall Pickering, 1993.

———. "The Horizontal and the Vertical in Mission: an African Perspective." *International Bulletin of Missionary Research* 7.4 (1983) 165–71.

———. *Translating the Message: The Missionary Impact on Culture*. Maryknoll, NY: Orbis, 2002.

Sarpong, Peter K. *Ancestral Stool Veneration in Asante: a Catholic Assessment*. Tarkoradi: St. Francis, 1980.

———. "Asante Christology." *Studia Missionalia* 45 (1996) 189–205.

———. *Sacred Stools of the Akan*. Accra-Tema: Ghana Publishing Cooperation, 1971.

Sawyerr, Harry. *The Practice of Presence: Shorter Writings of Harry Sawyerr*. Edited by John Parratt. Grand Rapids: Eerdmans, 1994.

Schlitz, Marc. "Yoruba thunder deities and sovereignty: Ara versus Sango." *Anthropos* 80.1–3 (1985) 67–84.

Schmidt, Brian. *Israel's Beneficent Dead: Ancestor Cult and Necromancy in Ancient Israelite Religion and Tradition.* Tubingen: Mohr, 1994.

Schoffeleers, Mathew. "Christ in Africa Folk Theology: The Nganga Paradigm." In *Religion in Africa: Experience and Expression*, edited by Thomas D. Blakely, Walter E. A. van Beek, and Dennis L. Thompson, 73–88. London: Currey, 1994.

———. "Folk Christology in Africa: The Dialectics of the Nganga Paradigm." *Journal of Religion in Africa* 19.2 (1989) 157–83.

Schottroff, Luise, Silvia Schroer, and Marie-Theres Wacker. *Feminist Interpretation: The Bible in Women's Perspective.* Minneapolis: Fortress, 1998.

Schreiter, Robert J., editor. *Faces of Jesus in Africa.* Maryknoll, NY: Orbis, 1991.

———. "Introduction: Jesus Christ in Africa Today." In *Faces of Jesus in Africa*, edited by Robert J. Schreiter, vii–xiii. Maryknoll: Orbis, 1991.

———. *The Ministry of Reconciliation: Spirituality and Strategies.* Maryknoll, NY: Orbis, 1998.

Schroeder, Edward H. "Lessons for Westerners from Setiloane's Christology." *Currents in Theology and Mission* 13 (1986) 71–77.

Schwarz, Hans. *Christology.* Grand Rapids: Eerdmans, 1998.

Selvanayagam, Israel. "When Demons Speak the Truth! An Asian Reading of a New Testament Story of Exorcism." *Epworth Review* 20.3 (2000) 33–40.

Setiloane, Gabriel M. *African Theology: An Introduction.* Braamfontein: Skotaville, 1986.

Shaw, Mark. "Salvation Outside Christian Faith." In *Issues in African Christian Theology*, edited by Samuel Ngewa, Mark Shaw, and Tite Tienou, 210–29. Nairobi: EAEP, 1998.

Shorter, Aylward. *African Christian Theology: Adaptation or Inculturation?* Maryknoll: Orbis, 1977.

———. "Folk Christianity and Functional Christology," *AFER* 24.3 (1982) 133–37.

———. *Jesus and the Witchdoctor: An Approach to Healing and Wholeness.* London: Geoffrey Chapman, 1985.

Sidhom, Swailem. "The Theological Estimate of Man." In *Biblical Revelation and African Beliefs*, edited by Kwesi A. Dickson and Paul Ellingworth, 83–115. London: Lutterworth, 1969.

Sigountos, J. G., and William V. Crockett, editors. *Through No Fault of Their Own? The Fate of Those Who Have Never Heard.* Grand Rapids: Baker, 1991.

Silverman, David. Doing Qualitative Research: A Practical Handbook. London: Sage, 2000.

Sire, James W. *The Universe Next Door: A Basic Worldview Catalogue*, 4th ed. Downers Groove, IL: InterVarsity, 2004.

Smith, Edwin. *African Beliefs and Christian Faith. An Introduction to Theology for African Students, Evangelists and Pastors.* London: United Society for Christian Literature, 1936.

———. *The Christian Mission in Africa: A Study Based on the Work of the International Conference at Le Zoute Belgium, September 14–21, 1926.* London: International Missionary Council, 1926.

———. "The Whole Subject in Perspective: An Introductory Survey." In *African Ideas of God: A Symposium*, edited by Edwin W. Smith, 1–35. London: Edinburgh, 1950.

Smith, Robert H. *Augsburg Commentary on the New Testament: Matthew*. Minneapolis: Augsburg, 1989.

Sobrino, John. *Christology at the Cross Roads: A Latin American Approach*. London: SCM, 1978.

———. *Jesus the Liberator: A Historical-Theological Reading of Jesus of Nazareth*. Maryknoll: Orbis, 1993.

Soyinka, Wole. *Myth, Literature and the African World*. Cambridge: Cambridge University Press, 1976.

Stein, Robert H. *Luke—The New American Commentary*. Vol. 24. Nashville: Broadman & Holman, 1992.

Stinton, B. Diane. *Jesus of Africa: Voices of African Christology*. Maryknoll, NY: Orbis, 2004.

Stroup, George. "Revelation." In *Christian Theology: An Introduction to its Traditions and Tasks*, edited by Peter Hodgson and Robert King, 88–114. London: SPCK, 1982.

Suenens, Leon-Joseph. *Renewal and the Powers of Darkness*. London: Darton Longman, & Todd, 1983.

Sugirtharajah, R. A. "Postcolonial Theory and Biblical Studies." In *Fair Play: Diversity and Conflicts in Early Christianity*, edited by Ismo Dunderberg, Christopher Tuckett, and Kari Syreeni, 541–52. Leiden: Brill, 2002.

Tanner, Kathryn. "Jesus Christ." In *The Cambridge Companion to Christian Doctrine*, edited by Colin E. Gunton, 245–72. Cambridge: Cambridge University Press, 1997.

———. *Jesus, Humanity and the Trinity: A Brief Systematic Theology*. Edinburgh: T. & T. Clark, 2002.

Taylor, John V. *The Primal Vision: Christian Presence amid African Religion*. London: SCM, 1963.

Tempels, Placide. *Bantu Philosophy*. Translated by Colin King. Paris: Presence Africaine, 1959.

Tesch, Renata. *Qualitative Research: Analysis Types and Software Tools*. London: Falmer, 1990.

Thiemann, Ronald F. *Revelation and Theology: The Gospel as Narrated Promise*. Notre Dame: University of Notre Dame Press, 1985.

Thomas, Douglas E. *African Traditional Religion in the Modern World*. North Carolina: McFarland, 2005.

Thompson, Jack. *Christianity in Northern Malawi: Donald Fraser's Missionary Methods and Ngoni Culture*. Leiden: Brill, 1995.

Thompson, Mark D. "The Uniqueness of Christ as the Revealer of God." In *Christ the One and Only: A Global Affirmation of the Uniqueness of Jesus Christ*, edited by Sung Wook Chung, 90–110. Grand Rapids: Baker, 2005.

Thompson, Michael B. "Arianism." In *Heresies and How to Avoid Them: Why it Matters What Christians Believe*, edited by Ben Quash and Michael Ward, 15–23. London: SPCK, 2007.

Thrower, James, editor. *Essays in Religious Studies for Andrew Walls*. Aberdeen: Dept. of Religious Studies, University of Aberdeen, 1986.

Thunberg, Lars. "Third World Theologies and the Appeal to History." *Studia Theologica* 40 (1986) 95–113.

Tienou, Tite. "Search for the 'African Past': Common Roots in African Theology and Philosophy." In *Issues in African Christian Theology*, edited by Samuel Ngewa, Mark Shaw, and Tite Tienou, 38–48. Nairobi: EAEP, 1998.

Tiessen, Terrance L. *Who Can Be Saved? Reassessing Salvation in Christ and World Religions*. Downers Grove, IL: InterVarsity, 2004.

Torrance, Thomas F. *Theological Science*. Oxford: Oxford University Press, 1969; T. & T. Clark, 1996.

Torres, Sergio, and Kofi Appiah-Kubi, editors. *African Theology en Route: Papers from the Pan-African Conference of Third World Theologians, December 17–23, 1977, Accra, Ghana*. Maryknoll: Orbis, 1979.

Tracy, David. *On Naming the Present: God, Hermeneutics, and Church*. London: SCM, 1994.

Turaki, Yusufu. *Christianity and African Gods: A Method in Theology*. Potchesfstroom: Postchefsroomse Universiteit, 1999.

————. "The Theological Legacy of the Revered Doctor Byang Henry Kato." *African Journal of Evangelical Theology* 20.2 (2002) 133–55.

————. *The Unique Christ for Salvation: The Challenge of the Non-Christian Religions and Culture*. Nairobi: International Bible Society, 2001.

Udoh, E. Ben. *Guest Christology: An Interpretative View of the Christological Problem in Africa*. Frankfurt Main: Peter Lang, 1988.

————. "Guest Christology: An Interpretative View of the Christological Problem in Africa." PhD diss., Princeton Theological Seminary, 1983.

Ugochukwu, Felix. *Christianity in Nigeria: The Way Forward*. Owerri: Springfield, 2004.

Ukpong, Justin S. "Christology and Inculturation: A New Testament Perspective." In *Paths of African Theology*, edited by Rosino Gibellini, 40–61. Maryknoll, NY: Orbis, 1994.

————. "Contextualization: A Historical Survey." *AFER* 29.57 (1987) 278–86.

————. "Developments in Biblical Interpretation in Africa: Historical Hermeneutical Directions." In *The Bible in Africa: Transactions, Trajectories, and Trends*, edited by Gerald O. West and Musa W. Dube, 11–28. Leiden: Brill, 2000.

————. "Inculturation Hermeneutics: An African Approach to Biblical Interpretation." In *Bible in a World Context: An Experiment in Contextual Hermeneutics*, edited by Walter Dietrich and Ulrich Luz, 17–32. Grand Rapids: Eerdmans, 2002.

————. "The Problem of God and Sacrifice in African Traditional Religion." *Journal of Religion in Africa* 14 (1983) 187–203.

————. "Toward a Holistic Approach to Inculturation Theology." *Mission Studies* 16.2 (1999) 100–124.

Ukwuegbu, Bernard. *Confrontational Evangelization: Foundations, Features, and Prospects*. Onitsha: Effective Key, 1994.

Unger, Merrill C. *Biblical Demonology: A Book of Spiritual Forces at Work Today*. Grand Rapids: Kregel, 1994.

Utuk, Efiong. *From New York to Ibadan: The Impact of African Questions on the Making of Ecumenical Mission Mandates 1900–1958*. Frankfurt: Peter Lang, 1991.

Uzukwu, Elochuku E. "Towards an African Christology." *Foundations of African Theology* 3 (1992) 1–24.

Van der Raaji, M. "An African Doctrine of God and Images of Christ." *Evangelical Review of Theology* 20 (1996) 233–39.

Vanhoozer, Kevin J. *First Theology: God, Scripture and Hermeneutics.* Downers Grove, IL: InterVarsity, 2002.

———. *Is there a Meaning in this Text: The Bible, the Reader, and the Morality of Literary Knowledge.* Grand Rapids: Zondervan, 1998.

Vos, Geerhardus. *The Self-Disclosure of Jesus: The Modern Debate about the Messianic Consciousness,* edited by Johannes G. Vos. Nutley. Presbyterian and Reformed, 1953.

Wachege, P. N. "Inculturation and Salvation within the African Context." *AFER* 43.1–2 (2001) 28–40.

Waliggo, J. M. "African Christology in a Situation of Suffering." In *Jesus in Africa Christianity: Experimentation and Diversity in African Christology,* edited by J. N. K. Mugambi and Laurenti Magesa, 93–111. Nairobi: Initiatives, 1989.

Walls, Andrew F. "Africa in Christian History: Retrospect and Prospect." *Journal of African Christian Thought* 1 (1998) 2–15.

———. *The Cross-Cultural Process in Christian History: Studies in the Transmission and Appropriation of Faith.* Edinburgh: T. & T. Clark, 2002.

———. *The Missionary Movement in Christianity History: Studies in the Transmission of Faith.* Maryknoll, NY: Orbis, 1996.

———. "Towards Understanding Africa's Place in Christianity History." In *Religion in a Pluralistic Society,* edited by J. S. Pobee, 180–89. Leiden: Brill, 1976.

Walvin, James. *An African's Life: The Life and Times of Olaudah Equiano, 1745–1797.* London: Continuum, 1998.

Wanamaker, Charles A. "Jesus the Ancestor: Reading the Story of Jesus an African Christian Perspective." *Scriptura* 62 (1997) 281–98.

Ward, Graham. *Christ and Culture.* Oxford: Blackwell, 2005.

Ware, Bruce A. *God's Greater Glory: The Exalted God of Scripture and the Christian Faith.* Wheaton: Crossway, 2004.

———. *God's Lesser Glory: The Diminished God of Open Theism.* Wheaton: Crossway, 2000.

Ware, Timothy. *The Orthodox Church.* New. ed. New York: Penguin, 1997.

Waruta, Douglas W. "Who is Jesus Christ for Africa Today? Prophet, Priest and Potentate." In *Faces of Jesus in Africa,* edited by Robert J. Schreiter, 52–54. Maryknoll, NY: Orbis, 1991.

Weaver, J. Denny. *The Nonviolent Atonement.* Grand Rapids: Eerdmans, 2001.

Weber, Joseph C. "Karl Barth and the Historical Jesus." *Journal of Bible and Religion* 32.4 (1964) 350–54.

Webster, D. D. "Liberation Theology." In *Evangelical Dictionary of Theology,* edited by Walter A. Elwell, 635–38. Grand Rapids: Baker, 1984.

Wessels, Anton. *Images of Jesus: How Jesus is Perceived and Portrayed in Non-European Cultures.* London: SCM, 1986.

West, Gerald. *The Academy of the Poor: Towards a Dialogical Reading of the Bible.* Sheffield: Sheffield Academic, 1999.

———. "The Bible and Theology." In *Doing Theology in Context: South African Perspectives,* edited by John de Gruchy and C. Villa-Vicencio, 15–25. Maryknoll, NY: Orbis, 1994.

———. *Contextual Bible Book.* Pietermaritzburg: Cluster, 1993.

———. "Reading the Bible Differently: Giving Shape to the Discourses of the Dominated." *Semeia* 73 (1996) 21-41.

West, Gerald, and W. Musa Dube, editors. *The Bible in Africa: Transactions, Trajectories, and Trends*. Leiden: Brill, 200.

Williams, Peter S. *The Case for Angels*. Carlisle: Paternoster, 2002.

Williams, Rowan. *Christ on Trial: How the Gospel Unsettles Our Judgement*. Grand Rapids: Eerdmans, 2000.

———. *On Christian Theology*. Oxford: Blackwell, 2000.

Wink, Walter. *Unmasking the Powers: The Invisible Forces that Determine Human Existence*. Philadelphia: Fortress, 1986.

Witvliet, Theo. "In Search of a Black Christology: The Dialectic of Cross and Resurrection." *Cross Currents* (1987) 17-32.

Wolde, van Ellen. *The Bright Side of Life*. London: SCM, 2000.

Wolterstorff, Nicholas. *Divine Discourse: Philosophical Reflections on the Claim that God Speaks*. Cambridge: Cambridge University Press, 1995.

Wright, G. Nigel. "Charismatic Interpretations of the Demonic." In *The Unseen World: Christian Reflections on Angels, Demons and the Heavenly Realm*, edited by Anthony N. S. Lane, 149-63. Grand Rapids: Baker, 1996.

———. *The Fair Face of Evil: Putting the Power of Darkness in Its Place*. London: Marshall Pickering, 1989.

Wright, N. T. *The Climax of the Covenant: Christ and the Law in Pauline Theology*. Edinburgh: T. & T. Clark, 1991.

Wright, N. T., and Marcus Borg. *The Meaning of Jesus: Two Versions*. London: SPCK, 1999.

Yates, Roy. "Jesus and the Demonic in the Synoptic Gospels." *Irish Theological Quarterly* 44 (1977) 39-57.

Yong III, Josiah U. *African Theology: A Critical and Annotated Bibliography*. London. Greenwood, 1993.

Zizioulas, John D. *Being as Communion: Studies in Personhood and the Church*. London: Darton Longman & Todd, 1985.

———. *Communion and Otherness: Further Studies in Personhood and the Church*. Edited by Paul McPartland. London: T. & T. Clark, 2006.

Index

Questions: Why the singular term Christ-E[nt?]

Like Ezigbo, we must come to our own understanding of revelation and hold it up to his
many references. General / [Special] - propositional

Engage the revealer Suppositions - are they
lacking? Pg. 153-4
— to get us into a spiritual mindset, how #64
do non-Africans entertain a spiritual mindset

☆ What is the difference in efforts for
☆ the 2 questions on # 175/176 → change in
outlook as affected by second part

What's the purpose of the Christ
Event if not to reveal God? A. pg. 187

What is the appropriate teach. of Af. Chrs?
#189
— Pt. to #192, How is God made
darker?

— How does Jesus both communicate and
interpret through acts?

— How does through revealing the # 200 idencChara.
and mission of God does he show his own?

Demonology — what is yours? -2 35
→ truthfulness or untruth fulness, no matter

Does God's appearance as a man make
that love? pg. 262

—

What are the rites of passage that need
to be redeemed in the African churches
and indigenous culture? What are ours?
p. 268

- poverty is a outcome of rejecting
Christ and relationship w/ God pg.28

key elem. of Rev.

#162 - Chalcedonian

#174 - rebuilding relat. w/ God

#172 - not a mush but real is Christ as God

#190 - Ch-Ev. is the litmus of God's revealing of God

#193 - In Christ, God is revealed through saving through seeing in <u>faith</u>

#201 Jesus has a pointed desire to reveal God for human's reinterpretation

#240 - Against self-accumulation part & parcel of the solution oriented approach

#252 - the goal of the C-E allows us to better know humanity, and the relationality of God to humans

#262 - as a man, God can reveal interest & love.

#266 - Jesus as a real community builder

#279 - Original sin not effective for indigenous ones

#291 - incarnation, critiques and gives hope

#296 - connects the gulf b/w grav. & construct. Christological